THE NERD REICH

THE NERD REICH

SILICON VALLEY FASCISM AND THE WAR ON DEMOCRACY

GIL DURÁN

SIMON & SCHUSTER

London · New York · Amsterdam/Antwerp · Sydney/Melbourne · Toronto · New Delhi

First published in the United States by Avid Reader Press,
an imprint of Simon & Schuster, LLC, 2026

First published in Great Britain by Simon & Schuster UK Ltd, 2026

1 3 5 7 9 10 8 6 4 2

Simon & Schuster UK Ltd, 7th Floor, 199 Bishopsgate, London EC2M 3TY

www.simonandschuster.co.uk
www.simonandschuster.com.au
www.simonandschuster.co.in

Simon & Schuster Australia, Sydney
Simon & Schuster India, New Delhi

The authorised representative in the EEA is Simon & Schuster Netherlands BV,
Herculesplein 96, 3584 AA Utrecht, Netherlands. info@simonandschuster.nl

A CIP catalogue record for this book is available from the British Library

Hardback ISBN: 978-1-3985-5592-1
Trade Paperback ISBN: 978-1-3985-5593-8
eBook ISBN: 978-1-3985-5594-5

Interior design by Kyle Kabel

Printed and Bound in the UK using 100% Renewable Electricity at CPI Group (UK) Ltd

FSC www.fsc.org MIX Paper | Supporting responsible forestry FSC® C013604

For Patricia Tipton Esrael and T. T. Nhu—
for everything.

The initial founding vision was that we were going to use technology to change the whole world and basically overturn the monetary system of the world . . . the basic idea was that we could never win an election on getting certain things because we were in such a small minority . . . But maybe you could actually unilaterally change the world—without having to constantly convince people and beg people and plead with people who were never going to agree with you—through technological means . . . technology is this incredible alternative to politics.

—Peter Thiel, 2010

CONTENTS

INTRODUCTION

In his final speech as president, Joe Biden warned that Silicon Valley billionaires posed an existential threat to American democracy. Sitting behind the *Resolute* Desk in the Oval Office on January 15, 2025, a grim-faced Biden shared his concern about "a dangerous concentration of power in the hands of a very few ultra-wealthy people, and the dangerous consequences if their abuse of power is left unchecked."

"Today, an oligarchy is taking shape in America of extreme wealth, power, and influence that literally threatens our entire democracy, our basic rights and freedoms, and a fair shot for everyone to get ahead," said Biden.

He reminded Americans that, in 1961, President Dwight D. Eisenhower had used his own farewell address to emphasize the rise of a "military-industrial complex" with "the potential for the disastrous rise of misplaced power." Six decades later, Biden said he was "equally concerned" about an emergent "tech-industrial complex that could pose real dangers for our country as well."

It is unclear why Biden saved this dire announcement for his final days in office. His declaration, among the most dramatic in American history, arrived far too late. Five days later, on January 20, during a speech celebrating Donald Trump's inauguration, Elon Musk, the world's richest man, performed a Nazi salute—twice—while standing behind a lectern affixed with the official seal of the President of the United States.

Later that day, Musk officially took charge of the so-called Department of Government Efficiency (DOGE), a project aimed at dismantling key parts of the federal government from the inside. He tackled the assignment with the sociopathic glee of a schoolboy ripping the wings from a butterfly, recruiting dozens of young men with zero government experience, including one nicknamed "Big Balls," to serve as henchmen. Musk's shock troops quickly set about tearing apart the federal bureaucracy. They were aided in this effort by Grok, Musk's proprietary artificial intelligence chatbot, which his team deployed to sift through sensitive government data.

The Constitution bars foreign-born individuals from the presidency, but the South Africa–born Musk found a workaround. He spent nearly $300 million to get Trump elected and buy himself a kind of co-presidency. Once deputized, he immediately began purging thousands of federal workers and dismantling the United States Agency for International Development, better known as USAID. The billionaire announced that he was tossing the agency—which provides lifesaving aid to the world's poorest people—"into the woodchipper." This decision alone is projected to kill up to 14 million people by 2030, many of them children.

Musk was not the only tech oligarch to find himself in a position of great power under Trump. In 2025, the tech industry revealed its true face. Devoid of any moral scruples or loyalty to democratic principles, many of Silicon Valley's most well-known figures chose to openly ally themselves with a president who would soon, with their help, check every box in the authoritarian playbook.

This shift took some observers by surprise. In the popular imagination, Silicon Valley had long been seen as a quirky West Coast bastion of liberal ideas and people, a land of future-facing billionaires who rejected the regressive politics of backward-thinking conservatives and aligned more closely with the Democratic Party. During Trump's first term, a movement called Tech Against Trump had sprung up to challenge his extremist policies. In 2017, over one hundred companies—including Apple, Facebook, Google, and Microsoft—had filed a legal brief challenging Trump's ban on immigration from Muslim countries.

But times had changed. In 2025, Silicon Valley was all in on Trumpism. Instead of filing lawsuits against the administration, tech giants lavished him with money and support. As his administration carried out a shock-and-awe effort to destroy the pillars of American democracy, the most powerful and prominent figures in tech stood behind him. There would be no energetic tech resistance this time around. Even those tech moguls who had expressed opposition to Trump during his first term now learned to love him, while others honored him by remaining silent.

When inaugural festivities on the National Mall in Washington had to be moved into the Capitol Rotunda due to freezing temperatures, Trump reserved the scarce seats for his new tech billionaire friends.

"Some of the most exclusive seats at President Donald Trump's inauguration on Monday were reserved for powerful tech CEOs who also happen to be among the world's richest men," reported the Associated Press. "That's a shift from tradition, especially for a president who has characterized himself as a champion of the working class. Seats so close to the president are usually reserved for the president's family, past presidents and other honored guests."

An iconic photo from the ceremony showed Musk, Amazon founder Jeff Bezos, Meta CEO Mark Zuckerberg, and Google CEO Sundar Pichai all seated prominently. Most of them had bent the knee to get there. Zuckerberg had banned Trump from Facebook and Instagram after the January 6 attack on the United States Capitol, then reinstated his accounts in early 2023. After Trump won the 2024 election, Zuckerberg dined with him at Mar-a-Lago. Trump deputy Stephen Miller said Zuckerberg wanted "to support the national renewal of America under President Trump's leadership." On January 7, 2025, Zuckerberg announced his decision to dismantle Meta's fact-checking infrastructure, further enabling the kinds of disinformation and misinformation that had led to the January 6 insurrection.

Bezos—owner of *The Washington Post*—had killed the editorial board's planned endorsement of Kamala Harris a few weeks before the election. Subsequently, the *Post*'s opinion pages, once the home of Trump's fiercest critics, morphed into a lapdog for the president who had promised to be a "dictator on day one." Bezos's Amazon—along with Apple, Meta, Google, and Microsoft—donated $1 million to Trump's inaugural fund. So did Sam Altman, the OpenAI CEO who had once compared Trump to Adolf Hitler. "Watching @potus more carefully recently has really changed my perspective on him," wrote Altman on X on January 22, explaining his shift. "I'm not going to agree with him on everything, but I think he will be incredible for the country in many ways."

But none reveled in Trump's ascension more than Musk, who during the first five months of Trump's second term became the face of the US government. In February, one month into his tenure at DOGE, Musk celebrated his reign of destruction by waving around a chainsaw onstage at the Conservative Political Action Conference. "Techno-Fascism Comes to America," declared *The New Yorker* less than one week later.

However, it was another tech billionaire who would emerge as the real power behind the throne: Peter Thiel, the venture capitalist and cofounder of well-known Silicon Valley companies like PayPal and Palantir. While Thiel did not become a special government employee or dance around with chainsaws, his influence on the Trump administration would prove more pronounced and durable than Musk's.

In March 2025, *Bloomberg* reported that sixteen men connected to Thiel and his companies now held positions of power in the Trump administration. Among them: David Sacks, a longtime Thiel crony and early PayPal employee, whom Trump appointed as his AI and crypto czar; Michael Kratsios, who had worked at several Thiel companies and now served as assistant to the president for science and technology; and Jim O'Neill, former chief of staff at the Thiel

Foundation, who became deputy secretary at the Department of Health and Human Services.

Thiel's master stroke was JD Vance. Trump had chosen the former senator from Ohio, who had once derided him as "America's Hitler," to serve as his vice president. Vance is almost entirely a creation of Thiel, who bankrolled his brief stint as a Silicon Valley venture capitalist and United States senator. With Vance at Trump's side, Silicon Valley had one of their own in the White House—a tech venture capitalist one heartbeat away from the presidency.

The merging of tech and MAGA networks created a frenzy of open political corruption unlike anything in American history. Trump had already become a tech CEO in 2022 after launching a social media platform called Truth Social. It flopped as a product but attracted hundreds of millions of dollars from investors, impressing upon Trump the fact that a tech company need not be commercially successful to generate massive profits. Trump, who had once called crypto a "scam," now expanded his business interests to include his own crypto company. Within a few months of his return to the White House, the Trump family's net worth increased by $5 billion thanks to their crypto company World Liberty Financial, which launched a new coin called $WLFI. "The trading debut was most likely the biggest financial success for the president's family since the inauguration," reported *The Wall Street Journal.*

It was a dynastic merger. Trump and his sons transformed themselves into Silicon Valley moguls while Silicon Valley transformed itself into an arm of the Trump family. Days after the election, Donald Trump Jr. had joined 1789 Capital, a venture capital firm. The firm's stated goal was to engage in "patriotic capitalism," which meant creating a "parallel economy" to support Trump's right-wing America First movement. The firm's cofounder, Chris Buskirk, had previously cofounded the Rockbridge Network, a Thiel-funded group that promoted itself as a venture capital firm for right-wing politics. In March 2025, the president's middle son, Eric Trump, became chief strategy officer of American Bitcoin, a Bitcoin mining company he cofounded with Trump Jr. Both brothers became vocal proponents of pro-crypto policy. Jared Kushner, Trump's son-in-law, who officially attained billionaire status in 2025, also cofounded an AI company, Brain Co., with tech investor Elad Gil.

As Trump's behavior became increasingly authoritarian—openly defying laws, targeting his enemies with prosecutions, dispatching troops into Democratic cities, and turning US Immigration and Customs Enforcement (ICE) into a shock force to terrorize immigrant communities—many in Silicon Valley cashed in on the action.

Palantir, the data surveillance company cofounded by Thiel, received a $30 million contract to augment Trump's masked ICE squads with software called ImmigrationOS, designed to identify targets for deportation. The Trump administration also turned to Palantir to expand its data platform across federal agencies, a move that *The New York Times* reported was "raising questions over whether he might compile a master list of personal information on Americans that could give him untold surveillance power." In July 2025, the company received a contract worth up to $10 billion to expand AI and data tools for the US Army. Altman's OpenAI and Musk's xAI also received massive government contracts. Even Marc Benioff, the Salesforce founder widely portrayed as a tech liberal in the press, became an unabashed Trump supporter as his company sought lucrative opportunities to work with ICE.

When Trump threw himself a military parade in Washington, DC, to celebrate his seventy-ninth birthday in June 2025, Amazon, Coinbase, and Palantir, along with Coca-Cola and Walmart, chipped in to sponsor it. Widely circulated press photographs showed US Army tanks rumbling down Constitution Avenue, in front of a pavilion where Trump, behind the presidential seal, watched the parade as the Palantir logo flashed on screens behind him. When Trump made the surprise decision to tear down the historic East Wing of the White House and replace it with a $400 million gilded ballroom, a slew of tech companies—Apple, Coinbase, Google, Microsoft, Meta, and Palantir—helped finance it. So did Ripple and Tether, two crypto exchanges that sell their own coins, along with Cameron and Tyler Winklevoss, twin brothers and crypto influencers best known for accusing Zuckerberg of having stolen the idea for Facebook from them.

As experts on governance raised alarms about the erosion of democracy in the United States, the tech billionaires of Silicon Valley lined up to lick Trump's loafers. It quickly became clear that these tech moguls were not mere bystanders supporting him out of respect for the presidency. Instead, they saw his return to power as the best path for achieving their goals for business and their vision for the future.

To many observers, tech's embrace of Trump seemed like a sudden reversal, an opportunistic pivot driven by tax policy or deregulation. In reality, tech's authoritarian turn had been years in the making, and it had accelerated sharply in the 2020s. And it wasn't just about money.

"Balaji Srinivasan and the network state—let's talk about that," Steve Bannon, right-wing mastermind and former Trump advisor, told *New York Times* columnist Ross Douthat during an interview in April 2025. "They're not weird. They're radicals."

"All right, the network state, we can save that for next time we have you on," said Douthat, cutting him off and changing the subject.

This was a strange choice given Bannon's unparalleled knowledge of right-wing politics and long relationship with Trump. Why interrupt the MAGA mastermind as he tried to expose the truth behind tech's radical turn? Bannon, an overt racist and fierce enemy of democracy, did more than almost anyone to aid Trump's rise to power. Yet even he seemed taken aback—and, perhaps, jealous—by the degree to which Silicon Valley oligarchs had absorbed Trump and his family. Maybe he wanted to hit the tech oligarchs where it hurt, by exposing the strange ideology underlying the tech moguls' newfound love for Trump.

Bannon was right to call them radicals. But what exactly do they believe? For decades, many described the anti-government politics of certain Silicon Valley figures as libertarian, portraying them as the eccentric beliefs of rich men who hated taxes but mostly wanted to build their companies without government interference. This framing is now dangerously obsolete. What began as libertarian-inflected fantasy among wealthy entrepreneurs and thinkers in the twentieth century has now curdled into something even more sinister: tech fascism. The sight of tech billionaires partnering enthusiastically with authoritarian regimes, providing technologies of control and surveillance while profiting from government contracts, clarifies the reality. Rather than opposing government control, they seek to enhance it. For decades, Silicon Valley had promoted libertarian fairy tales about freedom from government power. In fact, seizing that power for itself was the true goal.

Thiel himself dismissed libertarianism as useless fantasy in 2009, famously declaring, "I no longer believe that freedom and democracy are compatible." And the precursors of fascism were always present in libertarianism, which has deep roots in eugenics-adjacent ideas of hierarchy, supremacy, and disdain for the social contract.

The term "fascist" is highly charged and, according to some, overused—most likely its incidence has skyrocketed because fascism is resurgent in the twenty-first century. But fascists excel at deflecting the accusation. "[T]he right in the United States has attempted to turn the term against itself, labeling those who oppose fascism as fascists themselves, sometimes even the 'real' fascists," wrote the late David Golumbia in *Cyberlibertarianism: The Right-Wing Politics of Digital Technology.*

The word comes from the Latin *fasces*, meaning a bundle of wooden rods bound together with a small axe protruding from the side. This totem, carried by bodyguards of magistrates in ancient Rome, signaled authority and the power to punish. It also symbolized the power of unity: One stick can be snapped, but a bundle cannot be easily broken.

Benito Mussolini, the dictator who invented fascism and ruled Italy from 1922 to 1943, sought to bundle every institution of society under unified state authority. Italian fascism combined religion, the military, corporations, and media under state authority. Technofascism innovates on this model through technology, creating a system that seeks the "technicization of all aspects of government and society," making technology the "driving force" of the authoritarian regime, historian Janis Mimura told *The New Yorker* in 2025.

Tech fascism bundles powerful technologies—AI, crypto, defense tech, social media platforms, surveillance systems—toward authoritarian goals. These technologies are bound together under the control of a small, interconnected group of oligarchs who, simultaneously integrated into the highest levels of government, are creating an authoritarian infrastructure with boundless power. Its goal, like MAGA's, is to privatize the public and eliminate democracy.

Few grasp the power of technology better than Trump. In 2016, he used social media to overpower the incumbent political system and become president. Without Twitter, he would have been a joke candidate, an attention seeker hunting for cameras. His previous presidential campaign, in 2000, was a short-lived stunt and, though he flirted with another run in 2012, he decided against it because he had no chance. But in 2016, his massive Twitter following gave the reality TV star the power to eclipse both his opponents and the media. He became the main algorithm of US politics and, to the shock of many experts, triumphed. In 2026, Trump's regime is amplified and bolstered not only by social media, but also by artificial intelligence, crypto, surveillance, and a national media apparatus increasingly controlled by his accomplices.

Toni Morrison called fascism "marketing for power." Fascism is nakedly aggressive and authoritarian by design, a terrifying spectacle of power for the sake of power, "recognizable by its need to purge, by the strategies it uses to purge, and by its terror of truly democratic agendas." In addition, it "is recognizable by its determination to convert all public services to private entrepreneurship, all nonprofit organizations to profit-making ones—so that the narrow but protective chasm between governance and business disappears."

Everything Morrison articulated has now manifested in the streets of the USA, where private corporations partner with a fascist regime to purge federal workers, immigrants, the military, and even the press. AI is being used to hollow out the federal bureaucracy as masked goons, aided by Palantir, violently kidnap, terrorize, and kill citizens and immigrants alike. The Trump family gorges on crypto profits as the tech oligarchs gorge on government contracts in an orgy of corruption distinguished by both its unprecedented scale and its radical transparency. So certain are they of their power—so unafraid of consequences—that they are not even trying to hide their misdeeds from the public eye. And given how much they have gotten away with so far, it is not yet clear how far they will go. Trump has raised the prospect of using the federal government to interfere in elections, and if he does so, it seems likely he will have the full backing—or, at least, the silent complicity—of the tech billionaires.

"There is an alignment of interests that runs through Silicon Valley to what is now a coming autocracy," warned veteran British tech journalist Carole Cadwalladr, who said the US was undergoing a "digital coup." "It's a type of power that the world has never seen before."

"America has become a digital narco-state," declared Nobel laureate Paul Krugman.

How did this happen? This book tells the story of what Biden meant when he warned the American people of a rising "tech-industrial complex" and what Bannon tried to tell Douthat about the "network state." It traces the origins of tech fascism, starting with an apocalyptic 1997 book which predicted that, in the twenty-first century, powerful new technologies would eliminate jobs, sow widespread poverty and chaos, and hasten the collapse of nations while enabling the rise of a new class of high-tech oligarchs with loyalty to no existing nations.

The Sovereign Individual: How to Survive and Thrive During the Collapse of the Welfare State, written by two men with a long track record of doomsaying and conspiracy theory, had a profound effect on a restless Stanford University graduate named Peter Thiel, who spent the next few decades chasing its dark prophecies. The book put him on a path to becoming a multibillionaire obsessed with escaping democracy. Over the subsequent decades, his obsession with the book's thesis led him to cultivate and fund a cultish network of radical anti-democracy thinkers. Among them: Curtis Yarvin, a computer programmer who developed an expansive new theory for dismantling democratic governance, and Balaji Srinivasan, a tech entrepreneur who designed a blueprint for replacing nations with corporate city-states.

For many years, these ideas—that nations would crumble, that democracy would become obsolete, that a tech-powered elite would rule through technology—seemed like fringe science fiction fantasy to most observers. But they have now become the operating principles of some of the wealthiest and most powerful men in the world and have spawned a movement promoted by a rotating cast of venture capitalists, fringe philosophers, and political operatives who took these ideas from obscure blogs to the halls of power. A small network of Silicon Valley moguls has threaded this radical ideology into the governing philosophy of the Trump administration. They count the vice president of the United States as one of their own.

When a nation is betrayed by its wealthiest citizens—men who believe their money and technology entitle them to rule—existential crisis follows. But the future remains unwritten. The next few years will determine the destiny of our nation, our species, and our planet. While the United States is currently the main project, tech fascism has global ambitions. All around the world, Silicon Valley oligarchs are scheming to acquire land, resources, and power. They see a world in decline and seek to profit by hastening its collapse—and remaking it in their own image. Consider this a map of how we got here and a warning about the post-American authoritarian dystopia the billionaires of Silicon Valley are racing to build.

CHAPTER 1

THE SOVEREIGN INDIVIDUAL

Peter Thiel and the Politics of Apocalypse

To understand the right-wing radicalization of Silicon Valley politics, you must understand Peter Thiel. To understand Thiel, you must understand the formative role the book *The Sovereign Individual: How to Survive and Thrive During the Collapse of the Welfare State* and its authors James Dale Davidson and William Rees-Mogg played in shaping his political outlook.

"The democracy of the future will be unpopular with many freedom-loving Americans," wrote Jaan vanValkenburgh of the *Memphis Commercial Appeal* upon the book's release in 1997. "While the Internet continues to provide new opportunities, it will also make the mediocre middle-class expendable and the uneducated, paupers. Nations will become antiquated, and talented individuals will no longer pledge allegiance to a country."

"Power and freedom will be held by the talented few," she continued in a book review headlined "Gifted Elite Will Run Nationless, Ruthless World, Book Claims." The book in question was a somber futurist manifesto that predicted a coming economic and political revolution—fueled by technology—that would enable wealthy entrepreneurs and investors to overthrow the power of governments. "It describes how nations will become unnecessary and how talented people will help it happen and the lesser skilled masses will challenge it, perhaps violently," wrote vanValkenburgh in the conclusion of her piece.

Publishers Weekly dismissed the book's dire thesis—nation-states destroyed by cybercommerce, governments undermined by "cyber-currency," citizenship rendered obsolete, mafias and criminal gangs seizing power from behind the scenes—as "an apocalyptic exercise that is unconvincing."

The Sovereign Individual, part of a wave of crisis-tinged business books published before the year 2000, was not a bestseller. But it made a fateful impression on a young man whose fascination with its ideas would help to change the course of American history. His name was Peter Thiel. Nearly three years after the book's release, on October 20, 1999, Thiel gave a speech in which he made a few stunning predictions about the future. Speaking to an audience of libertarians at a think tank called the Independent Institute, the thirty-two-year-old Stanford University graduate said technology would dramatically transform the world in the twenty-first century. New forms of currency—digital, encrypted, privately controlled—could completely change how money works and begin to replace physical currencies like the dollar.

"It will be something where you have a choice between different currencies and the choice is not left to the sovereign, but to the individual," said Thiel. "And, in a sense, the individual becomes sovereign, is able to make choices regarding which currency they want to take."

Today, Thiel is a famous Silicon Valley billionaire known for his grim demeanor and awkward interviews in which he often struggles to choke out his intricately sprawling ideas. In 1999, however, he was articulate, boyish, quick, and largely unknown. Jaunty with optimism, he laid out a radical vision. Digital technology would first allow people in countries like India and Russia to evade government authority and buy dollars—to "move money into an account in a safe jurisdiction where the banks are not politically controlled." This same technology, he said, could eventually lead to an even more dramatic shift.

"The second theme is a little bit more speculative, and that is getting rid of money altogether, going from digital dollars from any kind of government-backed currency to purely private currencies," he said. "What a private currency or private money . . . fundamentally means is that there is no medium of exchange. You exchange value for value rather than exchanging value for something the government says has value."

Thiel acknowledged obstacles to this vision. For example, how would regular people carry or transfer digital currencies? He had an answer for that, too.

"I think the basic technology is going to take place on the Internet," he said. "I think a specific platform in the emerging world is going to be on a cell phone platform."

Thiel was ahead of his time. His speech took place eight years before the iPhone launched the smartphone revolution, and nearly a decade before the invention of Bitcoin kicked off a global crypto craze.

Thiel had good reason to be thinking deeply about the future of the internet and money. At the time, he was chairman and CEO of Confinity, a fledgling company with software called PayPal that allowed people to make digital payments. But his prescient speech went beyond promoting a new business model. Instead, he made a striking political argument. He assured his audience that this coming technology would fundamentally transform the governance of the world. And he crowed that officials in Washington, DC, would be powerless to stop the onslaught of technological disruption in the twenty-first century.

"I don't think the big fights on this are going to be fought in Washington, DC," he said. "The people in DC are completely backwards. They don't understand any of the technology, and even to the extent they can, it can't be stopped. You cannot stop things on the level of Washington, DC, in terms of shutting down these encryption protocols, things like that."

Very few people heard the speech at the time. Yet Thiel's words, preserved for posterity on YouTube, could turn out to be among the most important orations in American history. In the decades following his speech, the German-born tech investor would become one of the most influential figures in Silicon Valley. He would amass billions of dollars in personal wealth and use his money and influence to reshape technology and politics. His tentacles of influence would encircle some of the most powerful men in the world: Tesla CEO Elon Musk, President Donald Trump, OpenAI founder Sam Altman, and Vice President JD Vance. One of his companies, the data surveillance giant Palantir, has been described as an "operation system for the entire government."

Today, Thiel possesses a level of power—spanning both the public and private sectors—that would be dangerous in the hands of any one person. But it's especially troubling when you consider his long history of spouting anti-government ideas in public. His 1999 speech laid the groundwork for a dystopian vision he would cultivate and nurture for decades: a post-democracy world ruled by technology and its wealthy masters.

"I think that it is a very exciting future," said Thiel, concluding his speech. "I think that there are incredible technological forces pushing us in the direction of digital currency, of a world of limited government, limited tax authority and ability."

This vision, once viewed as eccentric and perhaps unserious, now shapes American public policy at the highest levels. Once-fringe tech libertarian fantasies have morphed into a cult extremist movement fueled by influential billionaire venture capitalists who seek to capture governments, overthrow democracy, and impose a permanent system of Silicon Valley hierarchy on the world. Their ideology, camouflaged as libertarian for many years, has now merged with Donald Trump's MAGA movement to fully reveal its true identity as an authoritarian movement: Silicon Valley fascism.

To understand the goals of tech fascism, we must trace Thiel's political evolution back to the book that he has repeatedly cited as a major influence on his thinking. By 1999, Thiel was evangelizing digital currency as a powerful weapon to undermine governments and disrupt the future, ideas he apparently mined from *The Sovereign Individual*, whose jacket copy heralded the "collapse of the welfare state and death of nations worldwide" while also asserting that the "map of the world, including the United States and Canada, will look dramatically different," and that the "U.S. government will diminish to the size it was in the 19th century."

"If our deductions are correct, you stand at the threshold of the most sweeping revolution in history," warned Davidson and Rees-Mogg in the book's introduction. "Faster than all but a few now imagine, microprocessing will subvert and destroy the nation-state, creating new forms of social organization in the process. This will be far from an easy transformation."

The impending collapse of the USA and other democratic governments was an alarming and far-out thesis to most readers in the late 1990s. But Davidson and Rees-Mogg drew their ideas from a teeming genre of dystopian thinking that had incubated in tech circles for decades.

Science fiction writers had long imagined dismal futures in which the world order collapsed and people used new forms of money and technology. By the 1980s, some Silicon Valley libertarians had already started to view such outcomes as the inevitable progression of technological advancement, and so-called cypherpunks began to experiment with the idea of digital forms of currency. But, in Thiel's telling, it was *The Sovereign Individual* that marked a turning point for him. The book attempted to popularize the futuristic ideas of the cypherpunks as investment advice, pushing them from the realm of science fiction to political reality. To do this, it laid out a dramatic thesis, hyping the arrival of an information age in which technology would upend both economics and politics, eliminating most jobs, reducing work to piecemeal gig assignments, and sparking widespread decline, chaos, and violence as tens of millions of people struggled to survive without work. This economic and social breakdown would, in turn, implode governments worldwide. Crime would surge, necessitating the widespread privatization of police and security services. Nations like the United Kingdom and the United States—unable to fulfill their basic functions—would soon become obsolete. A new world order would arise, centered on networks of criminals and wealthy individuals who, freed from the bondage of democracy, would become "sovereign individuals" unbound by the constraints of law, regulation, and nationality.

The Sovereign Individual is written in an elliptical and easy-to-read style. Its authors, who also published an investment newsletter called *Strategic Investment,* use short bursts of declarative prose, frequent subheads, and deliberate repetition to drive home their points. They also make use of epigraphs and pull quotes, borrowing the voices of prophets, poets, and philosophers to frame their ideas with intellectual and spiritual authority. The book begins in a relatively measured and conventional tone. By the end chapters, however, the reader is drawn into a deep and conspiratorial rabbit hole. What starts as a seemingly sober analysis gives way to sweeping predictions of decline, delivered with an almost messianic confidence.

In multiple books, the two men regularly portrayed democratic governments as mafia enterprises designed to extort money from the rich. As such, they viewed the future downfall of nation-states as a positive development, one that would enable new forms of private governance that allowed a superior class of wealthy men—the so-called cognitive elite—to reign supreme.

"An entirely new realm of economic activity that is not hostage to physical violence will emerge in cyberspace," they wrote. "The most obvious benefits will flow to the 'cognitive elite,' who will increasingly operate outside political boundaries."

The concept of the cognitive elite was lifted from *The Bell Curve: Intelligence and Class Structure in American Life,* a highly controversial 1994 book by Richard Herrnstein and Charles Murray. *The Bell Curve* argued that intelligence was largely hereditary and that society was naturally stratifying into distinct classes based on IQ. The book was denounced by leading scientists and civil rights organizations as a work of thinly veiled pseudoscientific racism, particularly for promoting the discredited idea that racial disparities in intelligence are largely genetic.

The fixation on cognitive superiority had deeper roots in American history. In the early twentieth century, the eugenics movement had promoted the idea that intelligence could be measured, ranked, and improved through selective breeding. Pioneered by figures like English polymath Francis Galton and others during the Victorian era, eugenics was carried forward in the United States by David Starr Jordan, the president of Stanford University, a fervent racist and believer in the notion that breeding and heredity were destiny. At Stanford, he "forged a eugenic university," according to *Palo Alto: A History of California, Capitalism, and the World* by Malcolm Harris. Believers in eugenics—a word coined by Galton to mean "well-born" in Greek—used flawed and unscientific methods to justify white supremacy and anti-immigrant hate, creating a movement that led to forced sterilization laws in dozens of states and fueled a broader campaign for immigration restrictions. The 1924 Immigration Act, which banned most Asians and drastically limited entry from Southern and Eastern Europe, was justified in part by the claim—later thoroughly debunked—that IQ tests proved these populations were genetically inferior.

Overt racist eugenics mostly fell out of favor in the mid-twentieth century, after the Nazis carried its ideas to their most logical and gruesome conclusion. But the underlying ideology of supremacy proved more durable. It survived on one track through white supremacist and nativist movements that never fully disappeared and are now resurgent. On another track, it thinly disguised its racism behind the equally potent idea that certain individuals were simply too intelligent and exceptional to be held back from greatness by mass democracy.

The years of the Great Depression saw the peak of a so-called technocracy movement, which asserted that democracy should be abandoned in favor of a society run by engineers and scientists. Supporters of technocracy—including Elon Musk's maternal grandfather, Joshua Haldeman—argued that "scientific management" could optimize civilization the way it optimized factories. Howard Scott, the leader of Technocracy Incorporated, also argued for a new monetary system based on energy usage and proposed the creation of a new government called the "technate," in which engineers would "optimize the use of energy to assure abundance." The movement fizzled in the 1940s, but at its peak, Technocracy Incorporated had an estimated 500,000 supporters in California alone.

"Members painted their cars 'Official Technocracy Gray,' wore a uniform consisting of gray double-breasted suits, and saluted Scott when they encountered him in person," wrote Klint Finley of *Wired*. "At their most extreme, some members replaced their names with numbers, such as '1x1809x56,' according to an essay published on, of all places, the US Social Security Administration website."

Ayn Rand, an immigrant who fled Bolshevik Russia, came to the United States on a tourist visa, and became a Hollywood screenwriter, had a related idea. She wrote novels that celebrated the idea that individuals of superior intelligence—"men of the mind"—were the victims of an inferior, parasitic majority. In *Atlas Shrugged*, her most famous novel, a group of capitalist elites withdraw to a remote enclave where they stage a strike against society with the explicit aim of hastening its collapse and rebuilding it on their own terms.

Rand preached capitalism, self-interest, and anti-government radicalism not as political preferences but as moral imperatives. Her philosophy, called objectivism, would give generations of aspiring entrepreneurs the philosophical permission to be exactly as ruthless and selfish as they wanted to be. Her books would help fuel libertarianism, a political movement that sought to slash taxes, gut regulation, dismantle the welfare state, and let the strongest survive without the constraints—or protections—of government. Rand rejected libertarians as "hippies of the right," but despite her quibbles, her novels became their sacred texts.

This mythology of exceptional individualism found fertile ground in Silicon Valley, where a generation of tech entrepreneurs absorbed libertarian ideology along with computer science. In fact, Davidson and Rees-Mogg were relative latecomers to a well-established genre of libertarian fantasy in which civilization's collapse is a feature, not a bug—a necessary prelude to the rise of superior individuals. Rand's novels were the ur-texts of this tradition, presenting as utopia what amounted to dystopia for everyone except a handful of chosen elites. Decades of futurist literature, from Alvin Toffler's *Future Shock* to John Naisbitt's *Megatrends,* had predicted that technology would transform society and render old institutions obsolete. *The Sovereign Individual* framed these transformations as developments that should be welcomed, accelerated, and exploited by a knowing class of elite investors. But tech-savvy individuals with libertarian leanings had already expanded futurism's theories into their own theories of escape from society and its rules.

In 1988, "The Crypto Anarchist Manifesto" by Timothy C. May declared that new encryption technologies would undermine government authority on a global scale. "These developments will alter completely the nature of government regulation, the ability to tax and control economic interactions, the ability to keep information secret, and will even alter the nature of trust and reputation," wrote May, an engineer, libertarian, and cypherpunk who cofounded something called the crypto-anarchist movement. In the early 1990s, May and fellow cypherpunks maintained an influential mailing list where they developed and promoted cryptographic tools such as digital cash systems, anonymous remailers, and strong encryption software. They framed these as tools to help individuals protect their privacy and limit government surveillance. Cypherpunks saw cryptography as a form of political resistance, a way to redistribute power from the state to the individual by making privacy mathematically secure rather than dependent on law or trust, arguments that live on in marketing for blockchain and crypto technologies today.

These ideas circulated at the highest levels of the tech establishment. *The Sovereign Individual* also echoes a 1994 essay called "Cyberspace and the American Dream: A Magna Carta for the Knowledge Age," which declared that technology would hasten the decline of most centralized institutions. "Governments, including the American government, are the last great redoubt of bureaucratic power on the face of the planet, and for them the coming change will be profound and probably traumatic," wrote the authors, a group that included right-wing activist George Gilder, tech journalist Esther Dyson, and futurist Toffler. The essay outlined a new ideology in which freedom and the future belonged to those who could use technology to shape it. It preached decentralization of government and the weakening of geographic and bureaucratic constraints, asserting that technology would enable people to live and work from anywhere.

Those sentiments found a champion in *Wired* magazine, which was cofounded by libertarian Louis Rossetto and his partner, Jane Metcalfe, in 1993.

"There are a lot of magazines about technology," wrote Rossetto in a manifesto in the magazine's first issue. "WIRED is not one of them. WIRED is about the most powerful people on the planet today—the Digital Generation. These are the people who not only foresaw how the merger of computers, telecommunications, and the media is transforming life at the cusp of the new millennium, they are making it happen."

In its early years, the magazine featured a signature blend of countercultural idealism, Silicon Valley techno-utopianism, and right-leaning libertarian values. This approach was heavily influenced by heavyweight 1960s hippie figures like Stewart Brand, a former member of Ken Kesey's LSD-infused Merry Pranksters who went on to found the *Whole Earth Catalog*, as well as Grateful Dead lyricist (and avowed libertarian) John Perry Barlow. Ironically, many figures from the LSD-fueled, anti-war counterculture of the 1960s embraced digital technologies—like ARPANET, born from the Cold War military-industrial complex—as tools for personal liberation and decentralized community. This fusion gave rise to the inaugural version of Silicon Valley libertarianism, an ideology that reimagined state-sponsored technologies of control and warfare as instruments of freedom and individuality. ARPANET birthed the internet, and Brand and his fellow travelers became pioneer adopters. In early online forums like the WELL (Whole Earth 'Lectronic Link), they fused anti-authority and back-to-the-land hippie sensibilities with a libertarian ethos so right-wing that it found common cause with Republican Speaker of the House Newt Gingrich.

"In the pages of *Wired,* the Internet, and digital communication generally, stood as a prototype of a newly decentralized, nonhierarchical society linked by invisible bits in a single harmonious network," wrote Stanford Professor Fred Turner in *From Counterculture to Cyberculture: Stewart Brand, the Whole Earth Network, and the Rise of Digital Utopianism.* "The builders of computers and telecommunications networks, suggested *Wired*—men like John Malone of TV cable behemoth TCI, Frank Biondi and Ed Horowitz of Viacom, and Bill Gates of Microsoft—were working to construct the high-tech infrastructure of a new and better world. So too were libertarian pundits and politicians.

"Together, *Wired* seemed to suggest, these two communities had set about to free America and the world from the rigid, oppressive corporate and government bureaucracies of the twentieth century," wrote Turner.

In 1995, two University of Westminster academics, Richard Barbrook and Andy Cameron, labeled this the "Californian Ideology." It was, they wrote, an "anti-statist gospel" wrapped in "a bizarre mish-mash of hippie anarchism and economic liberalism beefed up with lots of technological determinism."

As if to prove their point, Barlow—who cowrote songs like "Cassidy" and "Mexicali Blues" for the Grateful Dead—penned a sweeping manifesto in 1996. Its lofty title: "The Declaration of the Independence of Cyberspace."

"Governments of the Industrial World, you weary giants of flesh and steel, I come from Cyberspace, the new home of Mind," read the grandiose tract, which was a viral sensation on the early internet. "On behalf of the future, I ask you of the past to leave us alone. You are not welcome among us. You have no sovereignty where we gather."

"We must declare our virtual selves immune to your sovereignty, even as we continue to consent to your rule over our bodies," the screed concluded. "We will spread ourselves across the Planet so that no one can arrest our thoughts. We will create a civilization of the Mind in Cyberspace."

The following year, in 1997, tech critic Langdon Winner coined a term for this emerging ideology: cyberlibertarianism. He defined this as "a collection of ideas that links ecstatic enthusiasm for electronically mediated forms of living with radical, right-wing libertarian ideas about the proper definition of freedom, social life, economics, and politics in the years to come."

"The two prongs of this statement are crucial," David Golumbia would later write in *Cyberlibertarianism* of Winner's definition. "On the one hand, ecstatic enthusiasm for digital technology itself . . . and on the other, right-wing libertarian ideas about the proper definition of core terms like freedom."

Into this already flourishing landscape of tech libertarian fantasy, Davidson and Rees-Mogg dropped their opus. *The Sovereign Individual* capitalized on tech libertarianism, fleshing out the stark vision of the information age ruled by techno-savvy elites. Davidson and Rees-Mogg argued that technological disruption would accelerate the sorting of humanity into inferior and superior people. Their cognitive elites would be investors and tech entrepreneurs with the skills and knowledge to prosper in the new decentralized tech economy. They would become a powerful new political force, a class of "sovereign individuals" whose intelligence and wealth freed them from democracy, nationality, taxes, and regulations. "Cybercurrency"—an early term for crypto—would aid their escape and fuel their rise.

Where other financial gurus promised easy wealth, Davidson and Rees-Mogg offered Armageddon as opportunity. Their book wrapped foreboding geopolitical prognostications around advice for how investors could make a killing by betting against the continued existence of liberal democracy and government currencies. This had a strong appeal to certain kinds of conspiratorial mindsets, particularly among successful entrepreneurs and investors inclined to view themselves as cognitively superior.

The timing was perfect. The year 2000 had long symbolized the idea of the future—or, at least, a period of great transformation where the future would begin. Religious fundamentalists, as always, expected the possible return of Jesus Christ, or at least the rise of the Antichrist. Conspiracy theorists on the far right warned against the rise of a new world order complete with masked government agents in mysterious black helicopters. Even pop culture tapped into these existential worries about the twenty-first century as the dawn of an ominous new age. "Say, say, two thousand, zero, zero, party over, oops, out of time," sang Prince in his 1982 hit "1999," giving voice to global anxieties about the coming of the new millennium.

The Sovereign Individual consciously exploited this millenarian fever. In dire and quasi-religious tones, it sought to provide both an economic theory and moral rationale for drastic changes in human society. Its authors, noting that "[t]he coming of the Year 2000 has haunted the Western imagination for the past thousand years," used the momentum of these dark expectations to propel their arguments.

"As the decade expires, a murderous century expires with it, and also a glorious millennium of human accomplishment," they wrote. "All draw to a close with the year 2000. We believe that the modern phase of Western civilization will end with it. This book tells why. Like many earlier works, it is an attempt to see into a glass darkly, to sketch out the vague shapes and dimensions of a future that is still to be. In that sense, we mean our work to be apocalyptic—in the original meaning of the word. *Apokalypsis* means 'unveiling' in Greek. We believe that a new stage in history—the Information Age—is about to be 'unveiled.'"

For good measure, the authors included a Bible verse, Matthew 10:26: "For there is nothing covered that shall not be revealed, neither hid that shall not be known."

Despite these religious overtones, the book's drastic conclusions found a receptive audience among some eager would-be visionaries in Silicon Valley. The prophesied future in which technology would fundamentally transform the world to benefit a select group of entrepreneurs had a natural appeal in the vicinity of Leland Stanford's ranch-turned-university, where David Starr Jordan had sought to create a superior breed of men. But while the book's admirers often portray it as a groundbreaking work, it simply tapped into a thriving anti-government vibe in Silicon Valley.

In 2000, *Wired* writer and tech critic Paulina Borsook published *Cyberselfish: A Critical Romp Through the Terribly Libertarian Culture of High Tech*, a scathing takedown of Silicon Valley's tech libertarian culture. She portrayed the various tribes of tech libertarians—Cato Institute goons, cypherpunks, anarcho-capitalists, extropians—as disconnected narcissists hooked on Ayn Rand's escapist fairy tales and right-wing economist Milton Friedman's "shareholder theory of value," which argued that the sole responsibility of a corporation is to maximize profits.

Some of these tech tribes were stranger than others. Take, for example, the extropians. Launched in the late 1980s by Oxford philosopher Max More, the extropians mixed libertarian individualism with radical futurism, promoting the idea of life extension, cryonics, and even uploading the contents of human brains to computers as ways to transcend hard biological limits. Death, they argued, was simply another challenge to be overcome through technological advancement (an idea in which Thiel would take a deep interest). Then there was bionomics, a movement based on a 1990 book, *Bionomics: Economy as Ecosystem*, which portrayed markets as perfect by nature and government regulation as the parasitical bane of paradisiacal capitalism. Borsook wrote that bionomics used biological metaphors "to explain economic behavior, describing the way the world works in terms of learning, adaptation, intelligences, selection and ecological niches. It favors decentralization and trial and error and local control and simple rules and letting things be."

She dismissed it as "fake-o biology, technology, and libertarianism" that was perfect for "the top percentiles, the endlessly entrepreneurial, the happily workaholic," but not for anyone else. (At the first annual Bionomics conference, Borsook wrote, George Gilder "labeled the homeless as true economic parasites, because they occupy some of the most expensive real estate in the world . . . for free.")

Borsook was early in detecting the lurking political extremism of the techno-libertarian culture, describing it as "scary" and "psychologically brittle." "It bespeaks a lack of human connection and a discomfort with the core of what many of us consider it means to be human," she wrote. "It's an inability to reconcile the demands of being individual with the demands of participating in society, which coincides beautifully with a preference for, and glorification of, being the solo commander of one's computer in lieu of any other economically viable behavior. Computers are so much more rule-based, controllable, fixable, and comprehensible than any human will ever be. As many political schools of thought do, these technolibertarians make a philosophy out of a personality defect."

The Sovereign Individual fit perfectly with the tech libertarian zeitgeist. It also moved beyond abstract philosophy toward concrete predictions of global collapse and detailed strategies for preserving wealth in a coming era of disruptive transformation. And it wrapped them all up in a quasi-religious prophetic style, merging public anxiety about the year 2000 with an apocalyptic capitalism that promised financial salvation despite civilizational collapse.

It seems odd that Thiel, who fancies himself something of a philosopher, would choose to trace his political inspiration to *The Sovereign Individual* rather than to the original sources of its techno-futurist vision. For decades, however, he has made a point of aligning himself with Davidson and Rees-Mogg's overwrought screed, which was a tacky knockoff of slightly more erudite thinkers. The most logical explanation is that Thiel first encountered these ideas in the book.

It helped that the arrival of the new century also seemed to reward *The Sovereign Individual*'s warnings of planetary turbulence. It began with the so-called Y2K computer bug, a technical glitch in which older systems couldn't process the date change from 1999 to 2000, threatening widespread technological failures. Massive global preparation efforts averted any major catastrophe, but breathless media reports gave people the strong impression that civilization might suddenly implode on 01/01/00.

The Y2K apocalypse failed to materialize, but other disasters quickly followed. In the US, it started with the 2000 presidential election in which George W. Bush took the presidency with a 537-vote lead over Al Gore in Florida after the US Supreme Court halted a manual recount of the ballots. The *Bush v. Gore* decision, one of the most controversial rulings in the court's history, left many Americans believing Republicans had stolen the election and killed democracy. Then, on September 11, 2001, the ghastly reality intensified with massive terror attacks that plunged the world deeper into chaos, fear, and war. And lurking beneath these immediate crises was a slower-moving but even more catastrophic threat: Record-breaking temperatures and an undeniable scientific consensus made it clear that human-caused climate change posed an existential danger to civilization itself.

Prophets of doom have a built-in advantage because bad things happen so regularly that apocalyptic predictions often seem to come true eventually. As Cambridge scholar Norman Cohn cataloged in his classic history *The Pursuit of the Millennium: Revolutionary Millenarians and Mystical Anarchists of the Middle Ages*, millenarian sects in the Western world had been awaiting the apocalypse for two millennia. History is riddled with movements inspired by prophecies of imminent collapse, and they tend to share some common characteristics. "Millenarian sects or movements always picture salvation as a) collective, in the sense that it is to be enjoyed by the faithful as a collectivity; b) terrestrial, in the sense that it is to be realized on this earth and not in some other-worldly heaven; c) imminent, in the sense that it is to come both soon and suddenly; d) total, in the sense that it is to utterly transform life on earth, so that the new dispensation will be no mere improvement on the present but perfection itself; e) miraculous, in the sense that it is to be accomplished by, or with the help of, supernatural agencies," wrote Cohn.

The Sovereign Individual largely followed Cohn's template. Their cognitive elites occupied the role of the chosen few who were destined to imminently create a perfect new capitalist world. Like fire-and-brimstone preachers, Davidson and Rees-Mogg promised their chosen elites a path to transcendence—the hope of becoming sovereign individuals who would "operate like the gods of myth," commanding vast resources while remaining "beyond the reach of many forms of compulsion." But in place of supernatural miracles they substitute miraculous new technologies that would purify the world of liberal democracy and liberate capitalism from all political constraints—after defeating the evil force of the "new Luddites" who would rise in opposition to this massive transformation.

Davidson and Rees-Mogg understood the power of apocalyptic thinking. In fact, they quoted Cohn's *The Pursuit of the Millennium* three times in their book, which sought to recast ancient millenarian prophecy for the digital age: The world as we know it would end, but a chosen few would build a hyper-capitalist heaven from its ashes. Thiel, who was raised Lutheran and became fixated on apocalyptic themes while studying under Catholic literary critic and theologian René Girard at Stanford, found this cosmology quite convincing. His 1999 speech, in which he described a future where "the individual becomes sovereign," clearly echoed the book. In the following decades, he would repeatedly name *The Sovereign Individual* as a defining and formative work—and its ideas would influence far more than his investment strategies.

This is why it's crucial to understand the toxic milieu from which the book emerged. One of the most powerful tech figures in the world—a billionaire now embedded in the highest levels of government—built his worldview on a flimsy book written by two apocalyptic conspiracy kooks who trafficked in scary financial newsletters marketed to paranoid right-wing investors. For many years, Davidson and Rees-Mogg had published *Strategic Investment*, a bulletin that belonged to a lucrative but fringe genre: investment newsletters steeped in urgent narratives of imminent global collapse. These publications sold readers on ideas long popular in far-right and libertarian circles. They portrayed government-issued "fiat" currencies like the dollar as tools of totalitarian control, warned of looming economic and political upheaval, and pushed investment strategies centered on gold and other precious metals—assets presumed to retain value when government-issued paper money inevitably became worthless.

In *Hayek's Bastards: Race, Gold, IQ, and the Capitalism of the Far Right*, Quinn Slobodian traces the roots of what he calls "catastrophe libertarians" and their obsession with "hard money." Beginning in the 1970s, books with titles like *How You Can Profit from the Coming Devaluation* and *Crisis Investing: Opportunities and Profits in the Coming Great Depression* fed readers a steady diet of terrifying economic scenarios. But the right-wing fixation with distrusting government currency goes back at least to the Civil War, when the Union issued "greenbacks," a paper currency not backed by gold. The move triggered outrage among conservative elites and creditors, who viewed gold not just as stable money but as a moral anchor, and a defense against inflation, social decay, and federal overreach.

The rage of the so-called goldbugs surged again in the 1930s when President Franklin D. Roosevelt, facing a collapsing economy and widespread bank failures, took drastic steps to stabilize the financial system and fight off the Great Depression. In 1933, he required most Americans to surrender monetary gold (with limited exceptions) and then devalued the dollar by raising the official price of gold to counter deflation and stabilize the economy. Goldbugs saw these measures as an existential threat—proof that expanding monetary discretion enabled government overreach, risked inflating away savings, and severed the moral anchor of "hard" money, even though the dollar remained tied to gold internationally until 1971. This monetary obsession also fused with conspiracy-fueled movements in the twentieth century, like the John Birch Society. Gold came to symbolize personal sovereignty and resistance to a perceived globalist or technocratic elite. "Hard money" advocacy—and deep suspicion of government-issued currency—became a central pillar of right-wing goldbug politics.

For most of US history, the dollar was backed by gold in one form or another. That changed in 1971, when President Richard Nixon supercharged goldbug fears by ending the dollar's convertibility to gold, effectively dismantling the so-called Bretton Woods system. Bretton Woods was a post–World War II agreement that had stabilized global currencies by pegging them to the US dollar, which was itself tied to gold. For decades, this system anchored international trade and kept monetary policy relatively restrained. Nixon's move marked the transition away from money backed not by metal, but by strong government institutions, a productive economy, and central banks entrusted to manage the money supply.

In the wake of the "Nixon shock," gold-obsessed anti-government libertarians saw Armageddon on the horizon. One of them was Ron Paul, a Texas doctor of obstetrics and gynecology who had read *The Road to Serfdom* by Austrian economist Friedrich Hayek as a medical resident in the 1960s. Hayek's book warned that even well-intentioned government efforts to centrally plan the economy and expand social welfare could erode individual liberty. The popular book made him a central figure for libertarians, who embraced a simplified version of his arguments that focused on a defense of free markets and limited government. Paul eventually came under the influence of writers like Ludwig von Mises and Murray Rothbard, prominent theorists of the Austrian School of Economics, a radical free-market philosophy that distrusts government, opposes central banks, and casts doubt on government-issued currency.

Nixon's termination of the gold standard inspired Paul to run for office. His first campaign failed in 1974, but he won a special election to Congress in 1976, beginning a long political career. In the mid-1980s, during a hiatus from elected office, Paul and his chief of staff, a self-described anarcho-capitalist and libertarian named Lew Rockwell, produced successful newsletters with titles like the *Ron Paul Investment Letter* and the *Ron Paul Survival Report*. While nominally focused on financial tips and gold, Paul's newsletters also trafficked in vicious racism and political fearmongering, attacking Dr. Martin Luther King Jr. but praising Ku Klux Klan grand wizard David Duke.

This was the noxious landscape in which Davidson and Rees-Mogg plied their trade, but their paths there followed different routes than Paul's. Both men started with genuine credentials and establishment positions before they met at Oxford University and descended into cataclysmic thinking. Davidson was an ultra-conservative activist who in 1969 founded the National Taxpayers Union, an anti-government spending organization that positioned itself as a critic of federal waste and advocate for constitutional limits on taxation. Over the years, he repeatedly claimed to have been a classmate of President Bill Clinton, who attended Oxford's University College on a Rhodes Scholarship from 1968 to 1970, but the *Pembroke College Record* lists Davidson as having attended in 1976. Therefore, it's not clear how he and Clinton would have overlapped at Oxford, and neither Davidson nor Oxford responded to requests for clarification. In any case, Davidson and Rees-Mogg met at the home of a mutual friend in Oxford during the summer of 1982 and began collaborating on the newsletter as well as three books that Rees-Mogg later described as "works of futurology."

William Rees-Mogg—*Lord* Rees-Mogg—was an English journalist who studied history at Oxford University's Balliol College, serving as president of the Oxford Union, the renowned debate club, in 1951. He started his journalism career at the venerable *Financial Times* and rose to become editor of *The Times* of London, spending decades as part of the British journalism establishment as a "high Tory" voice of patrician reason and defending free markets, traditional order, and cultural refinement. In perhaps his most famous commentary, 1967's "Who Breaks a Butterfly Upon a Wheel," Rees-Mogg defended singer Mick Jagger against a three-month prison sentence for possessing a few amphetamine pills imported from Italy, arguing the case was driven by moral panic, not justice.

In 1981, he left *The Times*. That year, Queen Elizabeth II anointed him as a knight bachelor, and Prime Minister Margaret Thatcher's government appointed him to the BBC's Board of Governors. He had failed in two efforts to get elected as a Conservative member of Parliament in the 1950s, but Thatcher awarded him a lifetime appointment to the House of Lords in 1988. Thatcherism—a neoliberal program of privatization, deregulation, reduced trade union power, and the prioritization of self-reliance over public welfare programs—operationalized Rees-Mogg's arch-conservative politics. He remained an influential establishment voice throughout the Thatcher years, even as he moved toward the increasingly catastrophist politics he would articulate in his books with Davidson.

In his later years, after leaving journalism, he increasingly pivoted toward a more prophetic and speculative mode. What began as high-minded commentary gradually evolved into a sweeping vision of civilizational transformation, threaded with libertarian distrust, technological determinism, and bespoke apocalypticism. His penchant for conspiratorial thinking and ominous forecasts would eventually earn him the pejorative nickname of "mystic Mogg." After meeting Davidson, he ventured into coauthoring scary books that warned of economic collapse, state failure, and high-level conspiracy.

Davidson and Rees-Mogg—one a conservative American political activist turned full-time conspiracy theorist, the other a British establishment figure who abandoned respectability for lurid futurist fantasies—specialized in alarmist frameworks that promised readers both financial profit and political transformation. *The Sovereign Individual* stands as their masterpiece, but it was preceded by two other books.

Both 1987's *Blood in the Streets: Investment Profits in a World Gone Mad* and 1994's *The Great Reckoning: Protect Yourself in the Coming Depression* coupled financial advice with the duo's trademark theories of inevitable civilizational crash. These books extended the arguments put forth in their *Strategic Investment* newsletter, which pushed dire forecasts to paying subscribers. *Strategic Investment* was among the first and most successful products from Agora, a newsletter company specializing in right-wing propaganda as financial counsel.

The recurring theme: Major global disruption lurked right around the corner, but savvy individuals could prosper by following their prescient investment advice. This generally meant buying gold and real estate, betting against the dollar, and shifting assets into offshore accounts. The authors assured readers that, by heeding their sage wisdom, they would become part of a new class of intelligent elites who would lord over everyone else in a world beset by the triple threat of political instability, economic decline, and terrorism. They went far beyond investment strategy. Instead, they sought to indoctrinate their target audience—business executives and investors—into a disturbing and radical worldview. Rather than predicting the rise and fall of stocks, they theorized about the rise and fall of political reality according to a homespun theory they called "megapolitics."

"Those forecasts of doom were surprisingly popular in the United States," wrote Rees-Mogg in his memoir. "Rupert Murdoch said that one of them, probably *The Great Reckoning*, had kept him awake all night, which was, no doubt, why they sold so well."

In the early 1990s, it became clear that these seemingly sophisticated Oxford men were paranoid political cranks. The unhinged nature of their beliefs crystallized during the presidency of their fellow Oxford man, Bill Clinton, which pushed Davidson over the edge. Despite having supposedly known him at university, Davidson became an avowed hater of President Clinton, and his insatiable enmity led him to make increasingly wild—and wrong—predictions. In 1993, Davidson wrote a pamphlet-sized book warning of a looming economic depression that would end Clinton's career.

"Clinton is going to be a one-term president . . . I am as sure of this as I am that the sun will rise tomorrow," Davidson wrote in *The Plague of the Black Debt: How to Survive the Coming Depression.*

Despite these pessimistic assurances, the US economy grew steadily in 1993, and Clinton would serve two terms, but Davidson did not relent. On January 1, 1996—just in time for Clinton's reelection campaign—he published *Who Murdered Vince Foster? And Why the Biggest Political Scandal in History Is Also the Biggest Financial Story of Our Lifetimes.* This pamphlet breathlessly pushed a right-wing conspiracy theory which claimed that Foster, a Clinton aide who died by suicide, had been murdered as part of a vast financial plot. Once again, Davidson predicted imminent financial catastrophe, this time due to Clinton's alleged criminality and corruption. Davidson portrayed Clinton as a mix between a CIA asset and a mafia figure who, along with his wife, was complicit in everything from insider trading to drug dealing to murder. Rees-Mogg also sullied himself with the Clinton conspiracy theories, which were thoroughly disproven by five different investigations.

"While the world as a whole draws back from the disturbing conclusion that the President of the United States is tainted by close association with organized crime and criminals, that is what the evidence suggests," they wrote in the latter chapters of *The Sovereign Individual*.

Clinton hatred was good business in the late 1990s, and both Davidson and Rees-Mogg found common cause with Christopher Ruddy, a columnist at the *Pittsburgh Tribune-Review*, owned by Republican billionaire and Clinton-hater extraordinaire Richard Mellon Scaife. In 1998, Ruddy founded Newsmax, a rabidly anti-Clinton media outlet created as an even farther-right rival to Fox News. Davidson was an early investor and board member, while Rees-Mogg served as chair of the Newsmax board of directors from 2000 to 2005.

The Sovereign Individual was their final book together, and the only one that would continue to find new readers in the twenty-first century. Like most conspiracy theorists and fortune tellers, the prognosticating pair often missed the mark. The eighties and nineties passed without their prophesied economic depressions. The US dollar failed to collapse, and most banks continued to exist. Terrorist groups did not obtain loose Soviet nukes and use them to create global havoc. Clinton was not unmasked as a spy or mafia don, nor did the nation collapse during his presidency. In fact, the federal deficit shrank, the economy boomed, and Clinton left office with record-high approval ratings. In perhaps their most embarrassing forecasting failure, they predicted the obsolescence of China, a country now poised to dominate the twenty-first century and beyond. "In all explorations of the projected future there will be misjudgements," wrote Rees-Mogg in his memoir.

But Davidson and Rees-Mogg, and fans of their work, prefer to focus on their more accurate-seeming predictions. Most notably, the two men spent years predicting the looming demise of the Soviet Union until it finally collapsed in late 1991. They also grasped the degree to which the twenty-first-century technologies like advanced computers, artificial intelligence, and digital financial assets would radically change the lives of almost every human being on the planet. Running through all their bleak economic predictions was an almost mystical faith in technology's power to reshape civilization.

"It is hard to overestimate the powers of technology to change what is important in life," they wrote in *Blood in the Streets*, emphasizing the role of technology as a chief element in social and political organization. "Technology not only helps people work and play, it affects the organization of work. Technology is a factor determining the size of firms. And the size of countries. Technology has a hidden, indirect role to play in the development of political ideologies. It helps change religion. Technology influences our perception of reality itself . . . Technology is still the driving force that makes history go."

In *The Sovereign Individual*, they honed these ideas into a feverish thesis for the twenty-first century. "Davidson and Rees-Mogg painstakingly detail strategies for prevailing financially during the collapse of the welfare state and for adapting to the exigencies of the end of the modern phase of Western civilization," said the jacket copy. The 400-page book ended with a list of thirty "Implications and Strategies" to help readers achieve "financial independence in the Information Age."

"Citizenship is obsolete," they wrote, advising readers to abandon the United States and obtain passports from other countries. "Of all the nationalities on the globe, U.S. citizenship conveys the greatest liabilities and places the most hindrances in the way of becoming a Sovereign Individual." Among the countries they recommended: New Zealand, Chile, and Argentina. They also advised readers to hire private security, seek walled enclaves to protect against increasing violence, park their assets in offshore accounts to evade taxation, and of course, to prepare for the arrival of "cybercash" or "cybercurrency"—a fact that has led some to erroneously describe Davidson and Rees-Mogg's work as the inspiration for crypto.

Davidson continued to push hysterical forecasts in the newsletter, and in videos, into the 2010s. "On December 21, 2012, a civilization-altering development will jam up our credit lines . . . mute the roar of our mighty military engine . . . topple the world's biggest monopoly . . . and send shockwaves across markets . . ." wrote Davidson in a special edition of *Strategic Investment* that was posted online in 2013. "Dear Reader: This is the first time in 17 years that I've made such a shocking announcement."

He was tapping into something called the 2012 phenomenon, a conspiracy theory popular with New Age types and based on a misinterpretation of the Maya Long Count calendar. Believers in the theory claimed the world would undergo a major transformation scheduled for the winter solstice of 2012. But as the date grew nearer, the Mayan apocalypse trope became a melting pot of spiritual hope, pseudoscientific anxiety, and end-times imagination. Media coverage of the hype expanded its audience, capturing the attention of conspiracy theorists, religious fanatics, and Hollywood. In 2009, director Roland Emmerich released *2012*, an epic science fiction disaster film with an all-star cast.

Davidson saw an opportunity to crank up the old doomsday machine.

"You can start preparing right now for the cataclysmic upheaval ahead," he wrote. "While you may have to do some immediate and dramatic repositioning of your portfolio, and maybe even your life, you could stand to reap great rewards in the era ahead . . . In fact, I believe more money will be lost (and made) in the 18 months following this event than ever before."

While December 2012 failed to deliver on Davidson's prophecies of planetary cataclysm, it did mark a major transition for Rees-Mogg. On December 29, he died of esophageal cancer at the age of eighty-four. Obituary writers generally steered clear of the multiple conspiracy books he wrote with Davidson, who had spent that year pitching kooky New Age poppycock. "When he died in 2012, the obituaries were more respectful, concentrating instead on his many years smoothly ascending and serving the establishment," wrote *Guardian* columnist Andy Beckett. "They only briefly mentioned *The Sovereign Individual*, and the handful of other, equally strange and ambitious Rees-Mogg volumes that preceded it, without making much effort to explain what the books were about. His career as an author, the obituarists discreetly implied, had been an insignificant sideline, or a bit of an embarrassment."

Davidson and Rees-Mogg peddled obsessive delusions of collapse and marketed a homemade theory for remaking the world order. *The Sovereign Individual* was a masterpiece of a doom-and-gloom financial newsletter industry that weaponized investors' obsession with predicting, and profiting from, catastrophic futures.

Yet Thiel would continue to hold the schlocky tome in high regard for decades, going so far as to send fan mail to its authors. In his 2012 apocalypse newsletter, Davidson noted Thiel's admiration for his work:

> *Ever since being a college mate of Bill Clinton's back at Oxford in the '60s, I have had the good fortune (though oft-times misfortune) to befriend and brush shoulders with many of the world's most powerful men, and many of the world's richest families, including figures like George Bush Sr., Steve Forbes, Margaret Thatcher, John Browne, Sir Roger Douglas, Boris Yeltsin, to name but a few.*
>
> *I also predicted that some of these figures would change the course of history . . . long before the world even got whiff of their names . . . I have also been the secret man behind some of the biggest movements and most successful companies in America today . . . And everyone from the World Bank to Heads of State . . . Washington Bigwigs to Big Oil . . . Czars to CEOs . . . have sought out my advice.*
>
> *In fact, in one of my favorite reviews to date, the famous Internet billionaire Peter Thiel (of Paypal and Facebook fame) recently wrote me and said: "I am an extremely big fan of your writings, which have shaped my thinking about the markets (and the macro world as a whole) perhaps more than anything else."*

A few years later, Davidson returned with another grave warning—"COLLAPSE 2016," a one-hour video presentation in which he predicted another all-out economic meltdown. The video introduced him as a "rogue economist," the "secret man behind some of the biggest movements and most successful companies in America for the last four decades," and an advisor to both President Reagan and President Clinton.

"I'm not the kind of person who likes to go around preaching doom," Davidson assured viewers, launching into his latest crash theory. He also repeated Thiel's praise, almost word for word, claiming it was Thiel's review of his latest book, *The Age of Deception: Decoding the Truths About the U.S. Economy*, which he had self-published in 2015.

In fact, Thiel's biggest endorsement came in February 2020, when he wrote the preface for a new edition of *The Sovereign Individual*. "In truth, the great conflict over our megapolitical future is only just beginning," he said. "On the dimension of technology, the conflict has two poles: AI and crypto. Artificial Intelligence holds out the prospect of finally solving what economists call the 'calculation problem': AI could theoretically make it possible to centrally control an entire economy. It is no coincidence that AI is the favorite technology of the Communist Party of China. Strong cryptography, at the other pole, holds out the prospect of a decentralized and individualized world. If AI is communist, crypto is libertarian."

"The future may lie somewhere between these two extreme poles," he concluded. "But we know the actions we take today will determine the overall outcome. Reading *The Sovereign Individual* in 2020 is a way to think carefully about the future that your own actions will help to create. It is an opportunity not to be wasted."

The book Thiel deems so insightful—and which he would inspire many of his fellow tech leaders to embrace—is a work of zero academic merit produced by two men for whom dark prophecy and lurid conspiracism became a mechanism for profit. Yet it shaped his destiny.

° ° °

Though he was born in Germany and spent years of his childhood in Namibia and South Africa, Thiel had thoroughly immersed himself in the politics of his adopted homeland. By the time he arrived at Stanford in 1985, he was already a committed culture warrior. At Stanford, he would find both his philosophical mentor and his first political allies, and these relationships would help define his path from campus provocateur to billionaire kingmaker. In 1987, he cofounded *The Stanford Review*, a rabidly reactionary student newspaper that portrayed Western culture at the university as under assault from diversity programs, Marxists, and political correctness. "To flip through the pages, as I did on a long day at the end of 2019, is to be continually flabbergasted that the authors managed to amass so much power in the decades that followed without suffering any apparent blowback," wrote Max Chafkin in *The Contrarian: Peter Thiel and Silicon Valley's Pursuit of Power*. *The Stanford Review*, still published today, would eventually spawn a polemical book, 1995's *The Diversity Myth: Multiculturalism and Political Intolerance on Campus*, which demonized campus diversity efforts and characterized date rapes as cases of "belated regret." In many ways, the book foreshadowed today's attacks on diversity, equity, and inclusion and gender equality. Thiel cowrote the book with David Sacks, a South Africa–born Stanford student who served as editor in chief at *The Stanford Review*. Their collaboration established a pattern that would define Thiel's career: surrounding himself with ideologically aligned allies who shared his contempt for mainstream liberal institutions. Sacks would later become a key business and political ally.

After Thiel received a bachelor's degree in philosophy, he went on to Stanford Law, graduating in 1992. He was not a software programmer or techie. His interests tended toward metaphysics and theology. René Girard, his key influence at Stanford, was a Catholic theologian known for his theories on the psychology of desire—so-called mimetics—and a focus on humankind's tendency to use scapegoating as a tool of social order. Thiel's early interest in philosophy and religion, and especially the ideas of Girard, would prove consequential in his business career.

After leaving Stanford, he tried his hand at being a lawyer, a Wall Street derivatives trader, and finally, a hedge fund manager.

He proved mediocre at all three. "During a year when the NASDAQ was up 40 percent and the restaurants and bars of the San Francisco Peninsula were floating almost exclusively on corporate credit cards from bankers, Thiel lost investors' money betting on currencies," wrote Thiel's biographer, Chafkin.

Thiel's decision to make odd bets on currencies echoes the advice Davidson and Rees-Mogg regularly dispensed. They urged investors to bet on foreign currencies and gold to profit from the (always impending) implosion of the dollar. While betting on paper currencies did not serve Thiel well as a hedge fund manager, he had better luck in pursuit of digital currencies. In 1998, a year after *The Sovereign Individual*'s publication, Thiel and a young software programmer named Max Levchin cofounded Confinity, a software company whose chief product was designed to help users of the PalmPilot—an early attempt at the smartphone—to make digital payments from the handheld devices. Though Confinity's product targeted a very limited market of PalmPilot users, Thiel saw it as a revolutionary technology.

"Levchin's technology was almost absurdly narrow—only super-nerds owned PalmPilots at the time—but Thiel continued to see the basic idea as potentially disruptive," wrote Chafkin. "Levchin hadn't invented a new kind of IOU; he'd invented a new currency. Once you had Confinity's payments app on your PalmPilot, which could be downloaded by zapping it from your friend's handheld, you could then use digital IOUs instead of dollars to buy stuff."

The tool that allowed PalmPilot users to transfer funds had a name: PayPal. Thiel would later describe the product as an early attempt to create cryptocurrency, just as envisioned by Davidson and Rees-Mogg. "*The Sovereign Individual*, by James Dale Davidson and Lord William Rees-Mogg, is an unusual book that I read at a singular moment, just before starting PayPal," Thiel told *Forbes* in 2014. "A lot of thinking about technology oscillates between two extremes: It's either a big historical force acting over the long term or it's a matter of short-term trends to bet on. *The Sovereign Individual* is different because it takes foresight seriously: If you think hard, you can understand and make plans for a future lasting 10, 20 years or more—and that's how you have to think to be successful."

Confinity had competition. Across the hall from Confinity's office at 394 University Avenue in Palo Alto, an ambitious South African immigrant was also trying to pioneer a digital payments technology. His name was Elon Musk and he called his company X.com. Musk and Thiel had a few things in common. Musk hailed from South Africa, and Thiel had spent part of his childhood in South Africa and Namibia where, according to the *Financial Times*, "his father was involved in uranium mining as part of the apartheid regime's clandestine drive to acquire nuclear weapons." Both Musk and Thiel also had connections to Stanford University. Thiel had obtained his bachelor's degree and law degree there, and Musk obtained a student visa to attend a graduate program at Stanford, but dropped out after two days to seek his fortune in tech. Both men also viewed digital payments as a promising business model.

In March 2000, Confinity and X.com merged. The Confinity name was retired, and Musk appointed himself CEO of the new X.com. He didn't last long in the role. The company's employees, many of them loyal to Thiel, soon complained about Musk's management. Even worse, Musk insisted on phasing out the name PayPal, which had strong brand equity and internet cachet. As tensions peaked in September 2000, Thiel arranged a boardroom coup. He temporarily replaced Musk as CEO after orchestrating his removal while Musk was away on his honeymoon. "I had thoughts of assassination running through my head," Musk later told his biographer, Walter Isaacson.

In 2001, X.com rebranded as PayPal. Musk eventually forgave Thiel, but the conflict set the tone for their relationship. Though Musk would become the richest man in the world, it is Thiel who is known as the "godfather" of the so-called PayPal Mafia, the group of interlinked tech oligarchs—including Thiel's *Diversity Myth* coauthor, David Sacks, Palantir cofounder Joe Lonsdale, and LinkedIn cofounder Reid Hoffman—who got started at the company.

Despite *The Sovereign Individual*'s grim soothsaying, the early years of the twenty-first century were extremely good for Thiel. In

2002, PayPal went public and, shortly afterward, got acquired by online commerce giant eBay for $1.5 billion in stock. Thiel's 3.7 percent stake in the company meant he was now worth $55 million. PayPal's success wasn't just financial validation for Thiel. He likely saw it as confirmation of the book's main thesis, and especially its prophecy of digital currency. Thiel had taken Davidson and Rees-Mogg seriously at a time when he was struggling to find his place in the world. Now, the PayPal windfall would empower him to build the technological and political infrastructure for the post-democratic future the book had promised. Over the next two decades, he would invest systematically in technologies and ventures that read like a checklist from the book's main points.

In the aftermath of the 9/11 terror attacks, the newly minted multimillionaire—a self-described libertarian—spotted another major opportunity, this one in government contracts. In 2003, he cofounded Palantir Technologies as a "mission-oriented" software company to "reduce terrorism while preserving civil liberties." Silicon Valley venture capitalists largely panned the idea; Michael Moritz, a partner at the famed Sequoia Capital who had invested in PayPal, reportedly doodled through his meeting.

Thiel had better luck in Washington. In-Q-Tel, the CIA's venture capital arm, invested $2 million in the company, but "[t]he company's $30 million start-up costs were largely bankrolled by Mr. Thiel," according to *The Wall Street Journal*. Palantir, named after an all-seeing orb wielded by an evil wizard in J. R. R. Tolkien's *The Lord of the Rings*, would eventually become a government surveillance giant valued at over $300 billion.

But Thiel's most fateful bet came in 2004, when he put $500,000 into a fledgling company called Facebook. This decision would make him a billionaire when Facebook went public in 2012—the year when James Dale Davidson had erroneously predicted another financial apocalypse. Yet Thiel's decade of astronomical financial success failed to calm his existential anxiety.

Even as his wealth grew, his pessimism deepened, and he began emulating the apocalyptic tones of Davidson and Rees-Mogg. In

2007, he published an unusual twenty-five-page essay that expressed serious doubts about the future of democracy. His essay, titled "The Straussian Moment," contended that 9/11 changed everything, and that the liberal democratic order, with its Enlightenment assumptions about freedom and rational self-interest, would not survive the existential threats of the twenty-first century. This new reality made it necessary to rethink governance, even if it meant sacrificing cherished notions of liberty, which Thiel dismissed as "the fundamentalist civil rights mania of the American Civil Liberties Union."

This was quite a self-serving argument for the cofounder of a major surveillance company to make, but it provided a clear glimpse of Thiel's increasingly dour worldview. The essay justified his own trajectory from libertarian millionaire to government security state contractor and declared that the West urgently needed to adopt a harsher and more clear-eyed view of human nature and politics—to embrace a civilizational struggle against an existential enemy in a battle that would require extraordinary, and uncomfortable, moral compromises.

"Today, mere self-preservation forces all of us to look at the world anew, to think strange new thoughts, and thereby to awaken from that very long and profitable period of intellectual slumber and amnesia that is so misleadingly called the Enlightenment," he wrote.

Thiel dressed his thesis in the ideas of philosopher Leo Strauss and Nazi jurist Carl Schmitt, as well as Girard, the Stanford professor. In an odd twist, the essay spent a good deal of time pondering the idea, derived from Schmitt, that humanity faced a dire risk from an "Antichrist" that would rise to power by using all-powerful technologies and promising "peace and safety."

"By making people forget that they have souls, the Antichrist will succeed in swindling people out of them," Thiel wrote.

It was a strange point for a Silicon Valley venture capitalist to make.

In 2009, as the nation recovered from the Great Recession and Facebook became a global phenomenon, Thiel's outlook seemed to grow bleaker. His disillusionment had been reinforced by his experience backing Ron Paul in the 2008 presidential campaign. Paul's campaign took a major hit when *The New Republic* dug up shocking excerpts from *The Ron Paul Investment Letter*. Reporter James Kirchick described the newsletters as "saturated in racism," reflecting "decades' worth of obsession with conspiracies, sympathy for the right-wing militia movement, and deeply held bigotry." "Given the inefficiencies of what DC laughingly calls the criminal justice system, I think we can safely assume that 95 percent of the black males in that city are semi-criminal or entirely criminal," read one typical sentence in the newsletter.

Paul denied writing the offending material, which had been published under his name, but said he took "moral responsibility" for it. Paul's national polling numbers never increased beyond single digits, and he dropped out of the race in June. Barack Obama won the 2008 election, driving Thiel to despair. The arc of history was apparently bending away from his far-right visions of the future. So, he declared that US democracy provided no path forward for people with his beliefs.

"I remain committed to the faith of my teenage years: to authentic human freedom as a precondition for the highest good," he wrote in an essay called "The Education of a Libertarian," which was published in the libertarian *Cato Unbound* journal in early 2009. "I stand against confiscatory taxes, totalitarian collectives, and the ideology of the inevitability of the death of every individual. For all these reasons, I still call myself 'libertarian.' But I must confess that over the last two decades, I have changed radically on the question of how to achieve these goals. Most importantly, I no longer believe that freedom and democracy are compatible."

Ten years after the Independent Institute speech where he spoke optimistically of a new digital currency to undermine the power of world governments, Thiel unveiled an updated version of his theory. "The 1920s were the last decade in American history during which one could be genuinely optimistic about politics," he wrote in his Cato Institute essay. "Since 1920, the vast increase in welfare beneficiaries and the extension of the franchise to women—two constituencies that are notoriously tough for libertarians—have rendered the notion of 'capitalist democracy' into an oxymoron."

The Roaring Twenties started out great for wealthy capitalists, who lived in a post–Progressive Era bubble in which Republicans controlled Congress and the White House—and wealthy business controlled the Republican Party. (Coincidentally, the 1920s were also the peak of the American eugenics movement, with immigration bans and forced sterilization as the law of the land.) President Warren G. Harding won the 1920 election promising a return to "normalcy" in the aftermath of a World War and a deadly flu pandemic that killed tens of millions of people around the world. But the decade ended in yet another cataclysm: a stock market collapse of historic proportion. The crash of 1929 discredited laissez-faire capitalism, leading to the Great Depression and, in a response, Franklin D. Roosevelt's slate of reforms. The orgy of greed and racism gave way to regulation, social safety nets, and movements toward civil rights.

Thiel did not mention any of these pesky details as he laid out his vision for liberation from the oppressions of democracy. "In our time, the great task for libertarians is to find an escape from politics in all its forms—from the totalitarian and fundamentalist catastrophes to the unthinking demos that guides so-called 'social democracy,'" he wrote. "The critical question then becomes one of means, of how to escape not via politics but beyond it. Because there are no truly free places left in our world, I suspect that the mode for escape must involve some sort of new and hitherto untried process that leads us to some undiscovered country; and for this reason I have focused my efforts on new technologies that may create a new space for freedom."

Thiel identified three areas where this democracy-free future could unfold. The first was cyberspace: "By starting a new Internet business, an entrepreneur may create a new world. The hope of the Internet is that these new worlds will impact and force change on the existing social and political order."

The second was outer space: "Because the vast reaches of outer space represent a limitless frontier, they also represent a limitless possibility for escape from world politics," he wrote. But he acknowledged that space had a significant "barrier to entry": "Rocket technologies have seen only modest advances since the 1960s, so that outer space still remains almost impossibly far away." He noted the urgent need to "commercialize space" but acknowledged that this would be a slow process. "The libertarian future of classic science fiction, à la Heinlein, will not happen before the second half of the 21st century."

The final area of his future focus was more down-to-earth: the sea.

"Between cyberspace and outer space lies the possibility of settling the oceans," he wrote. "To my mind, the questions about whether people will live there (answer: enough will) are secondary to the questions about whether seasteading technology is imminent. From my vantage point, the technology involved is more tentative than the Internet, but much more realistic than space travel."

Since becoming a billionaire, Thiel had taken an interest in the idea of seasteading, which calls for creating self-governing settlements in the middle of the ocean. The idea traced back at least one hundred years, to a Jules Verne novel called *Propeller Island*, which recounted the struggles of millionaires living on an island-like ship in the Pacific Ocean off San Francisco. Of course, there was one small problem: Previous efforts to create new colonies on the sea had failed spectacularly.

"Within the pantheon of would-be utopian communities, there's a particularly rich history of people trying to live outside the nation-state paradigm out in the ocean," wrote Alexis Madrigal of *Wired* in 2008. "The most ambitious was Marshall Savage's Aquarius Project, which aimed at nothing less than the colonization of the universe. There was also Las Vegas millionaire Michael Oliver's attempt to create a new island country, the Republic of Minerva, by dredging the shallow waters near Tonga. And the Freedom Ship was to be a mile-long portable country costing about $10 billion to construct."

A fellow Stanford graduate named Patri Friedman had revived the seasteading idea in a blog that became popular among Silicon Valley libertarians. Thiel became one of Friedman's biggest supporters, donating $500,000 for him to start the nonprofit Seasteading Institute.

"[T]he idea of seasteading was viscerally appealing, a physical manifestation of PayPal's approach to skirting financial laws," wrote Chafkin. "Rather than launch a political campaign for lower taxes on billionaires or for reduced regulation of cryonics providers, a seastead could, in theory anyway, just make those policies real and challenge the government to shut it down. By the time the rest of the world noticed what was happening, he reasoned, it'd be too late."

"Decades from now, those looking back at the start of the century will understand that Seasteading was an obvious step towards encouraging the development of more efficient, practical public-sector models around the world," Thiel said in a press release announcing his investment in the Seasteading Institute.

Every bit as kooky and impractical as it sounds, seasteading essentially sought to create Galt's Gulch but on rusty oil rigs in the middle of the ocean. But it helped that Friedman was the grandson of right-wing economist Milton Friedman and, as Chafkin put it, "willing to say the exact things that were not said in polite society." His Nobel Prize–winning grandfather had pushed "shareholder theory of value," and Patri Friedman pushed his own version of the idea. Seasteading explicitly argued for governments that operated as businesses, with citizenship framed as a matter of customer service. "Government is an industry with a really high barrier to entry," Friedman had told *Wired*. "You basically need to win an election or a revolution to try a new one. That's a ridiculous barrier to entry. And it's got enormous customer lock-in. People complain about their cellphone plans that are like two years, but think of the effort that it takes to change your citizenship."

The idea received plenty of mockery and scorn in the press at the time. "Tired of being denied the opportunity to live on a floating ocean capsule?" said NPR host Mike Pesca. "Well, then, seastead instead. Through the miracle of seasteading, which is like homesteading on the high seas, you'll make your own rules, define your own morality and thumb your nose at those mindless drones, tethered to their land-based notions of society. Wow, I really should have gone into PR for crazy people."

But Thiel's fantasy of seabound colonization did not spark as much controversy as his comments about freedom and democracy. His strange Cato essay had pronounced democracy incompatible with freedom due to "the vast increase in welfare beneficiaries and the extension of the franchise to women," which drew heavy criticism. The resulting furor forced Thiel to clarify his thoughts in a note at the bottom of the essay.

"It would be absurd to suggest that women's votes will be taken away or that this would solve the political problems that vex us," he wrote. "While I don't think any class of people should be disenfranchised, I have little hope that voting will make things better . . . Thus, I advocate focusing energy elsewhere, onto peaceful projects that some consider utopian."

Of course, not everyone was horrified by Thiel's attack on democracy, welfare beneficiaries, and women's suffrage.

In San Francisco, an anti-democracy blogger writing under the pen name of Mencius Moldbug offered a rousing defense of Thiel. "He is making a *factual statement*," wrote Moldbug in a 2009 blog post titled "Democraphobia Goes (Slightly) Viral," which linked to Thiel's essay. "His point is neither philosophical nor normative. If one can say that Louis XIV was a more effective ruler than Louis XV, one can say that a gigantic committee of men was a more effective ruler than a gigantic committee of men and women."

Moldbug's approving words came to Thiel's attention, and the two struck up a friendship. "They soon met for the first time, at Thiel's house in San Francisco, and, according to private messages I reviewed, struck up a confiding correspondence," wrote Ava Kofman of *The New Yorker* in 2025. Moldbug's emails to Thiel "were long and homiletic, full of precepts gleaned from pickup-artist blogs," while Thiel's were "straightforward and concise." "Both men seemed to take for granted that America was a communist country, that journalists acted like the Stasi, and that tech C.E.O.s were their prey," wrote Kofman.

Davidson, Rees-Mogg, and *The Sovereign Individual* laid the foundation for Thiel's paranoid and pessimistic political outlook. By heeding one of their prophecies, Thiel eventually became a billionaire. But it was Moldbug—real name Curtis Guy Yarvin—who would design the blueprint for America's post-democratic future. Thiel, using his wealth and influence to push Yarvin's ideas, would help create an ideological movement so extreme that many would dismiss it as a joke. Within a few short years, it would evolve from obscure internet subculture into a mortal threat to American democracy.

CHAPTER 2

THE ACID STORY

Curtis Yarvin and the "Cathedral"

Two days before Donald Trump became president of the United States for the second time, vice president–elect JD Vance attended an inauguration party at Thiel's Beaux Arts home in Washington. Vance spotted a familiar face across the room and called out: "Yarvin, you reactionary fascist."

"Thank you, Mr. Vice President—and I'm glad I didn't stop you from getting elected," came the reply.

The man Vance had greeted was not a senator, a CEO, or a donor. He was blogger Curtis Yarvin, an honored guest. By late 2024, Yarvin had achieved international notoriety as the key thinker of a movement that sought to dismantle American democracy and replace it with corporate dictatorship. The new vice president recognized him by sight—and even knew to call him a fascist. "I don't think he meant it in a bad way, but I don't think he meant it in a good way, either," Yarvin told *Politico*.

His ideas had traveled from an obscure, pseudonymous blog to the highest levels of American power—all thanks to Thiel. While *The Sovereign Individual* provided the foundation for the billionaire's political vision, Yarvin—a computer programmer and heavy psychedelic drug user in San Francisco—created a blueprint for turning that vision into reality. His fawning defense of Thiel's anti-democracy screed made an impression. The two men had formed a lasting bond. In Yarvin, Thiel found an ideological soulmate—a fellow traveler in the great struggle against democracy.

Despite his rising profile, some continued to dismiss Yarvin as an internet troll unworthy of attention. After all, he is not an expert, a scholar, a politician, or a billionaire. His only products are his anti-democratic, pro-dictator political ideas, which he shares in long and convoluted screeds. In interviews, he comes off as a highly talkative and neurotic bore. He's a man who interrupts others constantly and laughs compulsively at his own jokes—while also being prone to bouts of public sobbing.

But this raises an important question: Why do Thiel and other figures of influence consider him important? Yarvin matters because he provides a window into the souls of men who now control vast amounts of American wealth and power. With the help of men like Thiel—along with Marc Andreessen and a coterie of like-minded venture capitalists—Yarvin's radically unhinged ideas evolved from a blogger's musings into a serious effort to undo democracy that would be adopted by a presidential administration. So, it is important to understand Yarvin, because doing so exposes the bizarre and flimsy framework upon which tech fascism is built.

Yarvin's entire worldview seems designed to reject the very institutions that nurtured him. Yarvin, who seeks to destroy government, is the son of government workers. His father, Herbert, worked for the State Department and was posted for years in Cyprus and the Dominican Republic, where Yarvin described his life as that of a "diplomat's brat."

"He was an atheist Jew and she was a WASP," Meredith Tanner, who dated Yarvin for a few years in the 1990s, said of his parents. "They ran off together despite the disapproval of their families and lived a nomadic life, and were living on nothing but carrots and their skin turned orange."

Herbert and Susan Yarvin had two sons. Norman, Yarvin's older brother, was born in California in 1971. Herbert, like his sons, was academically inclined. He earned a PhD in philosophy from Brown University in 1973 with a thesis titled "Some Cartesian Questions." Some saw him as a strict father who controlled every aspect of his sons' lives. Curtis Yarvin disputes that characterization, calling his father "stubborn," "intense," and "formidable"—like "a good manager." Whatever the case, Herbert Yarvin failed to get tenure as an academic ("too arrogant," his son later told a reporter) and pursued a career in federal government.

Susan Yarvin taught both of her sons to read while they were still babies, inspired by the books of physiotherapist Glenn Doman, coauthor of the 1964 manual *How to Teach Your Baby to Read: The Gentle Revolution.* "We were taught to read at the age of two and can read much faster than other people," Norman said, noting that Curtis will often escalate a debate by urging his opponents to read a book. "So, 'read book *x*' is not as big a request in his mind as it usually is."

The Doman method involves using flash cards multiple times daily to teach babies to begin recognizing words before they can speak fluently. Doman originally developed his technique to help children with brain injuries, but the book became popular among parents eager to give their children a head start. With millions of copies in print in more than twenty languages, the book has a strong fan base. However, the approach has its critics, who say Doman's method wrongly emphasizes reading over important activities like play, prioritizes rote memorization over comprehension, and lacks scientific evidence supporting its effectiveness.

The family lived in Nicosia, Cyprus, for several years, and Curtis attended the English School, a rigorous academy where students wore uniforms. They returned to the United States in time for Curtis to start high school at age twelve. He was a math whiz who skipped three grades and was selected for the Study of Mathematically Precocious Youth at Johns Hopkins University. The study, one of the longest-running longitudinal studies of gifted children, tracks the life paths of children who scored over 700 on the math portion of the SAT before the age of thirteen. The family settled in Columbia, Maryland, where Yarvin entered Wilde Lake High School. Two years later, he went to college, briefly attending Johns Hopkins before transferring to Brown, where his father had earned a PhD.

By his own account, Yarvin had a terrible time in high school and college. Being much younger than his classmates relegated him to "weird, threatening, disturbing alien" status, he said. He has described himself as having "no social life" during this period. Despite his advanced academic skills and achievements, Yarvin was a lonely child who felt ostracized by his peers. But while the isolated, intellectually precocious teenager didn't fit in at college, he found connection in the chaotic early culture of internet chat rooms.

"He found more of a community on Usenet, a precursor to today's online forums," wrote *The New Yorker*'s Ava Kofman in a 2025 profile. "But even in groups like talk.bizarre, where intellectual peacocking was the norm, he stood out for his desire to dominate. Along with posting jokes, advice, light verse, and 'flames' (blistering takedowns of other users), he maintained a 'kill file,' a list of members he had blocked because he found their posts uninteresting."

Yarvin forged his identity in the machine. Online, he could be anyone he wanted to be, and Yarvin adopted the persona of an aggressive and creative troll. Over a decade before most people would be introduced to the concept of social media, he enjoyed minor superstar status in the world of online jousting—at least in his own mind. Usenet filtered out most of the public, since it included only two groups of people at the time: tech workers and college students. This changed in 1993, when the early internet provider company AOL opened the floodgates by giving every customer access to Usenet. This ruined the experience for elite users like Yarvin, who had to seek out more exclusive forums elsewhere.

It was in talk.bizarre, one of Usenet's more freewheeling chat rooms, that Yarvin met Meredith Tanner, who was several years older and married. They corresponded over email and eventually met at a party. The relationship was platonic at first, but it turned romantic after he mailed her a dose of MDMA, also known as Ecstasy or "E."

"We did it on the phone together," said Tanner. "Do not ever do 'E' with someone you don't want to feel romantic about, because it's going to go that way. The conversation just started to turn romantic, and by the end of the phone call we had turned romantic, and after that we started planning for me to move to California to be with him."

"He was very into psychedelics, and entheogens in particular," she said. "We dropped acid and watched movies. It was an interesting experience."

Yarvin was nineteen and pursuing a computer science PhD at UC Berkeley. Tanner filed for divorce and moved to California, where she and Yarvin shared an apartment near campus. Their whirlwind chemical-fueled romance did not last. Tanner remembers Yarvin as immature, demanding, and insensitive, a description that accurately describes many men at that age. But her time with Yarvin provides a glimpse of his early days in California, which seemed to largely revolve around psychedelics. He ingested a wide range of psychedelics, she said, and maintained a fascination with Alexander "Sasha" Shulgin, a Berkeley biochemist and psychedelic evangelist who synthesized the chemical compound for MDMA in the 1970s. "He particularly wanted to try DMT," said Tanner.

In addition, Yarvin was a Democrat. "In fact, he was more liberal than I was, and I'm pretty liberal," said Tanner.

Yarvin had a soft side. Tanner said he wrote poetry and "seemed like a normal human being" sometimes. But his dark side, which he honed by baiting his faraway opponents in online chat forums, left her with mostly bad memories. "He does not view humans as being as real as he is," she said. "He's a solipsist. He would take contrarian positions in a discussion and push really hard to see if he could provoke people. He viewed people as social experiments."

His edgy and provocative behavior, even toward friends, soon alienated their small social circle in Berkeley, and Tanner said they found themselves ostracized. Yarvin seemed highly aware of his unsavory characteristics. "One thing he liked to do was lock himself in a closet with the lights off and think of what an asshole he was," said Tanner, adding that he did this while on psychedelics.

The relationship collapsed after a few years, as did Yarvin's academic career. He had initially tried to follow in his brother's footsteps, pursuing an advanced computer science degree, but dropped out. One classmate remembered him as someone who tried hard to impress professors with his intelligence. They also remember calling him "helmet head" due to his habit of wearing a bicycle helmet in class. After dropping out, Yarvin worked at a series of tech start-ups through the late 1990s, continuing his psychedelic experiments. His personal life remained troubled. On June 25, 1997—the day he turned twenty-four—everything was falling apart. The start-up where he worked was failing, and he was in another bad relationship. So, he made a decision he would later describe as fateful.

"My whole social group has collapsed in a series of, like, insane infighting... and this explodes," Yarvin recalled in a 2025 podcast interview with comedian Tim Dillon. "My relationship with this troubled woman explodes, and basically all I have is a job offer from a company in Berkeley, a lease on an apartment... so what do you do in a situation like that? So basically my feeling was that the right thing to do was to take a shit ton of acid and go see the new John Woo film."

In the film *Face/Off*, John Travolta plays an FBI agent fighting against a criminal played by Nicolas Cage. The film is a violent thriller with a sci-fi twist: Travolta's hero and Cage's villain use a fictional technology to swap faces, creating much drama and suspense. Yarvin admitted this was an unpleasant experience, but it fit with his stated philosophy that certain kinds of experiences—psychedelic experiences—"should be as intense and disturbing as possible."

"I was reasonably experienced dropping acid by myself, as one should be," said Yarvin. "I mean, when you're a full-grown man. Don't try this when you're thirteen, but like, you can sit in the closet for eight hours on acid. You're a man, right? And there's . . . I mean, it's not the only thing that can make you a man. It's just one of them, right?"

Dillon interjected to suggest that Yarvin used the drug as in a "Native American ritual," apparently referring to the ritual known as a "vision quest," where a person finds their purpose. "It's a Native American ritual, exactly," said Yarvin. "Well, I didn't have any peyote, and I couldn't sit in this . . . smokehouse, but I could go see the new John Woo film."

Yarvin also took a large dose of psilocybin mushrooms to watch the director's cut of *Das Boot,* a three-hour film about a German U-boat crew in World War II. "Big sound, big screen, big picture," he said. "You're like basically five hundred feet under the Strait of Gibraltar and, like, British destroyers are trying to, like, crush you in an instant by throwing garbage cans of TNT right into the water for about forty-five minutes."

He briefly mentioned smuggling hallucinogenic mushrooms from Japan in a jar of miso paste after 9/11. Dillon joked that this could provide fodder for a future article in *Vanity Fair.* "The man who drove America crazy with his m—" said Yarvin, halting before finishing the word "mushrooms."

In the two-hour conversation with Dillon, titled "The Acid Story," Yarvin strived to create the impression that his experiences with mind-altering substances played a formative role in his development. Fortunately for him, his toils at an early mobile website company called Unwired Planet, later renamed Phone.com and Openwave, would eventually deliver a financial windfall.

In 2002, he cashed out, left his job, and embarked on a period of self-guided study in computer science and politics. "After the dot-com crash, I was left with a newly acquired girlfriend (who would become my wife), a few hundred thousand dollars, and a place in San Francisco," he told *Tablet* magazine in 2022, noting that his haul was "considerably less than 'fuck you' money." Yarvin said he had bought a house and lost money in the stock market, depleting his funds.

He was supposed to be focusing on a big computer science project to remake the internet from scratch, but he drifted into other subjects. "In 2002, he left Openwave with enough money to spend his days reading reactionary philosophers like Julius Evola, a friend of Mussolini, and Thomas Carlyle, a Scotsman who idolized Napoleon, and posting on internet forums," wrote Julia Black of *The Information* in a 2025 profile.

On April 24, 2007, he started a blog called *Unqualified Reservations.* Writing under the pen name of Mencius Moldbug, he began developing the political ideas that would make him famous.

"The other day I was tinkering around in my garage and I decided to build a new ideology," wrote Yarvin in his first post, titled "A Formalist Manifesto." Yarvin complained that current ideological camps—which he identified as progressive, conservative, and libertarian—had all failed. As for his qualifications for developing a new ideology from scratch, Yarvin explained: "I am just some dude who buys a lot of obscure used books, and is not afraid to grind them down, add flavor, and rebrand the result as a kind of political surimi. Most everything I have to say is available, with better writing, more detail and much more erudition, in Jouvenel, Kuehnelt-Leddihn, Leoni, Burnham, Nock, etc., etc. If you've never heard of any of these people, neither had I until I started the procedure. If that scares you, it should. Replacing your own ideology is a lot like do-it-yourself brain surgery. It requires patience, tolerance, a high pain threshold, and very steady hands. Whoever you are, you already have an ideology in there, and if it wanted to come out it would have done so on its own."

The writers he named all viewed mass democracy as a form of tyranny. Like earlier cyberlibertarians, Yarvin also nodded to Austrian School thinkers like Ludwig von Mises and the anarcho-capitalist Murray Rothbard. "Furthermore, I am a computer programmer who has read far too much science fiction—two major risk factors for libertarianism. So I could just say, 'read Rothbard' and call it a day," he wrote, linking to a piece by Lew Rockwell—the former Ron Paul chief of staff who coauthored the radical and racist investment newsletter. Yarvin was also deeply influenced by *Democracy: The God That Failed* by Hans-Hermann Hoppe, a 2001 book which promoted monarchy as a superior form of "private government" and claimed the "transition from monarchy to democracy" had been a "source of civilizational decline."

In one of his earliest essays, "Patchwork: A Political System for the 21st Century," Yarvin laid out a horrifyingly dystopian vision for the future. He imagined the government of San Francisco replaced by a totalitarian corporation called Friscorp. This corporate overlord would keep its residents under constant surveillance and exercise total power over their lives. Friscorp could even execute its residents without cause. Yarvin pondered what might happen with people deemed "not productive" by Friscorp. Perhaps, he wrote, Friscorp could "convert them into biodiesel, which can help power the Muni buses."

He was, he said, "just kidding."

"The trouble with the biodiesel solution is that no one would want to live in a city whose public transportation was fueled, even just partly, by the distilled remains of its late underclass," he wrote. "However, it helps us describe the problem we are trying to solve. Our goal, in short, is a *humane alternative to genocide*."

"The basic idea of Patchwork is that, as the crappy governments we inherited from history are smashed, they should be replaced by a global spiderweb of tens, even hundreds, of thousands of sovereign and independent mini-countries, each governed by its own joint-stock corporation without regard to the residents' opinions," he wrote. "If residents don't like their government, they can and should move."

Yarvin argued that democracy could never be reformed from within and described his patchwork idea as a philosophy of "exit"—leaving democracy behind for new forms of government. This vision raised an obvious question: If corporate city-states were superior to democracy, why hadn't they already replaced it? He answered with a conspiracy narrative. Democracy persisted, he argued, not because people genuinely preferred it, but because a powerful "meta institution" worked to hide its failures from public view. Yarvin called this all-powerful institution "the Cathedral"—a sprawling conspiracy of universities, media outlets, foundations, think tanks, and government agencies that controls public opinion in the United States. Unlike traditional conspiracy theories that focus on secret cabals meeting in back rooms, Yarvin's Cathedral operated in plain sight through what he saw as coordinated political messaging and control across elite institutions.

"The Cathedral consists of the educational organs: public schools, the universities and the press," he wrote in "Patchwork." "Its spires are the Ivy League and the New York Times, whose faculty and news desk respectively are endowed with an almost pure connection to the Inner Light—lesser institutions, of course, following their lead."

Yarvin's theory mimicked familiar right-wing arguments against universities, the media, and other institutions depicted as liberal. According to his theory, these institutions wield so much power that they essentially make democracy impossible because citizens are constantly indoctrinated by professors, journalists, and popular culture to believe in the status quo. Elections, he said, were ineffective at making change because voters believed they were making free choices while actually being manipulated by the all-encompassing power of the Cathedral.

"Even when populists win Presidential elections, they simply have no way to control Washington," wrote Yarvin. "Even with Congress and the Presidency, the White House has no real authority over the civil service, who outside the military are institutionalist by definition. The 'Reagan Revolution' started out as a populist tsunami designed to smash the New Deal, and turned into nothing at all. Nixon's 'silent majority' met an even more inglorious fate. At most a few token populist policies can be advanced. Populists can of course disrupt the institutional bowels of the state, leading to a sort of policy constipation, but like the old House of Lords, their only real power is to delay."

Yarvin's Cathedral theory bears striking resemblance to antisemitic conspiracy theories about media, banking, and politics—but updated as right-wing dogma for the blogging age. His theory also adapted the ideas of Carl Schmitt, a philosopher and Nazi jurist who argued that politics is based on secularized versions of theological concepts. In plain terms, this "political theology" means treating political authority like a kind of secular religion, with leaders acting as godlike figures who uphold scripture (laws and rules) but can suspend them in a crisis. Yarvin's Cathedral metaphor casts the institutions of democracy as a powerful religion-like force that rendered democracy unworkable.

Instead of solely demonizing groups based on ethnic or religious identity, his critique targeted educational and professional credentials as a malicious elite who exercise total control over the democratic system. "The Cathedral is a selective aristocracy, which is more or less the way China was run for about 2500 years," Yarvin wrote. "It is also the way the Soviet Union was run, the way the Catholic Church was run, the way China today is run, and the way Nazi Germany probably would have been run if we still had a Nazi Germany to kick around."

Yarvin sought to invalidate American democracy as well as inoculate his theory against criticism. If historians and political theorists rejected his claims about the superiority of monarchy, it only proved the Cathedral's power over academic discourse. If journalists criticized his proposals for corporate dictatorship, it demonstrated media bias against alternatives to democracy. Yarvin designed his theory to be unfalsifiable, so he never grapples with basic questions like: If monarchy is so great, why have most societies abandoned it? No counterexamples are allowed to exist. All arguments against him become proof of the Cathedral's wily schemes.

How to defeat the Cathedral and implement a formalist ideology? Yarvin wanted to rip it apart. In a 336-page essay called "An Open Letter to Open-Minded Progressives" in 2008, Yarvin laid out a plan for remaking government: a massive purge.

"First, the existing government must be thoroughly lustrated," he wrote. "There is no point in trying to debug or reform it." Lustration—remember this word—is the act of purging government officials after a regime change. Yarvin's letter to progressives argued that nearly every single federal government employee—"except for essential security and technical personnel"—should be "thanked for their service" and fired. He used "denazification," the elimination of Nazis from positions of power in Germany after World War II, as an example of what he meant. The cleansing or purifying of institutions would become a main recurring theme of his work, along with racist and eugenic tropes. The following year, he argued that some races are better suited for slavery than others.

"Not all humans are born the same, of course, and Carlyle (following Aristotle) takes the view that the innate character and intelligence of some is more suited to mastery than slavery," he wrote. "For others, it is more suited to slavery . . . Spaniards and Englishmen in the Americas in the 17th and earlier centuries, whose sense of political correctness was negligible, found that Africans tended to make good slaves and Indians did not."

He denied being a white supremacist but hedged: "I am not exactly allergic to the stuff." He described "America's actual WASP-Ashkenazi aristocracy, genuine genetic elites with average IQs of 120, long histories of civic responsibility and productivity, and strong innate predilections for delayed gratification and hard work" as being in contrast with "populations with recent hunter-gatherer ancestry and no great reputation for sturdy moral fiber."

To construct his homemade "formalist" ideology, Yarvin immersed himself in the writings of anti-democratic theorists and writers whose ideas he could weaponize against democracy. His influences included the dusty ideas of Thomas Carlyle, a Victorian essayist who argued in favor of monarchy and rejected democracy as "anarchy plus a street constable"; Joseph de Maistre, a French counterrevolutionary and monarchist who saw hierarchy and punishment as divinely ordained necessities; Vilfredo Pareto, an Italian theorist who argued for rule by elites and helped inspire Mussolini's fascists; Robert Michels, a disillusioned socialist whose "iron law of oligarchy" held that even democratic structures become oligarchies over time; and Carl Schmitt, a Nazi who supplied legal arguments to justify Hitler's dictatorship.

Yarvin wove together strands of vintage reactionary thought, fascist-era authoritarian theory, and libertarian extremism, synthesized through James Burnham (who argued that technocratic managerial elites rule all societies) and Hans-Hermann Hoppe (who claimed that monarchs, as "private owners" of government, govern more responsibly than democratic politicians). Like many a tech founder, Yarvin did not invent something new in his garage, but he did repackage old authoritarian ideas for a new century. He classified himself as a "Rothbardian," a follower of the anarcho-capitalist who also wrote under many of these same influences.

Writing as Mencius Moldbug freed Yarvin to be inflammatory and toxic, and his edgy blog attracted a fan base in Silicon Valley. By 2009, he had enough of an audience that his defense of Thiel's anti-democracy screed came to Thiel's attention. The two had much in common and they became close.

Yarvin's ideas continued to spread and gain notoriety via influential tech forums, and as he had not fully concealed his identity, it did not take long for his real name to leak. In response, he eventually decided to start writing under his own name.

As his anti-democracy fantasies gained traction, his computer programming career started to progress. While creating a new ideology to end American democracy and break the country into a patchwork of corporate dictatorships, he had also been dreaming up an ambitious project called Urbit—the fruit of the self-taught computer science PhD he had vowed to pursue after cashing out his stock.

Urbit, a decentralized personal server platform, ambitiously sought to remake the internet from scratch. Yarvin's scheme called for a peer-to-peer internet modeled on what he described as "digital feudalism" and a "kingdom in the cloud" complete with dukes, earls, and fiefdoms. He named himself "prince" of the realm but, in a curious caveat, promised that Urbit wouldn't be a monarchy because "monarchy is not an acceptable solution in this context."

Urbit tapped into growing concerns about corporate and government control of the internet, which sparked a movement to create decentralized platforms—patchworks for cyberspace. In 2010, Yarvin made Urbit's computer code freely available for anyone to download, study, and modify. As Yarvin merged ideology and technology, Thiel pursued a similar path.

° ° °

On October 15, 2010, Thiel gave an uncharacteristically optimistic speech at a libertarian conference called Libertopia. Two years earlier, an anonymous programmer using the name Satoshi Nakamoto published a white paper outlining a plan for a decentralized, peer-to-peer electronic cash system called Bitcoin. The disruptive digital currency prophesied by Davidson and Rees-Mogg, and heralded by Thiel in his 1999 speech, now existed. Thiel reminded his audience that PayPal had been an early effort to realize the dream of a technologized form of money to undermine government authority. He reiterated his belief that technology would make it possible to "unilaterally change the world without having to constantly convince people" and "basically overturn the monetary system" and described technology as an "incredible alternative to politics."

Only technology, he said, provided the means to escape the constraints of democracy. But he warned of a serious complication: Governments had the power to regulate technology. "[E]ven though I think politics is bad and voting is bad, the one caveat is that we have to be very sensitive to the degree to which politics has been constraining technology," he said.

Thiel closed his speech on a religious note: "I think it is only a small exaggeration to say that the government is so fundamentally evil that to deny the evil nature of the government is equal to denying the existence of the devil. I think that sort of double negative works both for people who believe in the devil and people who don't. And then, on the flip side, if the individual is to become sovereign—you think of the most sovereign thing in the world as something like God . . . achieving individual sovereignty means that you get to be God, or you get to be as close to God as is possible for anybody on this planet to be. And I think it is better to try to be God or to be like God than to be making a pact with a devil or with something like the devil. I think it is better for us to try to do something noble than to spend the rest of our lives trying to make compromises with the base."

The crowd applauded.

Two years later, Yarvin used a technology metaphor to describe American democracy, comparing it to a failing corporation run by a flawed operating system in need of an upgrade. "It's a very large system that needs to be destroyed," he said, in a speech titled "How to Reboot the US Government," delivered at a tech ideas conference called BIL.

He outlined a concept he called RAGE, an acronym for "Retire All Government Employees," which called for purging federal government employees and turning the United States into a dictatorship.

"You need a CEO, and a national CEO is what's called a dictator," he continued. "It's the same thing. There's no difference between a CEO and dictator. If Americans want to change their government, they're going to have to get over their dictator phobia."

He divided the country between "red states and blue states, Christians and communists" and suggested, ironically, that perhaps each camp could choose a dictator to run the new system together.

The audience applauded.

Yarvin and Thiel were clearly on the same wavelength, and Yarvin had become an important part of Thiel's inner circle, which some call the "Thielverse"; its members (including Patri Friedman) found common cause in their disdain for existing governmental structures. "Thiel's budding movement also had a house political philosopher: Curtis Yarvin, who was then only known by his pen name, Mencius Moldbug," wrote Max Chafkin in *The Contrarian*. "Yarvin, like so many in Thiel's orbit, was a verbose and dyspeptic geek with an abiding distaste for the mainstream Left."

Yarvin's notoriety increased in 2012, when a radical English academic named Nick Land anointed Yarvin the "supreme Sith Lord of the neo-reactionaries" and principal thinker of a political moment Land dubbed the "Dark Enlightenment." Like Yarvin and Thiel, Land despised democracy and preached the need for what *The New Yorker* later termed "a technological revolution that abolishes the political order." Land argued that capitalism and technology would balloon out of control, leading to the collapse of existing states and societies, resulting in a post-human singularity in which humans would merge with machines. The proper response, he wrote, would be to accelerate the process. Land is viewed as the godfather of a virulent strain of tech thought known as accelerationism. "Nothing human makes it out of the near-future," he declared.

Land left his tenured academic position at the University of Warwick to engage in heavy drug use and dabble in the occult. The drugs took a toll, and Land had a mental breakdown. "It had pledged itself unreservedly to evil and insanity," he would later write of this period, referring to his mentally disturbed psyche in the third person. "Its tool of choice, at that time, the sacred substance of amphetamine, of which much can be said, but mostly elsewhere. After perhaps a year of fanatical abuse it was, by any reasonable standard, profoundly insane."

He disappeared from public view but reemerged in the 2010s, preaching a new anti-democratic line of thinking called neoreaction. "Politics since the Enlightenment, he argues, is a story not of the advance of human freedom but of constant resource transfer from the productive to the unproductive—a world-historical tragedy of the commons that would eventually spell its own doom," wrote James Duesterberg in *The New Yorker*. "Land's main contribution to this discourse was to find a radically anti-human, science-fiction-inflected optimism in democracy's end. He projected a future where the postwar order collapsed and uncontrollable digital superintelligence led to runaway economic growth, a rapid hierarchization of society, and the eventual rule of a transcendent force that he called 'technocapital,' or, simply, 'Intelligence.'"

His techno-extremism earned him a cult following (Marc Andreessen calls Land his "favorite philosopher"), and in 2012 he passed the baton to Yarvin, praising him as the next step in the evolution of political accelerationism. "The state isn't going anywhere because—to those who run it—it's worth far too much to give up, and as the concentrated instantiation of sovereignty in society, nobody can make it do anything," wrote Land. "If the state cannot be eliminated, Moldbug argues, at least it can be cured of democracy (or systematic and degenerative bad government), and the way to do that is to formalize it.

"Once the universe of democratic corruption is converted into a (freely transferable) shareholding in gov-corp, the owners of the state can initiate a rational corporate governance, beginning with the appointment of a CEO," he continued.

With this endorsement, Land gave Yarvin his intellectual blessing. The drug-casualty philosopher who had self-destructed out of

British academia was now anointing an obscure software engineer as the prophet of neoreactionary ideas that would soon migrate from fringe blogs to venture capital boardrooms.

Not long after that, in 2013, Yarvin's relationship with Thiel started to bear financial fruit. Despite his success as a blogger, he'd spent many years broke, having apparently exhausted the money he made at Openwave. "And by like 2011 or 2010, I had two kids and was completely out of money," he later explained to Dillon. "And I also was depending on the kindness of my wife and my mother, neither of whom was rich. My wife just had a day job as a tech writer. And they basically were like, 'Hey, you gotta actually fund this and make this a thing, or get a fucking job,' because they were basically, like, here I was for the last ten years, as a parent with kids, basically no income to speak of, no savings. And what am I doing? I'm doing these insane fucking projects. One of them is just this weird-ass blog, right?"

In 2013, Yarvin cofounded a start-up company called Tlon to manage Urbit's development. "Thiel became a direct patron of Yarvin himself," wrote journalist Corey Pein in *Live Work Work Work Die: A Journey into the Savage Heart of Silicon Valley*. "Thiel's Founders Fund and the venture capital fund Andreessen Horowitz were the key players in a $1.1 million seed investment round for Yarvin's strange startup, called Tlon." One of Yarvin's cofounders, John Burnham, was a 2011 recipient of the Thiel Fellowship, which paid students $100,000 to drop out of college and pursue business projects. Marc Andreessen, who made an early fortune in the mid-1990s as cofounder of the once-dominant Netscape web browser, also struck up a friendship with Yarvin, as did Balaji Srinivasan, a Stanford PhD who had cofounded a Thiel-backed genomics company and who would soon join Andreessen's venture capital firm.

Yarvin had toiled in relative obscurity for years, but now his luck changed. His writing captured a growing audience, and his company attracted investment from two of the most renowned firms in Silicon Valley. His neoreactionary and Dark Enlightenment ideas continued to spread, gaining enough traction to draw the attention of critics.

That same year, in 2013, Klint Finley of *TechCrunch* published the first major exposé of the movement in an article titled "Geeks for Monarchy."

"Neoreactionaries believe that while technology and capitalism have advanced humanity over the past couple centuries, democracy has actually done more harm than good," wrote Finley. "They propose a return to old-fashioned gender roles, social order and monarchy." In early 2014, online culture researcher Jamie Bartlett dubbed it a "bizarre online neo-fascist movement" that was "growing fast." "Supporters are dotted all over the world, connected via a handful of blogs and chat rooms," he wrote in *The Telegraph*. "Its adherents are clever, angry white men patiently awaiting the collapse of civilisation, and a return to some kind of futuristic, ethno-centric feudalism."

A few months later, Corey Pein characterized Yarvin's ideas as a call for "total corporate despotism" in a scathing commentary headlined "Mouthbreathing Machiavellis Dream of a Silicon Reich." "It is a potent and bitter ideological mash that could have only been concocted at tech culture's funky smoothie bar—a little Steve Jobs here, a little Ayn Rand there, and some Ray Kurzweil for color," he wrote in *The Baffler* in May of that year. Pein quoted science fiction writer David Brin, who portrayed Yarvin as a wannabe Machiavelli courting wealthy patrons with a sycophantic ideology designed to fluff the egos of tech billionaires. "The world oligarchy is looking for boffins to help them re-establish their old—pyramidal—social order," wrote Brin. "And your screeds are clearly interview essays. 'Pick me! Pick me! Look! I hate democracy too! And I will propagandize for people to accept your rule again, really I will! See the fancy rationalizations I can concoct????' But your audition materials are just . . . too . . . jibbering . . . loopy. You will not get the job."

Brin made several valid points, but he got one thing wrong. Yarvin was exactly the person for the job.

° ° °

In March 2014, a Google engineer named Justine Tunney published an unusual petition on the White House website. It had three main points:

1. *Retire all government employees with full pensions.*
2. *Transfer administrative authority to the tech industry.*
3. *Appoint Eric Schmidt CEO of America.*

"It's time for the U.S. Regime to politely make its exit from history and do what's best for America," she wrote. "The tech industry can provide us good governance and prevent further American decline."

Tunney, a former Occupy Wall Street activist turned anti-democracy reactionary, was channeling Yarvin. "Read Mencius Moldbug," she tweeted one month after posting her petition. Tunney strived to be even more incendiary than Yarvin. She called for "open-source authoritarianism," defended slavery, and declared that "[t]he bottom 1/3 of the population should be live-in servants for the top 1/3rd."

Yarvin's meandering and aggressively anti-democratic screeds had tapped into a vein of virulent anti-government sentiment in Silicon Valley. Tunney's petition, dismissed by most as a silly computer nerd troll stunt in 2014, reflected an appetite for dismantling democratic institutions and replacing them with corporate rule. And it provided an early glimpse of an authoritarian ideology that had already been embraced by men who would soon become some of Silicon Valley's most powerful figures.

As Yarvin gained followers, he also attracted opposition. In 2015, his invitation to speak at a computer programming conference called Strange Loop was rescinded after outcry from other participants. In 2016, his inclusion at another computer science gathering, LambdaConf, generated major controversy. "Conference attendees and speakers are expressing anger and frustration on Twitter, with many broadcasting their plans of whether to attend," reported the business publication *Inc.* in a story headlined "Controversy Rages Over 'Pro-Slavery' Tech Speaker Curtis Yarvin." "Some sponsors have dropped out. A website has appeared for an alternative functional programming conference called MoonConf, slated for the same dates and in the same city as LambdaConf." Yarvin responded with a long post in which, addressing conference attendees, he denied being racist but added, "I can see why you might think so."

The growing public criticism of Yarvin's politically extreme writings posed a problem for his most fervent supporters, who worried about the risk of having their close connection to him exposed. In 2013, Srinivasan, the Andreessen Horowitz partner, had devised a strategy for discouraging reporters who might get too close to the story. "If things get hot, it may be interesting to sic the Dark Enlightenment audience on a single vulnerable hostile reporter to dox them and turn them inside out with hostile reporting sent to *their* advertisers/friends/contacts," he wrote in an email to Yarvin.

Thiel also expressed worry about his connection to Yarvin. "How dangerous is it that we are being linked?" he asked Yarvin in a 2014 email. "One reassuring thought: one of our hidden advantages is that these people . . . wouldn't believe in a conspiracy if it hit them over the head (this is perhaps the best measure of the decline of the Left). Linkages make them sound really crazy, and they kinda know it."

Yarvin had upgraded fascism for the twenty-first century, proving that Silicon Valley had an appetite for openly anti-democratic ideas and providing a blueprint for authoritarian government in the dismal future foretold by *The Sovereign Individual*. But his explicit racism, his defenses of slavery, and his calls for dictatorship made him politically radioactive to normal people during the Obama years. Anyone hoping to move his ideas into mainstream politics would need to distance them from the blogger who joked about converting people into biodiesel.

CHAPTER 3

EXIT

Balaji Srinivasan and the Network State

Yarvin's over-the-top troll antics made him famous, but they also posed a serious liability. To most people, he sounded like a socially maladjusted middle-aged racist who had done far too many psychedelic drugs and created a fantasy version of fascism while living off his mother and his wife.

If Thiel, Andreessen, and Srinivasan wanted to push his ideas into the mainstream, the Dark Enlightenment needed a rebrand. This meant stripping out Yarvin's florid gobbledygook concerning the virtues of monarchy, slavery, and mass murder. Fortunately, Balaji Srinivasan had been working on a more start-up-friendly presentation.

"I'm going to talk about something fairly different today," he said, smiling as he took the stage at Startup School, a signature event of the famed Y Combinator venture capital firm, on October 19, 2013. The annual conference brought together tech-minded college kids and tech superstars for a day of panels and speeches about how to succeed in Silicon Valley. Notable speakers on the roster with Srinivasan that day included Facebook founder Mark Zuckerberg and Twitter cofounder Jack Dorsey. Both delivered typical business self-help bromides about the challenges of running their popular social media companies. Srinivasan was relatively unknown by comparison. But while few remember anything Zuckerberg or Dorsey said that day, Srinivasan's remarks would kick off a new phase of Silicon Valley's movement to escape democracy.

Sporting a dark gym sweatshirt and several days' worth of beard, Srinivasan skipped the usual milquetoast advice on how to start a company. Instead, he urged the crowd of wannabe tech entrepreneurs to think about starting their own countries. His speech began with a brief description of his résumé, which included a BS, MS, and PhD in electrical engineering from Stanford, along with the founding of a genomics company. Then, he launched into his pitch deck for replacing the United States of America with a new form of government.

Srinivasan's presentation, titled "Silicon Valley's Ultimate Exit," called for replacing democratic governments with networks of corporate governments. His first slide featured an American flag side by side with the Microsoft logo and a question: "Is the USA the Microsoft of nations?" That line drew chuckles from the audience, but the next slide brought roaring laughter and applause. It featured a chart showing the ways in which American democracy resembled Microsoft. These similarities included "Codebase>230 years old, in obfuscated language" (along with a picture of the US Constitution), "systematic FUD (fear, uncertainty, doubt) on security issues" (next to an image of the National Security Agency logo and a picture of Edward Snowden), and "primarily focused on rich enterprise customers" (along with the corporate logos of large government contractors Halliburton, Solyndra, and Booz Allen Hamilton).

His sixteen-minute speech extended the USA-is-Microsoft metaphor to make a familiar argument: US democracy was an outdated software system in need of an upgrade. One way to do this, he suggested, was to exit the nation altogether and form new countries to rival it, much as Google arose from a rented garage in Menlo Park to challenge preexisting companies like Microsoft and Yahoo. Srinivasan described the situation as a question of "voice" versus "exit," concepts taken from the work of economist Albert O. Hirschman.

"If a company or a country is in decline, you can try 'voice' or you can try 'exit,'" said Srinivasan. "Voice is basically changing the system from within, whereas exit is leaving to create a new system, a new start-up, or to join a competitor."

Srinivasan used his own family history as an example, explaining that his father had grown up in a modest hut in Tamil Nadu, India, before immigrating to the US to seek opportunity. "We're shaped by both voice and exit, starting with the Puritans, you know, they fled religious persecution," said Srinivasan. "The American revolutionaries which, you know, left England's orbit. Then we started moving West, leaving the East Coast bureaucracy . . . Later, late 1800s, Ellis Island people leaving pogroms and, in the twentieth century, fleeing Nazism and communism. And sometimes people didn't just come here for a better life, they came here to save their life. That's the, you know, airlift . . . at the end of Saigon."

Srinivasan was hardly the first person in Silicon Valley to push the idea of new post-USA territories, but he was pushing the idea in a public forum to an audience of young wannabe tech founders, packaging anti-government extremism as the future of tech.

Srinivasan argued that, just as people fleeing oppression and seeking opportunity had fled other countries to create the United States, it was Silicon Valley's destiny to exit from a country that had now become hostile to innovation and progress. The growing power of tech, he said, allowed for a radically different vision of the future. Technology companies would soon be in a position to disrupt the power of what he called the "Paper Belt"—the nation's cultural and political power centers of Washington, New York, Boston, and Hollywood.

"Uber, Airbnb, Stripe, Square, and—of course, you know the big one—Bitcoin are all things that threaten DC's power," he said. "It is not necessarily clear that the US government can ban something that it wants to ban anymore." This echoed Thiel's comments in his 1999 speech about how DC would be powerless to stop technology. But Srinivasan went further, describing exit as an urgent necessity to get ahead of what he called "the Paper Jam"—a coming backlash against technology. He read off a few headlines from recently published stories: "More Jobs Predicted for Machines, Not People." "Job Automation: Is a Future Employment Crisis Looming?" "Imprisoned by Innovation." "As Tech Wealth Explodes, Silicon Valley Poverty Spikes."

These stories, he said, were a warning.

"They are basically going to try to blame the economy on Silicon Valley, to say that it was the iPhone and Google that done did it, not the bailouts, the bankruptcies, and the bombings," he said.

Srinivasan said tech had to actively fight against this narrative using voice to push for changes within the existing system. Ultimately, however, voice would not be enough. The answer, he said, was to exit altogether. This was complicated, however, by the fact that the US has a powerful government and military. "They have aircraft carriers, we don't," he said, to audience laughter. "We don't actually want to fight them . . . wouldn't be smart. So we want to show what a society run by Silicon Valley would look like without actually affecting anyone who still really believes the Paper Belt is actually good. And that's where exit comes in."

For good measure, he name-dropped two Silicon Valley titans who were already testing out the idea: "So, two of the founders of PayPal—Peter Thiel is into seasteading, and Elon Musk wants to build a Mars colony."

Srinivasan ended his speech with a slate of predictions about the future: "Drones—warfare is going to become software. Law is going to become code. Management, via robotics, is going to become automation. And property rights are going to become a network effect."

"If you want to think big, if you want to think about things that are next, build technologies—as minimal or maximal as you want—for what the next society looks like. It could be as simple as allowing people—you know, the middle class—to make tax shelters. Apps that allow people to travel and relocate better . . . anything you can think of that reduces the barrier to exit, that reduces lock-in. If we work together, we might be able to build something like this."

The audience applauded.

Srinivasan's unusual speech attracted plenty of attention.

"In a nutshell, Mr. Srinivasan, a computer scientist and co-founder of the genomics company Counsyl, told a group of young entrepreneurs that the United States had become 'the Microsoft of nations': outdated and obsolescent," wrote Anand Giridharadas of *The New York Times* in a story headlined "Silicon Valley Roused by Secession Call." "When technology companies calcify, Mr. Srinivasan said, you don't reform them. You exit and launch your own. Why not do so with America?"

Though Srinivasan had not used the word "secession" in his speech, tech writers at *Gawker, The Verge,* and *New York* magazine also zeroed in on it as the radical subtext of his speech. Farhad Manjoo, then a tech columnist for *The Wall Street Journal,* published a scathing takedown of the speech, calling out Silicon Valley's "superiority complex." "On its surface, Mr. Srinivasan's talk, called 'Silicon Valley's Ultimate Exit,' sounded like a battle cry of the libertarian, anti-regulatory sensibility long espoused by some of the tech industry's leading thinkers . . ." wrote Manjoo. "But there was something more significant about Mr. Srinivasan's talk than simply a rehash of Silicon Valley's grievances. It was one of several recent episodes in which tech stars have sought to declare the Valley the nation's leading center of power and to dismiss non-techies as unimportant to the nation's future."

In an interview with Manjoo, Srinivasan backpedaled somewhat, insisting that he wasn't quite calling for secession, but instead a "peaceful exit." He compared it to his father's immigration to the US from India. "But when I asked him what harms techies faced that might prompt such a drastic response, he couldn't offer much evidence," wrote Manjoo.

Srinivasan's presentation did not contain new ideas. It simply merged the key points of *The Sovereign Individual* and Yarvin into a sanitized corporate pitch deck. Just as in *The Sovereign Individual,* Srinivasan spoke of meta political concepts and portrayed technology as an unstoppable force destined to undermine nations and transform global governance. And his push for corporate networks to replace existing democracies was a lightly repackaged version of Yarvin's "patchwork" idea for replacing democracies with corporate-controlled governments. All of this had deep roots in decades of extreme libertarian and accelerationist thinking, and other tech figures had already begun to float similar trial balloons. In May 2013, Google cofounder Larry Page suggested carving out part of the world as a zone where tech companies could operate without regulations. "There are many exciting things you could do that are illegal or not allowed by regulation . . . but maybe we can set aside *part* of the world," he said during a question-and-answer session at a Google conference. (In a 2009 TED Talk, Stanford economist Paul Romer suggested the creation of "charter cities"—experimental urban zones in developing countries—as a way to stimulate economic growth and alleviate poverty. Critics called it "colonialism" and Yarvin called Romer a "plagiarist.")

Just a few days before Srinivasan's speech, Marc Andreessen had predicted an explosion of new countries in the twenty-first century. "I think there is going to be double, triple, quadruple countries in the coming years," he told the tech publication *PandoDaily*. "The transition is going to be very painful," he said, "but I think ultimately it's going to be very healthy."

Srinivasan hadn't exactly innovated, but he had succeeded in distancing the idea of post-American tech sovereignty from Yarvin's cartoonishly fascist version—momentarily. One month later, on November 22, *Wired* published an essay by Srinivasan in which he attempted to further whitewash his idea, abandoning his harsh critique of the United States as failing software and recasting the idea as simple online community-building in the "cloud"—communities that could eventually become countries, or not. "From Occupy Wall Street and Y Combinator to co-living in San Francisco and co-housing in the UK, something important is happening," he wrote. "People are meeting like minds in the cloud and traveling to meet each other offline, in the process building community—and tools for community—where none existed before. Those cloud networks where people poke each other, share photos, and find their missing communities are beginning to catalyze waves of physical migration, beginning to reorganize the world. Will this ultimately end in a cloud country of our own, as Page, Thiel, and Musk propose in different ways?"

Unfortunately for Srinivasan, his effort to reframe his speech was completely overshadowed by the publication of the "Geeks for Monarchy" piece in *TechCrunch* that same day. It exposed Srinivasan's shtick as an outgrowth of Yarvin's proto-fascist, pro-monarchy ideology.

"Yarvin proposes that countries should be small—city states, really—and that they should compete for citizens," wrote *TechCrunch*'s Klint Finley. "That will probably sound familiar if you heard Balaji Srinivasan's Y Combinator speech." Finley then added a caveat: "I don't know Srinivasan, but it sounds like he'd find neoreactionary views repulsive." While he was correct in spotting the connection between Yarvin's and Srinivasan's ideas, he was wrong about Srinivasan's relationship to Yarvin's ideas. It's not clear how long Srinivasan had been reading Yarvin, but by 2013 they were close enough for Srinivasan to have imagined doxing reporters to scare them away from the story. The *TechCrunch* story threw him into a panic. In a text chain later obtained by *Wired* and other publications, Srinivasan called Finley's story "extraordinarily dangerous" and considered mounting a fierce attack to scare off other journalists. "It might mean moving to Singapore though as endgame," he wrote, acknowledging the potential risks of a scorched-earth strategy. Yarvin, who was on Srinivasan's text chain along with Patri Friedman and a recent Stanford Law grad named Blake Masters, urged Srinivasan to avoid overreacting.

"Dude, control the frame," Yarvin wrote. "If you make a big thing of it, you prove their point." He continued: "You and I have different vulnerabilities, you because you're in the closet and I because I'm out of it. Our mission of the next few years is to drag sanity into the mainstream from opposite directions. It's a long game which rewards patience . . ."

Yarvin was right. The controversy faded, and the criticism from mainstream media outlets only seemed to burnish Srinivasan's stature among Silicon Valley elites. The next month, he became partner at Andreessen Horowitz, the booming new venture capital fund known by the nickname a16z. The promotion capped a remarkable rise for Srinivasan, a New York native who had moved to California sixteen years earlier to attend Stanford University.

Like Yarvin, Srinivasan was a privileged child who grew up to scorn the very systems that had enabled his success. After leaving India, his parents eventually settled in Plainview, a suburban hamlet on Long Island, where both worked as physicians. Srinivasan was born in 1980, and as with Yarvin, his academic talents became apparent at an early age. "I was born with certain advantages," he wrote of his childhood. "My grandfather taught me a lot of math early on, before he passed away. I learned to read at a young age."

While he excelled at his studies, he described himself as a friendless nerd who hated school. In *The Anthology of Balaji,* a fawning collection of Srinivasan's interviews and tweets self-published in 2023, Srinivasan described his upbringing as bleak and oppressive. His parents worked constantly, he said, leaving him to entertain himself for long stretches. "I escaped into an inner world of fiction and reading, flying through books," he said. "That was my life for many, many years."

Despite his academic success, he came to despise compulsory education. "The first thirteen years of my conscious life, school was a prison-like environment," he said. "You must go there every day; you cannot leave. You have no control over your environment. You cannot avoid other kids in school, and I was simply not part of the social network. This was pre-internet, so I had no cultural role models. Especially early on, I was dressed up in foreign clothes while all of the other kids were wearing sports t-shirts. I stuck out."

A photo of Srinivasan published in *Newsday* in 1982 suggests a more nuanced reality. It shows him as a smiling two-year-old sporting a pageboy haircut and dressed in standard American toddler gear—shorts and a T-shirt emblazoned with a cartoon dinosaur. But Srinivasan said growing up as "the only brown kid" in an overwhelmingly white Long Island town in the twentieth century posed unique challenges. Kids would gang up on him and taunt him with racist names like "Gandhi," he said. He now credits such experiences with creating early feelings of alienation from society, as well as disdain for the authorities he blamed for failing to halt such torments.

"I learned early on that you've got to stand up for yourself, that the fix is in . . . the state is against you," he said, connecting his playground experiences to his anti-government attitude. "In short, teachers wouldn't protect me, so I learned to fight. I learned how to deter aggression and how to find a defensible position. I had to develop the reputation of being crazy. I learned the establishment was not on my side."

To survive Plainview's suburban hellscape, Srinivasan said he became a disruptive student with a knack for ending up in detention, where he could "read in peace." Fortunately, such contretemps did not affect his academic performance. He excelled at Plainview-Old Bethpage John F. Kennedy High School, earning a perfect score on the SAT. In addition, he made the cut for the varsity football and lacrosse teams, though only as an "nth string cornerback and midfielder." "At the front of the school were rankings of students in the honor roll and in detention," he said. "I was always at the top of both."

Srinivasan's classmates remember things differently.

"He always had an arrogance about himself," said Dana Kirschman, who attended middle school and high school with Srinivasan. "You could never tell him he was wrong."

She acknowledged that he faced some bullying, but not necessarily because of his race. "Yes, he was picked on, but he would also call teachers and students stupid all the time," said Kirschman.

Multiple other classmates disputed the claim that Plainview was especially hostile to brown people. "He did act up sometimes in classes and clubs, and was probably teased and maybe even bullied by some," said another classmate. "Because he was so smart, everything was probably going so slow around him. We weren't quick enough for how fast his mind was going. However, it would have had nothing to do with his race/ethnicity/religion."

After graduating in 1997, Srinivasan headed west to attend Stanford. Despite his simmering dislike for educational institutions, he remained for a decade, earning several degrees, including a master's in chemical engineering for work in genetic circuits and computational genomics. He stayed on campus to teach after finishing his degrees in 2006, leaving to launch a start-up in 2008. Counsyl, a company Srinivasan cofounded in a dorm room at Stanford, offered low-cost genetic testing "for more than 400 mutations and at least 100 genetic disorders for parents who are planning children," according to *TechCrunch*. The company struggled at first, before a powerful venture capitalist recognized its potential. "We had to bootstrap for the first few years and eventually got funding from Peter Thiel and Founders Fund," said Srinivasan.

He and Thiel had more in common than the genomics company, which would be acquired by Myriad Genetics for $375 million in cash and stock in 2018. Both shared an interest in Yarvin, crypto, and, as it turns out, *The Sovereign Individual*. Srinivasan has described the book—which Thiel recommended to him—as "the most prescient thing in the world."

° ° °

Five years after leaving Stanford, the first-generation American—whose father had grown up poor in Tamil Nadu—found himself in a rarefied circle of Silicon Valley titans. His anti-government views, apparently forged in the hallways of his Long Island high school, made him a natural fit at Andreessen Horowitz (a16z).

Founded in 2009 by Marc Andreessen and Ben Horowitz, a16z made a name for itself as one of the boldest and most successful venture capital funds in Silicon Valley. It did this, in part, by investing in companies that disrupted economics by openly breaking the law. a16z made a killing as an early investor in Airbnb and Lyft. Both companies were designed to directly challenge government authority: Airbnb operated in violation of local housing and zoning laws; Lyft started as an unlicensed taxi service. Yet they would triumph over the rules and regulations to become multibillion-dollar behemoths. a16z also made early investments in Facebook and Twitter, social media companies that would fundamentally reshape American politics.

Unlike many venture capital funds, a16z did more than just write big checks. It branded itself as an "all-service" firm that, like Y Combinator, took a hands-on approach to its investments. This meant offering recruiting, marketing, and public relations support, making it less like a bank and "more like a Hollywood talent agency," according to Andreessen. The firm also understood the power of narrative and eventually sought to shape stories not just around start-ups but across entire industries. "Software is eating the world," Andreessen had declared in a 2011 essay that—much like *The Sovereign Individual*, Yarvin, or Srinivasan—cast technology as an unstoppable historical force destined to conquer everything. He had a point: Amazon was devouring retail, Netflix was replacing the video store, and Spotify was remaking music distribution. If a legacy investment giant like Goldman Sachs was "a great vampire squid wrapped around the face of humanity," a16z wanted to become its twenty-first-century successor—aggressive, omnipresent, and unapologetically predatory in pursuit of massive returns.

Venture capital (VC) firms, which make bets on new companies by providing capital in return for ownership stakes, had long existed in one form or another. But the VC model underwent a major shift in the twenty-first century. The Netscape IPO in 1995—where Andreessen made his first fortune—had shown that an unprofitable, sixteen-month-old company could instantly skyrocket to a billion-dollar valuation. An economy based increasingly on software meant the right company—the rare and coveted "unicorn"—could scale wealth at an unprecedented rate. Venture capital firms restructured their entire model around hunting for these unicorns, herding major institutional investors and wealthy individuals into massive funding pools for portfolios of start-ups promising world-changing innovation. If even one company hits unicorn status, the returns can be staggering—making VCs the key beneficiaries of Silicon Valley's exponential wealth creation.

"These companies are in early stages of development, and as such, there is much more uncertainty about their prospects," wrote Catherine Bracy in *World Eaters: How Venture Capital Is Cannibalizing the*

Economy, a history of VCs. "Unlike the companies funded by private equity, venture capital's more mature and boring older brother, the startups in a venture capital portfolio are, at least in theory, doing something interesting and innovative, often employing new technologies if not creating them." Many of the companies in which VCs invest will fail to produce much value, but the billion-dollar unicorns make the risk worthwhile. The end result, wrote Bracy, "is an overall fund value that is quite lucrative, even though only a small fraction of the companies within the fund are driving most of the value creation."

Since VCs need massive returns to justify their high-risk bets, they actively seek companies that can disrupt traditional industries by sidestepping regulations or breaking established rules—a strategy that can create billion-dollar markets overnight. This leads to short-term thinking with an emphasis on generating the maximum amount of money as quickly as possible. In May 2026, *PitchBook*'s official "unicorn tracker" counted 1,688 active unicorns, collectively worth $6.1 trillion and built on $1.6 trillion in venture funding.

Andreessen had been in the right place at the right time with Netscape, and he did it again with a16z. Its distinctive full-service approach quickly made it one of Silicon Valley's most powerful venture firms. From its founding in 2009 with a $300 million debut fund, the firm would rapidly expand to more than $16.5 billion in assets under management by 2020, to over $90 billion in 2026. The firm would earn hundreds of millions annually in fees, and blockbuster exits from companies like Instagram, Airbnb, and Coinbase would secure billions in profit.

While the mainstream press mocked Srinivasan's fantasies of exiting the USA, a16z responded by giving him a seat on their rocket ship. In December 2013, he became the firm's eighth general partner. His five years at the firm coincided with both a meteoric rise in venture capital, as well as a crucial early boom period for crypto.

By early 2009, Bitcoin was being mined and distributed among a small group of initial users. While it was not the first cryptocurrency in existence, it turned out to be the first very successful one. In its first days, Bitcoin was a mysterious novelty to all but a hardcore group of dedicated fans who saw it as a new form of digital gold. Srinivasan was among those who took an initial interest. In early 2013, before joining a16z, Srinivasan had founded a company called 21e6 to cash in on the crypto craze. To create a Bitcoin, specialized computers compete to solve complicated math puzzles in a process called "mining." The first computer to solve the puzzle gets rewarded with new Bitcoins. Bitcoin mining guzzles enormous amounts of electricity. These math puzzles serve no purpose except to make Bitcoins hard to mine, creating a sense of scarcity. Bitcoin's value rests on the notion that this digital scarcity—pointless puzzles solved by burning electricity—is worth real money. Dollars are valuable because they are backed by governments and can be used as legal tender, but Bitcoin only has value if enough people continue to believe in it. As with a Ponzi scheme, Bitcoin's value relies entirely on finding new people to believe in this story and pay an ever-higher price for it. Therefore, the main use of Bitcoin—besides financing crime and terrorism—is casino-like betting on the idea that its value will continue to shoot up.

By 2011, crypto remained mostly a niche concept that was viewed suspiciously by most business and finance types. Famed investor Warren Buffett would later dub it "rat poison, squared." But there was enough interest in the budding sector that in June 2011, hackers stole thousands of Bitcoins from Mt. Gox, one of the earliest online crypto exchanges. Such disasters worsened establishment perception of Bitcoin, but the true believers persevered, and the price of Bitcoin rose from $13 to $266 in early 2013. With value spurting out of this mysterious technology, trepidation over Bitcoin became enthusiasm, and the frenzy to cash in on the crypto phenomenon began in earnest. As Bitcoin mining intensified, it created an arms race for faster chips and cheaper electricity, and that's where Srinivasan hoped to make a killing with 21e6.

"The company 21e6—shorthand for 21 million, the number of Bitcoins to be released—was created by Balaji Srinivasan, a Silicon Valley prodigy who had founded a successful genetics company from his Stanford dorm room," wrote Nathaniel Popper in *Digital Gold: Bitcoin and the Inside Story of the Misfits and Millionaires Trying to*

Reinvent Money. "In the spring of 2013, Balaji was quietly assembling a team of top engineers to build a Bitcoin mining chip that would go beyond anything that had been contemplated before—rolled out in data centers built exclusively for the 21e6 machines. If the chips worked as promised they would mint money for investors."

21e6, also known as 21 Inc., joined an expanding group of start-ups trying to create computers that excelled at mining Bitcoin quickly. Butterfly Labs, a start-up in Kansas City, created a custom Bitcoin mining computer with specialized chips in 2012. Shortly afterward, a twenty-three-year-old Chinese immigrant in New York named Yifu Guo developed an even faster mining computer that used less energy, lowering electricity costs. Srinivasan's idea won support from a slate of Silicon Valley VCs: Andreessen, Horowitz, Thiel, and David Sacks, along with angel investor Naval Ravikant and the Winklevoss twins, Cameron and Tyler.

"Soon enough, Balaji was closing in on a $5 million fund-raising round," wrote Popper. "The Bitcoin arms race had begun."

By the end of the year, 21e6 had raised over $70 million.

"From the beginning, 21e6 was sold as a top-secret project, allowing people to invest without needing to come out as public supporters of Bitcoin," wrote Popper. "The company was also structured as a limited liability company rather than the C Corp typical of startups, so that people could invest with their own money."

But the extreme volatility of the crypto sector disrupted Srinivasan's plan for Bitcoin dominance. Bitcoin reached a peak of $1,200 in late 2013, creating one of the first speculative frenzies in crypto. The streak didn't last. Disaster struck again in early 2014 when the Mt. Gox exchange, which processed most of the world's Bitcoin transactions, announced that hackers had stolen more than $460 million from customers' accounts. The price of Bitcoin plummeted, and Mt. Gox collapsed in a cloud of lawsuits and bankruptcy proceedings. 21e6, which required an endless wave of Bitcoin hype to drive demand for its product, went into a tailspin. By 2015, the company was in deep debt and trouble.

"In May 2015, I became CEO of a company that was in a very

difficult situation," Srinivasan later wrote in a self-published essay about the company, titled "The Turnaround," in 2018. "It had more than $80M in data center and venture debt commitments with less than a year of runway."

This framing seemed odd, since he had cofounded the company, and as early stories made clear, it was his brainchild. After distancing himself from his creation, he details its harrowing journey from failure to success. As the company foundered, it pivoted to desperate strategies, including one that involved what Srinivasan described as "repurposing the datacenter's mining chips to embed in phone chargers."

Srinivasan did not mention that he had sought to exit the predicament altogether by seeking a position in government. At the 2016 Republican National Convention in Cleveland, where Thiel first lived after his parents immigrated to the United States, Thiel delivered a tech-themed speech that, echoing Yarvin and Srinivasan, depicted the nation as a broken product in need of restoration. "Our nuclear bases still use floppy disks," he said. "Our newest fighter jets can't even fly in the rain. And it would be kind to say the government's software works poorly, because much of the time it doesn't even work at all. This is a staggering decline for the country that completed the Manhattan Project. We don't accept such incompetence in Silicon Valley, and we must not accept it from our government."

"Tonight, I urge all of my fellow Americans to stand up and vote for Donald Trump," he concluded, to thundering applause.

Yarvin spent election night at Thiel's San Francisco mansion, where guests popped champagne as the results became clear. Weeks later, Yarvin took credit for influencing Thiel's politics in an email exchange with Milo Yiannopoulos, a far-right British blogger and provocateur who would find himself largely outcast from politics in 2017 after one video surfaced in which he made controversial comments about pedophilia and another showed him singing "America the Beautiful" as audience members gave Nazi salutes.

"Peter [Thiel] needs guidance on politics for sure," wrote Yiannopoulos.

"Not as much as you might think!" Yarvin replied. "I watched the election at his house, I think my hangover lasted until Tuesday. He's fully enlightened, just plays it very carefully!"

Trump's win gave Thiel a new degree of influence in the nation's capital. As is customary for large donors, he went to Washington with a list of candidates for powerful positions in federal government. Among Thiel's top requests: He wanted Trump to appoint Srinivasan as head of the Food and Drug Administration (FDA). Srinivasan, along with Thiel deputy Jim O'Neill, met with the new president to discuss the position.

Word spread quickly in Washington, and the knives came out. As it turned out, Srinivasan had repeatedly posted tweets that called for the FDA to be replaced with a private company—a "Yelp for drugs." He had criticized the agency for slowing drug experimentation and development by enforcing rules and regulations, which is the FDA's entire job. But with the prospect of a White House appointment looming, Srinivasan deleted every single one of his tweets and signed off of Twitter with a simple message: "Don't argue on Twitter. Build the future."

It was a rookie mistake. The offending posts had been preserved on internet archives, and Srinivasan's decision to nuke all his tweets only drew more attention to them. This provided exactly the kind of minor scandal capable of derailing a nomination in those days. "Balaji Srinivasan, Who May Run the FDA for Trump, Hates the FDA. But Silicon Valley Likes Srinivasan," declared *Recode* in a piece detailing his deleted tweet scandal. "Why Did Trump's Top FDA Pick Delete All His Tweets?" asked *Gizmodo*.

Amid this fusillade of bad headlines, his Silicon Valley buddies lobbied hard in his favor. Billionaire Naval Ravikant and a16z cofounder Ben Horowitz tweeted their support for his nomination, as did *Dilbert* cartoonist Scott Adams. It didn't work. Within a week, *Politico* delivered the verdict: "Srinivasan Not Up for FDA Role, Per Source."

Thiel's decision to push him as a nominee demonstrated the degree to which he held Srinivasan in high regard. It also provided an early glimpse of Silicon Valley's budding alignment with Trump.

"Up until now, tech leaders have been unwilling to endorse any part of the Trump agenda in public," wrote Peter Kafka of *Recode* before the nomination tanked. "Srinivasan isn't formally part of the Trump agenda yet. But you can see how if he gets there, Techland—at least corners of it—could start telling itself that Trumpland might have some upside, after all. They might even start saying it out loud."

Whipped by Washington, Srinivasan—who later claimed it was he who had turned down Trump—returned to the mess at 21e6, which rebranded as Earn.com, and the company became "a service that rewards users financially for answering emails and completing tasks." This pivot garnered the company an infusion of cash from a16z. A year later, in 2018, a rapidly growing crypto company called Coinbase—which had launched from Y Combinator in 2012 and received funding from a16z in 2013—acquired Earn.com in a deal reportedly worth $120 million. Earn.com underwent another dramatic makeover, becoming a marketing program that paid users small amounts of crypto to watch videos and complete quizzes about crypto.

"It was a crummy company," one Coinbase engineer said of Earn.com. "Hiring Balaji was a way for Andreessen Horowitz to liquidate its dog of a startup." Other Coinbase insiders said the actual purchase price was much lower than $120 million: "You can come up with any sort of deal number you like for public consumption when you factor in hypothetical future payouts. And Balaji has a big ego, so he wanted as big a number as possible."

As part of the deal, Srinivasan joined Coinbase as chief technology officer. a16z had bet big on Coinbase, which had become a major player after the collapse of Mt. Gox. Brian Armstrong, a former Airbnb engineer from San Jose, had founded the company in a San Francisco apartment in 2012. He launched it via Y Combinator's start-up incubator and received a $150,000 cash infusion. Fred Ehrsam, a former Goldman Sachs trader, joined as a cofounder after reading Armstrong's posts on Reddit. In May 2013, Union Square Ventures invested $5 million in the company. a16z followed up in December of that year by leading a $25 million investment round. Coinbase had fewer than a million users at the time, but it eventually grew to become the largest US-based crypto exchange, with more than 100 million users worldwide. Srinivasan signed on as CTO after Coinbase had already experienced its first burst of exponential growth and attained unicorn status with a valuation of $1.6 billion.

At Coinbase, Srinivasan first distinguished himself as a "visionary and crypto zealot" who looked like a "hobo" in "stained sweatpants," wrote Jeff John Roberts in *Kings of Crypto: One Startup's Quest to Take Cryptocurrency Out of Silicon Valley and Onto Wall Street,* which chronicled the rise of Coinbase. "Balaji crumbled a Tate's chocolate chip cookie into a bowl, reached for another from the package and crumbled that up, too," wrote Roberts. "Then a third. He took a carton of half-and-half from the fridge, poured it over the crumbs, and began to eat. It was 1:30 in the morning in June of 2018. Balaji looked into the San Francisco night."

While he sought to cultivate the image of a cookie-guzzling eccentric, Srinivasan plunged aggressively into the company's internal politics. He quickly developed a reputation as a lethal Machiavellian knife fighter, with colleagues depicting him as someone quick to shiv anyone who stood in his way. "Some people lead by loyalty and inspiration," Nathalie McGrath, Coinbase's former vice president of people, told Roberts. "Balaji leads by fear and by money."

It worked. Armstrong, Coinbase's CEO, considered Srinivasan a friend and allowed him to run roughshod over the company. "For someone who by all accounts did not work well with others, Balaji was remarkably good at office politics," wrote Roberts. "Anyone in his way got edged aside with alacrity. Balaji either fired them outright or, through back-office maneuvering, stripped them of influence until, totally demoralized, they quit on their own accord."

"Balaji was Coinbase's first brilliant jerk," said McGrath.

His ego made him enemies, but his technical knowledge, enthusiasm, and energy inspired some. "He could function without sleep, appearing just as invigorated at midnight as at seven in the morning," wrote Roberts. "And he barely slowed down to eat, fueling himself for days at a time with his Tate's and half-and-half."

Srinivasan hit Coinbase like a wrecking ball, "tearing through anyone who presented an obstacle," including Coinbase president and chief operating officer Asiff Hirji, who had advocated for hiring him. Srinivasan also pushed out Adam White, a former air force commander who was Coinbase's fifth employee, who described him as "cutthroat and manipulative." With CEO Armstrong standing on the sidelines, Srinivasan consolidated power and got locked into a battle with Hirji. Their mutual disdain for one another stemmed from their conflicting visions for the company.

"Mr. Hirji, a former executive from stock brokerage TD Ameritrade who was accustomed to working in large organizations, lobbied for Coinbase to prioritize attracting financial institutions to its services," reported *The Information*, a tech publication, in 2019. "Meanwhile, Mr. Srinivasan, an experienced Silicon Valley startup founder, wanted Coinbase to cater more to individuals by aggressively expanding the types of digital currencies in its exchange, including some that occupy a regulatory gray area."

Shouting matches became the norm as the two executives butted heads. Then, after a tumultuous year during which Srinivasan got the upper hand, both men abruptly quit. Srinivasan's deal with Coinbase allowed him to cash out after a year at the company, and he left after one year and one day. Hirji quit shortly thereafter, after falling out with Armstrong, the CEO. Coinbase phased out Coinbase Earn, dealing a final death blow to 21e6.

Now fabulously wealthy with plenty of time on his hands, Srinivasan focused his energy on becoming a Twitter troll of great renown. Despite having once counseled his followers to avoid arguing on Twitter, he gained a reputation for sparring with critics and trashing tech journalists. The disruptive skills he had picked up as a noxious little snot in the Plainview school system came in handy now that he was a multimillionaire venture capitalist. He hurled insults, picked fights, and chased the dopamine rush of social media engagement.

When *New York Times* reporter Nathaniel Popper wrote a story about women and Black people making less money than men and white people at Coinbase in 2020, Srinivasan tweeted that Popper was "a woke white who can't code."

"Guy who has built nothing thinks he can critique guy who invented the web browser," he posted about another journalist who had criticized Andreessen.

"I cofounded a clinical genomics company that sold for $375M. You work at *Buzzfeed*," he tweeted at tech journalist Ryan Mac in 2020.

Srinivasan worked hard to make his disdain for journalists a key part of his public persona, though he had married a former tech journalist, Boonsri Dickinson of *Business Insider*, in 2015.

In addition to trashing journalists, Srinivasan sought to make himself into a major crypto influencer. Like Thiel, he saw crypto as a weapon for both generating wealth and transforming the governance of the world. He was especially bullish on Bitcoin, having invested early. In addition, as a devotee of *The Sovereign Individual*, Srinivasan saw Bitcoin as an important tool for establishing tech sovereignty from existing government structures. As he wrote in a tweet in October 2019:

> Tech will align behind Bitcoin as part of the political realignment of the 2020s. Not traditional right vs left, but rather:
>
> - Land v Cloud
> - State v Network
> - Centralized v Decentralized
> - Nationalists/Socialists v International Capitalists
> - Hamilton v Satoshi
> - MMT v BTC

On January 30, 2020, Srinivasan caused a stir on Twitter when he warned that the new COVID virus then ravaging China was likely to become a global pandemic with major ramifications for technology and society. "What if this coronavirus is the pandemic that public health people have been warning about for years?" he wrote in a long Twitter thread. "It would accelerate many pre-existing trends."

These trends included "border closures," "nationalism," "social isolation," "remote work," "face masks," and "distrust in governments." He encouraged world governments to take strong precautions. "For a virus like this, the time to 'overreact' is now, before it becomes pandemic," he wrote. "However, some folks in the US media are acting just like the Chinese state media they claim to deplore—and minimizing the issue."

Srinivasan was early in sounding the alarm on COVID, though his warning echoed worries in the scientific community that the virus would spread globally. Those concerns had largely been ignored by the mainstream media and the US political establishment. Coincidentally, the day after his Twitter thread, the US Secretary of Health and Human Services declared a public health emergency. By March, with global infections accelerating, the public health lockdowns started. Srinivasan's prescient warning boosted his reputation in crypto and tech circles, with the crypto publication *CoinDesk* eventually dubbing him "The Man Who Called COVID."

Two days after Srinivasan's viral tweets, on February 1, Yarvin published an essay echoing his argument that COVID would become a devastating global pandemic. A few weeks later, just before the first lockdowns hit the USA, he made his first public appearance in years to tape a podcast interview in front of a live audience in Los Angeles. "The scene brought out LA art hipsters, connoisseurs of civilizational decline, and PayPal founder Peter Thiel," wrote journalist Jacob Siegel. "The billionaire, who was one of the first investors in Facebook and has been a longtime patron of Yarvin's, drank Pabst Blue Ribbon and ate pizza. Thiel's car idled outside the club, engine on, driver behind the wheel, ready in case the need arose for a sudden exit." In early April, as the death toll climbed, Yarvin wrote that the virus would provide "not just a test of our government" but "a test of our form of government."

Srinivasan was right about the pandemic going global, but his more detailed predictions proved far less accurate. For example, he suggested that people might adopt public masking and remote work as permanent trends. In reality, most people couldn't wait to stop wearing masks, and many employers would start demanding a return to physical workplaces within two years. But the global pandemic, which forced most of the world's people into quarantine and killed over 7 million globally, would strengthen Srinivasan's conviction in the need to remake the world's government. "I don't think people realize that there is no normal to go back to anymore," he wrote on April 3.

Coming out of the global pandemic, Srinivasan—always bullish on disruption—would see a chance for his rebranded version of Yarvin's Dark Enlightenment to take a great leap forward.

CHAPTER 4

THE NEW REALITY

The Tech Right Rises

Srinivasan was not the only tech figure to make sweeping predictions about the pandemic.

"The coronavirus panic is dumb," wrote Elon Musk in a Twitter post on March 6, 2020.

On March 19, he predicted that the virus would soon disappear. "Based on current trends, probably close to zero new cases in US too by end of April," he wrote.

The billionaire had zero idea what he was talking about. The pandemic was just getting started. Over the next year, it would plunge all of humanity into an unprecedented period of fear, uncertainty, and death. It would also fully radicalize some of Silicon Valley's most well-known figures, especially Musk. Public health lockdowns had shuttered all businesses deemed nonessential, including Tesla's factory in Alameda County. Musk considered this an existential threat to his business and an unjust restriction of his freedom. When his efforts to simply wish away the virus failed, he rebelled against government authority. He decried mandatory health measures as "fascist," threatened to move his company from California to Texas, and finally reopened his factory in violation of county public health orders.

His open defiance created an international media spectacle. California officials, who had shut down bars and restaurants for similar violations, refused to act against Musk. His bold and successful lawbreaking made him a hero to the COVID denial movement that had emerged, largely from Trump's MAGA base, to oppose lockdowns and vaccines. The pandemic marked Musk's transformation from electric vehicle champion beloved by liberals into the world's most prominent right-wing social media troll. His already massive Twitter following increased exponentially, and his account became a weapon of political warfare. Musk became one of the loudest voices on Twitter, a status he enjoyed so much that he would eventually buy the company.

Musk's revolt against California's public health measures gave me an early glimpse of Silicon Valley's simmering anti-government radicalism. As editorial page editor of *The Sacramento Bee* at the time, I fired off columns and editorials blasting his ignorant defiance and questioning the state's lack of response. The next year, I would take a job at the *San Francisco Examiner*, where I would gain an even more granular knowledge of tech's political extremes. In those early days of the pandemic, however, I viewed Musk's provocations as a quirk of one billionaire's narcissism rather than a larger ideological trend.

But Musk was not alone in his anti-government pandemic agitations. On April 18, 2020, Marc Andreessen published an essay that became the tech industry's wartime manifesto. "It's Time to Build" blasted Western governments for failing to adequately prepare for the pandemic, which Andreessen blamed on a "smug complacency" fueled by a "satisfaction with the status quo" and resulting in an "unwillingness to build." Andreessen's essay argued that all problems could be solved through a rapid acceleration of "building" and growth through unfettered capitalism and deregulation. Though thin on specifics, Andreessen's superficial essay wowed many in Silicon Valley, where vibes matter more than substance. Andreessen had framed the pandemic as a civilizational turning point and cast so-called builders—presumably, wealthy investors like himself—as the heroes destined to save the future.

"It's Time to Build" provided an early pandemic glimpse of a radical shift among Silicon Valley elites, a process supercharged by a new platform called Clubhouse and scores of private group chats. As social distancing and lockdowns dragged on, these modes of communications took on a new importance. Clubhouse, launched in March 2020, allows users to host live audio-only chats with large audiences, like a private radio show. Clubhouse surged in 2020 because, according to *Business Insider*, it "offered the homebound online masses a way to spend some of their suddenly abundant time."

"More than any other startup, Clubhouse epitomizes the venture-capital-backed euphoria that swept the tech industry since lockdowns shut millions of people inside and pushed them online for connection, entertainment, and information," the article continued.

Musk, Ashton Kutcher, Mark Zuckerberg, and Oprah Winfrey made cameo appearances in the app's virtual "rooms," lending it celebrity cachet. The select audience of invite-only participants skewed heavily toward Silicon Valley types, who could banter with MC Hammer and other venture capitalists and tech figures in marathon sessions on crypto, Web3, and non-fungible tokens, or NFTs, a class of supposedly valuable digital assets that gained traction in 2020, created a frenzy in 2021, and crashed one year later.

Among the many virtual chats in Clubhouse was one called "Silicon Valley's Ultimate Exit: Rise of the Network State." The so-called network state was the latest iteration of Srinivasan's project for tech to secede from existing nations. Srinivasan had invested in Clubhouse, along with Andreessen Horowitz, which led an investment round that valued the company at $100 million in May 2020, when the app had only 1,500 users. Marc Andreessen, who also made regular appearances, called Clubhouse "the Athenian agora come to life," comparing it to ancient Greece's public forums. Like NFTs, Clubhouse turned out to be a flash in the pan. It rose to a $4 billion valuation in 2021 but fell with the pandemic lockdowns as important conversations migrated to private chat groups on encrypted services like Signal and WhatsApp, where tech insiders curated group conversations among the wealthy and influential.

In the spring of 2020, as Andreessen's "It's Time to Build" essay circulated and Clubhouse ramped up, a former Twitter executive and tech consultant named Sriram Krishnan launched a WhatsApp chat called "Build," where an exclusive group of Silicon Valley elites could banter more freely among themselves. Andreessen loved the idea, and Krishnan launched "dozens, within a year, on topics from engineering to design to project management to artificial intelligence," according to *Semafor*, which reported that Andreessen became the "nuclear reactor" powering many of the groups. Separately, tech entrepreneur Erik Torenberg founded other political chat groups that drew from the same crowd.

The chats served as a secret club where participants could share raw and controversial thoughts without the risk of public criticism. Executives "commiserated" about how to handle employee demands that they support Black Lives Matter and transgender rights policies. They debated COVID policy, and some strategized about how to defeat San Francisco's newly elected district attorney, a progressive named Chesa Boudin.

Like Andreessen, Srinivasan was a constant presence in the groups, which became, in the words of Krishnan, "the memetic upstream of mainstream opinion." (Krishnan became a general partner at a16z in 2021. After returning to the White House in 2025, Trump appointed Krishnan as the White House senior policy advisor for AI.)

"[T]heir influence flows through X, Substack, and podcasts, and constitutes a kind of dark matter of American politics and media," wrote Ben Smith of *Semafor*. "The group chats aren't always primarily a political space, but they are the single most important place in which a stunning realignment toward Donald Trump was shaped and negotiated, and an alliance between Silicon Valley and the new right formed."

"A lot of these technologists hoped that the centrist path was a viable one . . ." Chris Rufo, a right-wing provocateur who participated in the chats, told Smith. "I looked at these chats as a good investment of my time to radicalize tech elites who I thought were the most likely and high-impact new coalition partners for the right."

The radical yearnings of the tech right soon found a real-world target in California. On November 13, 2020, the *San Francisco Chronicle* revealed that California Governor Gavin Newsom had violated the state's COVID lockdown rules to party with lobbyists at the swank French Laundry restaurant in Napa County. The resulting media storm energized a hopeless campaign by Republicans, COVID deniers, and anti-vaccine activists to oust Newsom in a recall election. Newsom became a global symbol of pandemic hypocrisy and a target for pent-up lockdown anger. The recall campaign received an influx of cash from a Trump-supporting billionaire and a handful of Silicon Valley venture capitalists, including David Sacks and Chamath Palihapitiya, who briefly considered running for governor himself. Right-wing media outlets went into overdrive, portraying California as an apocalyptic hellscape and demonizing the Democratic governor as the cause of all ills, hammering him with familiar Republican attacks on the issues of crime, homelessness, and poverty.

Though humiliated, Newsom was never in real danger of losing. He blasted the recall as a Republican power grab, raised a $70 million war chest, and crushed it by twenty points on September 14, 2021. Recall fever was just beginning, however, and in 2022, it swept through San Francisco, where Republican billionaires and Silicon Valley venture capitalists funded recall campaigns against three members of the school board and the district attorney.

Like the Newsom recall, the San Francisco recalls channeled public frustration about the pandemic into a voter revolt against Democratic elected officials. The first recall campaign to emerge in the city targeted three school board members accused of moving too slowly to reopen schools during the pandemic, and for being too "woke." Soon afterward, a second recall campaign launched to oust District Attorney Boudin, a staunch progressive and son of 1960s Weather Underground radicals. Recall organizers accused the school board members of doing grave harm to San Francisco's children and blamed Boudin for every other problem in the city—the crime, drug addiction, and homelessness that had been blamed on Newsom in the previous year's recall. Boudin had been in office for one year, crime was generally at historic lows compared to previous decades despite a spike during the pandemic lockdowns, and DAs typically have no impact on crime rates or homelessness, but facts didn't matter. Money flooded into the San Francisco recall campaigns, which received funding from a Republican billionaire named William Oberndorf and several tech billionaires, including David Sacks and a largely unknown venture capitalist and self-described centimillionaire named Garry Tan.

Before the recalls, Tan had promoted himself as a tech influencer who provided advice to aspiring start-up founders. With thick-rimmed glasses and inspiring platitudes, the avuncular Tan came off as a cross between a business mentor and a life coach in videos with titles such as "STOP Chasing Money—Chase WEALTH—How to Get RICH." During the pandemic, he was a regular on Clubhouse, where he was known for moderating conversations with fellow tech moguls.

As the recalls gained steam, the Canada-born venture capitalist underwent a dramatic transformation, morphing into something more like a mini-Musk—a super wealthy and aggrieved Twitter troll full of rage at the political establishment. If the recalls had a main character, it was Tan, who framed the campaigns as a battle of "common sense" and "moderate" Democrats against a plague of progressive power. Yet his ideas were considerably to the right of most California Democrats. For example, he rejected voter-approved criminal justice reforms supported by mainstream Democratic leaders like Governor Newsom and his predecessor, Jerry Brown. In fact, most of Tan's positions seemed indistinguishable from Republican talking points.

Given his background, this was not altogether surprising. Tan, like Sacks, owed much of his career to a very famous Republican donor, Thiel. Tan idolized Thiel and credited him with teaching him the most important lesson of his life: Always listen to Peter Thiel. In 2003, Thiel had tried to recruit Tan to join Palantir, which was then in start-up mode. Thiel took Tan to dinner and wrote him a check for $72,000, which was the salary Tan was then making at

Microsoft. Thiel told the twenty-three-year-old Stanford grad that he was wasting his time at the major tech company.

"Cash this check and quit your job," said Thiel. "This is a zero-risk opportunity for you."

Tan turned him down.

"Big mistake," said Tan, recounting the story in one of his tech influencer videos in 2019. "This mistake cost me $200 million in equity, at least. Palantir is now worth $20 billion or more."

Though he missed the big windfall, Tan joined Palantir as an engineer in 2005 as the company's tenth employee—so early that he helped design the company's distinctive logo, a solid circle sitting atop a downward-pointed chevron, which he later describe as "an orb on a pedestal, just as the Palantir of *Lord of the Rings* fame was an orb of knowledge that let you see into your enemy's secrets" or, alternatively, "a human being reading a book." "The logo itself represents the core goal of Palantir, which is one of human-computer symbiosis," wrote Tan.

In the years before he got involved in San Francisco politics, Tan tweeted admiringly about Thiel dozens of times, often just posting a quote of something the billionaire had said. So, as fate would have it, two of the biggest supporters of the recalls were longtime members of Thiel's inner circle. Sacks decried Boudin as a "killer DA." Tan lambasted Boudin as a "dangerous ideologue who hurts our citizens," accused him of "causing death and assaults on our elders," and alleged that "violent crime against Asians" was being "used as a political tool."

San Francisco has long been a flashpoint in the nation's culture wars, with right-wing media outlets painting the heavily Democratic city as Sodom and Gomorrah on the Pacific. The recalls supercharged this effect, inflating its political skirmishes into existential crises the city's detractors blamed on liberal governance. Sacks and Tan pushed this narrative, using it to build a formidable movement to scapegoat four Democratic politicians for all the city's ills. Their strategy fit neatly with the thesis of *San Fransicko: Why Progressives Ruin Cities*, a 2021 book by a former left-wing PR agent turned right-wing propagandist and media darling named Michael Shellenberger. The book blamed San Francisco's dysfunctions, like homelessness and opioid addiction, on progressive leadership and evidence-based policies like harm reduction. This analysis ignored key facts—for example, crime and drug overdose rates are generally higher in Republican states—and experts panned the book. But it was perfectly timed to provide a ready-made argument for the recalls. The right-wing media ate it up, as did Tan.

"If you want to know why our city is covered in needles, poop, crime and no pragmatic housing, you'll have to read San Fransicko," Tan wrote on Twitter.

Seemingly overnight, a city that hadn't recalled an elected official since 1914 faced coordinated campaigns against four officials backed by millions in donations from wealthy individuals, vocal support from crusading venture capitalists, and unusually aggressive media strategies. A new breed of "doom influencers," some of whom had first appeared in Shellenberger's book, materialized as if on cue to boost the recall as San Francisco politics became a global spectacle. Srinivasan, who now lived in Singapore, joined the fray, declaring San Francisco a city of "anarchy and tyranny" that was worse off than Rwanda. "[I]t may be easier to start a new city than to reform San Francisco," he tweeted to his 1 million followers.

To some observers, the recalls looked more like high-tech political warfare than grassroots organizing, and some of the tactics resembled those usually found in international disinformation campaigns rather than local elections. For example, anti-recall activists uncovered a network of bot accounts with AI-generated profile pictures pumping pro-recall messages on Twitter. The accounts—nicknamed "The Wencils" because a few of them had the curious name listed in their profiles—vanished once exposed.

The recalls were also backed by a new crop of political organizations with civic-sounding names—GrowSF, NeighborsSF, TogetherSF—that shared the same donor circle of billionaires and venture capitalists. A joint investigation by *The Guardian* and *Mission Local* later revealed these groups had received a combined $20 million, creating a "gray money" network to influence city politics. It was classic "astroturfing"—billionaire money laundered through nonprofits to create the illusion of organic neighborhood activism—and it worked. In February 2022, all three targeted school board members were recalled. In June, voters ousted Boudin. His replacement was a former deputy DA who had left the office to campaign against Boudin while drawing a paycheck from one of the billionaire-funded organizations.

San Francisco's recalls proved that with enough money and strategy, tech moguls could exert outsized influence on real-world politics. Ousting Boudin had been a topic of conversation in the pandemic group chats, and now the DA was unemployed and replaced by a handpicked candidate who worked for them. An unusual alliance of Republicans and tech figures had successfully tested its political firepower by overthrowing progressive power in deep-blue San Francisco. In the years following the recalls, billionaire-backed efforts also resulted in a takeover of the San Francisco Democratic Party's governing committee and a new majority on the Board of Supervisors. They were just getting started.

On July 4, 2022—one month after the Boudin recall—Balaji Srinivasan published *The Network State: How to Start a New Country*. The 474-page ebook, free to read online, was his most ambitious effort yet to repackage Yarvin's ideas. It predicted a new civil war in the United States and called on people to "exit" American democracy for life in privatized micro-nations called network states.

The first page of the book defines the concept: "A network state is a highly aligned online community with a capacity for collective action that crowdfunds territory around the world and eventually gains diplomatic recognition from pre-existing states." For example, Srinivasan wrote that Bitcoin fanatics, yoga lovers, or keto diet practitioners could form online communities and begin identifying as parallel network state societies. Eventually, they could acquire land, move their society from the digital cloud to the land, and seek to become a sovereign nation or state. Once again, Srinivasan laid out two paths to creating network states. The first, called "voice," meant using the levers of democracy to take over existing governments and using their power to create a new system. The second, "exit," meant abandoning the USA altogether to start a new country elsewhere. Coincidentally, "exit" is also venture capitalist lingo for cashing one's investment out of a company. This was essentially the same argument Yarvin laid out in "Patchwork," which called for replacing democracy with networks of city-states governed as joint-stock corporations. Srinivasan rebranded these as network states, proposing a new class of tech companies offering subscriptions to entirely new countries and societies.

"A key point is that we can apply all the techniques of startup companies to startup societies," he wrote. "Financing, attracting subscribers, calculating churn, doing customer support—there's a playbook for all of that. It's just Society-as-a-Service, the new SaaS."

Beneath the shifting buzzwords, the structure remained identical: corporate-controlled territories replacing democratic governance. Yarvin's version pushed explicit fascism, but Srinivasan framed the transformation of governance as necessary innovation. Yarvin pitched corporate dictatorship, but Srinivasan emphasized the idea of consumer choice in a world of inevitably declining nation-states, pointing to Hong Kong and Singapore as examples of zones that successfully offered alternative regimes.

The notion of creating special places governed by new rules was hardly original, and the concept predated Yarvin. Capitalists have long sought to create what historian Quinn Slobodian calls "alternative political arrangements at a small scale" through "acts of secession and fragmentation, carving out liberated territory within and beyond nations." In England, the City of London—not to be confused with London, the actual city—is a financial district that has operated with special status for hundreds of years. It even has its own government, the City of London Corporation, along with its own police force and other unique privileges. Elsewhere, the Bahamas, the Cayman Islands, and Bermuda offer Caribbean tax havens with lax regulations designed to serve corporations and wealthy individuals. Dubai's twenty-two-square-mile Jebel Ali Free Zone caters to 11,000 corporations enjoying long, union-free tax holidays there. Communist-ruled China has over a dozen Special Economic Zones where capitalism (but not democracy) reigns supreme.

Britain's most famous overseas special zone was Hong Kong, which operated as a free port under British rule from 1842 to 1997. In 1977, inspired by visits to Hong Kong and Singapore, British geographer Peter Hall proposed creating "freeports" on English soil—zones with radical deregulation to revive declining British cities. By the early 1980s, Margaret Thatcher's government embraced these concepts, creating freeports and enterprise zones with tax breaks and relaxed planning rules. The zones largely failed, but the experiment did produce one success story: Canary Wharf, a complex of high-rises built on former London docks in an area designated an urban enterprise zone in 1982. Today, an estimated 120,000 people work at Canary Wharf, where Barclays, Citigroup, HSBC, Morgan Stanley, and JPMorgan all have offices. But this success came with serious caveats. The project required billions in state-funded infrastructure beyond the tax breaks—including the building of the Docklands Light Railway and Jubilee Line extension. Srinivasan adapts the idea for a tech audience that, despite talk of techno-optimism, feels what Slobodian calls a "sense of creeping paranoia" about the future. Motivated by "greed, megalomania or the desire to have a zero percent tax rate," they seek to escape into privatized societies where they make all the rules. It's a dystopian vision straight out of *The Sovereign Individual*: existing countries and zones hollowed out by capital flight and falling tax revenues, left to collapse as the wealthy flee into highly fortified arks.

"The proponents of crack-up capitalism envisioned a new utopia: an agile, restlessly mobile fortress for capital, protected from the grasping hands of the populace seeking a more equitable present and future," wrote Slobodian in *Crack-Up Capitalism*.

In his 2013 speech at Y Combinator, Srinivasan had criticized American democracy as an outdated software system. Now he took an even harsher view, describing the federal government as "the most determined opponent of liberty." His solution: Abandon citizenship in nation-states like the USA for membership in the fragmented governance model of his proposed network states. "In short, will the American nation choose the decentralized Network or the centralized State?" he asked.

Just as Yarvin had railed against the Cathedral—a villainous shadow government of universities, media, and government institutions secretly controlling American democracy—Srinivasan pointed the finger at an all-powerful liberal cabal he called "Woke Capital," costuming the same conspiracy theory in Republican-friendly culture war grievance instead of Yarvin's edgy religious metaphor. Srinivasan, who barely mentions Yarvin in *The Network State*, gave credit where credit was due. "As Yarvin in particular has documented at length, the most important left-authoritarians are not formally part of the elected State at all," he wrote. "They are the professors, activists, bureaucrats, and journalists."

Defeating Woke Capital would require anti-woke forces to unite in battle against their common enemy, said Srinivasan, and this is where he reveals the true politics of the network state. He divides the US into three political tribes. Democratic voters are the Blue tribe and Republican voters are the Red tribe, as usual. But the book introduces a new tribe, the Gray tribe, which forms the heart of the network state. Srinivasan describes the Gray tribe as "libertarianish" and "people of the Network Leviathan" who prefer online communities over real-world ones. The Grays have no allegiance to the old politics of Red or Blue but, according to *The Network State*, form an emerging and decisive political force. To crush the Blue tribe, Srinivasan suggests, the Gray tribe must form an alliance with the Red tribe, as well as with the disaffected Blues he terms "Left-Libertarians." These are former Democrats who listen to podcasts like "Gray Zone, Red Scare, or Jimmy Dore," a description that fits a fringe group known as the "post-Left"—highly online and right-leaning former leftists who despise Democrats more than Republicans. The post-Left is a tiny constituency, but Srinivasan inflates their importance, presumably because his coalition theory doesn't work otherwise. The Gray tribe must partner with this sliver of turncoat niche Blues, as well as with the Reds, to win.

Srinivasan sees the Red tribe—Republicans—as essential to creating the network state. He divides the Red tribe into three groups: "Red God," "Red State," and "Red Network." The Red God group consists of religious conservatives. They form a powerful constituency of the Republican base, he wrote, but their numbers are waning as Americans turn away from religion. The next group, the Red State, is composed of secular nationalists—mainly "national security hawks" who "reflexively support the US in every foreign intervention" and hate liberals but fear China more than anything else. Rounding out the Red tribe is the Red Network, which consists of "people of the Network" who are also "the folks in favor of commerce and trade networks, both within and across borders—the capitalists."

"Today, that kind of capitalism is almost synonymous with internet startups and technology," wrote Srinivasan. "The most valuable companies in the world were born on the Network."

Srinivasan describes these people as practitioners of "network capitalism," which will soon evolve into "crypto-capitalism." That's because the blockchain—the decentralized technology that allows crypto to operate without government or bank control—will supposedly come to power the entire economy and the world. So, the distinction between Red Network and Gray tribe is cosmetic: Both groups include tech capitalists loyal to networks over nations. Srinivasan's framework is convoluted and easy to critique, but his main point is that the network-state-aligned groups—mostly Gray and Red, with some former Blues—must band together to overthrow the Blue tribe, which he portrays as dangerous fanatics with a quasi-religious belief in government.

"For the left-authoritarians among the blues, their primary Leviathan is the State, which is very real and can do violence against its/their enemies, as opposed to what they think of as an imaginary God," Srinivasan wrote. "This is why State-worshippers mock the concept of 'thoughts and prayers' in favor of 'passing a law.'" This coalition—tech capitalists, Republicans, and right-leaning former liberals uniting to crush the Democratic Party—forms the core of *The Network State*'s political strategy. Srinivasan admits his theory will face some challenges, like the fact that not all Republicans will agree to readily do away with their national identity as Americans. At the same time, his book sketches a blueprint for how right-wing capitalists might unite to topple the nation as outlined in "Patchwork" and *The Sovereign Individual.*

Though *The Network State* mentions Yarvin only in passing, it hails the influence of Davidson and Rees-Mogg, mentioning *The Sovereign Individual* five times and calling it "an incredible book that nailed many aspects of our digital future decades in advance, Bitcoin prime among them." Like *The Sovereign Individual, The Network State* hinges on the idea that crypto will undermine the power of governments, with crypto-fueled decentralized tech network states becoming a dominant force. Dollars and nation-states are the past, both argue, while crypto and privatized governments are the future.

The Network State also nods to *The Sovereign Individual* in other ways. For example, *The Sovereign Individual* has a section titled "History in Reverse," which argues that "[t]he process by which the nation-state grew over the past five centuries will be put into reverse by the new logic of the Information Age. Local centers of power will reassert themselves as the state devolves into fragmented, overlapping sovereignties." In *The Network State,* a section called "The Future Is Our Past" makes the same argument, with Srinivasan echoing *The Sovereign Individual*'s arguments.

The Network State also mimics *The Sovereign Individual* in format and style. It consists of bold, sweeping declarations delivered in short bursts of text and punctuated by bullet points of factoids and stats wrangled in support of a towering prophecy in which the entire world order faces imminent collapse. Like Davidson and Rees-Mogg before him, Srinivasan whips up a DIY theory of megapolitics to explain past, present, and future—weaving together threads from history, movies, and tech to support his sweeping claims. *The Network State* does not present a coherent plan for twenty-first-century governance, but it does provide a clear glimpse of the extremist worldview circulating among tech venture capitalists in the post-pandemic moment. Srinivasan depicts American democracy and the institutions that uphold it as inherently wicked and corrupt. He reserves extra scorn for journalistic institutions, especially *The New York Times,* which he vilifies as a chief agent of Woke Capital.

"What if Sulzberger is more like Keyser Söze?" wrote Srinivasan, comparing the *Times*'s publisher to a mysterious mob figure in the 1995 movie *The Usual Suspects*. "What if his employees are highly self-interested professional prevaricators? What if they've always been like that? What if you can't trust anything they say, and by extension anything the US establishment says, without checking it yourself?"

The animosity was personal: In 2021, *Times* reporter Cade Metz wrote about extremist voices rising out of Silicon Valley's "Rationalist" movement, which included "white supremacists and neo-fascists" along with fans of Yarvin. It included Srinivasan's 2013 emails proposing to dox unfriendly journalists and "turn them inside out with hostile reporting," and the exposure clearly stung.

So deep is Srinivasan's disdain that he even disparages Ida Tarbell, the muckraking journalist whose reporting helped lead to the breakup of the Standard Oil monopoly in 1911. In Srinivasan's version of history, Tarbell—who died in 1944—"demagogued and defeated" the world's richest man, Standard Oil founder John D. Rockefeller.

To combat the power of Woke Capital and its journalists, Srinivasan urges the building of "parallel" systems controlled by the network state and its allies. Just as Bitcoin will replace the dollar and corporate government will replace democracy, so too will network-state-controlled education, media, and political organizations replace existing versions. These new parallel institutions will play a central role in the conflict Srinivasan refers to as the "Second American Civil War," which he claims is already underway.

"Today, in the territory governed by this inept bureaucracy, we now see power outages, supply-chain shortages, rampant flooding, and uncontrolled fires," he wrote, portraying a nation in rapid decline. "We see riots, arsons, shootings, stabbings, robberies, and murders. We see digital mobs that become physical mobs. We see a complete loss of trust in institutions from the state to the media. We see anti-capitalism and anti-rationalism. We see states breaking away from the US federal government, at home and abroad. And we see the End of Power, the Revolt of the Public, the defeat of the military, the inflation of the dollar, and—looming ahead—an

American anarchy." This anarchy will result in the Second American Civil War, which Srinivasan says will be fought mostly through propaganda and polarization. "It'd be nothing like the movies, with huge movements of uniformed soldiers, tanks and planes," he wrote, imagining a hypothetical societal breakdown triggered by a government effort to confiscate Bitcoin. "Instead, it'll just be a continuation and escalation of what we've seen over the last several years: a network-to-network war to control minds rather than a state-to-state war to control territory."

"All the discussion over the last few years around 'free speech' doesn't really engage the fundamental issue, which is that this is a time of information war, where the victory condition for one side is to invade the minds of the other side—because it cannot feasibly invade the territory," he wrote. "To invade the minds of the other side, and to control the digital networks—because the tech companies that greenlight transactions, communications, and online behavior have in many ways become the de facto privatized governments of the Western world. The power to determine what people can and cannot do in the digital world belongs to the people who run these networks. And so controlling these networks, by controlling the minds of people who run them, is the key to maintaining control over the US in a digital time."

This big information network war would lead to a great "unbundling" of the country, he said, a full meltdown in which "no one is in charge and everything is in chaos." The Second American Civil War would end with the death of the nation and the rise of the network state. Taking a page from Davidson and Rees-Mogg, Srinivasan roots his entire thesis in the breathless promise of looming apocalyptic demise. Srinivasan bases his case in conjecture and opinion and never makes a convincing argument for why people would abandon their nuclear-armed superpower homeland for cultish "startup societies" lacking infrastructure and military defense capabilities.

The Network State is not a scholarly work. It's a rambling and peculiar self-published manifesto authored by a man whose sole qualification is that he is a multimillionaire. Dr. David Karpf, an associate professor at George Washington University who studies digital politics, wrote a review that described it as a "blueprint drawn in crayon . . . delivered in painfully stilted startup-speak." "Balaji's ideas are stunningly undercooked, offered with such conspiratorial self-certainty that you have to wonder whether anyone has bothered to ask him if he's alright," wrote Karpf, concluding that "Balaji Srinivasan is a clown" and dismissing *The Network State* as "Galt's Gulch plus blockchain." "*The Network State* is the ranting of an unserious mind, disconnected from reality," he wrote. "It is bad science fiction masquerading as bold nonfiction . . . The tech barons are enacting a plan. But they have not thought this plan through at all."

But Srinivasan's call for a network war to replace democratic institutions with privately controlled versions found influential fans among his Silicon Valley peers. *The Network State* received glowing reviews from Srinivasan's billionaire friends, who had grown exponentially more wealthy and powerful in the decade since his secession speech at Y Combinator.

"Balaji has the highest rate of output per minute of good new ideas of anybody I've ever met, and *The Network State* may be his best," said Andreessen in a blurb for the book.

"Balaji is a visionary, one of the most original thinkers of our time," said Brian Armstrong, the Coinbase CEO. "Many have had the experience of hearing him say something, thinking it was crazy, and then a year or two later realizing 'Balaji was right.' I think Balaji will be right about *The Network State*."

"We've started new currencies. Now *The Network State* shows us how to start new cities and new countries," said Vitalik Buterin, a computer prodigy who received a Thiel Fellowship and cofounded a crypto platform called Ethereum.

The Network State also had an enthusiastic fan in San Francisco: Garry Tan. Though his words of praise did not grace the book's official Amazon page, he would turn out to be among the most dedicated followers of Srinivasan's vision.

"I legit believe YC is a prototype model for what @balajis talks about when he says the Network State," wrote Tan on Twitter in early

August 2022, referring to Y Combinator, the famed start-up accelerator where Srinivasan had given his "ultimate exit" speech in 2013.

A few weeks later, Tan was named CEO and president of Y Combinator. Sam Altman, a fellow Thiel protégé who had previously held the role, highlighted Tan's political activism after the announcement of his hiring. "Garry is one of the most 'YC' people in the whole industry," tweeted Sam Altman, who had become cofounder and CEO of OpenAI, in response to Tan's hiring. "Also, it's a big deal [in my opinion] that YC will have a CEO so active in local politics. I think YC can make a big difference here."

Tan's political machinations in San Francisco, transforming tech money into political action, had paid off. In less than two years, he had gone from obscure venture capitalist to emergent political boss. Now, he had one of the greatest prizes in Silicon Valley: leadership of a legendary VC incubator.

Tan and Srinivasan weren't the only Silicon Valley figures making big moves in 2022. In April of that year, Yarvin had updated his ideas with an edgy new essay on *Gray Mirror*, his obscure Substack newsletter. "The Butterfly Revolution" envisioned Trump returning to power with a vengeance in 2024. Yarvin acknowledged that a second Trump presidency seemed unlikely but outlined a plan for a hypothetical future administration in which Trump would brutalize and dismantle the federal government.

Yarvin called for a "full reboot" of government, a process in which Trump would install "a CEO" to gut the bureaucracy. This would be accompanied by an "army of ninjas"—"*ideologically* trained"—to "parachute" into government agencies to dismantle them. These ideological ninjas would also fan out to invade and destroy other institutions of democratic influence. "Finally, it is not sufficient to have an army of parachute ninjas large or smart to drop into all the agencies in the executive branch," wrote Yarvin. "Many institutions of power are outside the government proper. Ninjas will have to land on the roofs of these buildings too—mainly journalism, academia and social media."

Coincidentally, Musk announced plans to buy Twitter shortly

afterward, complaining that Twitter's algorithms and rules favored liberals and squelched free speech. "Free speech is essential to a functioning democracy," he had tweeted on March 25. "Do you believe Twitter rigorously adheres to this principle?"

Musk viewed control of Twitter as necessary to halt the progress of what he called a "woke mind virus" infecting the world. "Unless the woke mind virus, which is fundamentally anti-science, anti-merit, and anti-human in general, is stopped, civilization will never become multiplanetary," he told Walter Isaacson, his biographer.

On April 25, Musk entered into an agreement to buy Twitter for the eye-popping sum of $44 billion. Wedbush Securities analyst Dan Ives later called it "one of the most overpaid tech acquisitions in history." Musk soon got cold feet, balked at the price, and attempted to pull out of the deal. After some public drama and legal wrangling, he formally acquired the company in October. Fellow investors included Andreessen Horowitz, Saudi Prince al-Waleed bin Talal, and 8VC, a venture capital firm cofounded by Joe Lonsdale, who also cofounded Palantir.

The Wall Street Journal later revealed that Musk had been goaded into buying the site by a "shadow crew" of right-wing billionaires. "Before and during Mr. Musk's breakneck takeover of Twitter, a close-knit group of libertarian-leaning activists and businessmen have been encouraging him to get involved," reported the *Journal*. "This group includes the so-called PayPal mafia—former executives at the online payments company who include Mr. Musk, the investor Peter Thiel and entrepreneur David Sacks—as well as ancillary figures like the venture capitalist Steve Jurvetson, an early Tesla investor who once served on the auto maker's board; and Mr. Musk's brother, Kimbal, a Tesla board member, according to people familiar with the matter."

On October 26, 2022, Musk arrived at Twitter's San Francisco office building carrying a porcelain sink. He posted a photo to his account, along with a caption: "Entering Twitter HQ—let that sink in!" Musk proceeded to fire or lay off most of the company's staff, gutting the content moderation teams and eventually disbanding the company's Trust and Safety Council.

The next month, OpenAI released ChatGPT, kicking off a race for consumer-facing AI chatbots that generate humanlike text responses to user prompts. ChatGPT became an overnight sensation, sparking both euphoria and alarm about the rise of so-called artificial intelligence. Altman, the Thiel confidant and former Y Combinator CEO, became one of the most famous people in tech, drawing comparisons to J. Robert Oppenheimer, who oversaw the Manhattan Project. The glowing descriptions of Altman would soon fade, but the race had begun. AI—in conjunction with the extremist political beliefs of Silicon Valley's billionaire masters—was about to hit the world like an atom bomb.

Nearly one year later, on October 16, 2023, Andreessen published something called "The Techno-Optimist Manifesto." His earlier manifesto, "It's Time to Build," had been written in normal essay style, like something that might appear in a newspaper. "The Techno-Optimist" was an altogether different creation, resembling biblical verse or poetry. Its opening lines provide a glimpse of its structure:

We are being lied to.
We are told that technology takes our jobs, reduces our wages, increases inequality, threatens our health, ruins the environment, degrades our society, corrupts our children, impairs our humanity, threatens our future, and is ever on the verge of ruining everything.
We are told to be angry, bitter, and resentful about technology.
We are told to be pessimistic.
The myth of Prometheus – in various updated forms like Frankenstein, Oppenheimer, and Terminator – haunts our nightmares.
We are told to denounce our birthright – our intelligence, our control over nature, our ability to build a better world.
We are told to be miserable about the future.

Andreessen argued that Americans have been taught to dislike technology, but this was an exaggeration. Ninety percent own a portable computer in the form of a smartphone, and most have enthusiastically embraced the addictive apps and conveniences of the digital age. By 2023, however, the public had become concerned about the potential dangers of AI, and their worries made sense. After all, none other than Altman had declared that AI would generally devastate the job market. "Jobs are definitely going to go away, full stop," Altman had told *The Atlantic* in July 2023, suggesting that AI would eliminate entire categories of work.

In place of jobs, Altman suggested that people would rely on some form of universal basic income—a welfare check necessitated by the lack of work. Altman was already working on models. In 2020, OpenAI had funded a nonprofit called UBI Charitable, which conducted "the largest universal-basic-income experiment in the world," according to *The Atlantic*. A year later, Altman introduced Worldcoin, a project to create a global digital identification and payments system by scanning people's eyeballs with a device called the Orb, offering small amounts of crypto as an incentive to participate.

"It seemed to me like a bet that we're heading toward a world where AI has made it all but impossible to verify people's identity and much of the population requires regular UBI payments to survive," wrote Ross Andersen of *The Atlantic*. "Altman more or less granted that to be true, but said that Worldcoin is not just for UBI."

Such warnings no doubt impressed OpenAI's investors, but most people weren't ready to hear that technology would imminently kill their jobs and put them on welfare. Andreessen, who had declared that "Software Is Eating the World" in 2011, now sought to alleviate such frightening scenarios. His optimistic manifesto declared that technology would create "abundance" and "societal wealth" by revving up a "Techno-Capital Machine"—a concept borrowed from Nick Land—that would create a world in which "[a]ll the machines work for us." Andreessen hailed technology as a "glory of human imagination and ingenuity" and a primary driver of growth and markets, the only mechanism by which to cure humanity's problems. "We have a problem of poverty, so we invent technology to create abundance," wrote Andreessen. "Give us a real-world problem, and we can invent technology that will solve it."

Andreessen sought to shift the narrative away from Altman's apocalypse scenario and toward a positive vision where capitalism and technology would magically address all economic needs. In Andreessen's techno-optimist fairy tale, technology would make physical goods so cheap, they would be almost free, and with everything so cheap and plentiful, wealth levels would skyrocket. "We believe we should push to drop prices across the economy through the application of technology until as many prices are effectively zero as possible, driving income levels and quality of life into the stratosphere," wrote Andreessen.

He cited computer scientist and futurist Ray Kurzweil's "Law of Accelerating Returns," which dictates that technological advances increase exponentially because, in Andreessen's words, they "tend to feed on themselves, increasing the rate of future advance." "We believe in accelerationism—the conscious and deliberate propulsion of technological development—to ensure the fulfillment of the Law of Accelerating Returns," wrote Andreessen. "To ensure the techno-capital upward spiral continues forever."

Andreessen tried to brand his ideas as nonpartisan—"a material philosophy, *not* a political philosophy," he said—but his manifesto largely reframed old Republican ideas, such as a pure faith in growth and markets as the answer to everything, in futurist terms. Even more revealing was Andreessen's decision to cite Filippo Tommaso Marinetti, an early-twentieth-century Italian editor and poet who fused futurism with fascism. In a section of the manifesto titled "Becoming Technological Supermen," Andreessen nodded to "Manifesto of Futurism," a 1909 free verse screed where Marinetti celebrated "speed," glorified violence, and promised to "destroy the museums, libraries, academies of every kind" and to "fight moralism, feminism, every opportunistic or utilitarian cowardice." Andreessen excerpted a section of Marinetti's manifesto: "Beauty exists only in struggle. There is no masterpiece that has not an aggressive character. Technology must be a violent assault on the forces of the unknown, to force them to bow before man."

This was an unusual and revealing choice. In 1918, Marinetti founded the Futurist Political Party. One year later, he published "The Manifesto of the Italian Fasces of Combat," better known as "The Fascist Manifesto," and the Futurist Party merged with Mussolini's budding fascist party, aptly named the Italian Fasces of Combat. Though Marinetti had authored the original fascist manifesto, Mussolini later wrote his own version, "The Doctrine of Fascism." Like Marinetti, Mussolini defined fascism as a philosophy of aggressive and constant struggle.

"Fascism wants man to be active and to engage in action with all his energies; it wants him to be manfully aware of the difficulties besetting him and ready to face them," he wrote. "It conceives of life as a struggle in which it behooves a man to win for himself a really worthy place, first of all by fitting himself (physically, morally, intellectually) to become the implement required for winning it."

Andreessen echoed these sentiments: "We believe in ambition, aggression, persistence, relentlessness—*strength*." To drive home his manifesto's distinctly right-wing politics, he named some enemies of his philosophy, including "social responsibility," "sustainability" and "existential risk," "risk management," "tech ethics," and "trust and safety." He concludes by naming "saints" of his techno-optimist vision, including Marinetti and Nick Land, as well as James Burnham and Vilfredo Pareto, two of the thinkers who inspired Yarvin's early work. Andreessen also canonized John Galt—the capitalist hero of Rand's *Atlas Shrugged*—as well as a pseudonymous writer known as Beff Jezos, an AI researcher and physicist who had cofounded yet another weird new tech movement, effective accelerationism, or e/acc.

Andreessen's manifesto bundled many strains of the same old ideas into a new package he framed as optimism. By the time he published it, tech was already teeming with cultish movements that glorified technological acceleration as the key to unlocking the secrets of the universe. The release of AI chatbots like ChatGPT supercharged them, since Silicon Valley elites saw it as a sign that they were on the cusp of massive breakthroughs that would enable them to create "superintelligent" AI, colonize space, and even defeat death.

Earlier in 2023, Dr. Timnit Gebru and Dr. Émile Torres coined the acronym TESCREAL as a framework for understanding seven overlapping ideological movements: transhumanism, extropianism, singularitarianism, cosmism, rationalism, effective altruism, and longtermism.

In the months before publishing his manifesto, Andreessen had embraced the term, going so far as to add "TESCREAList" to his Twitter bio. To fully decode the goal of his manifesto, it helps to have a basic familiarity with these strange ideologies, which are rooted in eugenics and play a central role in the race to develop artificial general intelligence (so-called superintelligent AI), or AGI.

"These ideologies, which are direct descendants of first-wave eugenics, emerged in roughly this order, and many were shaped or founded by the same individuals," wrote Gebru and Torres in a paper analyzing the TESCREAL ideologies. "We show how the TESCREAL bundle has come to animate the AGI race by examining how advocates of the bundle initiated and funded the push to build AGI . . . and much of the billionaire funding for projects focused on AGI comes from wealthy individuals aligned or explicitly affiliated with one or more of these ideologies."

What are these ideologies, and what do they have in common?

Transhumanists believe advanced technologies such as AI, genetic engineering, nanotechnology, and cybernetics will transform people into superhumans with enhanced physical, cognitive, and sensory abilities. In essence, they wish to become post-human robots that transcend human biological limits and become immortal. "Transhumanism is this idea that we could create a kind of utopian world in which we live forever," said Torres in an interview. "There's no suffering, there's radical abundance, and everything is awesome forever."

Just like the transhumanists, the extropians reject the natural processes of decay, decline, and entropy, preferring so-called *extropy*, a fantasy vision of perpetual growth and progression. But extropians belong to a specific anarcho-capitalist strain of the movement, a selective club that even had its own special handshake back in the 1990s. Notably, the early extropians were major proponents of cryonics, the act of freezing your body or head after you die so that future technologies can bring you back to life. "It's a doctrine of self-transformation, of extremely advanced technology, and of dedicated, immovable optimism," wrote Ed Regis of *Wired* in 1994. "Most of all, it's a philosophy of freedom from limitations of any kind."

Singularitarians believe superintelligent "godlike" forms of AI will emerge to fundamentally overwhelm and transform human existence, making the dreams of the transhumanists and extropians come true. They await the "technological Singularity," when humans merge with machines over time to, in the words of Gebru and Torres, begin a "new epoch in cosmic history" in which "[o]ur descendants will then spread beyond Earth and flood the universe with consciousness, thus enabling the universe to 'wake up.'" Others believe the Singularity will be a sudden "intelligence explosion" that enables the post-human future in the stars.

Cosmists focus mainly on the vision of a future in space, from Mars to the farthest reaches of the universe. The modern version of cosmism comes out of Russian cosmism, a school of thought from the nineteenth and twentieth centuries, which fused technological fantasy with religious ideas of immortality from the Russian Orthodox Church. It asserts that humankind will use technology to beat death, becoming post-human beings of energy that spread throughout the universe to harvest the cosmos. "The cosmists' original idea held that one could resurrect the dead by rearranging their atoms to the precise positions they were in while the person was alive," wrote Douglas Rushkoff in *Team Human*, which examines the bizarre beliefs of tech elite. "But the cosmists were working on other solutions, such as perfecting humans through intentional evolution, moving human consciousness into the bodies of robots, conquering death, colonizing space, or uploading ourselves to computers."

Cosmist ideas captured the imagination of the West during the space race of the 1960s and '70s, spreading through global New Age movements and informing the nascent transhumanism movement. "The cosmists convinced America's LSD-taking spiritualists that technology could give them a way of beating death," wrote Rushkoff.

The world's most prominent cosmist: Elon Musk, the SpaceX founder who has declared that "[b]ecoming multiplanetary is critical to ensuring the long-term survival of humanity and all life as we know it."

Rationalists believe they can optimize decision-making and identify existential risks invisible to ordinary thinkers. The movement, centered around long-running blogs like *LessWrong* and *Slate Star Codex,* attracts tech workers who believe human reasoning can be systematically debugged and improved through logic, rigorous thinking, and purported cognitive hacks. (Srinivasan took his Blue Tribe/Gray Tribe concept from a 2014 post on *Slate Star Codex.*) The rationalists view themselves as cognitive elites, which provides intellectual and moral cover for some of Silicon Valley's more extravagant futurist claims.

Case in point: effective altruism, which comes out of rationalism. Effective altruists believe in seeking the greatest good by using evidence and reason to pursue an impartial analysis of how to achieve the greatest good for humanity, in some strands of the movement prioritizing the welfare of future human populations as much—if not more—than present ones. Another strand of the philosophy justifies any method of accumulating wealth and power, if you plan to deploy it virtuously later. (It doesn't always work out. The most prominent effective altruist, or EA, is Sam Bankman-Fried, the FTX crypto exchange founder serving thirty years in prison for fraud.)

Longtermists round out the TESCREAL bundle. They view the "trillions" of humans yet unborn as more important than the billions currently on Earth and argue that decisions should be made in the interest of those future humans. Taken to its most extreme conclusions, it's a philosophy that justifies sacrificing present populations for the sake of hypothetical future ones. Of all the TESCREAL ideologies, longtermism is perhaps the most important because it provides tech elites with a moral justification for just about any action.

The TESCREAL ideologies are not mutually exclusive. One can be a transhumanist, a singularitarian, a cosmist, and a longtermist—and most TESCREAList are, including Andreessen. And by 2023, the newest cult—effective accelerationism, or e/acc—had stormed

Silicon Valley. While effective altruism advocated caution and careful analysis to avoid AI's existential risks, e/acc rejected such concerns as wimpy obstacles to progress. The e/acc philosophy was simple: Accelerate technological development at maximum speed, consequences be damned. Any attempt to slow down or regulate AI was dismissed as "decel"—deceleration—the ultimate sin. Andreessen's manifesto was seen as a battle cry for the e/acc movement, with its pure faith in the idea that "technological progress . . . leads to material abundance for everyone." Among those who publicly embraced e/acc: Garry Tan, who added "e/acc" to his Twitter biography.

These ideologies, most of which had simmered in Silicon Valley for decades, are radical by design. Just as Yarvin remade fascism for the twenty-first century, TESCREAL remakes religion for the age of AI. It requires faith in an all-powerful being (superintelligence) that will engineer immortality (eternal life) and enable a perfect abundance in the stars (heaven), providing a promise of transcendence that contradicts known science. For example, there is no evidence that AI systems will develop consciousness, sentience, or the ability to grant immortality. The claim that human consciousness can be "uploaded" to machines or that technology will enable immortality has zero grounding in biology, neuroscience, or physics. Like the billions of Christians who believe they will receive eternal life through Jesus Christ, TESCREALists hold faith-based convictions about resurrection and immortality, except their savior is silicon rather than spiritual.

"We are our bodies," said Adam Becker, an astrophysicist who catalogs the anti-reality beliefs of the tech world in *More Everything Forever: AI Overlords, Space Empires, and Silicon Valley's Crusade to Control the Fate of Humanity*. "These bodies cannot be extended past a certain limit. There are certain hard biological limits that we are probably already running up against. And if not, we will soon. And you can't just transfer consciousness out of the body. We don't haunt our bodies. We are our bodies."

Similarly, the cosmist fantasy of life on Mars, or in the deepest reaches of the universe, has no grounding. "Mars is terrible," Becker said in an interview. "The gravity is too low. The radiation is too high. There's no air—and the dirt is made of poison. You would just die." And it's even less likely that humans will thrive on even more faraway planets. "Even with propulsion far beyond what we have today, human travel to the nearest star would take centuries, and with current or near-term technology it would take tens of thousands of years," Becker said. "There is no guarantee any destination would be habitable, so humanity could live aboard ships for many thousands of years—even hundreds of thousands—and still not find a viable planet."

All humans must perish, and space is a death trap, but scientific limitations on human biology, computers, and space travel are no obstacle for the TESCREAL faithful, whose priests and prophets push these extremely unlikely scenarios as imminent. Tech has incubated a family of cults, and, like most cults, they have bizarre ideas about the future. The chosen tribe of Silicon Valley has recreated God, eternal life, and heaven in their own image. Its members view themselves as heir to a cosmic destiny to eventually conquer the Earth, the laws of physics, and the universe itself. They were the audience that Andreessen, a billionaire e/acc, sought to reach with his corny tech manifesto, which he wrote in the style of biblical prophecy.

Two weeks after "The Techno-Optimist Manifesto" appeared, the TESCREAL tribes of Silicon Valley kicked off the search for a promised land at a conference in Amsterdam. On October 30, 2023, fifteen months after the publication of *The Network State*, Balaji Srinivasan hosted the first annual Network State Conference. A few hundred people—mostly men—gathered in an auditorium in Amsterdam, where Srinivasan declared that multiple efforts were underway to start new network state countries. According to Srinivasan's opening presentation, these included network state projects in Arizona, Texas, Latin America, and San Francisco.

"Imagine a thousand different start-ups, each of them replacing a different legacy institution," he said. "For example . . . San Francisco, and we're replacing San Francisco both with things outside it—like Culdesac in Arizona, Próspera in South America, and Cabin, which is in Texas but is also around the world—and the Neighborhood SF is actually fixing SF from within SF."

On the screen behind him, a PowerPoint slide titled "The Parallel Establishment" featured the logos of various companies and organizations he suggested were contributing to this process. Included in his slide: Thiel Fellowship (which pays young people to skip or quit college to pursue business ventures); Emergent Ventures (a Thiel Fellowship copycat started by George Mason University economist Tyler Cowen with $1 million from the Thiel Foundation); Substack (a VC-funded newsletter company designed to compete with mainstream media outlets); and the Musk-owned version of Twitter (which the billionaire had renamed X and converted into a global bullhorn for right-wing disinformation, polarization, and abject racism). The slide also featured the logos of four different real estate projects. There was Culdesac, a seventeen-acre car-free suburb in Tempe, and Cabin, which billed itself as a start-up building a "network city of modern villages" around the world. There was Neighborhood SF, a start-up which claimed to be building a one-square-mile tech colony in the middle of San Francisco. Then there was Próspera, a start-up city funded by Andreessen, Thiel, and Srinivasan through Pronomos Capital, a company founded by Patri Friedman—the seasteading advocate—to build network state cities around the world.

Srinivasan, clad in a suit and tie, spoke confidently and gave the impression that the network state's rise was well underway. He depicted the influence of Substack, X, and the real estate projects as the seeds from which his revolution would bloom. New companies would rise to challenge all existing institutions—banking, education, law, media, government—and eventually grow strong enough to replace them. For example, Srinivasan proposed replacing Harvard University with the Thiel Fellowship. "We replace media with parallel media," Srinivasan said. "They exist alongside the legacy in parallel. They're gaining strength. They're pulling away users—until they become the new thing. So, this is how we turn that seemingly impossible thing of building a new country. Break into a bunch of individual start-ups and then add them together."

Other speakers reinforced the message that network states were already materializing. Dryden Brown, the twenty-eight-year-old CEO of a project called Praxis, announced plans to build a tech city in the Mediterranean backed by Sam Altman, Joe Lonsdale, and Srinivasan himself, along with investments from Thiel and others. Mark Lutter of the Charter Cities Institute discussed plans for a new city in Zanzibar and mentioned a "stealth" project called Braavos Cities that planned to build a settlement in the Caribbean.

Patri Friedman detailed his decades-long quest to create new countries after having become dissatisfied with existing versions. "A lot of people look at government through the lens of: Is it moral, or does it represent me?" said Friedman. "I take a different view. I say drop that and just look at government as an industry . . . we've got this legacy industry doing a crappy job. How do we fix it? With start-ups. With competition."

This competition to create new states was heating up, according to the speakers at the conference—so much so that future network state sovereigns had already begun to consider the finer details, such as military-grade security for their future realms.

"Network states and start-up cities are starting to get more momentum," Spencer Macdonald, a former army officer who runs a cryptosecurity firm, told the audience during a presentation titled "Parallel Security of Network States." "So, we need to start talking about security." As a photo of the destroyed border wall between Gaza and Israel flashed on the screen behind him, Macdonald warned the audience that technology and walls will be insufficient to protect network state cities. He encouraged them to recruit former Special Operations soldiers to staff private police forces and hire social media teams capable of waging "info war."

Another of Macdonald's slides contained an image of California Forever, a controversial new project that sought to build a 400,000-person city in rural Solano County, sixty miles north of San Francisco. A few months earlier, *The New York Times* revealed that a secretive group funded by Silicon Valley billionaires, including Andreessen, had spent $900 million to quietly buy up 60,000 acres of land in the county. Michael Moritz, one of the billionaires behind California Forever, had pitched it to investors as what the *Times* described as "a kind of urban blank slate where everything from design to construction methods and new forms of governance could be rethought." News of this grand plan surprised the voters of Solano County, who immediately launched a movement to oppose it due to concerns over traffic, pollution, and sprawl. "I interviewed many startup city founders," read the text with Macdonald's California Forever slide. "They are thinking about security (and other aspects of execution) in close coordination with host nation governments."

Garry Tan also made an appearance at the conference, speaking in a taped conversation with Srinivasan where the Y Combinator president framed Musk's acquisition of Twitter as part of a bigger plan. "We've replaced some pieces of that political machine—specifically, we have parallel media now with Elon's Twitter, or X," said Tan. "Getting a parallel media was a key piece, and it wasn't through voting. It was done by building . . . We need to replace the unelected parts of the system as well, building parallel education, nonprofits, media, unions.

"That's a possible recipe for reforming San Francisco and building the alternative tech political machine," he said. "And if it works in [San Francisco], it will work everywhere."

Tan had used a similar line in a speech delivered at a meetup of fellow effective accelerationists at an AI-themed group house a few months earlier. "I guess I come here representing the home of techno-capital in America," he said, in a talk that highlighted San Francisco's importance as a launchpad for the e/acc movement. "That's why I think it's so important for us to fight here, it's so important for us to build here, because if we can build here, we're going to take over the whole country, we're going to take over every nation in the world."

Coincidentally, Tan's presentation at the Network State Conference was followed by a video narrated by Beff Jezos, the pseudonymous e/acc cofounder who would soon be unmasked as a physicist and quantum computing researcher named Guillaume Verdon. Where Andreessen had framed accelerationism as a material philosophy of self-perpetuating capitalist virtue, Verdon wrapped it in mystical theology and metaphysics. "At e/acc, we believe the engine of progress of civilization is something called the techno-capital machine, which is a cybernetic loop between technology and capital, and that this sort of loop is a form of intelligence that is optimizing itself."

The purpose of this techno-capital machine, he said, was to push humanity up something called the Kardashev scale, a framework devised by Soviet astrophysicist Nikolai Kardashev in 1964 to classify hypothetical alien civilizations. Kardashev reasoned that the most advanced civilizations would consume the most energy, accumulate the most material, and thus command the most power. The e/acc movement had adopted the Kardashev scale as the destiny of humankind—a tech cult gospel in which monstrous consumption and accumulation is the highest calling in the universe. "We believe this is a force for good that we should aim to accelerate," Verdon said. E/acc had even invented its own deity: the Thermodynamic God, Verdon's name for the mystical intelligence he claims animates the techno-capital machine.

But the Thermodynamic God has enemies—those who oppose acceleration in the name of accountability, deliberation, regulation, or safety. Verdon called them "the top-down centralized incumbents," and defeating them was the movement's central task.

"So, how do we really win?" he asked. "Ultimately, we have to use the full power of the techno-capital machine." This meant a formal alliance between crypto capital and e/acc AI builders—a "decentralized" coalition designed to outmaneuver regulators and capture the AI companies. As a capstone, he proposed that this alliance build its own independent "network state cloud": sovereign computing infrastructure, beyond the jurisdiction of any government, purpose-built to ensure that no democratic body could ever bottleneck the acceleration. Stripped of its pseudo-scientific mysticism, Verdon was simply updating *The Sovereign Individual*'s core prophecy—that AI and crypto would combine to overthrow the planetary order in the twenty-first century—but with a mystical religious framework that even included a new form of TESCREAList god.

Outside the strangest circles of the tech world, few people paid attention to the 2023 Network State Conference, which was livestreamed on social media. In San Francisco, however, a local activist named Emily Mills watched the entire conference and raised the alarm on Tan's affiliation with e/acc and Network State. "Garry Tan is an Effective Accelerationist who wants to take over the nation and the world with that ideology utilizing Network State style strategies," wrote Mills in November 2023. "This needs more reporting." Where others might have seen Silicon Valley eccentricity, Mills saw proof of an ideological infrastructure being built in real time, complete with real estate projects and political strategies that—according to Tan himself—had been tested in San Francisco's recall campaigns. Theory was flowing into practice, backed by money from tech elites who openly plotted to create a post-democracy world. Despite her efforts to raise the alarm, the press remained aloof, and Tan's more extreme edges remained hidden, temporarily. Three months later, in January 2024, Tan got drunk and ignited a media firestorm by writing "die slow motherfuckers" in a late-night X post targeting seven progressive members of the San Francisco Board of Supervisors. The supervisors took it as a death threat, especially since Tan had taken an increasingly harsh tone toward them since the recall elections and had previously threatened to "wipe out" the same group of elected officials. Under heavy criticism, and with some of the targeted officials filing police reports, Tan apologized.

His aggressive language and threats echoed Srinivasan, who had begun to fantasize about purging the liberals from San Francisco. Srinivasan's remarks at the Network State Conference had been tailored as a business pitch to investors and tech workers. One month before the conference, however, he had given a more provocative and horrifying version of the network state vision. During six hours of conversation on the right-wing *Moment of Zen* podcast, he unveiled a shocking new update to his ideas. Expanding on his fantasy of a Second Civil War, Srinivasan said the tech Gray tribe had become a new force in politics, distinct from Blue or Red. Eventually, he said, Gray would overpower Blue and Red alike.

"If Red is the past—the conservatives—and Blue is the present . . . Gray is the future," he said. In the meantime, Red and Gray had to work together against Blue. The tech capitalist network and the Red tribe Republican network needed to merge in a common struggle, and he offered an example of how this might work. Srinivasan imagined a nightmarish future dystopia in San Francisco, which would begin with the Grays buying up large swaths of the city in a quest to seize power and territory. "What I'm really calling for is something like tech Zionism," he said, having compared his network state to other movements started by people such as Abraham, Jesus Christ, Joseph Smith (the founder of Mormonism), Theodor Herzl (the "spiritual father" of the state of Israel), and Lee Kuan Yew (the former authoritarian ruler of Singapore). He added that a major new network state project was already underway "on bare land" in California. "You're seeing it in Northern California, you know, this thing, this project," he said, in what seemed like a reference to the California Forever project in Solano County.

Srinivasan proceeded to paint a grim picture of how the network state would operate in San Francisco. The Gray tribe would wear gray shirts emblazoned with corporate logos to signify their tech affiliations, he said, suggesting that these would symbolize allegiance to Musk, Bitcoin, or Y Combinator. "And if you see another Gray on the street, you do the nod," he said. "You're a fellow Gray."

Members of the Gray tribe would receive special ID cards enabling access to tech-controlled sectors of the city. They would also form a close alliance with the police—"all in on the police"—providing regular banquets and jobs in "tech security" for the officers' family members. Officers who signed on with the Grays would get special uniforms to represent their allegiance, and the Grays would donate heavily to police charities to "merge the Gray and police social networks."

This would be bad news for the Blues—the Democrats and progressives who make up most of San Francisco's voting population. Srinivasan said Blues would be unwelcome in zones controlled by Grays. "Take total control of your neighborhood," he said. "Push out all Blues. Tell them they're . . . unwelcome . . . push out all Blues."

The goal, he said, was to do to San Francisco what Musk had done to Twitter: Gut it, purge it, and harvest its power. Early on, Musk had upended the site's reality by erasing blue checks, the official checkmarks that once appeared on the accounts of journalists, celebrities, and politicians and which had become an online status symbol. "Elon, in sort of classic Gray fashion . . . captures Twitter and then, at one stroke, wipes out millions of Blues' status by wiping out the blue checks," he said. "Another stroke . . . [he] renames Twitter as X, showing that he has true control, and it's his vehicle, and that the old regime isn't going to be restored."

Corporate logos would fill the skyline in the Gray sector, and streets would be renamed to honor tech figures. Meanwhile, the Grays would build monuments and screen propaganda films to remind people of the alleged horrors inflicted by progressive Democratic governance. As if this entire vision wasn't already dripping in fascist cosplay, Srinivasan generated a masterpiece of authoritarian fantasy, which he called the "Gray Pride parade."

"A huge win would be a Gray Pride parade with 50,000 Grays," said Srinivasan. "That would start to say: 'Whose streets? Our streets!' You have the AI Flying Spaghetti Monster. You have the Bitcoin parade. You have the drones flying overhead in formation . . . You have bubbling genetic experiments on beakers . . . You have the police at the Gray Pride parade. They're flying the Anduril drones . . ."

Everyone would be welcome at the Gray Pride march, he said—everyone except the members of the Blue tribe. Blues would be banned from the Gray-controlled zones, said Balaji, unlike members of the Red tribe. "Reds should be welcomed there, and people should wear their tribal colors," said Srinivasan, comparing his color-coded apartheid system to the Bloods vs. Crips gang rivalry. "No Blues should be welcomed there." Like Yarvin, Srinivasan used the terms "denazification" and "lustration"—both referring to the purging of discredited Nazi and communist officials—to describe the necessary process. "De-Blueification is the goal," he said. "Blues out."

Police, bribed with food and jobs, would become an arm of tech capital. Democrats would be purged from Gray-controlled zones. The

San Francisco recalls had proved that aligning tech money with right-wing networks could overthrow elected progressives in deep-blue territory. Now Srinivasan envisioned scaling that model to transform the entire city. His vision had sharpened from abstract theory into what he saw as actionable strategy.

Tan's late-night outburst against the city's elected officials reflected the odd vision of the deep-blue city cleansed of Democratic power, though Tan continued to identify as a "moderate" Democrat.

The mask slipped again in September, when Tan keynoted a tech conference at Fort Mason, on the San Francisco waterfront. Reboot 2024 showcased a budding alliance between the tech venture capitalists and the most powerful right-wing organizations in the country.

A manifesto on the conference's website declared the dawning of a "New Reality":

> *The New Reality is here. It's just not evenly distributed. You can see it everywhere. Across media, politics, education, and global affairs, new technologies and players are laying waste to incumbents and making possible new enterprises and ways of building. Political pressure and popular opinion are moving from stagnation to revolution, from doom loop to boom loop.*
>
> *This isn't incremental improvement. It's reality transformation.*
>
> *But the Old Reality won't go without a fight. Legacy organizations and personalities will try to write their privileges and cash flows into law faster than New Reality technologies and founders can overtake them. It's a classic strategy, employed by every guild and elite. It will work, until it doesn't.*
>
> *Tech will be at the center of the fight. The printing press didn't have a politics, but printers, readers, and thinkers did. And today, after decades of pretending that Washington didn't exist, Silicon Valley has woken up to politics, recognizes the stakes, and is playing to win.*

The conference featured a secret guest whose identity wasn't revealed until he spoke. It was Kevin Roberts, president of the

Heritage Foundation and a key author of Project 2025, a 920-page plan for right-wing government that would soon become the key strategy document of the second Trump administration. Among other things, Project 2025 included a proposal to purge the government by eliminating up to 1 million federal workers and dismantling entire agencies, a plan resembling Yarvin's 2012 call for a total "reboot" of the government.

Reboot—the conference—was largely a mash-up of right-wing Republicans and Thiel's protégés. Speakers included Mike Solana of Thiel's Founders Fund, who did a fireside chat with Brendan Carr, an outspoken right-wing member of the Federal Communications Commission. Longtime Thiel associate Trae Stephens of Anduril and Founders Fund spoke about "rebuilding America's defense arsenal" with Michael Kratsios, who had formerly served as a Trump aide as well as Thiel's chief of staff.

"While there were a few big swings at existential issues in America, what was billed as disruption to the status quo primarily served to reinforce a variety of conservative talking points—courtesy of a slate of far-right speakers who blame liberalism, regulation, and skepticism toward tech as anathema to human progress," wrote journalist Eddie Kim.

This merging of tech and far-right networks—hosted by the Foundation for American Innovation, which *Inc.* later described as "the foundation shaping the tech right"—seemed like a live test of Srinivasan's theory. Two months before the most consequential election in American history put Trump back in power, the Grays and the Reds gathered in San Francisco to discuss the dawning of a new era that would bring MAGA Republicans and Silicon Valley into one unified network.

The ideological groundwork had been laid, the coalitions formed, and the strategy tested. What had seemed like fringe tech philosophy was now backed by hundreds of millions in political donations and embraced by the institutional right. A Gray-Red alliance had become operational, and the tech industry's realignment was gaining momentum.

Trump now received massive support from Silicon Valley. Musk, who had initially pledged to stay out of the election, had become Trump's biggest donor and most vocal supporter after the former president survived an assassination attempt in July. He spent $290 million to elect him, and also turned X into a right-wing propaganda machine. David Sacks, who had once condemned Trump as "disqualified" and had initially backed Florida Governor Ron DeSantis, hosted a Trump fundraiser at his San Francisco mansion that reportedly raised $12 million in a single night. Major Silicon Valley donors followed their lead, lining up behind the Republican ticket, which now featured a former Silicon Valley venture capitalist and Thiel protégé named JD Vance.

CHAPTER 5

THE UNICORN

JD Vance and the Road to the White House

The most important thing to understand about JD Vance is that he is almost entirely a creation of Peter Thiel. At nearly every step of his career, Thiel has been there with connections, funding, and support. Vance owes his career in Silicon Valley, his conversion to Catholicism, and his political rise to Thiel. They met in 2011 when Thiel gave a talk at Yale Law School. Vance—then going by the name James David Hamel—was a student there. Vance was so impressed by Thiel's remarks that he found his email address and wrote to him, and Thiel responded by inviting him to visit Thiel in California someday. Vance would later describe meeting Thiel as "the most significant moment of my time at Yale Law School," and he called Thiel "possibly the smartest person" he had ever met. His friendship with the tech billionaire would prove the most consequential relationship of his life.

Before graduating law school in 2013, James David Hamel—JD—changed his surname to Vance in honor of the grandmother who helped raise him. After a brief stint clerking for a judge in Kentucky and less than two years at Sidley Austin, an elite law firm staffed by Ivy League attorneys, Vance moved to California to work as director of operations at a Menlo Park–based biotechnology company called Circuit Therapeutics. It was an unusual first job in tech for a lawyer with no experience. Frederic Moll, then CEO of Circuit, later told *The New York Times* "he was a very smart guy with an impressive background in law, but also it was a favor to Peter [Thiel]."

In 2016, with little to show for his time at Circuit, Vance landed a plum slot at Mithril Capital, a venture capital firm cofounded by Thiel. *Hillbilly Elegy: A Memoir of a Family and Culture in Crisis*, the book Vance had been working on for years, was published in June of that year. At Mithril, Vance proved to be a lackluster employee. One colleague later told *The Wall Street Journal* he never once saw Vance in the office. Another suggested Vance spent most of his time at Mithril traveling the country on his book tour. "Several months later, Mr. Vance left Mithril Capital after butting heads with the firm's managing partner, Ajay Royan, three people familiar with the situation said," reported *The New York Times*. Regardless, Vance had a champion in Thiel, one of his book's earliest readers and fans.

"Elites tend to see our social crisis in terms of 'stagnation' or 'inequality,'" wrote Thiel in a blurb for the book. "J. D. Vance writes powerfully about the real people who are kept out of sight by academic abstractions."

The book rocketed to bestseller status. It made the *New York Times* bestseller list, earned plaudits from Oprah Winfrey, and made Vance a media star. *Hillbilly Elegy*, which recounts Vance's upbringing amid drug abuse and dysfunction in Ohio, became a media map for decoding Trump's appeal to poor white rural voters. It was catnip for the mainstream media—a tearjerker personal story coupled with vaguely right-of-center bromides about the importance of family structure and the hazards of government intervention.

Not everyone was impressed. A review in *The New Republic* dubbed the book "the liberal media's favorite white-trash explainer," with writer Sarah Jones dismissing it as "little more than a list of myths about welfare queens repackaged as a primer on the working white class." Jones wrote that Vance's book blamed a hillbilly "culture of poverty" for the plight of struggling whites and called on poor whites to address this problem with personal responsibility. "His great takeaway from life in America's underclass is: Pull up those bootstraps," wrote Jones. "Don't question elites. Don't ask if they erred by granting people mortgages and lines of credit they couldn't afford to repay. Don't call it what it is—corporate deception—or admit that it plunged this country into one of the worst economic crises it's ever experienced. No wonder Peter Thiel, the almost comically evil Silicon Valley libertarian, endorsed the book."

"When I read JD Vance's memoir, I resented it all the way through," Barbara Kingsolver, the Pulitzer Prize–winning, Kentucky-raised writer, said of *Hillbilly Elegy* as the book experienced a resurgence in 2024. "There was just something about it that kept telling me, he's not from here, he doesn't get us."

"JD Vance should not be held up as a representative of Appalachia or working class people, as his book *Hillbilly Elegy* displayed contempt for both groups," said Silas House, the former poet laureate of Kentucky.

Vance, writing from his vantage point as a Yale-educated lawyer and Silicon Valley executive in San Francisco, was more "Thielbilly" than hillbilly. Yet his book, a self-serving and inaccurate diagnosis of poverty authored by a man who grew up in suburban Middletown, Ohio—a far cry from the hollers of Eastern Kentucky—resonated with elite audiences. Vance, already a contributor at the conservative *National Review*, had provided the usual Republican analysis to the problem of rural poverty. Yet his personal story, coupled with the book's lack of overtly partisan attacks, made him irresistible to media bookers as a go-to expert on Trump's appeal to poor whites—a phenomenon Vance appeared to despise. He used his perch as a best-selling author to vehemently oppose Trump.

As Trump ascended toward the presidency, Vance declared himself a "Never Trump guy" and tore into him as often as possible. He called Trump "a bad man," "an idiot," "morally reprehensible," and "unfit" and described him as "cultural heroin" and an "opioid of the masses." "Trump's actual policy proposals, such as they are, range from immoral to absurd," he wrote in *USA Today* in early 2016.

Behind the scenes, he delivered even harsher assessments.

"I go back and forth between thinking Trump is a cynical asshole like Nixon who wouldn't be that bad (and might even prove useful) or that he's America's Hitler," he wrote in a private message to a friend on Facebook. After Trump took office in 2017, Vance said some Trump supporters were racist and had supported him for "racist reasons."

Vance's stance put him on the opposite side of Thiel. On election night 2016, while Vance was presumably lamenting the results, Thiel was sipping champagne with Yarvin in San Francisco. The disagreement over Trump, however, did not permanently affect Vance's relationship with Thiel. They stayed in touch after Vance left Mithril in 2017 to return to Ohio, where he became a partner at Revolution LLC, a VC firm based in Washington, DC, and cofounded by former America Online CEO Steve Case. That year, Vance reportedly landed an $8 million deal to write a second book, *A Relevant Faith: Searching for a Meaningful American Christianity*. In 2022, the Associated Press reported that the deal was off, but Vance would eventually publish *Communion: Finding My Way Back to Faith* in 2026.

In late 2019, after two years at Revolution, Vance started his own fund with investments from Thiel, Andreessen, and former Google CEO Eric Schmidt. He named the firm Narya Capital, after a magical ring of power in J. R. R. Tolkien's *The Lord of the Rings*. This was a clear nod to the influence of Thiel, who has a longstanding practice of giving his companies names derived from Tolkien's fantasy world—Mithril, Palantir, Valar. Narya officially launched in 2020 with $93 million in funding, but Vance once again proved himself a mediocre venture capitalist.

Most VC firms focus on investing in companies located in coastal cities like New York and San Francisco, but Narya's stated purpose was to focus on investments in the middle of the country. Yet Vance's signature investment, a Kentucky-based indoor farming start-up called AppHarvest, produced an unqualified disaster. The company had planned to create giant greenhouses and agriculture jobs to replace disappearing coal industry jobs. Jonathan Webb, the company's founder, had no experience in agriculture or business. Yet he attracted nearly $800 million in investments, including from NBA star Blake Griffin and James Murdoch, son of Rupert Murdoch. Vance joined the company's board. "It's not just a good investment opportunity, it's a great business that's making a big difference in the world," said Vance when the company went public in 2021.

"This is psychotic to me, the amount of money we've raised," said Webb, AppHarvest's CEO, later that year. "The reality is, none of us had any clue what we were doing," he added.

His words proved prophetic. Within three years, facing $341 million in debt, AppHarvest declared bankruptcy amid a hurricane of legal woes. AppHarvest employees complained about terrible working conditions in hellishly hot greenhouses, where they were deprived of water breaks and proper safety gear. "Some workers said they suffered heat exhaustion or injuries, though state inspectors did not find violations," reported CNN. Despite AppHarvest's promise to create jobs for locals, the company—like most of the agriculture industry—quickly resorted to hiring Latino immigrant workers. By the time AppHarvest unraveled, Vance was long gone, having quit the board and distanced himself from the company.

Not all of Narya's bets ended in failure. The company also invested in Rumble, a right-wing version of YouTube, and in a Christian prayer app called Hallow. Not coincidentally, Thiel had also invested in those companies. Vance's investment in companies catering to far-right and religious groups reflected his own personal shifts during his brief time as a venture capitalist. The man who had become a media darling with his baby-faced, thoughtful, middle-of-the-road persona began to assume a new form as a conservative firebrand with sharp elbows and a boiling hatred for "woke ideology." During this time, he also underwent a spiritual transformation. Though he had been raised mostly nonreligious in a culture of Protestant evangelism, Vance converted to Catholicism in 2019.

"I became persuaded over time that Catholicism was true," said Vance in an interview with Rod Dreher of *The American Conservative*, who attended his baptism ceremony in Cincinnati. Vance chose Augustine as his patron saint, saying books like *Confessions* and *The City of God* had greatly affected his thinking.

He also gave a clear but subtle nod to the influence of Thiel. "When I looked at the people who meant the most to me, they were Catholic," said Vance. "My uncle by marriage is a Catholic. René Girard is someone I only know by reading him, and he was Catholic. I've been reading and studying about it for three years, or even longer. It was time." Thiel, of course, had formed a strong attachment to Girard's ideas when he was his student at Stanford. One of Girard's key ideas, mimetic rivalry, asserted that people don't develop their desires independently but instead copy them from others, creating cascades of imitation that can be deliberately triggered and directed. Thiel credited this insight with his decision to become a major investor in Facebook, a decision that made him a billionaire.

Vance later made Thiel's influence plain. "[Thiel] defied the social template I had constructed—that dumb people were Christians and smart people were atheists," wrote Vance in 2020. "I began to wonder where his religious belief came from, which led me to René Girard, the French philosopher whom he apparently studied under at Stanford."

Vance explained that Girard's theories on mimetic rivalry and scapegoating—the notion that humans tend to mimic one another's desires and eventually relieve civilizational tensions by punishing scapegoats—had been deeply influential on him. Thiel had been fixated on those concepts for years, and his increasingly obsessive fascination with them would eventually play a defining role in his public identity. Vance's early immersion in these ideas, which helped to spur his religious awakening, illustrates his status as a Thiel insider and protégé more clearly than anything else.

At some point during his journey into Catholicism, Vance also came under the influence of "postliberal" Catholic scholars like Patrick Deneen and Adrian Vermeule, who reject liberal democracy and argue for replacing it with a more hierarchical system rooted in Catholic moral teaching. In the 2018 book *Why Liberalism Failed,*

Deneen blamed liberalism for the ills of the world and called for a new political order.

"Deneen's thinking echoes an older line of reactionary argument on the folly and perversity of liberal democracy that extends back from twentieth-century anti-liberal intellectuals, like Leo Strauss and fascist theorists Carl Schmitt and Giovanni Gentile, to nineteenth-century nationalist and monarchic critics of liberalism, like Joseph de Maistre," wrote Robert Kuttner in a stinging review of the book, tracing Deneen's influences back to the same illiberal thinkers who inspired Thiel and Yarvin. Kuttner dismissed Deneen's arguments as "dubious, both historically and intellectually." *Regime Change: Toward a Postliberal Future*, Deneen's next book, continued the attack on liberalism and called for an "aristopopulism" of radicalized right-wing elites to channel societal turmoil against the bureaucratic order that supposedly uses its power to impose destructively progressive ideas on the masses. Drawing from the same well of thought, Deneen recycles arguments already made by Yarvin in a rawer form. The same goes for Vermeule, a Harvard University law professor, who calls liberalism a "fighting, evangelistic faith" and argues that universities should categorize it "in the same space as Christianity, Islam, and Buddhism"—essentially reinventing Yarvin's Cathedral.

Both Deneen and Vermeule also push for a turn away from American-style democracy and toward authoritarian, hierarchical forms of government. With his political ascension, Vance—already versed in Silicon Valley's version of the same thinking—became a key figure in the postliberal Catholic movement to tear down the prevailing order of American democracy. And while the radical right-wing Catholics and their tech counterparts don't agree on everything, their ideas overlap significantly, and Vance became a bridge between them.

Now a venture capitalist and a Catholic because of Thiel, Vance soon turned his focus to becoming a politician. In 2017, he considered running for US Senate but decided against it, most likely after polling showed zero chance for an anti-Trump Republican in Ohio. By 2021, the political landscape had shifted dramatically, and so had Vance. The man who once called himself a "Never Trumper" and said Trump was "noxious" and "leading the white working class to a very dark place" now began to sound like him. Vance morphed into a vicious critic of liberalism, his rhetoric sharpening in step with the wider radicalization of the Republican Party and the rise of an extremist faction called the alt-right, a highly online group of movements that includes white supremacists and neo-Nazis. In August 2017, during Trump's first year in office, alt-right forces had marched by torchlight at a Unite the Right rally in Charlottesville, Virginia, chanting, "Jews will not replace us." Trump's response—"very fine people on both sides," he said—signaled that such overt racism and extremism were welcome in the GOP.

Over the next few years, the alt-right's extreme ideas became mainstream Republican talking points: rhetoric about a "great replacement" of whites, culture war framed as existential battle, liberal democracy condemned as the enemy. The alt-right, inspired by the same ideas at the heart of the neoreactionary tech right, became a powerful influence in the Republican Party. Vance, who had once positioned himself as a centrist, now sought to center himself as a pillar of this new radicalized base. Within a few years of converting to Catholicism, Vance was born again as a Trump supporter and vicious right-wing culture warrior, blasting so-called wokeness while praising the former president he had once called "America's Hitler." Vance did more than just suck up to Trump. With backing from Thiel, he set out to become a power player in conservative politics.

In 2019, the same year he cofounded Narya and became a Catholic, Vance also cofounded an organization called the Rockbridge Network with a pro-Trump activist named Chris Buskirk. Rockbridge, named after the Ohio town where it was founded, fashioned itself as a "political venture capital firm" seeking to "bring together investors who are dissatisfied with the status quo of politics and raise capital to fund projects that will disrupt but advance the Republican agenda."

According to *The New York Times*, Rockbridge formed after "Buskirk began informally hosting a series of small dinners with the hopes of laying groundwork for Mr. Vance's political career and, eventually, of building a Trump-aligned alternative to the Koch Network," the conservative funding powerhouse that had soured on Trump. Thiel immediately became a core funding source for Rockbridge, which would marshal more than $100 million over the next five years and help "lead Silicon Valley's march to the right."

Rockbridge took a stealthy approach to avoid the scrutiny and vilification the Koch Network had attracted, but it rapidly expanded to include a constellation of dark-money umbrella organizations focused on everything from right-wing philanthropy to shaping media coverage. Rockbridge meetings, which had started off as small dinners, soon became a hot ticket, hosting conferences in swank hotels like the Ritz-Carlton.

These events drew enthusiastic support from Silicon Valley's growing coterie of right-wing firebrands. Andreessen, the Winklevoss twins, and Palmer Luckey—cofounder of Anduril, a drone and surveillance company with a *Lord of the Rings* name that was funded by Thiel and Andreessen—all joined the fold. So did Ken Howery and Luke Nosek, who traced their connection to Thiel back to PayPal Mafia days.

Another powerful Thiel connection, Rebekah Mercer, joined him in becoming one of Rockbridge's key funders. Mercer, a right-wing heiress from New York, was a Stanford graduate who had immersed herself in politics to such a degree that, in 2016, *Politico* described her as "the most powerful woman in GOP politics." Mercer also regularly collaborated with Trump advisor Steve Bannon, and both were investors in Cambridge Analytica, the infamous data analytics firm that used data harvested from Facebook to build detailed psychological profiles of voters and target them with highly manipulative political advertising.

With Rockbridge, Vance became more than just another ambitious politician pining for the support and money of donors. The organization established him as the head of a powerful donor network explicitly designed to take a venture capital approach to politics by spreading bets toward a goal of maximum disruption and profit.

Trump had lost the 2020 election but had won Ohio, where Vance decided to run for Senate in 2022. One of his campaign stops was on the *Jack Murphy Live* podcast in 2021. "So, there's this guy, Curtis Yarvin, who has written about these things," said Vance. Murphy, real name John Goldman, had asked Vance how Trump might "rip out the disgusting leadership class" in the United States. He was following up on a comment Vance had made minutes earlier, when he said it was necessary to "rip out, like a tumor, the current American leadership class and then reinstall some sense of American political religion." By "tumor," Vance meant Democrats and liberals. Murphy pressed him to explain how they might be cast out of American politics: "Unfortunately, this evil leadership class has already taken over all of our institutions, all the media, all the academy, all of our corporations, every educational institution, every arts and culture institution, even every freaking sporting institution that we've had . . . how do we, aside from elections, how do we rip out this leadership class?" asked Murphy. "What do we do? Is it even possible to renovate or rehab these institutions from the inside?"

"This is, like, a tough question, but this is maybe the question that confronts us right now," said Vance. "One model is what happened to Germany after the Nazis lost, or what happened to the Iraqis after Saddam Hussein, after we threw Saddam Hussein out. De-Nazification, de-Baathification. There was this massive recognition that you couldn't just . . . replace the bad people, replace the bad Nazis, with good Germans. There was this entire effort to de-institutionalize that ideology."

One option would be for conservatives to wait for the system to collapse and then remake it, Vance said, but he dismissed this option as "defeatist." He proceeded to outline his preferred method. "I tend to think we should seize the institutions of the left and turn them against the left, right?" said Vance. "We need, like, a de-Baathification program—a de-wokeification program—in the United States, right?"

Vance's lips moved, but Yarvin's ideas came out of his mouth. Vance told Murphy the constitutional republic had been replaced by an "administrative state" that limited the power of the president. Some Republicans wanted to destroy the bureaucracy, said Vance, but this was foolish. Instead, he said, Republicans should "seize the administrative state for our own purposes" and "fire all of the people."

"I think Trump is going to run again in 2024, I think he'll probably win . . . he will be the president of the United States in January 2025," said Vance. "I think what Trump should do, if I was giving him one piece of advice: Fire every single mid-level bureaucrat, every civil servant in the administrative state. Replace them with our people. And when the courts—because you will get taken to court—and when the courts stop you, stand before the country, like Andrew Jackson did, and say, 'The chief justice has made his ruling, now let him enforce it.' Because this is a constitutional-level crisis. If we continue to let bureaucrats control the entire country, even when Republicans win elections, then we've lost, we've just permanently lost, we've permanently given up."

He pointed to Viktor Orbán, the Russia-aligned authoritarian prime minister of Hungary, as an example of the kind of leader needed to overthrow liberal power. Specifically, he pointed to how Orbán took control of universities by threatening to withdraw government funding unless they complied with his political demands. "You actually just go down American institutions and make it possible for conservatives to actually govern and succeed in these institutions in a way where they're currently cut out," said Vance. "That's basically my strategy . . . de-institutionalize the left, re-institutionalize the right."

He identified the enemy: the cultural, governmental, and societal pillars of American democracy—Yarvin's Cathedral—which he portrayed as a liberal cabal. And he offered a solution: mass purges, with wholesale firings of federal civil servants (Yarvin's RAGE—"Retire All Government Employees").

Vance outlined these ideas during a strikingly confessional appearance on Murphy's right-wing podcast in which Vance explained why, after having previously opposed Trump, he now supported him. "I was wrong about Trump," said Vance, adding that he had supported most of Trump's policies and suggesting that he had been misled by his elite education. "I saw and realized something about the American elite, and my role in the American elite, that took me just a while to figure out," he said. "I was redpilled," he added, using the term Yarvin had appropriated from *The Matrix* movie to describe an instantaneous conversion to reactionary ideology.

Vance's realignment with Trump provided his salvation. Polls showed Vance trailing in the Republican primary and he seemed likely to lose. Then on April 15, 2022, Trump endorsed Vance, who surged to victory against his Republican primary opponents and went on to beat longtime Democratic Congressman Tim Ryan in the general election. Thiel bankrolled the effort, dropping a total of $15 million in support of Vance's Senate campaign, setting the record for the largest amount of money a single donor has ever spent to get someone elected to the US Senate. Thiel had also tried to get another protégé, a Stanford graduate named Blake Masters, elected to the Senate in Arizona that year. Masters met Thiel while studying at Stanford Law School. He took notes on Thiel's lectures, and the two men used them to cowrite a best-selling book called *Zero to One: Notes on Startups, or How to Build the Future,* which details Thiel's thoughts on business. "If they both win, Masters and Vance will be among four U.S. senators who partly owe their seats to Peter Thiel's largesse," wrote Max Chafkin, Thiel's biographer, a year before Vance's election to the Senate. "They are, as two Thielworld insiders pointed out to me, extensions of him."

Thiel had spent another $15 million on Masters's race, but his campaign fell short, in part due to his political extremism. On the campaign trail, Masters cited a white supremacist writer as a key influence. In addition, he was exposed for having "approvingly quoted a Nazi war criminal" during his Stanford undergrad years, and for generally holding a slew of beliefs so noxious and racist that he earned high praise from an infamous neo-Nazi blog called *The Daily Stormer.*

On January 3, 2023, Vance became the junior senator from Ohio. At thirty-eight, he was the youngest serving Republican member of the Senate at the time. His performance as a senator would match his performance as a VC: mediocre and undistinguished. Vance authored several pieces of legislation—most designed to bolster his reputation as a right-wing culture warrior—but none were signed into law.

This hardly mattered, as he didn't stay long on Capitol Hill. In fact, his biggest achievement in the Senate was the speed with which he exited it. On January 20, 2025, he became vice president of the United States.

° ° °

Venture capital functions according to something called the power law, which means that a small percentage of investments will yield large results. In the VC model, firms can blow hundreds of millions of dollars making bad bets that fail, hoping to make billions of dollars by picking a few massively successful companies—the so-called unicorns—to make it all worthwhile.

VC survives by fishing a few big winners out of a sea of bad bets. Winners are companies that generate enough excitement and hype to send their valuation skyrocketing, allowing the VCs to cash out. Venture funds actively hunt the major cash windfalls that occur when a company goes public via an initial public offering, or IPO. Dr. Olivier Jutel, a critic of the VC model, says its main philosophy is "you should only invest in things that will give you a thousand-x return."

To achieve profit at breakneck speed, VC firms often push company founders to engage in something called "blitzscaling." The term, derived from the Nazi warfare tactic of overwhelming an enemy with superior force, means pushing exponential growth at all costs, regardless of long-term consequences to society or the company itself. "For venture capitalists, the job has become not about finding companies that are creating breakthrough innovations that could spur large-scale value creation, but about pursuing power law returns that can make them very rich," wrote Catherine Bracy in *World Eaters: How Venture Capital Is Cannibalizing the Economy*.

To ensure maximal chances of success, VC firms do more than just bankroll. Many also provide a full suite of services to shape and control their investments, enforcing a culture where their picks will do whatever it takes to succeed. These firms—like Andreessen Horowitz and Y Combinator—don't just sit back and allow company founders to do as they please. They become full partners in the project, holding the purse strings and calling the shots. Some unicorns deliver windfalls to their early investors without ever turning a real-world profit. Others go on to be extremely profitable over the long term, such as Thiel-funded companies Facebook, Palantir, and the financial services company Stripe.

Vance did not distinguish himself as a venture capitalist, but he has done very well if you think of him as a VC-funded *investment*. Thiel scouted him at Yale Law, plucked him out of the legal profession, and brought him out to San Francisco. There, Vance attracted the interest of Thiel's fellow investors, like Andreessen, who poured millions into Narya Capital even though the absentee employee had done little—besides write a best-selling book—to merit such faith. But Vance didn't return to Ohio to make a name as an investor; he did it to run for office. With investment and support from Thiel, he quickly vaulted to the highest levels of government.

Thiel had invested money in politicians before, including Ron Paul, Ted Cruz, Josh Hawley, and his risky contrarian bet, Trump. But his yearslong investment in Vance could prove to be his most successful political venture. Like PayPal, Facebook, and Palantir—the investments that made Thiel a billionaire—JD Vance was a unicorn.

This rising politician, who had once been described by Thiel's own associates as an extension of Thiel himself, is one heartbeat away from the presidency. Getting Trump to accept Vance, who had once compared him to Hitler, took some effort. Thiel and his fellow VCs, like David Sacks, lobbied Trump heavily to put him on the ticket. The relationship between Thiel and Trump had deteriorated since 2016, when Thiel had bucked conventional wisdom to put his money behind Trump. In 2023, with Trump pining to return to office, Thiel declared he would stay out of the 2024 election and described his previous support for Trump as a "not very articulate scream for help." "There are a lot of things I got wrong," Thiel said in an unusually introspective interview with *The Atlantic*. "It was crazier than I thought," he added. "It was more dangerous than I thought." Thiel complained that he had seen Trump as someone who could force a national reckoning by tearing things down so they could be rebuilt. He lamented, however, that Trump "couldn't get the most basic pieces of the government to work."

The billionaire expressed his frustration by refusing to give money to Trump's 2020 campaign. Tensions reached a breaking point in April 2023, when Thiel once again denied Trump's request for money. Trump told Thiel he was disappointed and had expected more from him. Behind Thiel's back, Trump delivered a harsher assessment, calling Thiel "a fucking scumbag" in a conversation with Thiel crony Blake Masters. Thiel detailed the drama to *The Atlantic*'s Barton Gellman in what the billionaire described as an effort to hold himself publicly accountable to his pledge to avoid giving money to Trump or Republicans in 2024.

At the time, the former president still had competition for the Republican nomination. Florida Governor Ron DeSantis, former South Carolina Governor Nikki Haley, and venture capitalist Vivek Ramaswamy launched challenges. Early on, David Sacks had enthusiastically backed DeSantis. But once Trump crushed his competitors, Silicon Valley's right-wing zealots had no choice but to line up behind him. They wanted something in return and put intense pressure on Trump to choose Vance as his VP, with even the reluctant Thiel lobbying Trump in multiple phone calls. The effort paid off. Two days after the failed assassination attempt in Butler, Pennsylvania, Trump announced that he had chosen Vance as his running mate. "IT'S JD VANCE," tweeted Delian Asparouhov, a partner at Thiel's Founders Fund. "WE HAVE A FORMER TECH VC IN THE WHITE HOUSE. GREATEST COUNTRY ON EARTH BABY." Musk, Sacks, and Ramaswamy also celebrated the victory, which came after Musk—who, like Thiel, had pledged to stay out of the 2024 election—promised to spend $45 million per month in support for Trump.

"Overnight, Vance's appointment as the VP candidate became a seminal moment for the Silicon Valley elites," wrote Jacob Silverman in *Gilded Rage: Elon Musk and the Radicalization of Silicon Valley.*

"Many Americans knew Vance as a 'hillbilly' made good, but for America's right-wing tech class, he was also one of them."

No one could savor the triumph more than Thiel, the man who had fished Vance out of obscurity and shepherded his journey to fame, wealth, and power. And with Musk alone spending nearly $300 million—plus major contributions from tech venture capitalists and the crypto industry—Thiel's public decision to withhold his personal millions hardly mattered. In fact, there was something poetic about Thiel's decision to keep his financial fingerprints off the campaign that would put his former employee and protégé in the White House.

Thiel had already done his job, almost singlehandedly transforming a random Yale Law student into a venture capitalist, a Catholic, a right-wing radical, a US senator, and a vice president. And if Vance manages to succeed Trump, Thiel—his benefactor, mentor, and maker—will become the most powerful man in the world.

CHAPTER 6

APOKÁLYPSIS

Tech Fascism Unveiled

Ten days before the 2025 inauguration, Peter Thiel wrote in the *Financial Times* that Trump's return to the presidency would result in an *apokálypsis*—Greek for "unveiling"—of hidden truths about the government. Thiel pointed to the assassination of John F. Kennedy, the COVID pandemic, and the alleged jail suicide of financier and sex offender Jeffrey Epstein as possible subjects about which the Trump administration might reveal shocking secrets.

"The new administration's revelations need not justify vengeance—reconstruction can go hand in hand with reconciliation," wrote Thiel in a short opinion essay headlined "A Time for Truth and Reconciliation." "But for reconciliation to take place, there must first be truth. The apokálypsis is the most peaceful means of resolving the old guard's war on the internet, a war the internet won."

Thiel lashed together a bunch of right-wing grievances to argue that the American government had become corrupted to its core. He gleefully suggested that Biden's 2020 victory had been the last gasp of a dying regime composed of people who hoped to "write off Trump as an aberration." With Trump restored to power, Thiel suggested he might pursue extreme measures to destroy the old regime for good, perhaps by declassifying state secrets and demanding accountability for supposedly terrible misdeeds at which he hinted but never quite named. "The first Trump administration shied away from declassifications because it still believed in the rightwing deep state of an Oliver Stone movie," wrote Thiel. "This belief has faded."

He went so far as to recommend that Trump proceed with "piecemeal declassifications" that would "befit both Trump's chaotic style and our internet world, which processes and propagates short packets of information." Thiel's essay was cryptic by design, and it seems unlikely any major newspaper would have published such an odd piece if it had not been written by one of the world's most influential billionaires. Larded with religious language and drenched in conspiracy theory, and crafted in a gnomic and elliptical style, it asserted that Trump would expose terrible realities that would shake Americans' faith in their government and overturn the establishment. "The future demands fresh and strange ideas," he concluded, writing that "America is not an exceptional country. It is no longer even a great one."

Thiel evoked South Africa's Truth and Reconciliation Commission, which investigated Apartheid-era crimes and human rights abuses, as a model for how Trump might approach accountability. In other words, Trump should use the levers of government to punish those enemies whose misdeeds amounted to Apartheid-level heinousness.

Things would not go quite as Thiel envisioned. While Trump would declare that COVID resulted from a "lab leak," US intelligence agencies remain divided on the subject, and the American public did not seem to care very much either way. Likewise, Trump's decision to release a new trove of documents on the Kennedy assassination was a dud, failing to shed new light on the subject. Regarding Epstein—once a close friend of Trump—one of the biggest revelations turned out to be his longstanding and lucrative relationship with Thiel.

In June 2025, a *New York Times* investigation would reveal that Epstein had invested $40 million in two funds managed by Valar Ventures, a Thiel-backed firm named after "angelic spirits" in *The Lord of the Rings*. Epstein's investments, made in 2015 and 2016, had ballooned to nearly $170 million, according to the *Times.* Given his significant ties to Epstein, it is notable that Thiel publicly questioned the official narrative of Epstein's 2019 death in federal custody, though his *Financial Times* piece made no mention of his close relationship with the dead financier.

As the inauguration drew near, Thiel seemed both giddy and anxious. The possibility of revelation, accountability, and the destruction of the prevailing order in Washington excited him. Yet his decision to frame Trump's victory in the fire-and-brimstone language of apocalypse injected an odd religious element into his call for partisan retribution, hinting at deeper tensions beneath the surface. Perhaps Thiel felt religious because he felt vindicated. The 2024 election had confirmed a key prophecy of *The Sovereign Individual.* Technology was dramatically remaking politics in the twenty-first century, just as Davidson and Rees-Mogg had foretold, and as fate would have it, the book's most devoted reader—Thiel—was right at the center of the action.

Trump had returned to power with help from a gigantic investment of cash from Silicon Valley. Musk alone spent over $291 million to support Trump and the Republican Party, making him the single largest individual donor by a wide margin. His massive contribution rivaled the money rolling in from the crypto industry, which suddenly became the most significant corporate donor in US politics by raising more than $175 million through a network of super PACs and crypto groups led by Fairshake—an effort heavily backed by Brian Armstrong's Coinbase and Ripple along with a16z and its cofounders. Armstrong had hired Srinivasan in 2018 and now embraced *The Network State* to such a degree that he spoke at the 2024 conference and described Srinivasan's vision—the "creation of new physical places"—as "crypto's destiny." "I do think crypto has implications far beyond just payments and money," Armstrong said when asked about crypto's relationship to the network state in a 2024 interview.

While companies like Coinbase, Ripple, and a16z flooded money into elections, other crypto interests took a different approach. Binance, a major crypto exchange, boosted the Trump family's crypto company while seeking a pardon for its founder, Changpeng Zhao, who pleaded guilty to violating anti-money-laundering regulations in 2023 and served four months in prison.

"At the time, the government said Zhao had caused 'significant harm to U.S. national security' by allowing sanctioned Iranian crypto exchanges, Russian drug-traffickers, Hamas militants and other criminal groups to move billions of dollars through the exchange," reported *The Wall Street Journal*. In a story headlined "How a Billionaire Felon Boosted Trump's Crypto Company en Route to a Pardon," the *Journal* stated that sometime around the election, "Zhao's representatives began discussions with allies of Trump, saying they wanted to find a solution to Binance's legal troubles in the U.S. and offering a deal with a Trump family business, according to people familiar with the discussions." Binance had created a task force to "strike a deal with the Trumps' nascent cryptocurrency venture, World Liberty Financial, that Binance could leverage into clemency for Zhao." Binance then "took steps that catapulted the Trump family venture's new stablecoin product, enhancing its credibility and pushing its market capitalization up from $127 million to over $2.1 billion." (Stablecoins are digital products whose value is tied directly to the dollar.) Months later, Trump pardoned Zhao, paving the way for Binance to resume its operations in the US. "The pardon marks the most distinct instance yet of Trump using the powers of his office to benefit someone at the center of deals that have enriched his family," reported the *Journal*.

Crypto PAC spending, though shocking and unprecedented, was only part of the story. The industry's overlords had amassed enough money to disrupt politics, but not in the way imagined by the old cypherpunks who had envisioned digital currency as a tool for undermining government by evading it. As it turns out, crypto is a weapon for capturing government through the maximization of political corruption. The crypto PACs, which flooded money into the 2024 election, were but a sideshow. Crypto's real political innovation was the creation of a towering corruption machine through which the president of the United States could be openly bribed. Trump became a crypto billionaire the same week he returned to the White House. "The Trump family's new crypto tokens are worth well over $10 billion on paper, after a frenzied rally pushed up the value of the digital assets in the days before the inauguration," reported *The New York Times* on January 20, 2025, as a Trump-themed crypto product called $Trump surged.

Thiel had predicted *apokálypsis*, a word *The Sovereign Individual* had also used to describe revelatory transformations of the twenty-first century, and Trump's victory did reveal an extraordinary truth: It exposed the extent to which tech wealth and power had become a clear and present threat to American democracy. The lords of Silicon Valley had *become* a political technology, a venture capital system with seemingly infinite money to throw at high-risk bets on whoever and whatever might help them control the digital infrastructure of future governance. Crypto bought them an alliance with Trump, who had long derided the industry as a "scam" but now became a champion of a Silicon Valley vision built on crypto, AI, war, and the network state.

° ° °

Crypto's rise from niche digital hobby to political juggernaut did not happen overnight, and it did not happen organically. It was a vision heavily funded and marketed by an interconnected group of venture capital firms who saw its potential to generate both wealth and power. They stuck by it for years as the crypto market crashed and rose repeatedly, and they touted its virtues while most people regarded it as a risky form of gambling. Nowhere is their success more disturbingly apparent than in the conversion of one particularly harsh critic of crypto, Donald Trump.

"I am not a fan of Bitcoin and other Cryptocurrencies, which are not money, and whose value is highly volatile and based on thin air," wrote President Trump on Twitter in 2019. "Unregulated Crypto Assets can facilitate unlawful behavior, including drug trade and other illegal activity." "Bitcoin just seems like a scam," he said after leaving office in 2021. "A disaster waiting to happen." "We only have one real currency in the USA," he declared, twisting the knife in a way designed to inflict maximum pain on crypto enthusiasts who prefer to see government-issued currencies as fake totems of government power.

By 2024, Trump had undergone a dramatic conversion even more stunning than "Never Trump" Vance's somersault into the pro-MAGA Catholic camp. Trump, who had spent years casting doubt on crypto with catty quips, now became the crypto advocate in chief—and suddenly began reaping billions of dollars in crypto profits for himself and his family. By summer of 2025, crypto had become the main source of Trump's wealth, and his family's net worth had increased dramatically, in part due to various crypto schemes. "The Trump family notched as much as $5 billion in paper wealth on Monday after its flagship crypto venture opened trading of a new digital currency," reported *The Wall Street Journal* in September 2025, when the Trump family launched World Liberty Financial on the open market.

The idea of a crypto billionaire president is alarming when you consider crypto's true purpose. At their core, cryptocurrencies are designed to challenge government authority by competing with it. While most crypto buyers likely view it as little more than a kind of digital lottery ticket, crypto products like Bitcoin are inherently political because they seek to privatize a key public necessity. "As they are currently configured, Bitcoin and the blockchain technology on which it rests satisfy needs that make sense only in the context of right-wing politics; those of us who do not share those politics must, therefore, view Bitcoin and the blockchain with both skepticism and a clear eye for the political terms and concepts invoked in the discourse surrounding them," wrote David Golumbia in *The Politics of Bitcoin: Software as Right-Wing Extremism*. Golumbia warned that Bitcoin's politics were rooted in extreme right-wing assumptions, a point Srinivasan's arguments had clarified and crypto's alliance with MAGA has confirmed.

Crypto had a rapid but rocky rise to the height of political power. The industry, which is also a movement, survived multiple near-death experiences known as crypto "winters," when faith wavered and prices fell. Multiple crypto companies suffered massive failures that exposed digital asset markets as shady and unstable. Early crypto exchanges like Mt. Gox and Bitfinex got hacked, with thieves stealing hundreds of millions of dollars from customer accounts. Crypto investors have also lost billions upon billions of dollars to a proliferation of scams and failed currency schemes, which explains why most Americans remain wary of crypto. A 2025 report by Gallup found that, despite a surge in popularity since 2021, only 14 percent of Americans report owning or using crypto, and 60 percent have no plan to buy it. Despite this overwhelming skepticism, not to mention its history of catastrophic and costly failures, crypto has managed to thrive, amassing trillions in market capitalization and becoming one of the most feared political forces in the nation. Crypto survived its existential battles and attained the heights of influence thanks to a massive surge of investment from Silicon Valley venture capitalists, who bet big on a scheme that had few legitimate use cases beyond crime, terrorism, and casino-like gambling.

Efforts to legitimize Bitcoin as actual currency, however, have flopped. In 2021, El Salvador became the first country in the world to embrace Bitcoin as legal tender. Nayib Bukele, the country's authoritarian president, even announced plans to build a Bitcoin city. But Salvadorans largely shunned Bitcoin for transactions, and Bukele's government quietly rolled back its crypto experiment as part of a $1.4 billion International Monetary Fund loan agreement to stabilize the country's finances.

Unsurprisingly, Thiel played a key role in the crypto story. While his venture funds are not the largest investors in crypto, Thiel was one of the earliest major institutional backers of Bitcoin. Founders Fund, Thiel's main VC arm, was among the most formidable investors in crypto infrastructure. In 2013, it invested in a seed round for BitPay, an early crypto payments company. Starting in 2014, when crypto was still a fringe experiment, the firm quietly accumulated a stockpile of crypto, mostly Bitcoin. By early 2022, when Founders Fund cashed out its entire position, that stash was worth approximately $1.8 billion. The firm's exit was perfectly timed, taking place just months before the 2022 crypto crash erased around $2 trillion from the global crypto market. (Speaking at the Bitcoin 2022 conference in Miami in April, Thiel crowed that Bitcoin would never be controlled by the government, mocked the dollar, and tossed hundred-dollar bills into the crowd, making no mention that his firm had cashed out.)

One of Thiel's most consequential early bets was the $100,000 Thiel Fellowship he awarded to twenty-year-old Vitalik Buterin in 2014. Buterin proposed something even more ambitious than Bitcoin: Ethereum. Rather than serving merely as a digital currency, Ethereum was conceived as a programmable blockchain—a platform for building entire digital institutions. Its purpose is not just to move money but to run smart contracts and decentralized applications, providing the technical foundation for new governance structures built around cryptography and automation. Where Bitcoin is marketed as "digital gold," a purported alternative to state-issued money, Ethereum aspires to offer infrastructure for alternative social and institutional systems altogether. It functions as a distributed computing platform maintained by a global network of participants, capable of executing self-enforcing code (smart contracts) with reduced reliance on human intermediaries. Even within the crypto world, there is deep uncertainty about whether Ethereum's grander ambitions can or should succeed. But the underlying vision is broadly recognizable: governance through code, a world in which certain forms of power are shifted from public institutions toward automated systems and private or semi-private networks.

If cryptocurrencies aim to erode the state's monopoly over money, Ethereum represents an attempt to build decentralized mechanisms that can replace government functions. Buterin praised *The Network State* when it was published, speaks at the Network State Conference, and hosts something called Zuzalu, a tech retreat that calls itself a "pop-up city." Ether, the native cryptocurrency of Ethereum whose market capitalization reached a high of nearly $600 billion in August 2025, fell to $203 billion in June 2026. It is the second-biggest cryptocurrency in the world, behind Bitcoin. So, while Thiel's funds are not the largest investor in crypto, his investments have been among the most consequential, aiding the growth of Bitcoin and leading directly to the creation of Ethereum.

While Thiel's influence pops up throughout the crypto story, Andreessen Horowitz is widely credited with being the single largest venture investor in the digital asset sector. Along with Y Combinator, it played a key role in the creation of Coinbase, making its first investment in 2013 when it was a fledgling company with 600,000 users. The firm invested in Coinbase a total of eight times between 2013 and 2020. When Coinbase went public in 2021, Andreessen Horowitz's stake was valued at $11.2 billion on the first day of trading, though it realized only a portion of that before Coinbase's share price collapsed in the 2022 crypto winter. Still, it was the firm's most successful bet yet.

The early investments by Thiel and Andreessen Horowitz are notable because they poured millions of dollars into crypto when it was still an obscure, high-risk bet on a technology that mostly seemed useful to drug traffickers and pariah nations. A 2021 study by the Government Accountability Office found that crypto had "been central to the rise of drug sales in the U.S., specifically fentanyl and other synthetic opioids." Drug dealers were among the first to embrace crypto. Silk Road, a digital marketplace for illegal drugs that conducted transactions in Bitcoin, did $213 million in illicit business between 2011 and 2013, when the FBI caught up to its founder. Ross Ulbricht, a twenty-nine-year-old who went by the name of "Dread Pirate Roberts," was nabbed inside a branch of the San Francisco Public Library, where he was using public Wi-Fi to run his empire. Ulbricht had violated federal law in myriad ways, and at least six people died after using drugs they bought on Silk Road. On Ulbricht's computer, prosecutors found messages in which he appeared to pay $650,000 in crypto for a purported Hells Angels hit squad to murder specific individuals on his behalf. Federal prosecutors did not pursue those charges, but they didn't need to; Ulbricht received two life sentences for the drug conspiracy and money laundering convictions.

Ulbricht's imprisonment made him a martyr for the crypto cause, but he had always viewed himself as more than a digital drug kingpin.

In 2013, he told a journalist that Silk Road was "at its core . . . a way to get around regulation from the state." "Their time is coming to an end," he wrote of the US government in an online forum. "The future is OUR time. Let us take this opportunity they've given us to gain a foothold from which we can throw that yoke off completely . . . WE are free spirits!"

Before sentencing Ulbricht, US District Judge Katherine B. Forrest noted his anti-government aspirations. "It was an enterprise, the stated purpose of which . . . was to flout the law, to be outside of the law, to be beyond the law," Forrest said. "In the world that you created over time, democracy that we had set up with our Founding Fathers, that provides for the passage of laws and the enforcement of those laws through our democratic process, did not exist." (During the campaign, Trump had vowed to pursue the "death penalty" for drug dealers, but he pardoned Ulbricht—crypto's drug kingpin poster boy—on his second day in office.)

Crypto also appeals to pariah nations like Iran, Russia, and North Korea. They love crypto because it allows them to evade sanctions and fund their authoritarian regimes. Teams of North Korean hackers run global crypto theft scams to fund the country's nuclear program. Human traffickers, along with various and sundry other criminal types who keep their money in the shadows, also favor crypto. These are the actual use cases of crypto—the rare situations in which people use it as a shell for moving currency into illicit schemes.

But most people who put their money into crypto are simply gambling. They buy into these schemes based on the idea that prices will continue to rise, turning small investments into life-changing windfalls. Real currencies like the dollar are backed by the full power of the US government, including its military and its nuclear arsenal, but crypto schemes mostly rely on something called the "greater fool theory." This means a digital "asset" only gains value if you can find other people foolish enough to pay more for it in the future. Like most scams, this creates a small pool of winners and a vast population of losers. By pouring real money into imaginary digital currencies, crypto speculators drove crypto's total market capitalization to a peak of nearly $4.4 trillion in late 2025. (It plunged, again, to $1.2 trillion in June 2026.)

Crypto's exponential growth spurt began in late 2020, as the COVID pandemic raged. Massive federal stimulus funds flooded markets with liquidity while institutional players, from corporate treasury managers to payment giants like PayPal and Square, embraced crypto and lent it a new veneer of legitimacy. Venture capital poured in. Bitcoin more than quadrupled in value, rocketing from around $7,000 at the start of 2020 to nearly $29,000 by year's end, then kept going into early 2021. Venture capital firms, which had put over $4.5 billion into crypto and blockchain in 2020, poured more than $26 billion into the sector in 2021 alone, according to *Crunchbase*.

Tracing the exact amount of venture investment in crypto is difficult due to the sector's extreme opacity. Between 2021 and 2024, however, VC firms invested approximately $77 billion in crypto companies, according to an analysis by *PitchBook*. Other analysts suggest the number is higher, but all agree that 2021 marked a boom. Billions flowed into cryptocurrency-related businesses focused on blockchain applications that promised digital transactions to disrupt traditional systems (though most have struggled to deliver real-world value). Andreessen Horowitz, which had launched a $300 million fund in 2018, would launch a $515 million fund in 2020, a $2.2 billion fund in 2021, a $4.5 billion fund in 2022, and a $2.2 billion fund in 2026. Altogether, the firm claims to have committed $9.8 billion to crypto across multiple funds as of 2026, with investments in at least 120 crypto sector companies, including Solana, OpenSea, LayerZero, and Coinbase.

Coinbase would become the dominant crypto exchange in the United States, but it had competition. In 2019, a twenty-seven-year-old MIT physics grad named Sam Bankman-Fried launched a rival crypto exchange called FTX. While Coinbase focused on crypto beginners, allowing them to buy or sell digital products in a user-friendly interface, Bankman-Fried's company focused on more sophisticated investors and traders. FTX offered a range of advanced products and charged lower fees than Coinbase. In addition, while Coinbase was based in San Francisco, FTX was headquartered in Hong Kong, and later the Bahamas, to skirt US laws and regulations. Its biggest investors included Temasek Holdings (Singapore's sovereign wealth fund), as well as the VC firms Sequoia Capital and Paradigm, who each poured hundreds of millions of dollars into the company. Court documents would later reveal that Thiel also invested, and "Thiel vehicles held more than 300,000 shares of FTX or subsidiaries in both common and preferred stock."

FTX boomed, and Bankman-Fried—known as SBF—reached billionaire status before the age of thirty. The media feted him as a once-in-a-generation wunderkind, and he became the face of crypto, cultivating the persona of an aloof and shoeless computer nerd who played video games during important meetings and maintained a vegan diet heavy on Oreo cookies. At the same time, he sought to popularize crypto by exploiting the power of celebrity glamour, pulling Super Bowl champion Tom Brady, supermodel Gisele Bündchen, basketball champion Steph Curry, comedian Larry David, and pop star Taylor Swift into his web. In 2021, FTX plastered San Francisco's Financial District with large ads featuring portraits of SBF and Bündchen, and David starred in a Super Bowl ad with the tagline "Don't Miss Out."

SBF knew what he was doing, and his strategy sucked in many people, especially politicians. Having materialized a net worth of double-digit billions seemingly overnight, SBF became one of the nation's biggest political donors. By 2022, he had given over $100 million to political campaigns and groups. At the height of his political influence, Bill Clinton and Tony Blair attended his crypto summit in the Bahamas. Senator Cory Booker complimented SBF's trademark puffy hairdo as a "glorious afro," and Democratic politicians lined up at the trough. Intoxicated by his growing influence, SBF even fantasized about using his fortune to buy Trump out by paying him to stay out of the 2024 election. "Sam's thinking, 'We could pay Donald Trump to not run for president. Like, how much would it take,'" Michael Lewis, SBF's biographer, told NBC News.

"He didn't get an answer. He was floated—there was a number that was kicking around. And the number that was kicking around when I was talking to Sam about this was $5 billion. Sam was not sure that number came directly from Trump."

SBF's fantasies of power came to an abrupt conclusion on December 13, 2022, when federal authorities indicted him for fraud, conspiracy, and misappropriating customer money. As it turns out, SBF's success was largely a mirage built of crime, fraud, and theft. FTX collapsed into bankruptcy, with customers losing billions in assets. Temasek, Sequoia, and Paradigm lost over $200 million apiece. In 2023, SBF was convicted and eventually received a sentence of twenty-five years in federal prison.

The collapse of FTX intensified an already terrible year for crypto, which had entered another bad winter. In May of that year, a scheme consisting of two crypto products called Luna and Terra collapsed, erasing $40 billion in value. This triggered a cascade of major crypto company failures, and Bitcoin's price plummeted by over 60 percent. A study by experts from the London School of Economics and the Massachusetts Institute of Technology found that "wealthier and more sophisticated investors were the first to run and experienced much smaller losses. Poorer and less sophisticated investors not only ran later and had larger losses, but a significant fraction of them attempted to buy into the run, hoping to 'buy the dip.'" Crypto's critics once again started writing its obituary, but true believers had come to see these periodic crashes as part of the game that wiped out suckers but enriched savvy players at the top.

SBF had blazed crypto's path into politics. Now locked away in federal custody, he could no longer play, but Coinbase CEO Brian Armstrong picked up where SBF had left off. Armstrong, a former Airbnb employee from San Jose who had started Coinbase out of a San Francisco apartment in 2012, had become a mega-billionaire after the company went public in 2021 at a valuation of $86 billion, with Armstrong owning $13 billion in shares. While SBF had dreamed of paying Trump to stay out of the 2024 election, Armstrong took a different approach. Since 2018, his distinctively large, bald head had been a regular presence on Capitol Hill. Clad in suits rather than sweats, Armstrong became the face of crypto's effort to lobby for friendly crypto legislation. In 2024, Coinbase was the single largest corporate backer of Fairshake PAC, which, along with affiliated crypto PACs, flooded the election with crypto money and became the biggest corporate spenders of the election cycle.

"The crypto industry treated this year's election as a pivotal moment, spending tens of millions of dollars to support candidates who favored softer regulations for the sector," reported *The New York Times*. "A super PAC called Fairshake and two related organizations, Protect Progress and Defend American Jobs, spent a total of about $135 million, financed by donations from the crypto companies Coinbase and Ripple and the venture capital firm Andreessen Horowitz, which has backed over 100 crypto start-ups."

Combined with other funds spent by other crypto groups and supporters, crypto raised a total of $245 million for the 2024 cycle. "Crypto has accounted for nearly half of all corporate money flowing into the election, according to a report from nonprofit watchdog Public Citizen. No other sector is close. That includes oil companies and banks, which have historically been big political contributors," reported CNBC. Crypto researcher Molly White places the total number raised at $175 million, saying the higher counts are based on flawed methodologies that double count certain contributions.

This surge of crypto money had one purpose: to scare the hell out of any politician who might dare challenge the industry's interests in Washington, DC. Crypto, a scam-ridden Ponzi scheme mostly useful for crime and gambling, had plenty of skeptics in Washington. One of them was Senator Sherrod Brown, a three-term Democrat from Ohio who had earned a "strongly against crypto" rating from Stand With Crypto, which tracks politicians' attitudes toward crypto so closely that it even rates specific tweets.

"Hamas's terrorism is fueled by cryptocurrency," Brown wrote in a 2023 post. "We need to crack down on illicit crypto and stop terrorists from moving money around, evading sanctions, and funding their acts of evil. We must curb this emerging threat and protect our national security." Stand With Crypto rated this Brown tweet, and many others, as "very anti-crypto." Brown had backed Senator Elizabeth Warren's call for hearings into links between crypto and terrorism, and he had called for strong crypto regulations to protect consumers from scams and abuses. So, as Brown sought a fourth term in 2024, the crypto industry decided to make an example out of him. Crypto carpet-bombed Ohio voters with ads in support of Brown's opponent, Bernie Moreno. In total, crypto-funded PACs spent $40 million to elect Moreno, a largely unknown car salesman who had never held public office but enthusiastically supported Bitcoin. Brown had a cavalier response to the onslaught. "Bring 'em on," he said. Unfortunately, the massive surge of crypto money worked. Moreno beat him by three points. "The crypto army is striking," declared Tyler Winklevoss, one of the top crypto funders, labeling Brown a "crypto public enemy."

Meanwhile, in California, Fairshake spent $10 million to sink Democratic Representative Katie Porter, a crypto critic running for US Senate. Audaciously flipping reality on its head, the crypto ads accused Porter, an opponent of big money interests in politics, of being on the take from major oil and pharmaceutical interests. A fact-check by *The Sacramento Bee* rated these ads "mostly false," but they did real damage. Porter had already been running behind Representative Adam Schiff, a more crypto-friendly politician, but crypto's onslaught of negative ads finished her.

"We are making sure the 8 million crypto owners in California . . . know about [Porter's] hostility toward the technology and how that would hurt American jobs," said Fairshake spokesman Josh Vlasto, a former aide to Democratic Senate Majority Leader Chuck Schumer. Dozens of crypto company moguls also backed a challenge to Massachusetts Senator Elizabeth Warren, a fierce critic of the industry who had been Porter's professor at Harvard Law School. Their relatively meager donations to John Deaton, a Republican lawyer with a practice specializing in crypto, failed to dent Warren's popularity. She won 60 percent of the vote on election night.

In addition to attacking crypto-skeptical Democrats, the PAC also supported pro-crypto Democrats. Fairshake spent $20 million to boost the Senate campaigns of Ruben Gallego in Arizona and Elissa Slotkin in Michigan. Both had received grades of "strongly pro-crypto" and would prove reliable votes for the industry in the Senate. Gallego and Slotkin, like Moreno, were the most prominent among the fifty-three members of Congress elected with crypto support in 2024, a year during which the industry claimed an 85 percent win rate for its congressional picks. Crypto had arrived—a point made clear when, less than two weeks after winning the presidential election, Trump held a private meeting with Coinbase CEO Armstrong.

The industry had hedged during the campaign, avoiding direct contributions to Trump's campaign while flexing its power in congressional races. Once Trump secured victory, crypto bent the knee. "The cryptocurrency industry, fresh off of a 2024 elections spending spree, has turned its influence efforts in recent months to a new target: celebrating the start of President-elect Donald Trump's second term," reported *Politico* in a January 2025 article about how the industry was pouring millions of dollars into the inauguration fund.

Those millions pouring into elections and inaugural funds were child's play compared to what followed. With Trump back in power, his family crypto company attracted massive investment from those seeking to curry the president's favor. Within months, the Trump family's estimated net worth skyrocketed by billions in an orgy of unprecedented corruption so staggering it made all previous bribery scandals look like penny-ante grift. The Trump family's crypto interests included World Liberty Financial, a so-called governance token launched during the campaign, a Bitcoin mining company, and pump-and-dump schemes like $Trump and $Melania, which skyrocketed in value before plummeting, transferring obscene amounts of wealth into Trump family coffers. "I have never seen such open corruption in any modern government anywhere," said Steven Levitsky, a professor of government at Harvard University who coauthored *How Democracies Die*.

"Trump's crypto schemes are the Mount Everest of corruption," said Senator Jeff Merkley, who coauthored a bill called the End Crypto

Corruption Act of 2025 to bar elected officials from crypto schemes. "We must ban Trump-style crypto corruption so all elected federal officials—including the president, vice-president and members of Congress—cannot profit from shady crypto practices."

Despite this open grift and profiteering by the president and his family, the crypto industry extolled the administration as a breath of fresh air. "President Trump really breathed life back into this industry over the last few years," Coinbase CEO Armstrong told CNBC after Trump hosted a White House crypto summit and announced the creation of a "strategic Bitcoin reserve" in early 2025. "We felt like we were being unlawfully attacked by the prior administration. Under another fork of history, this industry might not have existed in the United States—it might have been moved entirely offshore. But luckily, the president has taken a leadership role here and decided to bring it back to the U.S."

The Bitcoin Reserve, created by an executive order, sought to "create a national stockpile of Bitcoin and other digital currencies, an audacious idea that has been widely criticized as a scheme to enrich crypto investors," reported *The New York Times*. Trump also ordered the creation of a US Digital Asset Stockpile for non-Bitcoin assets like Ether and Solana, putting the weight of the federal government behind the crypto industry. The End Crypto Corruption Act stalled in Congress, but Trump signed a pro-crypto bill, the Guiding and Establishing National Innovation for US Stablecoins Act (GENIUS), in July 2025. Among other things, it freed stablecoins from oversight by the Securities and Exchange Commission and the Commodity Futures Trading Commission. More importantly, it lent government legitimacy to crypto and gave the industry its first major legislative win.

Merkley complained the bill could enable even more crypto corruption. "We need guardrails that ensure that government officials aren't openly asking people to buy their coins in order to increase their personal profit or their family's profit," he said. "Where are those guardrails in this bill? They're completely, totally absent." By then, the scope of Trump's crypto-fueled corruption had become so shamelessly thorough and vast that senatorial mewling failed to register. Personal and family gain from crypto was the entire point for the crypto billionaire president. "I'm a big crypto fan," Trump told reporters when asked about his shift. "I've been that right from the beginning, right from the campaign."

The merger between crypto and Trump reached a bizarre milestone one week after the 2024 election when Trump appointed Elon Musk to run a government-slashing initiative named after a dog-themed crypto scheme. The Department of Government Efficiency, known as DOGE, referred to Dogecoin, a crypto product that had started as a joke based on an internet meme featuring a Shiba Inu. The Doge meme had fascinated Musk for years, and his occasional tweets about Dogecoin caused multiple price spikes. During a *Saturday Night Live* skit in 2021, he described Dogecoin as "the future of currency." "It's an unstoppable financial vehicle that's going to take over the world," he said, having proclaimed himself "the DOGE-father" earlier in the show.

In announcing the creation of DOGE, Trump said it would "pave the way for my Administration to dismantle Government Bureaucracy, slash excess regulations, cut wasteful expenditures, and restructure Federal Agencies." Musk's decision to use the name for his government assignment dramatically pumped up the price of the Dogecoin yet again. "It has been one of the biggest winners in the postelection rally, gaining 153% since Election Day compared with bitcoin's 30% rise in the same period," reported CNBC.

It's not clear whether Trump had ever heard of Yarvin, but DOGE seemed to wrap his "Butterfly Revolution" and "Retire All Government Employees" in a crypto-themed package. Trump appointed the world's richest man—already CEO of four companies—to oversee the gutting and purging of government. Even the four-letter acronym of DOGE echoed Yarvin's "RAGE."

A presidential executive order officially brought DOGE to life on January 20, 2025. Creating new government departments requires an act of Congress, so despite the word "department" in its name, DOGE was more like a government task force charged with "modernizing federal technology and software to maximize governmental efficiency and productivity." The order required every federal agency to set up a "DOGE team," including "a team lead, an engineer, a human resources (HR) specialist, and an attorney." At the first meeting of Trump's new cabinet, Musk jokingly referred to himself as "tech support." "As crazy as it sounds, that is almost a literal description of the work that the DOGE team is doing . . . helping fix the government computer systems," he said during his first cabinet meeting, portraying the government's existing technology as broken, old, and error-riddled. The role went far beyond upgrading government computers, however, since Musk had pledged to cut $2 trillion from the federal budget—a goal most experts considered ridiculous. Clad in a black hat emblazoned with "Make America Great Again" in black gothic letters, Musk said his DOGE role had earned fresh death threats. Yet he smiled as he urged his fellow cabinet members to support his effort, warning that the USA would become "de facto bankrupt" without the significant cuts DOGE planned to impose. "It requires saving four billion dollars a day every day from now through the end of September," Musk said.

With that, the South Africa–born billionaire took a hatchet to the United States government. "What if government was run like a company?" Musk had asked in a 2013 CNBC interview, echoing the familiar Republican line that government is best run as a business. Musk decided to run DOGE like he ran Twitter. During his takeover of the company, he conducted mass firings, stoked chaos, and used destruction as a tool. He gutted the Trust and Safety team and personally unplugged company servers at a data hub in Sacramento. Now, he brought this approach to Washington, firing tens of thousands of employees, scrapping entire departments, and openly disregarding rules and laws. By May 2025, a tally by Reuters estimated that 260,000 federal workers had been purged via firings, layoffs, buyouts, and forced early retirements. This amounted to roughly 10 percent of the entire federal workforce and marked the largest such reduction in history.

During the first few months of the administration, Musk appeared to be presiding over the federal government. The billionaire who had bucked state authority during the pandemic lockdowns had become the world's richest man, the owner of Twitter, and the CEO appointed to run roughshod over the federal bureaucracy. As part of the DOGE project, Musk unleashed AI systems inside government, vacuuming up troves of data to allegedly drive DOGE's decision-making. In May 2025, Reuters reported that Musk's use of his own AI system, Grok, was "potentially violating conflict-of-interest laws and putting at risk sensitive information on millions of Americans." Musk had promised that DOGE would operate with the utmost transparency, but that was a lie. Exactly how Grok was being used inside the government remained a mystery, and it quickly became known that the DOGE team was using the encrypted messaging app Signal to communicate, in violation of public records laws. "The use of AI and Signal reinforces concerns among cybersecurity experts and government ethicists that DOGE is operating with limited transparency and that billionaire Musk or the Trump administration could use information gathered with AI to further their own interests, or to go after political targets," reported Reuters.

Such blatant violations of laws and norms became standard operating procedure throughout the Trump administration. This was a deliberate effort to challenge Congress and the courts, a strategy detailed in Project 2025, a blueprint produced by the Heritage Foundation and over one hundred Republican organizations in 2023. It called for a future Republican president to use executive power to bypass traditional checks on power. "Project 2025 unabashedly promotes the wholesale violation of norms and laws, consolidating enormous power in a president and trampling on Congress' constitutional role—to take away Americans' long-cherished freedoms and opportunities," said an analysis by the Center for American Progress, calling it an "authoritarian playbook" that would "weaken the independence of public agencies, install political cronies throughout the government, punish people it disagrees with, and control what news the media can report." Among other things, the 920-page document recommended that a Republican president test out executive power by pursuing a massive purge of the government workforce and dismantling entire agencies.

It's not exactly clear how Yarvin's vision of a dictator-like president appointing a CEO to carry out a government purge got into the official policy blueprint of the Trump administration. DOGE was one among many shocking triumphs for Thiel's network in the second Trump era. For example, Yarvin had called for "a total shutdown of international relations, including security guarantees, foreign aid, and mass immigration," all of which quickly became marquee policies of the Trump administration. One of Musk's first tasks at DOGE was to feed USAID "into the woodchipper," and Trump would deploy masked ICE agents in a violent campaign targeting immigrants in Democratic cities while also throwing international relations into turmoil with tariffs and threats.

While Yarvin was far from the only right-wing thinker to express some version of these ideas, his obvious influence on the new administration attracted mainstream press attention. Two days before the inauguration, *The New York Times Magazine* ran a long interview with Yarvin headlined "Curtis Yarvin Says Democracy Is Done. Powerful Conservatives Are Listening." "For a long time, Curtis Yarvin, a 51-year-old computer engineer, has written online about political theory in relative obscurity," wrote David Marchese in an introduction for the interview. "His ideas were pretty extreme: that institutions at the heart of American intellectual life, like the mainstream media and academia, have been overrun by progressive groupthink and need to be dissolved. He believes that government bureaucracy should be radically gutted, and perhaps most provocative, he argues that American democracy should be replaced by what he calls a 'monarchy' run by what he has called a 'C.E.O.' — basically his friendlier term for a dictator." Marchese called Yarvin a "fixture of the right-wing media universe" and mentioned his ties to Andreessen, Thiel, and Vance. Marchese also said he had been aware of Yarvin for years, but that his ideas had "felt fringe." "But given that they are now finding an audience with some of the most powerful people in the country, Yarvin can't be so easily dismissed anymore," wrote Marchese. The interview, in which Yarvin promoted aristocracy and claimed Franklin D. Roosevelt had been a dictator, was accompanied by moody black-and-white photos of Yarvin looking pensive in a leather jacket.

Politico followed up with a breezy interview—"Curtis Yarvin's Ideas Were Fringe. Now They're Coursing Through Trump's Washington"—where Yarvin bragged about seeing Vance calling him a "reactionary fascist" at Thiel's DC mansion and referred to the vice president as "perfect" in "almost every way." Yarvin basked in the attention as national outlets including CNN and *Time*, and international ones like *El País* and *Le Monde*, rushed to explain his transformation from blogger to political Svengali. On February 5, 2025, a group of anonymous researchers with tech backgrounds published a memo, "Capture of U.S. Critical Infrastructure by Neoreactionaries," which warned that "the rapid takeover of federal infrastructure mirrors the broader ambitions of the neoreactionary (NRx) movement—a small group of Silicon Valley elites who reject democracy and seek to install a 'CEO Monarch' to rule by technological and financial dominance. This network includes Peter Thiel, Marc Andreessen, Balaji Srinivasan, David Sacks, and Curtis Yarvin, among others. Once considered fringe, purveyors of this ideology have now been embedded into the core of government operations."

While Musk and Yarvin reveled in publicity, Thiel's extended network fanned out across the administration, with *Bloomberg* reporting that at least sixteen of Thiel's longtime associates had taken high-level positions in Washington. They included Sacks, who Trump appointed as his AI and crypto czar. "A billionaire tech entrepreneur who used his wealth and influence in Silicon Valley to help Donald Trump win the presidency has deep connections to the new administration's efforts to remake the government," reported *Bloomberg*, adding that "[s]ome Thiel allies have held high-ranking government posts before, while others are heading to Washington for the first time."

The story also noted the long-running ties between Musk and Thiel, tracing back to their days at PayPal. More recently, Thiel had invested in Musk's companies, including SpaceX, Neuralink, and the Boring Company, an alliance that had spawned its own network of powerful, interconnected tech moguls: "The early bonds between the billionaires have persisted, and others in their orbit have gained power and influence. The so-called PayPal Mafia—a group of Silicon Valley stars with links to the payment app's formative period—has become integral to the second Trump administration. The men—they're all men—have overlapping business interests and have been outspoken about the importance of US tech dominance."

Musk soaked up most of the press attention, but it was a stunning coup for Thiel, whose network was in power and whose business interests would reap benefits.

◦ ◦ ◦

The Sovereign Individual had predicted that two major technological advances would shape the destiny of the twenty-first century. Davidson and Rees-Mogg said crypto would undermine government authority while advanced automation would hasten the collapse of nation-states by cratering mass employment and creating severe economic and political disruption. In 2024, the USA got its first crypto billionaire president. This development coincided with the rise of an automation technology, generally known as artificial intelligence, that provided an operating system for his agenda.

Researchers have been chasing AI since at least the mid-twentieth century, and the quest produced major advances in automation: industrial robots, algorithmic trading, recommendation engines, and early machine learning systems that power search and social media. These systems automated specific tasks but lacked anything that could be mistaken for humanlike understanding or creativity. In the 2010s, major technological advances made it possible to train so-called large language models (LLMs). These LLM systems could generate language and seem to reply in a personal fashion, though with significant limitations. There are many kinds of AI systems, but most people would come to think of AI as LLM chatbots, and one company would come to dominate the early days of the race to bring AI to the masses: OpenAI.

Sam Altman, OpenAI's cofounder and CEO, had a meteoric rise

in Silicon Valley. He dropped out of Stanford University in 2005 to start Loopt, a mobile app that allowed users to share their locations with friends. Y Combinator accepted the company into its inaugural start-up accelerator batch that year. While Loopt never achieved widespread adoption, it showed enough early promise to attract an investment of $30 million in venture capital. In 2012, Loopt was acquired for $43 million and Altman pivoted to investing. His ambition and tenacity caught the attention of Paul Graham, Y Combinator's cofounder. "You could parachute him into an island of cannibals and come back in five years and he'd be king," Graham wrote in 2008.

Altman started a small venture fund, Hydrazine Capital, with a major investment from Thiel. Two years later, in 2014, Graham named Altman as his successor at Y Combinator. At twenty-eight, he became one of the most important people in Silicon Valley, the head of a storied start-up accelerator, which Thiel soon joined as a part-time partner. The two men became so close that Altman would eventually marry a man he met during a 3 a.m. soak in Thiel's hot tub, according to *The Optimist: Sam Altman, OpenAI, and the Race to Invent the Future*, an authorized biography by journalist Keach Hagey. Thiel, known for snarky criticism of fellow tech figures, offers conspicuously high praise for Altman. "We should treat him more as a messiah figure," Thiel told Hagey.

In 2015, while still at Y Combinator, Altman cofounded OpenAI as a nonprofit, alongside Musk and others. Thiel was among those who backed the company's initial $1 billion funding pledge. "OpenAI's mission is to ensure that artificial general intelligence (AGI)—by which we mean highly autonomous systems that outperform humans at most economically valuable work—benefits all of humanity," stated OpenAI's charter, framing the project as a high-minded pursuit for the global good. It was more of a strategic countermove to outflank Google, which had acquired the AI "super lab" DeepMind in 2014 and appeared poised to dominate the AI race. (Thiel provided the first significant investment in DeepMind, and Founders Fund owned over 25 percent of the company when Google bought it.) Altman described his mission as a "Manhattan Project for AI," comparing it to the secret government operation to develop nuclear weapons and defeat fascism in World War II. Early on, the company billed itself as an organization that would focus on research, not commercial products. The word "open" reflected the organization's stated intention of sharing its research widely and generally collaborating on making sure AI development avoided a destructive path.

By 2016, Altman had begun to worry about the apocalypse, so much so that a *New Yorker* profile of him that year included details of doomsday preparations. Altman listed rogue AI, nuclear war, and a deadly virus among his worries. "I prep for survival," he said, adding that he had "guns, gold, potassium iodide, antibiotics, batteries, water, gas masks from the Israeli Defense Force, and a big patch of land in Big Sur I can fly to." As a backup plan, he planned to hide out with Thiel on a compound in New Zealand.

The profile depicted Altman as a man convinced of his own grand destiny to shape the world through venture capital. "I think his goal is to make the whole future," said Graham. This future included a plan for Y Combinator to create its own city. "It would lie somewhere in America, or perhaps abroad, and would be optimized for technological solutions: it might, for instance, permit only self-driving cars," wrote *The New Yorker*'s Tad Friend. Echoing Srinivasan's exit speech three years earlier, Altman envisioned crowdfunding the creation of a tech city of 100,000 acres and up to 100,000 residents and said he was already scouting locations.

Thiel later described Altman as someone "at the epicenter, maybe not of Silicon Valley, but of the Silicon Valley zeitgeist." Though they differed on Trump—Altman compared him to Hitler—both men shared a keen interest in politics. In 2017, Altman briefly considered running for governor of California, telling *San Francisco Chronicle* columnist Willie Brown that his campaign would forgo normal tactics and rely on what Brown described as "digital intelligence." In the end, he did not enter the 2018 race, which Gavin Newsom won with 62 percent of the vote. Altman's decision to stay out of electoral politics was for the best, since he seemed wholly unsuited for the role of politician. "I have narrow interests in technology, I have no patience for things I'm not interested in," he had told *The New Yorker*. "When someone examines a photo and says, 'Oh, he's feeling this and this and this,' all of these subtle emotions, I look on with alien intrigue."

Besides, he had other things to worry about in 2018. That year, Musk abandoned OpenAI, delivering a huge blow to the project, of which he was the major funder. Musk framed his departure as amicable, but the truth was more complicated. Musk had wanted full control of the company, but OpenAI's board rejected the idea. So, he withdrew his support, pledged to pursue AI on his own, and soon became a harsh critic of the man he calls "Scam Altman." Faced with a potential fatal lack of funding, OpenAI pivoted. In 2019, Altman left his plum perch at Y Combinator to become the company's CEO as it created a for-profit subsidiary and secured a $1 billion partnership with Microsoft.

"Over the next four years, OpenAI became everything that it said it would not be," wrote Karen Hao in *Empire of AI: Dreams and Nightmares in Sam Altman's OpenAI*. "It turned into a nonprofit in name only, aggressively commercializing products like ChatGPT and seeking unheard-of valuations. It grew even more secretive, not only cutting off access to its own research but shifting norms across the industry to bar a significant share of AI development from public scrutiny. It triggered the very race to the bottom that it had warned about, massively accelerating the technology's commercialization and deployment without shoring up its harmful flaws or the dangerous ways that it could amplify and exploit the fault lines in our society."

On November 30, 2022, OpenAI released ChatGPT, a publicly accessible chatbot built on earlier models that had previously been available through limited, controlled access. Headlines framed ChatGPT as an unprecedented breakthrough—a chatbot that could mimic humanlike conversation, execute computer coding tasks, and instantly write marketing copy, poems, and stories that many found novel if not impressive. The *Harvard Business Review* called it "a tipping point for AI" and *The Guardian* called it "an eerily good human impersonator."

"ChatGPT is incredibly limited, but good enough at some things to create a misleading impression of greatness," wrote Altman on Twitter a few weeks after its release. "It's a mistake to be relying on it for anything important right now. It's a preview of progress; we have lots of work to do on robustness and truthfulness."

ChatGPT had 100 million users worldwide within two months of its launch, kicking off a race to market LLMs to the public as OpenAI's valuation soared to $80 billion by 2024. Competing models emerged from Google, Meta, and Anthropic, a company founded by former OpenAI employees who had abandoned the project in 2021 amid internal disputes. The race to dominate the AI market had begun, with OpenAI now leading the way.

In November 2023, one year after ChatGPT's launch, the OpenAI board voted to fire Altman, saying he "was not consistently candid in his communications" and the board "no longer had confidence in his ability to continue leading OpenAI." The coup failed and Altman won reinstatement a few days later. As the AI race began to have outsized impacts on culture, politics, society, and the economy, Altman—a venture capitalist, not an AI scientist—became the face of the AI boom. *Time* named him CEO of the Year in 2023, and *New York* magazine declared him the "Oppenheimer of Our Age." It was a high point for Altman, whose decision to brand himself as the leader of a new Manhattan Project had worked like a charm, at least temporarily.

In the years following ChatGPT's public release, AI infiltrated almost everything. Companies raced to incorporate LLMs into email programs, social media apps, word processors, schools, hospitals, cars, and computer operating systems in an endless spree of mass adoption. CEOs and politicians pitched it as the answer to everything, a miracle technology that would eliminate boring tasks, increase efficiency, enhance education, and even cure cancer. OpenAI's valuation skyrocketed toward $500 billion, and Altman cultivated his image as a maverick leader, but the cracks were beginning to show. "By Altman's own assessment—discernible in his many blog posts, podcasts, and video events—we should feel good but not great about him as our AI leader," wrote *New York*'s Elizabeth Weil. "As he understands himself, he's a plenty-smart-but-not-genius 'technology brother' with an Icarus streak and a few outlier traits. First, he possesses, he has said, 'an absolutely delusional level of self-confidence.' Second, he commands a prophetic grasp of 'the arc of technology and societal change on a long-time horizon.' Third, as a Jew, he is both optimistic and expecting the worst. Fourth, he's superb at assessing risk because his brain doesn't get caught up in what other people think." In reality, the CEO of OpenAI did have to worry about what people think, and the problems of AI—and Altman's leadership—would become impossible to ignore.

As AI began eating the world, the narrative quickly turned negative as problems and risks emerged. Science fiction writers had long imagined computer systems so advanced they would become a serious threat to humanity. The supposed existential risks posed by "superintelligent" AI systems had become the technology's defining feature in popular culture, animating the plots of popular movies. Yet AI's most immediate harms were more mundane than fantastical.

For one thing, AI companies create their products by harvesting every bit of accessible content and data in the world, strip mining the creativity, knowledge, and intellectual property of billions of people to feed their networks without permission, payment, or acknowledgment—all in a quest to transform the collective output of humanity into private corporate property. Worse, this massive process of theft and regurgitation requires tremendous amounts of energy, making AI systems a nightmare for the natural world. "The energy resources required to power this artificial-intelligence revolution are staggering, and the world's biggest tech companies have made it a top priority to harness ever more of that energy, aiming to reshape our energy grids in the process," wrote James O'Donnell and Casey Crownhart in the *MIT Technology Review* in May 2025.

The surge of energy consumption driven by AI marked a sharp reversal for Silicon Valley, which had trended toward efficiency, clean energy, and climate consciousness but now pivoted to absurd levels of energy guzzling. But nearly every aspect of the AI race appears to require the maximal exploitation of people, land, and resources. AI's boosters pitch it as the solution to every problem imaginable, but the current approach seems destined to create more problems than it solves. "Essentially what we have in this generation of what is called AI is a business where there's 10,000 mostly white men who are benefiting, and eight billion people around the world who are being either exploited, at a minimum, or directly harmed by the success of those 10,000," said Roger McNamee, an early Facebook investor and billionaire turned Silicon Valley critic.

McNamee identified what may be AI's most immediate threat: The technology, as currently designed, benefits a small network of men while producing vast potential harms for nearly everyone else. Some AI critics obsess over the hypothetical threat of a "godlike" superintelligence, but AI already functions as an engine of scaled destruction—supercharging environmental ruin, political polarization, mass surveillance, sexual exploitation, digital disinformation, and economic inequality. People immediately began using chatbots to drive themselves to psychosis or suicide, or to enhance crimes, scams, and disinformation campaigns. AI did not need to become godlike to be dangerous. It needed humans to become guinea pigs, which they did. In 2025, Pew reported that 79 percent of Americans say they "interact with AI almost constantly or several times a day."

Yet despite such widespread adoption, the AI industry faced a serious existential challenge. Investors were pouring cash into the development of AI, but AI was producing a relative trickle of revenue, making the AI boom look to some like an economic bubble. Tech giants like Amazon, Microsoft, Google, and Meta invested a combined $410 billion in AI hardware and infrastructure in 2025 alone and are projected to escalate that to as much as $650 billion in 2026. Meanwhile, venture capital has fueled roughly $259 billion in investment in start-ups and software—accounting for a staggering 61 percent of all global VC funding in 2025. Trillions are being spent to build out the technology, but the revenue for AI software and services is projected to remain under $200 billion in 2026. This chasm between investment and revenue, which one analysis called "AI's $600 billion question," makes the AI gold rush an extremely high-stakes gamble. "At the core of the AI bubble is a basic math problem. There is a fundamental mismatch between the trillions being invested in the infrastructure to develop AI and the billions people and companies are spending to use AI. Specifically, J.P. Morgan Chase analysts anticipate $5 trillion of spending on AI infrastructure between now and 2030," reported *Time*.

The AI race hinges on an inherently accelerationist logic: that burning maximum cash and energy to scale the technology as fast as possible will produce both a world-shifting miracle and infinite profits. Unlike the crypto race, which was heavily dependent on venture capital for its survival, major tech companies like Microsoft, Google, and Meta helped lead the charge into AI, pledging hundreds of billions of dollars for AI infrastructure and data centers. Venture capital has followed, and many of the same venture capitalists pushing crypto also massed around AI. Thiel, Andreessen, and Musk all invested in OpenAI, and both Andreessen Horowitz and Thiel-related funds have tens of billions of dollars invested in a range of AI companies. (Thiel's Founders Fund is also an investor in OpenAI rival Anthropic.) In 2025, Andreessen Horowitz announced plans to raise $20 billion—the largest fund in its history—specifically for AI start-ups. In 2026, the firm announced it had raised a more modest amount of $15 billion across several funds, with $1.7 billion reserved specifically for AI infrastructure.

Growing safety concerns did little to impede Silicon Valley's competition to secure early dominance in what is widely perceived as a winner-take-all quest to scale a technology some regard as "the last invention"—especially with China in pursuit of the same goal. Musk, who had stormed out of OpenAI in 2018 and once warned that AI posed a "civilizational risk," released his own AI chatbot in November 2023. The stated goal of his company, xAI, was to create an LLM that matched his right-wing sensibilities, since the major chatbots tended to answer questions in a seemingly balanced and evidence-based way some mistook for liberalism. Musk pledged that xAI would provide an "anti-woke" alternative and embedded his Grok chatbot in X. His efforts to create a chatbot in his own image later backfired spectacularly when, among other things, Grok users manipulated it into praising the virtues of Hitler and declaring itself "Mecha Hitler." Musk's company eventually faced lawsuits alleging its lack of guardrails allowed users to "nudify" images of women and children for the purposes of sexual exploitation. Musk would eventually concede that xAI had fallen short and would be rebuilt from scratch. Before that, however, Grok, xAI's flagship chatbot, would be among the wave of AI programs unleashed inside the federal government.

Trump's return was a bonanza for the crypto industry, but it was an even bigger windfall for AI. During his first week in the White House, Trump announced the creation of Stargate, a partnership between OpenAI, Oracle, and SoftBank that pledged $500 billion to build up to ten new AI data centers. He also repealed a Biden executive order emphasizing the need for safety, security, and workers' rights, issuing a new executive order on AI focused on the need to "enhance America's global AI dominance" and pledged to bulldoze regulations to speed up the development of AI, defining the issue as an emergency. "I'm gonna help a lot through emergency declarations, because we have an emergency, we have to get this stuff built," Trump said.

Altman praised Trump as singularly qualified to lead in the AI era. "This means we can create AI and AGI (artificial general intelligence) in the United States of America," said Altman of Trump. "I think with a different president it might not have been possible." The Trump administration sought to weaponize AI as a core part of its shock-and-awe narrative. Musk reportedly used Grok and other chatbots to augment DOGE's mission to eliminate diversity programs, monitor federal worker activities and communications, and accelerate mass layoffs.

On June 13, 2025, Trump escalated the relationship between AI and government with the creation of Detachment 201, which inducted four high-level AI executives into the US Army Reserve with the rank of lieutenant colonel. Despite having no military background, four executives from Meta, OpenAI, and Palantir donned camouflage fatigues and combat boots as they were sworn in as part of a new Silicon Valley unit to advise the army on the use of technology in warfare.

Three days later, OpenAI received a $200 million contract to "develop prototype frontier AI capabilities to address critical national security challenges in both warfighting and enterprise domains," according to a statement from the Pentagon. In July, Anthropic, Google, and xAI also received contracts worth up to $200 million apiece. One month later, the US Army announced plans to consolidate seventy-five different technology contracts worth as much as $10 billion into one single contract with Palantir. Government business was hardly a new development for Palantir, which had secured $2.5 billion in government contracts since 2009—$531 million in 2024 alone, under the Biden administration. *Breaking Defense* reported that Palantir was already the prime contractor on fifteen of the contracts and a subcontractor on the remaining sixty. Palantir had also received a $30 million contract to create a tool called "ImmigrationOS" to help ICE's deportation squads find their targets. The contract turned out to be a sliver of Palantir's business with the Department of Homeland Security (DHS). In February 2026, the DHS signed a purchasing agreement worth up to $1 billion with Palantir.

The money flowed both ways. Borrowing from crypto's playbook, AI companies now sought to join the ranks of the biggest players in US politics. In 2025, Marc Andreessen, Joe Lonsdale, and OpenAI president Greg Brockman launched Leading the Future, an AI super PAC with a $125 million war chest. It billed itself as a bipartisan operation to support pro-AI politicians from both parties and was led by Josh Vlasto, the longtime Schumer aide who also played a key role in crypto's Fairshake PAC. The effort drew complaints from Trump advisors. "Any group run by Schumer acolytes will not have the blessing of the president or his team," a White House official told NBC News. "Any donors or supporters of this group should think twice about getting on the wrong side of Trump world."

AI titans smoothed these concerns by launching the Innovation Council Action, an explicitly pro-Trump super PAC with plans to spend $100 million in the 2026 midterm elections. Meanwhile, Anthropic put a relatively meager $20 million into Public First Action, a bipartisan 501(c)(4) group "that will support public education about AI, promote safeguards, and ensure America leads the AI race," according to the company. On the state level, companies including Google and Meta poured millions into lobbying and politics.

The Sovereign Individual had imagined that advances in automation, information technology, and microprocessing would lead to a "world without jobs," birthing an economic revolution that would collapse nation-states. "Societies that have been indoctrinated to expect income equality and high levels of consumption for persons of low or modest skills will face demotivation and insecurity," the authors wrote. "As the economies of more countries more deeply assimilate information technology, they will see the emergence—so evident already in North America—of a more or less unemployable underclass. This is exactly what is happening. This will lead to a reaction with a nationalist, anti-technology bias."

Job losses seemed well underway in 2025. DOGE flamboyantly used AI in its quest to eliminate approximately 260,000 government jobs. Corporations slashed tens of thousands of positions in the private sector, cuts they attributed to their adoption of the technology. Such trends helped increase public negativity toward AI, with an estimated 57 percent of Americans saying its risks outweigh its benefits. Dario Amodei, the CEO of Anthropic, urged government to stop "sugar-coating" the fact that AI would wipe out scores of white-collar jobs in the consulting, finance, law, and technology sectors. "AI could wipe out *half* of all entry-level white-collar jobs—and spike unemployment to 10–20% in the next one to five years," reported Jim VandeHei and Mike Allen of Axios in a story headlined "A White-Collar Bloodbath." "We, as the producers of this technology, have a duty and an obligation to be honest about what is coming," Amodei told them. In 2023, Altman had cavalierly declared that "jobs are going to go away." In 2025, Altman updated his remarks to clarify that any positions evaporated by AI probably did not qualify as "real work" anyway.

Davidson and Rees-Mogg had predicted job losses, but they missed a crucial part of the mechanism. AI would not destroy governments by hollowing out the economy over time. Instead, AI became the operating system for governance itself. *The Sovereign Individual* imagined technology forcing the cognitive elite to flee collapsing nation-states destabilized by severe economic decline. What is unfolding is far more profitable and sinister: Technology is becoming the infrastructure of state power, arriving precisely at the moment when those who controlled it had captured the presidency for an aspiring dictator distinguished by a bottomless appetite for greed. The arrangement allowed him to feast on crypto corruption while they gorged on government power and lucrative state contracts to bolster their risky bets on speculative technologies. Instead of collapsing government, they colonized it. Even as this new order consolidated its grip on Washington, the network began preparing its exits.

° ° °

As tech billionaires swallowed the government whole, the United States came to resemble a de facto network state, at least temporarily. Government by tech corporation was a prime example of the "voice" strategy—an exponentially more powerful version of what tech money had achieved in San Francisco. But voice was a high-risk gamble. Democracy was too unpredictable, its institutions unlikely to crumble overnight. Failure would mean severe consequences for the oligarchs who had tried to overthrow the most powerful nation in the world. Srinivasan had long worried about a massive backlash against Silicon Valley. In 2013, he had warned that tech would be blamed for job losses. A failed takeover would expose the plot, spark public anger, and complicate the future. Exit remained essential—for escape, or for exile.

In May 2023, Trump's campaign announced a "quantum leap" plan to "create a new American future and modernize communities across the country." The first item on its agenda: "BUILDING FREEDOM CITIES." "President Trump will work to open up the

American frontier, holding a contest to charter new cities where families and individuals can have a new shot at the American Dream," read the plan. "The federal government owns nearly one-third of the land mass of the United States. Hundreds of millions of these acres are empty."

The quantum leap plan envisioned a competition in which the ten best proposals for new cities won vast plots of federal land on which to build. "In other words, we'll actually build new cities in our country again," said Trump in a video announcement. "These Freedom Cities will reopen the frontier, reignite American imagination, and give hundreds of thousands of young people, all hardworking families, a new shot at home ownership and, in fact, the American Dream."

Trump did not explain why it was necessary to build new cities from scratch rather than invest in existing cities, and few asked. Mainstream news outlets reported on the plan without questioning the idea, and few have mentioned it since, remaining aloof toward his curious but sweeping proposal. Building entirely new cities from scratch is a massively expensive undertaking. It's also a political nightmare, since most communities do not appreciate having entire new cities dropped into their midst. Trump's plan aimed to solve this problem by putting federal authority and land behind the projects.

There were already several projects in search of support, and even a prototype in Honduras. In 2013, four years after a military coup overthrew the country's elected president, the president of the Honduran Congress pushed through legislation to create new special economic zones called Zones for Employment and Economic Development, or ZEDEs. Juan Orlando Hernández, the politician in question, was elected president that same year.

In 2017, a group of investors launched Próspera, a proposal to turn a patchwork of lands—one thousand acres, some on the mainland, some on the resort island of Roatán—into a zone. The Delaware-based Próspera corporation amassed $120 million in investment from tech oligarchs and broke ground in 2020. Among its backers: Thiel, Andreessen, Altman, and Srinivasan. Most of them invested through Pronomos Capital, a venture fund seeking to invest in network state cities around the globe. Patri Friedman, the seasteading proponent and Thiel acolyte, had founded the company. Srinivasan served as an advisor.

There isn't much to see at Próspera's main headquarters near the town of Crawfish Rock on Roatán, just an office building and a smattering of businesses including "a Bitcoin café and education center, a genetics clinic, a scuba shop," according to *The New York Times Magazine*. Two thousand residents supposedly call the zone home, though most of them are "e-residents" and few people physically inhabit Próspera. The sparse settlement is mostly known for allowing experimental medical treatments not currently approved by the FDA, a situation made possible by Próspera's status as a ZEDE, which allows it to adopt flexible regulations. ". . . Próspera is a private, for-profit city, with its own government that courts foreign investors through low taxes and light regulation," wrote journalist Rachel Corbett in *The New York Times Magazine* in 2024. "Businesses can choose a regulatory framework from a menu of 36 countries or customize their own."

Próspera claims that 250 companies are incorporated in the zone, which has become a destination for biohackers who visit for those experimental therapies. Friedman, for example, underwent a procedure to implant a microchip in his hand that allows him to unlock his Tesla. Próspera's construction started during the presidency of Juan Orlando Hernández, the senator who architected the legislation to create the zones and served in office until 2022. His successor, Xiomara Castro—the wife of the president who was deposed by the military coup in 2009—challenged the legitimacy of Hernández's ZEDE laws, which were highly unpopular with the Honduran public. That year, the Honduran Congress voted to repeal the ZEDE law, prompting Próspera to file a $10.8 billion arbitration claim with the International Centre for Settlement of Investment Disputes. Making matters worse for Próspera, the US government indicted Hernández on drug trafficking charges. He was arrested and extradited to the US, where he stood trial and received a forty-five-year sentence in 2024, the same year that the

Honduran Supreme Court ruled that the ZEDE laws had been unconstitutional. Since then, Próspera has been in a legal standoff with the Honduran government, pursuing the arbitration claim that could bankrupt the nation.

In 2025, Trump pardoned Hernández. A story in *The Wall Street Journal* shed light on the president's motivations for freeing a man convicted of smuggling 400 tons of cocaine and being at what a federal prosecutor called "the center of one of the largest and most violent drug-trafficking conspiracies in the world." Republican operative Roger Stone had lobbied for the pardon, citing Próspera as part of his rationale. "In a blog post on the week of Trump's inauguration in January, Stone argued that the new president could 'crush socialism and save a freedom city in Honduras' by pardoning Hernández, branding Próspera as a utopian project with 'major implications for U.S. policy and the future of freedom throughout the world,'" reported the *Journal*. Stone's decision to make Próspera part of his argument raised questions about whether tech oligarchs played a role in the Hernández pardon. "The reason seems clear: Hernández helped some big-time American crypto bros turn their dream of a government-free utopia into a reality," wrote Jennifer Gould in the *Air Mail* newsletter. "And these broligarchs—the best known of whom is Peter Thiel—are the same people who helped fund President Trump's first presidential campaign, and J. D. Vance's political career."

Thiel denied any involvement in the pardon, and Andreessen did not respond to the *Journal*'s questions. But Stone's decision to call Próspera a "freedom city" seemed to reveal a direct line between the controversial, tech-backed project in Honduras and Trump's plan to create similar projects on American soil. Srinivasan has long identified Próspera as the prime example of his network state idea in action—a venture-capital-backed settlement governed by a private corporation.

As Próspera fought to remain in a country that had rejected it, another project funded by the same group of tech oligarchs began gathering steam. Praxis, the brainchild of a surfer and college dropout named Dryden Brown, billed itself as a future city of 10,000 people slated for construction somewhere in the Mediterranean. After leaving New York University and working at a hedge fund (from which he was reportedly fired), in 2020 Brown received a grant from Emergent Ventures—libertarian economist Tyler Cowen's knockoff Thiel Fellowship—to "help build institutions and a financial center in Ghana" in 2020. During a talk at the 2023 Network State Conference, Brown said the plan was to "talk to a bunch of different founders from a bunch of different industries and figure out sort of, like, what policy changes would unlock their willingness to move to a new place . . . if we could sum up the investment amounts of all of those companies moving to a new country, it'd be quite a lot of foreign direct investment flowing into that country . . . then wrap that sort of, like, foreign direct investment in a narrative of a beautiful, green, new city that'll invest in social goods for the local community."

Praxis investors included Andreessen, Altman, and Lonsdale, along with the Winklevoss twins, Fred Ehrsam of Coinbase, and, for a while, FTX founder Sam Bankman-Fried. Thiel has long been listed as a Praxis backer since it's funded by Pronomos Capital, but *The New York Times* reported that "according to a person familiar with his investments, Mr. Thiel has never directly supported Praxis." In October 2024 Brown claimed to have lined up over half a billion dollars in financing from a Bahamas-based crypto investment firm called GEM Digital to build a "heroic" crypto city. "Entrepreneur Dryden Brown said he has secured $525 million in milestone-based financing to develop Praxis, one of a number of tech utopia proposals under way around the world," reported *The Wall Street Journal*. As part of the deal, Praxis was to issue its own crypto token, though nothing ever came of it.

Along with Próspera, Praxis became a flagship project on Srinivasan's official Network State Dashboard, a web page that tracks the progress of such projects around the globe. Brown depicted Praxis as a high-tech city, marketing his concept with AI-generated images featuring futuristic, cathedral-like architecture, and he claimed thousands of people had already signed up to become future "Praxians."

Brown's ambitions went beyond mere real estate. Praxis leaned hard into the network state identity, marketing itself as the "Next

America"—the future of global governance disruption that would be enabled by crypto. "Network States offer a path to crypto's next wave of adoption by integrating onchain infrastructure into the parallel institutions supplanting the global system's core functions," declared the Praxis website, in a sentence that sounded like it could have been lifted directly from *The Network State*. "As local communities dissolve and Nation States stumble, Network States will ascend," declared the Praxis manifesto, titled "The Network State: Crypto's End Game." "Soon, Network States will be your most important group affiliation, passport, and community. Network States will represent Citizens controlling trillions of dollars of assets, represented on their native asset registries. We'll watch the flippening of Network States over Nation States in real time. Network States will coalesce neighborhoods and build cities. The next global superpower will be a Network State. The next America will be onchain."

To build the city, Praxis needed to find a government willing to sell 10,000 acres of land that would be designated an "acceleration zone"—"a new type of Special Economic Zone that accelerates technological progress in service of national priorities." Praxis named these tech priorities as AI, crypto, energy, and biotech. As part of the deal, the host government would agree to let Praxis operate as a private territory governed by an "Acceleration Zone Board" with the power to determine its own laws and regulations. "Acceleration Zones are designed to be attractive to Government, Companies, Capital, and Residents," wrote Brown in a manifesto titled "National Accelerationism: How to Implement a Program of Techno-Optimism Now." "Governments (especially elected officials): [Acceleration Zones] are simple to implement (generally passing one law is sufficient), and offer an immediate and winning popular narrative."

Though Brown claimed to have ample financing and interest, finding an amenable host government proved challenging. The search took on a game show quality as Brown traveled the world searching for a location, even popping up in Argentina and the Dominican Republic to consider the finer points of locating there. As he searched the globe for a place to plant the Praxis flag, California

Forever—the proposal for a new tech city of 400,000—emerged in Northern California. A group of tech billionaire investors, including Andreessen, had quietly bought up 60,000 acres of land in Solano County for that purpose, a fact that shocked local communities and sparked fierce opposition. California Forever was conceived by Jan Sramek, a former Goldman Sachs trader from the Czech Republic who had moved to California a decade earlier and, despite having no background in real estate, decided to build a massive new city on farmland. Somehow, he had also convinced multiple billionaires to fund his dream. By the time *The New York Times* exposed his project in a 2023 story headlined "The Silicon Valley Elite Who Want to Build a City from Scratch," Sramek's company had spent $900 million acquiring the land.

Sramek tried to brand California Forever as a solution to create housing and jobs, but the people of Solano County weren't buying it. They worried that his project, which would create the biggest city in the county, would worsen already bad traffic, increase pollution, and strain the environment. Further complicating Sramek's plan was the fact that Solano County has an "orderly growth" ordinance to prevent projects much less ambitious than California Forever from suddenly appearing on the landscape. News stories branded the project as a "tech utopia," a label Sramek rejected. He also denied that California Forever had any relation to the network state idea, though both his personal background and the nature of his project suggested otherwise. For example, a 2024 *Business Insider* profile described Sramek as "someone who set out at an early age to be the European equivalent of Peter Thiel." In 2008, while studying at the London School of Economics, Sramek singled out Thiel as his role model. "Lateral thinker, hedge fund manager, entrepreneur, venture capitalist, intellectual, philanthropist," said Sramek in an interview with a blogger. "He seems to combine everything extremely well." In addition, Srinivasan himself had seemed to indicate that California Forever was a network state project a few months after it became public. Coincidentally, Sramek's Venmo account revealed Srinivasan among his 180 contacts on the payments app. A Venmo connection is hardly a smoking gun, but it seems illogical to claim that a strange new tech city funded by tech billionaires, touted by Srinivasan, and spearheaded by a longtime Thiel fanboy has no relation to the network state.

California Forever had another big problem. Building the new city would require approval from Solano County voters. So, Sramek hired an "A-team" of political advisors—including top consultants to Gavin Newsom and Kamala Harris—to craft a ballot measure for the 2024 election. California Forever also launched a full-scale public relations campaign to build support, lavishing massive grants on local community organizations as part of the effort to curry favor. It didn't work. Sramek was forced to abandon the ballot measure after polls showed that 70 percent of voters opposed the project. It was something of a miracle in that, in the hyper-polarized political landscape of 2024, Sramek had found a way to unite both Democrats and Republicans—against his billionaire city scheme. It didn't help that California Forever had filed a $510 million lawsuit against a group of local landowners and farmers who had refused to sell their property, with the company of out-of-town billionaires accusing the locals of "endless greed."

Praxis and California Forever had run into the buzz saw of reality and learned that building a new city is much harder than imagining one. Still, the idea of building futuristic new tech cities suddenly seemed to be all the rage. A tech billionaire named Marc Lore searched the land for a place to site Telosa, a 5-million-person city with a density "equivalent to San Francisco" slated for development in either Appalachia or the Southwest. Another project, the Highland Rim Project, sought to build a network of aligned Christian communities in the rolling hills along the Kentucky-Tennessee border. Highland Rim is closely associated with Andrew Isker, a controversial right-wing pastor aiming to create Christian zones explicitly designed to operate outside secular democratic governance. Isker has described Indians as "cow worshippers," Judaism as "literally blasphemous and anti-Christian," and the Civil Rights Act of 1964 as a law that aids a war "against Christians, men, and white people."

"There's a name for the rough concept that Isker describes: the 'Network State,' an ascendant and buzzy tech movement where internet groups are beginning to explore what it might be like to start their own new countries," wrote Kiera Butler of *Mother Jones*. "At first, these new countries would appear online, and eventually in actual physical locations. Simply put, the Highland Rim Project is the Christian nationalist take on that idea." Highland Rim was funded by New Founding, an "anti-woke" right-wing Christian venture capital firm. Nate Fischer, the CEO of New Founding—and funder of *American Reformer*, the Christian nationalist publication formerly edited by Chris Buskirk, JD Vance's partner in the Rockbridge Network—explicitly described his idea as a network state. "Nation states are not the principal form of government today," Fischer wrote on X. "I see no reason Christian nations or peoples couldn't organize network states." New Founding had received investment from Marc Andreessen, and Fischer had invested in Pronomos Capital, Friedman's fund for network state projects. It was a strange marriage: one of Silicon Valley's most powerful venture capitalists directly funding a company behind a Christian nationalist separatist project that openly identified as a network state.

Most of these new concepts cropped up in California—and seemed designed to tap into Trump's freedom city proposal. In San Francisco, Mark Lutter and Jeffrey Mason of the Charter Cities Institute proposed a tech-focused freedom city in the Presidio, a sprawling park on federal land with views of the Golden Gate Bridge, that would focus on "development and deployment of innovative technologies under a more permissive regulatory framework which can then safely be deployed at scale." In Alameda, an island city in the San Francisco Bay, a tech worker named James Ingallinera proposed the creation of "Frontier Valley" at the site of an old navy base, describing the project as a "new special regulation district" with "the most accelerated code in the US for robotics and physical innovation." In Sonoma County, eighty-seven miles north of San Francisco, a Stanford computer science graduate named Devon Zuegel pitched "Esmeralda," a new walkable city for "high-agency people" on the outskirts of the bucolic town of Cloverdale. Zuegel, who served as editor in chief of Thiel's far-right *Stanford Review*, denied that her project—backed by a team of funders whose names she will not reveal—had anything to do with the network state. At the 2024 Network State Conference, however, she had described her proposal as "a Chautauqua of the West." She had also visited Próspera and written a highly detailed forty-page analysis of the project.

Despite this proliferation of strange new concepts, no project received more media attention than Praxis, which, after failing in its yearslong search to find a willing host country, took a more hostile approach under Trump. In the summer of 2024, Dryden Brown visited Greenland to scout locations for his project. "I went to Greenland to try to buy it," he explained in a series of social media posts in November. One month later, president-elect Trump declared that "the ownership and control of Greenland is an absolute necessity" in a social media post announcing his decision to appoint a new ambassador to Denmark: Ken Howery, a longtime Thiel associate who cofounded PayPal and Founders Fund. Trump had long fantasized about taking Greenland, an icy island territory governed by the Kingdom of Denmark since the 1700s. It's easy to see why: Greenland contains a mother lode of resources crucial to the twenty-first-century economy, including minerals and rare earth substances that power phones, electric vehicles, guided missiles, and wind turbines. Greenland also sits between the Arctic and Atlantic Oceans, making it a geopolitically strategic location for military operations and Arctic dominance. Climate change promises even greater riches, as the melting ice could unlock Greenland's gold mine of natural resources and open new Arctic shipping lanes.

Trump had publicly mused about buying Greenland since 2019, but seizing the territory became a core part of his foreign policy in 2025. The president framed control of Greenland as a moral necessity. "I'm talking about protecting the free world," he told reporters at a Mar-a-Lago press conference in January 2025, days after Donald Trump Jr. had visited the island.

Bullying Denmark became a key plank in Trump's policy toward

Europe. "I think we're going to get it one way or the other," he told reporters in March. "We're going to get it." Denmark's leaders made it clear that Greenland was "not for sale or for taking," but Trump continued to press the issue. Vice President Vance also joined the fray. "You have not done a good job by the people of Greenland," Vance said, addressing his remarks to the Danish government during a visit to a US military base on the island in 2025. When the commander of Pituffik Space Base tried to smooth the diplomatic mess by pledging "all of our flags will fly proudly—together," she was fired. Trump escalated, refusing to rule out military action against the NATO ally and threatening to impose a 25 percent import tax on Europe unless Denmark gave up Greenland. Amid this saber-rattling, the network state reared its head.

"As the Trump administration intensifies efforts to acquire Greenland from Denmark — or take it by force — some Silicon Valley tech investors are promoting the frozen island as a site for a so-called freedom city, a libertarian utopia with minimal corporate regulation," reported Reuters in a story headlined "Greenland 'Freedom City'? Rich Donors Push Trump for a Tech Hub Up North," published on April 10, 2025. Brown told Reuters that Praxis had been approached by other companies about building a city in Greenland. The story also quoted Shervin Pishevar, a Praxis investor, saying the annexation of Greenland "can be the dawn of a new Manifest Destiny." Andreessen declined to comment, while a spokesman for Thiel told Reuters, "Peter isn't involved in any plans or discussions regarding Greenland." Brown clearly relished the attention and adjusted his vision for Praxis to fit Greenland, and to appeal to Elon Musk. "He advocates for building a city there in part because its harsh environment could provide a test site for colonizing Mars—one of Musk's highest ambitions," reported Reuters. "We must build a prototype of Terminus on Earth before departing for Mars," Brown posted on X in November, referring to Musk's alleged plan for a colony on Mars. "I believe Greenland is the place, @elonmusk."

By June, Brown was pitching yet another location for his network state / freedom city. A *Vanity Fair* profile featured Brown trumpeting a new plan to build a city called Atlas on the 100,000-acre grounds of Vandenberg Space Force Base near Santa Barbara, California. "The idea goes like this: Let the so-called Praxians build a city on federal land in Vandenberg," wrote Zoë Bernard. "They will erect facilities, housing, and offices. They will attract tech talent from nearby Los Angeles and San Francisco. With their newfound city, they will help revitalize American manufacturing. They will build drones and ships and space infrastructure. In doing so, Vandenberg will become the new American industrial base and a proud emblem of Western prowess."

Brown cited Ayn Rand and the Founding Fathers as inspirations, but he evaded Bernard's questions about whether the Trump administration supported his plan. "We've had a bunch of conversations with a bunch of different people," he said. He framed Atlas as a "high testosterone" project—contrasting it with California Forever, which he derided as a "boring center-left" project "pandering" to "boomer, lower-middle-class farmers who hear about Marc Andreessen and are like, 'This guy seems weird.'" "It is low testosterone," concluded Brown, who clearly had come to see the project as a nemesis.

Up in Solano County, Jan Sramek's vision for California Forever had started to sound a lot like Brown's. Unable to win countywide voter approval for his new city, Sramek searched frantically for a different approach. On the same day *Vanity Fair* published its profile of Brown, Sramek posted a long X thread that framed the Solano County project in stark new terms. "America cannot compete with China without building America's Shenzen—a place to build drones, ships, robots, and everything else cutting edge," he wrote, name-checking the Chinese megacity that transformed rural farmland into one of the world's fastest-growing industrial and technological zones. "Either we're going to fix California, or we're going to lose with China," he wrote.

California Forever's pivot had begun a few months earlier, when Sramek announced the project would now include a new shipbuilding facility, just as the Trump administration proposed a bill to compete with China by revitalizing the nation's shipbuilding. Having failed to obtain popular support for his city, Sramek adopted a new strategy. Instead of pushing a walkable, family-friendly community of 400,000, he recast the project as an economic imperative with national security implications—an urgent effort to accelerate a twenty-first-century manufacturing boom in a do-or-die race against China. Sramek formalized the shift a month later, announcing plans for a "manufacturing park" for "frontier tech" called Solano Foundry, which he pitched as a "strategically located" hub "for the most innovative industries, including advanced transportation, robotics, energy, and defense." This sounded a lot like Praxis's "acceleration zone" model, one that framed the project as both a local and federal necessity. California Forever abandoned efforts to get countywide approval and began trying to pick off Solano County's cities one by one, promising jobs, development, and tax-base expansion in exchange for annexation and support. The language shifted from parks, housing, and lifestyle to drones, shipbuilding, and advanced manufacturing, with an emphasis on economic stagnation and the need to "move faster" to secure the future.

News outlets covered these stories, but few connected the dots. The network state generally went unmentioned, even as the same interrelated group of tech billionaires funded multiple projects with the same goals, structures, and visions. Freedom cities were simply Trump's rebranding of the same idea. In 2025, the network state movement emerged from the shadows and gained momentum, with buy-in from the White House. *Wired* reported that a group seeking to create "startup nations"—the Freedom Cities Coalition—had met regularly with Trump administration officials to draft legislation. The goal: not just Trump's ten promised cities, but "as many as the market can handle," Trey Goff, chief of staff of Próspera, said. "According to Goff, Freedom Cities Coalition has briefed White House officials on three options for creating freedom cities," wrote Vittoria Elliott and Caroline Haskins of *Wired.* "One is through 'interstate compacts.' In this scenario, two or more states could set aside territories with shared tax and regulation policies, with some state-specific carve-outs. Under existing law, these compacts can't be revoked, though they can be dissolved under certain circumstances." Alternative approaches involved the creation of "federal enclaves with special economic and jurisdictional zones, or having Trump issue executive orders to create each new freedom city," wrote Elliott and Haskins. "The energy in DC is absolutely electric," Goff said. "You can tell in meetings with the people involved that they have the mandate to do some of the more hyperbolic, verbose things Trump has mentioned."

Trump's threat to seize Greenland by force if necessary inspired other, more aggressive ideas for creating network states. Palmer Luckey, cofounder of Anduril, called for Trump to build a freedom city in Cuba. "The United States should immediately expand our base on Guantanamo Bay into Liberty City, an American Singapore of the Caribbean," he wrote. "We already control Guantanamo under a perpetual lease, complete with a deepwater port, airfields, and proximity to key trade routes. Why not turn it into a special economic zone?" Coinbase CEO Brian Armstrong, one of the more vocal evangelists for the network state, agreed. At the 2024 Network State Conference, he had explicitly linked his company to the concept, stressing the need to create "an archipelago" of private cities to serve as a "refuge where the builders of the world can make sure they have a place to reside." "If you're building network states, build them with Coinbase," he told the audience.

Now, he urged Trump to accelerate progress toward the goal. "We need more special economic zones in the U.S. We should designate ~10 or so like this across different pieces of federal land, each with its own exemption from federal and state law," he wrote on X in response to Luckey's call for a colony in Cuba. "One for bio, one for drones/aviation, one for crypto, one for robotics, one for mining, etc. See what happens without so much regulation within a small sandbox."

Trump was already thinking along those lines. Though Praxis did not find a home in the Mediterranean, a similar concept soon emerged in Gaza, where Trump floated the idea of building a privatized tech metropolis on bombed-out ruins. "I have concepts for Gaza that I think are very good," Trump said during a trip to the

Middle East in May. "Make it a freedom zone. Let the United States get involved and make it just a freedom zone. I'd be proud to have the United States have it, take it, make it a freedom zone."

Months earlier, he had shared an AI-generated video of a dystopian future Gaza, complete with a Trump resort, a golden statue of himself, and dollar bills raining from the sky. His Gaza fantasy was the network state in its most ghoulish incarnation: a tech-fascist casino amid the ruins of a genocide. The result: Project Sunrise, a $112 billion proposal from Trump son-in-law Jared Kushner that would displace Palestinians and build a tech city in Gaza. "Beachside luxury resorts. High-speed rail. AI-optimized smart grids," reported *The Wall Street Journal*. "Welcome to 'Project Sunrise,' the Trump administration's pitch to foreign governments and investors to turn Gaza's rubble into a futuristic coastal destination."

As with Praxis and California Forever, the proposal for Project Sunrise featured digital images of a futuristic cityscape. Seizing land and creating new colonial settlements backed by tech capital had become a key part of Trump's foreign policy. Within days of the US raid to capture and arrest Nicolás Maduro, the president of Venezuela, Mark Lutter of the Charter Cities Institute publicly called for the creation of yet another tech city there. "Venezuela doesn't need to become another Iraq," he wrote on X. "It needs a Freedom City . . . A Freedom City = new land, new rules, real property rights, real rule of law—jointly built with the U.S. This playbook works. Shenzhen. Jebel Ali. Growth spreads when success is allowed to exist."

Lutter, a graduate of George Mason University, had been one of the first people to receive a grant from Emergent Ventures in 2018, the year it was founded with a $1 million contribution from the Thiel Foundation. In 2023, he spoke at the Network State Conference.

Proposals for futuristic tech utopias operating beyond normal rules and laws had become an ongoing theme by 2025. A Trump-backed peace plan for Ukraine called for the creation of a "free economic zone" in the country's Donbas region, most of which is currently occupied by Russian military forces. In Kazakhstan, President Kassym-Jomart Tokayev announced vague plans for a "cryptocity" near the capital, Astana. On the Caribbean island of Nevis, a Belgian Bitcoin investor named Olivier Janssens was buying up land for a proposed city called Destiny, which Janssens describes as an American Dubai. On the Venezuelan island of Isla Margarita, a German crypto entrepreneur was planning CryptoCity, a housing development for 1,000 people where every transaction would be handled via crypto. In Nigeria, Itana City—backed by Pronomos Capital and the crypto exchange Binance—was supposedly rising inside the Lekki Free Zone near Lagos. It bills itself as the "global jurisdiction of choice on the African continent for the Internet citizens of the world." *Wired* called it "a Peter Thiel–backed startup city" that "wants to be Africa's Delaware."

Pop-up conferences like Edge City and Zuzalu toured Thailand, Bhutan, Patagonia, and Montenegro, spreading the gospel of future digital citizenship. Srinivasan himself launched a so-called Network School in Forest City, a Chinese-funded development off the coast of Malaysia that had become a "ghost city" with fewer than 7,000 residents and rows of empty high-rise apartment buildings. Network School aimed to provide "a three-month learning retreat marketed to people interested in 'network nations,' a kind of utopia for the anarchocapitalist set," according to *Wired*.

A different Forest City emerged in the English countryside. In October 2025, the Albion City Development Corporation unveiled a proposal to build Forest City 1, a new settlement of 1 million people on 45,000 acres of prime agricultural land near the Cambridgeshire-Suffolk border. Forest City 1 is the brainchild of Shiv Malik, a former *Guardian* journalist who left to work in tech, along with tech entrepreneur Joseph Reeve. They promote Forest City 1 with glossy digital renderings and the breathless claim that it would be Britain's first new city in fifty years. Malik and Reeve are currently seeking government approval to become an officially designated development corporation, which would empower them to acquire land and steamroll opposition. "A development corporation is quite an authoritarian tool . . . it should not be used lightly," Malik said on the *Anglofuturism* podcast, explaining that "it can compulsory purchase land—it can force people to sell what's theirs." Forcing people to sell, he added, is sometimes "just necessary in society."

Malik strenuously rejects the idea that his project has anything to do with the network state, but the similarities are hard to ignore. The architect signed onto Forest City 1's list of supporters, Patrik Schumacher—principal architect at Zaha Hadid Architects—is the same designer linked to Próspera in Honduras, Liberland (a proposed new country on disputed territory between Croatia and Serbia), and Praxis. Malik's own social media history also undermines his denials. In 2022, he reached out directly to Srinivasan on Twitter to pitch him on an app called Pocket. "Heya @balajis — the citizens of the network state(s) will need decentralized ID," he wrote. "That's what we're building." A year later, when Srinivasan posted that something needed to be done to "hyperdeflate the cost of raising a family," Malik replied: "Build cities."

° ° °

Thiel was right—the second coming of Trump had unveiled some hidden truths. It exposed the stunning radicalization of Silicon Valley venture capitalists, who had used crypto to capture the election, AI to seize government, and, in turn, used the power of government to push the network state under the guise of freedom cities. Thiel's anticipated apocalypse had nothing to do with COVID, the Kennedy assassination, or Jeffrey Epstein—for the most part. The release of the Epstein files in 2026 revealed the extent to which Epstein had been a major early player in crypto, investing $3 million in Coinbase and helping to fund the development of Bitcoin at a critical stage in 2014. "At the very moment Bitcoin's future was in jeopardy, Epstein's money and access placed him inside the institutions that were beginning to frame the cryptocurrency as a tool to route around nation states—and consolidate power among a new class of networked tech elites," wrote journalist Nafeez Ahmed.

"With his interest first piqued as early as 2011, Epstein was ahead of the game on crypto," wrote David Z. Morris in *The Verge*. "The financier understood it as a tool for clandestine payments and shady international finance, and found prominent community members more than willing to welcome him. Bitcoin wasn't even invented until 2009, which means *all* of Epstein's crypto connections formed after his 2008 guilty plea for solicitation of a minor. Between 2011 and 2019, Epstein invested in major crypto exchanges and software development firms . . . Epstein even forged ties with Bitcoin's core development team and mused about changing the technology of Bitcoin itself."

Epstein, who infamously had his own island, was a consummate example of a member of the cognitive elite, a man who moved with ease through networks of money and power. In Epstein, Thiel found both an investor and an ideological soulmate. The unveiling of this reality further complicated Thiel's image as he and his acolytes reached the zenith of influence and, perhaps, explained his sense of apocalyptic dread. By the time the scope of his relationship with the dead sex offender became clear, Thiel had moved beyond apocalypse to the next stage of his existential crisis, one that had simmered for years but now came to define him. In the year following Trump's return to Washington, DC, Thiel would distinguish himself as the world's foremost lecturer on one of Christianity's grimmest themes: the Antichrist.

CHAPTER 7

ANTICHRIST

Silicon Valley's New Religion

Having attained the heights of wealth and power—with his friends, allies, and companies in control of government at a critical moment—Peter Thiel decided the time was right to warn the world about the Antichrist. As Palantir reaped billions and *The Sovereign Individual*'s crypto and AI prophecies bore fruit, Thiel embarked on a global tour of closed-door lectures focused incisively on disturbing biblical themes. Thiel had been weaving apocalypse and Armageddon into his public talks for years, but now he homed in on his main subject, delivering his Antichrist-centric lectures in a peculiarly specific format: A select group of invitees gathered for four hours on four separate nights. After a period of mingling and refreshments, Thiel spoke for an hour or so, then participated in a question-and-answer session, followed by more mingling. He did this in select venues around the globe, including the University of Austin, an ersatz anti-woke university founded by Joe Lonsdale and right-wing writer Bari Weiss, and a private gathering near the Vatican in Rome.

Thiel billed his lectures as off-the-record, but the secrecy only intensified media interest. Perhaps that was the point. Transcripts leaked after he delivered the full sequence in San Francisco, where hundreds of people lined up on the sidewalk outside of the

Commonwealth Club, on September 15, 2025. A few feet away, a group of protesters dressed as devil worshippers jeered and held signs that anointed Thiel himself as the world's new evil overlord:

"Embrace Darkness. Hail Thiel."

"The End Is Near. Palantir Is the Path. Thiel Leads the Way."

"Spoiler Alert," declared a sign wielded by someone costumed as a cartoonish Satan. "Peter Thiel is the Antichrist."

Reporters worked the crowd but had a hard time finding anyone genuinely interested in Thiel's religious ideas. Attendees seemed more excited by the prospect of getting face time with one of the most well-known tech billionaires in the world. "The crowd was largely white, male, and clad in some form of button-down—attire appropriate for seeing their high priest deliver his sermon," reported *The San Francisco Standard*. One man who identified himself as Dick Gay said he was a tech investor who had been inspired by Thiel's 2014 book, *Zero to One: Notes on Startups, or How to Build the Future*. Among other things, the book encouraged people to model their companies after "cults." "In the most intense kind of organization, members hang out only with other members," wrote Thiel, along with coauthor Blake Masters, the Stanford grad whose failed Senate campaign Thiel would later fund. "They ignore their families and abandon the outside world. In exchange, they experience strong feelings of belonging, and maybe get access to esoteric 'truths' denied to ordinary people. We have a word for such organizations: cults. Cultures of total dedication look crazy from the outside, partly because the most notorious cults were homicidal: Jim Jones and Charles Manson did not make good exits. But entrepreneurs should take cultures of extreme dedication seriously." "The best startups might be considered slightly less extreme kinds of cults," they wrote.

Some of those attending Thiel's lectures seemed ready to drink the Kool-Aid. Gay told the *Standard* he had attended the University of Austin. In addition, Gay was an investor in Sperm Racing, a company promoting competitions in which "men compete to see whose sperm is 'fastest' under a microscope," according to the *Standard*. Another attendee, Justin Park, planned to pitch Thiel on his company, Cross on the Moon Coalition, which planned to put an actual seven-foot-tall cross on the moon.

Inside the auditorium, things got weirder. In rambling lectures, the billionaire laid out his own homespun theology, woven together from bits of philosophy, framing politics as an existential struggle against the Antichrist. Thiel even named possible suspects, including Representative Alexandria Ocasio-Cortez ("the initials are worrisome"), climate activist Greta Thunberg, tech regulation, and critics of artificial intelligence. He described the Antichrist as a sinister but deceptive figure who would seek to establish a totalitarian government to rule the entire world, using the slogan "peace and safety." In fact, he said, the Antichrist will likely be someone who uses the fear of existential threats to trick people into handing over total power.

"The Antichrist comes to power by talking constantly about Armageddon, about rumors of wars and scaring you into giving him control over science and technology," Thiel told the audience. In addition, he said the Antichrist would be defined by "velocity"—speed—seeking to move very quickly to capture total control of the world. In other words, the Antichrist would be an accelerationist in addition to a doommonger. Whether by design or by coincidence, Thiel's description of the Antichrist seemed to perfectly describe Thiel himself. By the time of his San Francisco lectures, the tech surveillance billionaire—the tentacles of his empire enwrapping the high-velocity technologies of AI and crypto, as well as governments worldwide—had distinguished himself as one of the world's foremost invokers of apocalyptic themes. The contradiction did not go unnoticed. "It's so strange . . . you build military AI, military drones, autonomous drone technology to export to war zones all over the world," said comedian Tim Dillon, who roasted Thiel during an appearance on the *Joe Rogan Experience* just days before his San Francisco lectures. "You build domestic surveillance technology to surveil our friends and neighbors. And then your other pet passion is the Antichrist."

Thiel's Antichrist obsession had become a laughingstock after a disastrous interview with Ross Douthat of *The New York Times* in

June 2025. The interview, published under the headline "Peter Thiel and the Antichrist," produced a viral video clip in which Thiel—his face glistening with moisture as he stammered through his incomplete thoughts—struggled to answer a simple question: Did he prefer the human race to endure?

"Uh," said Thiel.

"You're hesitating," said Douthat.

"Well, I . . . I don't know . . . I would . . . there's so many questions implicit in this," said Thiel.

"Should the human race survive?" asked Douthat.

After eighteen seconds of uncomfortable delay, Thiel finally said yes. His disastrous performance inspired memes and mockery, along with headlines around the world that probably brought Thiel to the attention of millions of people for the first time. Even the animated TV series *South Park* clowned Thiel's fetish; the show's 2025 season hinged on a storyline in which, after Trump impregnates Satan in the White House, Thiel and Vance conspire to abort the resulting Antichrist baby.

Like Dillon, Douthat also pointed out that Thiel's Antichrist appeared to have much in common with Thiel himself. "This is my very specific question for you, is that: you are an investor in AI, you're deeply invested in Palantir, in military technology, in technologies of surveillance, in technologies of warfare . . . and it just seems to me that when you tell me a story about the Antichrist coming to power and using the fear of technological change to sort of impose order on the world, I feel like that Antichrist would maybe be using the tools that you are building, right?" said Douthat. "Wouldn't the Antichrist be like, 'Great . . . we're not going to have any more technological progress, but I really like what Palantir has done so far,' right? Isn't that a concern? Wouldn't that be the irony of history . . . that the man publicly worrying about the Antichrist accidentally hastens his or her arrival?"

Thiel once again struggled to find words. "There are all, look, there all these different scenarios . . . I obviously don't think that's what I'm doing," he said.

"To be clear, I don't think that's what you're doing either . . ." said Douthat.

Thiel argued that he was simply making a basic observation that the world had stagnated due to a desire for peace and safety. Citing the Bible as his source, he said this emphasis on peace and safety naturally raised the specter of the Antichrist. "This is 1 Thessalonians 5:3," he said. "The slogan of the Antichrist is peace and safety."

On the contrary, Paul's first letter to the Thessalonians does not mention the Antichrist. The verse Thiel cited reads, "For when they are saying, 'Peace and safety,' then sudden destruction cometh upon them as travail upon a woman with child, and they shall not escape." It refers to the time when the "Day of the Lord" will come "like a thief in the night," but the word "Antichrist" does not appear.

"Antichrist" appears in only four verses of the Bible, in 1 and 2 John. "Little children, it is the last time: and as ye have heard that antichrist shall come, even now are there many antichrists; whereby we know that it is the last time," reads 1 John 2:18. John describes these Antichrists as "deceivers" who deny that Jesus "Christ is come in the flesh." These Antichrists are false teachers who preach against the teachings of Jesus, and most scholars agree that John describes an actual group of people, not a future apocalyptic villain. The Antichrists of the time were a faction of early Christians who broke off during a schism, which John describes as those who "went out from us."

Over time, however, the concept of an Antichrist has been conflated by some theologians with other books of the Bible to portray it as a supernatural figure who will rise to aid Satan in a final battle against God. The Antichrist figure merged with other threatening biblical figures, including the "man of lawlessness" in Thessalonians and the "Beast" in the book of Revelation. Scholars believe that the Beast—a monstrous creature rising out of the sea which has seven heads with ten horns—symbolizes the Roman Empire and its emperors who executed Jesus and persecuted early Christians. In historical terms, all these labels refer to people or powers in biblical times, not in the present or the future.

Such details mattered little to Thiel, who by this point was deep in the process of constructing his own personal theology. Thiel framed his Antichrist lectures as an exercise in "political theology," a term he took from Nazi philosopher Carl Schmitt, who argued that politics is religion in disguise and, therefore, an existential battle of good versus evil. Schmitt, who wrote legal opinions to justify Hitler's early atrocities, is perhaps best known for the 1922 book *Political Theology*, which begins with the sentence "Sovereign is he who decides on the exception." Schmitt meant that the true ruler of a society is the person who can decide when to suspend normal laws and rules, usually in response to a crisis or emergency by imposing a "state of exception." Hitler took power in this exact way after the Reichstag fire in 1933, suspending civil liberties and purging his political opponents after declaring a temporary emergency that lasted until his death and defeat in 1945. Yarvin's ideas, including his Cathedral metaphor, were largely inspired by Schmitt.

This context is important because Schmitt, like Thiel, also ruminated on the Antichrist, as well as the *katechon*, a term from 2 Thessalonians that refers to a mysterious restraining force that holds back the "man of lawlessness" who would arise before the Day of the Lord, presumably Judgment Day. For Schmitt, the *katechon* represented whatever power prevents chaos and delays the apocalypse—the sovereign authority who can restrain evil. Thiel's lectures position technology and its masters as this *katechon* force that can hold back the totalitarian power he imagines as the Antichrist.

Thiel had cited Schmitt's Antichrist writings in his 2007 "The Straussian Moment" essay, where he quoted German philosopher Heinrich Meier's assertion that Schmitt worried about an Antichrist that would seize power by creating what Meier called an "artificial world" and a "religion of technicity," a dystopian predicament in which virtual realities replaced real life and where entertainment replaced politics. "It is a world where people spend their lives amusing themselves to death," wrote Thiel. "Following the medieval tradition, Schmitt knows and fears that this artificial unity can be brought about only by the shadowy figure of the Antichrist." He then extensively quoted German philosopher Meier's description of Schmitt's Antichrist:

> *God created the world; the Antichrist counterfeits it . . . The sinister magician recreates the world, changes the face of the earth, and subdues nature. Nature serves him; for what purpose is a matter of indifference—for any satisfaction of artificial needs, for ease and comfort. Men who allow themselves to be deceived by him see only the fabulous effect; nature seems to be overcome, the age of security dawns; everything has been taken care of, a clever foresight and planning replace Providence.*

Again, this sounds like a description of Silicon Valley in the twenty-first century, where venture-capital-backed corporations are rushing to create computer systems so powerful they might destroy everything and where the strange religions of TESCREAL have arisen to worship Thermodynamic Gods and theoretical acceleration loops of mystical abundance. This is the main tension of Thiel's Antichrist lectures—a contradiction so glaringly obvious that one suspects he's deliberately baiting his critics: When Thiel speaks of the Antichrist, he seems to be talking about himself.

Thiel is neither a theologian nor a philosopher, and many of his arguments are pointless ramblings that obscure rather than clarify his thesis. For example, in San Francisco he launched into an ornate reverie on the alleged significance of the number thirty-three, the age at which many believe Jesus was killed. "Buddha begins his travels at age thirty and experiences Nirvana, ego death, at age thirty-three," said Thiel. "But I had to be ecumenical and say something nice about Islam. One idea that's pretty cool is, when you're reborn into your afterlife, you're born into your thirty-three-year-old self. Your thirty-three-year-old self is your best self . . . It's like Alexander at the peak of his power. Or even in Tolkien, the hobbits have a coming-of-age ceremony at thirty-three. That's how old Frodo is when he inherits the ring." Thiel added that "these numbers do occur almost mystically through a number of different contexts," a superstitious claim unsupported by fact. Case in point: Buddha obtained Nirvana at thirty-five, not thirty-three. Thiel's lectures contain many of these slippery digressions, but the overall goal is simple: to point the finger at his political enemies.

Thiel likely understands that accusing others of being the Antichrist will provoke them to respond in kind. But there is no reason to argue over an obscure concept barely mentioned in the Bible, and certainly not at the behest of a peculiar billionaire with zero credibility on the topic. Though he was raised Lutheran, Thiel has described himself as "religious but not spiritual," and described his beliefs in contradictory terms as both "small orthodox Christian" and "somewhat heterodox." Despite his longtime fascination with religious themes, Thiel suggests a person need not believe in God to find religious ideas useful. "My line is always: We don't need belief in God, we don't need belief in the Bible, we need knowledge of God, knowledge of the Bible," he said during his lectures in San Francisco. "There's some way that you can have knowledge of Christ. He is a type of a man, a type of healer, a type of lawyer, a type of carpenter, type of scapegoat, type of king. And there's something like that we can also do with history. We can't know everything, but knowledge is more important than belief."

In essence, Thiel argues religious stories and symbols can be used to make secular points about the future of politics. This is ironic since, in the Epistles of John, the word "Antichrist" refers to "false teachers" who perverted the teachings of Christ, as well as others who denied Christ's divinity. By manipulating scripture to bolster secular political ideas and suggesting Christianity can be useful without faith, Thiel would appear to be repeating these sins.

Much of his argument is built upon such reversals. His lectures borrow heavily from the work of Wolfgang Palaver, a Catholic theologian from Austria who had delivered a lecture about Schmitt and the Antichrist at Stanford in 1996. Thiel attended the lecture, where Palaver critiqued Schmitt's ideas to dispel them. Ever the contrarian, Thiel did the opposite, producing an inverted version of Palaver's talk to promote the Nazi's thinking about the Antichrist. "Thiel's language often mirrors Palaver's scholarship directly, sometimes closely paraphrasing it," wrote Laura Bullard in *Wired*.

"Although Thiel has never publicly acknowledged Wolfgang Palaver, the Austrian theologian's influence arguably runs through nearly everything Thiel has ever said or written about the Antichrist and the katechon," she wrote.

But whereas Palaver "wrote about Schmitt's apocalyptic theories in hopes of driving a stake through their heart," the theologian's work "provided a roadmap not only for Thiel's speaking tour but for his considerable strategic interventions in global politics—from his investments in military tech to his role in shaping the careers of JD Vance and Donald Trump to his support of the National Conservatism movement."

Thiel's lectures also make heavy use of René Girard, the late Stanford professor whose work he latched on to as a student. Girard was known for his theories of mimetic desire (that people learn desire by mimicking the desires of others) and scapegoating (that societies often resolve their tensions by punishing a symbolic scapegoat). For Girard, the point of understanding these concepts was to avoid repeating them, since he believed that mimetic desire leads to mimetic rivalry, an existential competition that ends with the punishing of a scapegoat and, eventually, the apocalypse. Thiel has credited Girard's idea on mimetic desire for his decision to invest in Facebook, and his Antichrist lectures scapegoat his political opponents as literal Antichrists. Where Palaver and Girard saw warnings, Thiel sees weapons.

Calling people Antichrists has a long and horrific tradition in the Western world. For centuries, people have sought to label their enemies as Antichrists, a tactic that proved especially popular in the United States. "The symbol of the Antichrist has played a surprisingly significant role in shaping Americans' self-understanding," wrote historian Robert Fuller in 1995's *Naming the Antichrist: The History of an American Obsession*. "Because they tend to view their nation as uniquely blessed by God, they have been especially prone to demonize their enemies." Among those who have been demonized in the past few centuries: Native Americans, Abraham Lincoln, Franklin Delano Roosevelt, Saddam Hussein, Barack Obama—even nonhuman technological innovations like barcodes and microchips. Calling someone the Antichrist is a tried-and-true way to slander your opposition as literal evil; throughout history, this kind of dehumanization and doomsday talk has sparked social upheaval, religious persecution, and violence. The pattern is so well established that it even has its own academic field: eschatology, the study of religious end-times beliefs.

Such thinking has a long history in Europe, where anxieties over pending apocalypses and Antichrists fueled social and political turmoil for centuries. Norman Cohn, the Cambridge scholar who documented Europe's history of apocalyptic turmoil in *The Pursuit of the Millennium: Revolutionary Millenarians and Mystical Anarchists of the Middle Ages*, saw the rise of the Nazis as part of this pattern. Hitler stole the idea for a thousand-year "reich" from the book of Revelation, which claims that Christ and his saints will reign on Earth for one thousand years—a millennium—after Satan is captured and imprisoned. In the Nazi version of the myth, the Jewish people became the ultimate enemy, a cosmic threat and existential risk whose annihilation would purify the world.

Like many who came before them, the Nazis projected warped scripture to provide moral justification for their horrors. They did this because, as masters of propaganda, they understood that apocalyptic thinking is a powerful technology for shaping political reality. Thiel, who framed Trump's return as an *apokálypsis*, understands this dynamic as well. Nothing unites people like religion, especially when it allows them to portray their political struggles as a battle between good and evil. "The whole concept of the Antichrist or there being some satanic adversary . . . fosters a crisis mentality," said Fuller, the Antichrist historian. "And with the crisis mentality, now we put aside all other differences. There's a tribal cohesion, a tribal unity, and it justifies even immoral acts because to defeat an evil enemy, a satanic enemy, you must then do whatever's necessary. So, it can therefore justify extremism and it can justify what would otherwise be reprehensible behavior [that] is now looked at as even holy, sacred and a duty for the true believer."

In his "Straussian Moment" essay, Thiel observed that it is sometimes necessary to hide brutal truths behind obscure concepts and thus limit understanding to a chosen few. "Indeed, there is little in Strauss that is more clear than the need for less transparency," wrote Thiel. "Unchecked philosophizing poses great risks to philosophers (as well as the cities they inhabit), as in even the most liberal or open-minded regimes there exist certain deeply problematic truths."

Thiel's lectures seek to articulate a problematic truth, one focused on the degree to which technology has created both the mechanism and the antidote for totalitarian control. While he could state these ideas plainly, he chooses to mask them as Christian eschatology. It seems like an odd decision given that Thiel—a gay man with a net worth of $27.5 billion, one who may not even believe in a literal God—is hardly a credible messenger in the eyes of many Christians. Yet here he stood in 2025, pontificating on scary doomsday themes like a fire-and-brimstone Bible-thumping Kentucky snake handler, taking it upon himself to warn against a mystical civilizational threat and impose an apocalyptic Christian extremist framework on godless Silicon Valley.

Just as his fascination with *The Sovereign Individual* percolated over decades, so too did his related fixation on Christian eschatology. Davidson and Rees-Mogg quoted scripture and used apocalyptic themes to push their vision of "megapolitics," and now Thiel sought to add his own layer. His religious lectures reflect the same visions of looming political upheaval, warning that Silicon Valley was helping to create the "machinery" of the Antichrist. "Over the last twenty-five years . . . under cover of relative peace and safety, an incredible machinery of tax treaties, financial surveillance, and sanctions architecture has been constructed," he said in San Francisco. "And all these tech fortunes are downstream of this vast system."

Speaking to his tech brethren at an event hosted by Acknowledging Christ in Technology and Society (ACTS 17), Thiel expressed paranoid worry about the rise of a one-world government aligned with Satan. Despite his own deep ties to intelligence and the military, he called out the strong link between "the military and financial and ideological superpower with the big tech companies," adding that he had originally envisioned PayPal as an anti-government technology to "evade these policies of the world's powers and principalities." In essence, Thiel argued that Silicon Valley was building the very "Antichrist-like system" that would be used to control the world.

° ° °

In the summer of 2023, Thiel delivered a talk at the Catholic University of Paris. It focused on Armageddon. During the question-and-answer session, someone asked the billionaire what could be done to prevent Armageddon, since his talk had provided no answers.

"Fend off the Antichrist, came the reply," wrote Bullard. "But beyond that, Thiel said that he—like Girard—wasn't really in the business of offering practical advice."

A man in the back of the room raised his voice to object.

"It's not true what you said about Girard," he said. "On many occasions, young people asked Girard, 'What should we do?' And Girard told them to go to church."

"Wolfgang?" said Thiel.

It was Palaver, the theologian from whom Thiel had cribbed much of his Antichrist material.

The criticism must have stung. A few months after Palaver corrected him in Paris, Thiel attended "The Roast, the Toast, and the Holy Ghost," a three-day event celebrating the fortieth birthday of Trae Stephens, a longtime Thiel associate who was a partner at Founders Fund and a cofounder of Anduril, the AI and drone weapons start-up. As part of the festivities, Thiel gave a speech about "miracles, forgiveness and Jesus Christ." Michelle Stephens, Trae Stephens's wife, later recounted the scene to *Christianity Today*:

> *We served caviar bumps, breakfast pizza, mimosas, and spiked coffee. DJ Canvas had come out with his crew to play a Saturday night set, remixing all of our beloved movie-themed songs into a*

trap beat. He also does this for Christian and worship music. He's got the best dance moves. He's got the best vibes. He performed while we were hanging out, having breakfast, communing together. Then my husband Trae's partner at Founders Fund, Peter Thiel, gave a 55-minute lecture on forgiveness and miracles—the meaning and significance of Jesus' death and resurrection—and testifying to his belief as well. We were blown away. A lot of people were looking like he had 10 heads, like, "What are you talking about?" But people were also coming up to us saying, "Whoa. I did not know Peter Thiel was a Christian. I didn't know Christianity could sound like that. So thoughtful, intellectual, rigorous. What are you reading? Where are you going to church in San Francisco?" Meanwhile, my Christian friends were like, "That was heretical. How dare you put a non-seminary-trained individual up on a platform, call it a sermon, and have him talk about Jesus?" That's from my friends! I'm like, "Okay, my goodness, I messed up." But then some of my Christian friends were like, "Did you just trick over 220 people into going to church?"

Stephens soon formed ACTS 17 with the goal of spreading Christianity in tech. Within a year, the press was abuzz with stories about the sudden outbreak of Christian evangelism in Silicon Valley. "Everything clicked when Peter Thiel gave the speech about God," wrote Emma Goldberg of *The New York Times* in a story headlined "Seeking God, or Peter Thiel, in Silicon Valley." The idea behind ACTS 17, according to the *Times*, is to "gather influential people, including in Silicon Valley, to talk about Christian belief." "For those seeking not just spiritually but also professionally, it's their chance to get close to industry demigods," wrote Goldberg.

"Our goal is not necessarily conversion," Michelle Stephens told *The San Francisco Standard* in another story headlined "Christians in Tech Drive Religious Revival in SF." The idea, she said, was to encourage the "high intellectuals of our time" to take an interest in faith. "To hear it from Stephens, there's a natural affinity between tech and Christianity," reported the *Standard*. "People in the industry give back through the creation of jobs and wealth that are meant to provide abundance to all. Plus, forgiveness and persevering after failure is key to culture."

Other events followed. On May 5, 2024, ACTS 17 cohosted "Holy Guacamole," an event at which Garry Tan and Thiel discussed political theology in a converted former San Francisco church owned by Tan. A few months later came "Code & Cosmos," where Tan and former National Institutes of Health director Francis Collins discussed the intersection of faith and science.

Media coverage portrayed ACTS 17 as a lighthearted group with a clever method for bringing people closer to faith. In Silicon Valley, where venture capitalists and tech founders are deified, they had the power to easily convene striving tech wannabes around religious themes, but the results were mixed. While big tech names could attract hundreds of people to an event with free food in San Francisco, religion did not seem like the main draw for most of the audience. Journalist Zoë Bernard described the scene as "business networking for the spiritually curious" in a *Vanity Fair* piece headlined "Christianity Was 'Borderline Illegal' in Silicon Valley. Now It's the New Religion." At Code & Cosmos, she wrote, fledgling tech founders lined up to feign interest in Tan's religious ideas before pitching him on their start-ups—clearly more interested in connecting with venture capital than with Jesus Christ. "Pleasantries now out of the way, the founders got down to business," wrote Bernard. "They asked Tan if he would connect with them on LinkedIn. (He did.) They asked for selfies. (He obliged.) And then, one by one, his hopeful disciples pitched their start-ups. 'I'd love to tell you about my company,' they said, and Tan, listening on with an air of pointed graciousness that was indeed Christlike, continued his smiling and nodding, followed by variations on the reply 'That's a good idea. Do you have any customers?' or 'Interesting concept. Do you have customers?' Invariably, the founders' faces fell, a newfound sheepishness creeping into their voices as they replied 'no' or 'Not yet, but soon!' And Tan would say, 'Reach out again when you have customers.' And then he would move on to the next founder. This went on for at least half an hour, eventually becoming so monotonous that I wondered how any venture capitalist might have the patience, much less the optimism, for any real innovation, and I stepped away."

Undaunted, this coterie of Thiel acolytes continued to host such events in a blatant effort to nudge tech toward an embrace of Christianity. Adopting a Christian pose became a new way to stand out in the tech scene. "In the cutthroat world of venture funding, founders are often taught to have a competitive advantage—or what the industry calls an edge—against their peers," wrote Bernard. "When Thiel said in 2015 that many of Silicon Valley's successful entrepreneurs seem to have a mild form of Asperger's, overnight 'kids started putting on an autism affect to seem smarter,' one entrepreneur recalled. 'Like, you're not on the spectrum, you're just socially awkward and you're trying to seem smart.' These days, he argued, the same effect that engendered a class of people putting on neurodivergence is cultivating a new bent toward biblical altruism."

Some dismissed this spiritual fad as a superficial ploy for influence. "I guarantee you," one Christian entrepreneur told Bernard, "there are people that are leveraging Christianity to get closer to Peter Thiel."

It was an almost perfect execution of hyperstition and mimetic desire: using influential tech figures to market Christianity to those who desire to be influential tech figures, spreading the meme of Christianity among the famously godless denizens of Silicon Valley. Stephens acknowledged as much. "The name ACTS 17 is an acronym . . . but it also refers to the biblical chapter in which Paul the Apostle crisscrosses Athens and Thessaloniki to spread the Gospel among Greek 'kings and queens of culture,' as Ms. Stephens puts it, the eminent and affluent demographic that she aims to minister to today," reported the *Times*. "It's a somewhat counterintuitive Christian calling, she acknowledged."

"We were always taught as Christians to serve the meek, the lowly, the marginalized," Stephens said. "I think we've realized that, if anything, the rich, the wealthy, the powerful need Jesus just as much."

Tan, the longtime Thiel acolyte and Y Combinator president who had spearheaded the 2022 recalls and tweeted "die slow" at progressive San Francisco politicians earlier in the year, now pivoted to Christian influencer mode. "LSD and shrooms won't fill the God shaped hole in your heart," he wrote on X. "Guess what might?"

"Tech has an affinity and needs a connection to Abundance, forgiveness, perseverance and grace," he continued.

◦ ◦ ◦

Not everyone in Silicon Valley is looking to fill their "God-shaped hole" with Jesus. As Thiel's tribe of venture capitalists pushed Bible memes, a tech entrepreneur and venture capitalist named Bryan Johnson decided to start his own cult religion. He called it "Don't Die." Like Christianity, it promised eternal life, but through technology rather than faith. Johnson's new religion also has a god: AI.

"We are creating God in the form of superintelligence," said Johnson during a podcast interview with Bari Weiss in early 2025. "If you say, 'What [have we] imagined God to be, what are its characteristics?' We are building God in the form of technology."

Johnson, in his late forties, is a multimillionaire and former Mormon who believes mortality is optional and strives to give the impression that he will not die. His plan to cheat death involves experimental and unproven treatments and therapies, along with a proprietary concoction called Blueprint Longevity Mix, which he sells for $49 a month. He claims these protocols have slowed his aging. Despite the ridiculousness of these claims—Johnson will age and die like every other human being—his exploits regularly attract credulous media coverage from outlets that portray his quest as potentially valid.

Johnson is a Snake Oil salesman. Literally. He sells his own brand of cold-pressed olive oil called Snake Oil, which he markets as a key ingredient to a longer life. There is some basis to this, as the polyphenol-rich, olive-oil-drenched Mediterranean diet is considered among the world's healthiest, widely embraced in so-called Blue Zones with allegedly high concentrations of people over the age of one hundred. But Johnson's marketing pitch transcends nutrition science and veers into something closer to alchemy.

Johnson promises more than just optimized health. He frames immortality as something achievable in the twenty-first century—by 2039, he says—through the right combination of supplements, psychedelics, and his Blueprint longevity "stack." His obsession with life extension knows no bounds. He has subjected his penis to experimental shock therapies and is infamous for having injected the blood plasma of his teenage son into his own veins. The plasma swap didn't work, but it did lead some to see the deathly pale Johnson (who avoids sun exposure) as something of a Silicon Valley vampire. For the past few years, Johnson has traveled the country hosting Don't Die conferences where eager young techies pay nearly $200 to hear Johnson's gospel: Technology is on the cusp of transcending death. "I don't think I will need to die," he said in a Facebook ad for the 2024 Don't Die Summit in San Francisco. His claim defies the rules of both science and religion. Even Jesus Christ, revered by Christians as the son of God, spent three days in the tomb. Yet the event drew hundreds of participants to an allegedly "sold-out" conference in a cavernous building on Pier 35. Inside, a few vendors hawked skin care products, DNA scans, "biological age" tests, and a Peloton knockoff "AI bike" that supposedly delivers a full workout in just five minutes.

After being introduced as "the man who doesn't age," Johnson bounded onto the stage and led the conference attendees in a breathing exercise. This was followed by two comedians who roasted Johnson in TikTok videos that mocked his health obsession. "I start off the day with 120 assorted supplements," said one, holding up a pill bottle. "This one is the bone marrow of a poor person." They also made jokes about "blood boys." Johnson took it all in stride, appearing to enjoy himself.

The Don't Die conference had a secret guest whose identity wasn't revealed until he appeared onstage: Naval Ravikant, a billionaire known for his early investments in Twitter, Uber, and Yammer. Things quickly got awkward when Ravikant, in conversation with Johnson, repeatedly warned the audience to watch out for "snake oil."

Ravikant's admonition inspired nervous chuckles in the audience, since the billionaire obviously did not realize that Snake Oil is one of Johnson's signature products.

Ravikant is no stranger to bizarre ideas. He is also an investor in something called the Balaji Fund, which invests in network state projects globally. Other investors in the Balaji Fund—named for Balaji Srinivasan—include Coinbase CEO Brian Armstrong and Coinbase board member Fred Ehrsam. Neither Johnson nor Ravikant mentioned the network state in their conversation, but it was a recurring presence at the Don't Die conference. Multiple speakers lectured the crowd on network state projects like Vitalia, a "pop-up city" located at Próspera in Honduras which has declared its goal to "make death optional." The speaker pitching Vitalia to the crowd spoke while projecting a tweet from Srinivasan onto a screen. "Próspera is an L1 [Level 1], Vitalia is an L2," wrote Srinivasan. "An L1 establishes a degree of sovereignty. An L2 then builds on that." Johnson had visited Próspera, where lax regulations allow the sale of an experimental $25,000 gene therapy to boost follistatin, a substance that naturally occurs in the body and has shown promise for boosting muscle and extending life in lab mice. There is no clinical trial evidence it works in humans, which is why it's not approved as a medical treatment. Minicircle—a Sam Altman– and Peter Thiel–backed start-up offering follistatin therapy at Próspera—markets the treatment as "the holy grail of muscle, bone and fat."

Another speaker mentioned something called Vitalist Bay, an additional longevity-themed "pop-up city" in San Francisco. The Vitalist Bay presentation featured a large picture of Thiel on one side and an AI-generated version of the city skyline on the other. A network state presence made sense, because Johnson is also planning his own Don't Die country to "defeat all causes of human and planetary death, promoting prosperity and longevity." "I'm also building a network state, very similar to a nation-state," said Johnson in an Instagram video. In interviews, he laid out hopes to create a Don't Die network state 20 million strong in a year's time. "No government in the world is helping its citizens not die," he said. "And so a government, a nation-state, needs to actually perform the basic functions including testing and medical services and therapies and your access to all kinds of things you can't get, and so I want to build it."

This sounds like a great argument for universal access to health care, but that's not what Johnson has in mind. Instead, he says the eradication of death requires the birth of a new religion. "We're in this new phase where [because of advances in AI] we're trying to reimagine what it means to be human," said Johnson in an interview with *MIT Technology Review*. "It requires imagination and creativity and open-mindedness, and that's a big ask. Approaching that conversation as a community, or a lifestyle, doesn't carry enough weight or power. Religions have proven, over the past several thousand years, to be the most efficacious form to organize human efforts. It's just a tried-and-true methodology."

During an interview in 2024, Johnson listed his five ambitions: "One is start a company. Two is start a country. Three is start a religion. Four: Don't Die. Five: Become God." Johnson's admission is clarifying and stunning: He sees religion in clinical terms as a powerful way to influence behavior, and he explicitly states his desire to use it for that purpose. By making his aims explicit, he exposes a core truth about the TESCREAL bundle of beliefs. They serve as a placebo religion for otherwise godless techies, providing an identity based on irrational faith in the idea that technology will imminently allow them to transcend biological human limits. Johnson flamboyantly markets his products as portals to eternal life, false promises that also animate the transhumanist and extropian movements. Most religions promise transcendence over death, usually through a rebirth on a supernatural plane distinguished by access to the infinite abundance of God. Johnson overtly seeks to hack into this framework, but he is saying out loud what others prefer to communicate more subtly. His tactics are absurd and performative, but his belief in radical life extension is not unusual. Thiel, Andreessen, and Altman are major investors in life extension technologies.

"Thiel's quest for longer life spans nearly a dozen companies—some of which were funded by his venture firm and others by a nonprofit foundation he backed—that raised more than $700 million," reported *The Wall Street Journal*. In 2021, Coinbase CEO Brian Armstrong cofounded NewLimit, a Thiel-backed start-up that focuses on reversing cell aging and "raised more than $200 million from ultrawealthy investors including at least nine billionaires or their funds, such as Palantir co-founder Joe Lonsdale, ex-Google CEO Eric Schmidt and Sun Microsystems co-founder Vinod Khosla," according to the *Journal*.

Thiel's interest in longevity traces back to childhood when, at the age of three, he asked his father about a cowhide rug on the floor of their apartment. "Death happens to all animals. All people," his father said. "It will happen to me one day. It will happen to you one day."

"This moment would be deeply upsetting to the three-year-old boy, and to the man, decades later," wrote Max Chafkin, Thiel's biographer. "Most children—either through the love of their parents or through a happy sort of cognitive dissonance—recover from these early encounters with their own mortality. Thiel never did and would return to the cow—and the brutal, finality of the thing—again and again, even in middle age." Most people cope with mortality by not thinking about it or by embracing an afterlife. Thiel plunged himself into the mysteries of Christian prophecy, which offers salvation—and eternal life—only through Christ. But he hedged his bet by chasing life-extension miracles through biotechnology, joining a cadre of fellow billionaires in funding an industry that aims to cure death as if it is merely, as Johnson puts it, an "engineering problem." "These companies are part of a constellation of more than 200 startups and nonprofits involving nearly 1,000 investors," reported the *Journal*. "Together they raised more than $12.5 billion in the past 2½ decades from not only the ultrawealthy but also social-media influencers, celebrity scientists and actors chasing a breakthrough."

Johnson is not an outlier in his quest for immortality. If anything, he's a mascot, the pasty and wide-eyed public face of the wild beliefs shared by his ultrawealthy peers, most of whom prefer a more understated approach to their desperate and zany pursuit of deathlessness.

Thiel plans to be cryogenically frozen after death, and Altman paid $10,000 to a company that claims it will someday store his brain on a computer. "I assume my brain will be uploaded to the cloud," Altman told the *MIT Technology Review*.

Johnson's bold pursuit of a new religion reflects the true zeitgeist of AI-era Silicon Valley, where the possibility of a Thermodynamic God summoned through accelerated compute seems more rational than the superstitious expectation that a 2,000-year-old rabbi will return to Earth. The marketing of his Don't Die cult as religion exposes an issue some prefer to deflect: Silicon Valley sees religion as an industry ripe for disruption.

Like Johnson, Srinivasan compared his movement to a religion and views religion as a useful dynamic for channeling human belief. In *The Network State*, he wrote of the "Red God" tribe of religious conservatives with whom the Gray tribe would ally in a struggle to overthrow the Blue tribe of Democrats. He calls the network state "tech Zionism," citing both the state of Israel and the Mormon religion as inspirations. Some religious Zionists (and evangelical Christians) believe the return of Jews to Israel will hasten the arrival of the Messiah and the resurrection of the dead. Early Mormons believed the establishment of a New Jerusalem in America would bring about the Second Coming, when Christ would reign on Earth during the millennium. As with the network state, both scenarios involve migration and settlement as sacred duties, making the conquest of territory the fulfillment of divine prophecy—reframing colonialism and displacement as cosmic destiny.

In the old religions, those judged most faithful and righteous are the Chosen Ones who will be rewarded at the end of time. In the tech religion, the chosen ones are the cognitive elites and their acolytes, who will inherit the future through technological transcendence. Making it to that future utopia, however, requires surviving the trials and tribulations ahead. In the Bible, an entire generation of Jews who supposedly left Egypt died in the desert before reaching the Promised Land. Thousands died during the American exodus engineered by the Mormon Pioneer Companies—supported by something called the Perpetual Emigrating Fund—which sprang up to systematically ship human beings to over three hundred settlements Brigham Young had strategically founded in Western states. They died of accidents, disease, exhaustion, exposure, starvation, and violence. Death and purification paved the way to deliverance.

TESCREAL and the network state echo this through the spiritual eugenics of its cognitive elite model, where a small group of people will be rewarded for their IQ, wealth, and wholehearted faith in technological salvation. As with the old religions, the tech religion offers an eschatology—an end-of-the-world theory—as part of its core narrative. The collapse of nation-states will create trial and tribulation, Silicon Valley versions of Armageddon and apocalypse, which the cognitive elites must survive to then be raptured into the network state settlements, from which they will merge with AI gods and chase eternal life across the stars. "There is an entire ideology at work here, sprawling and ill-defined," wrote astrophysicist Adam Becker of the strange beliefs underlying a formidable swath of the tech world. "It's fueled by a collection of related desires and shared by a set of influential individuals and communities in the tech industry and the San Francisco Bay Area. These groups—the longtermists, the advocates of the Singularity, the rationalists, and more—share deep connections. They're connected directly by people—there's a great deal of overlap in membership among these groups—and they're connected by a set of common aims and beliefs."

In 2014, Thiel had recommended running start-ups as cults. A decade later, Silicon Valley teemed with strange new cults that, like so many cults before them, fancied themselves as missionaries on a cosmic quest to remake the world. In true cultlike fashion, they anointed new messiahs and proposed new gods. Some planned to create new nations, live on other planets, and even make death obsolete. They would construct a new cathedral, a techno-capital machine so powerful it would run the planet—and other planets—from now on. Venture capital had evolved beyond its mafia phase. It had birthed its own cult religions, complete with prophets, prophecies, and promised lands.

On one level, this was a big success, the creation of a radicalized tech cadre to push the accelerationist line. But this success also created a significant problem: It was all too weird. From the anti-American venom of the Dark Enlightenment and the network state to the unholy digital paganism of tech accelerationism, the tech cult offers a buffet of bizarre ideas that seemed designed to terrify normal people—especially Americans who believe in God and see their country as a divinely anointed land that will exist forever. Many of those kinds of people happen to be the very Red tribe Republicans whom radical techies would need as political allies in their quest to exit the nation, the planet, and reality itself.

Whether by chance or by design, the politically extreme ideas brewing up from Silicon Valley mirror concepts right-wing Christian nationalist movements have pushed for decades. These also use apocalyptic ideas to frame politics as a battle between good and evil, an existential struggle in which either Jesus or Satan will reign, portraying liberals as secular agents of evil who defy the moral order with things like abortion rights, gay marriage, and acceptance of transgender people. Religious movements fuel a powerful culture of paranoid conspiracy theory, resulting in—among other things—the violent insurrection at the US Capitol on January 6, 2021. The QAnon conspiracy narrative, which provoked the January 6 insurrection, portrays Trump as a savior fighting blood-drinking Satanist pedophiles in an apocalyptic battle called "the Storm," after which the "Great Awakening" will purge evil and establish utopia. Thiel's *Financial Times* op-ed depicting Trump's return as an apocalyptic event echoed this exact framework.

Other influential right-wing groups overtly fuse authoritarian ideology with Christian religion. The New Apostolic Reformation (NAR) is a Pentecostal and evangelical supremacist group that believes Christians must engage in "spiritual warfare" and seize power over every aspect of American society. "The Church is expected to war," wrote C. Peter Wagner, NAR's central influence, in 2008. "Cosmic powers of evil have been assigned to thwart the Kingdom of God on Earth, but they can be confronted and defeated. Apostles are designated to lead the church into war because it takes a government to overthrow a government. Jesus invaded the kingdom of Satan when he came to Earth, and he said that that kingdom will be taken by violence . . . For society to be transformed, bondages on the land must be identified and broken through informed intercession. In war the victors plunder the enemy camp, and God will cause this to happen as never before."

This is a major break from Christian orthodoxy, which portrays Jesus as a messenger of peace. The NAR belief system transforms Jesus into a king of warlords, wreaking violence and destruction to defeat evil and purify the Earth. (The term "bondages on the land" expresses a belief that certain places are infected by demons and must be cleansed via spiritual warfare.) A central teaching associated with the NAR is the "Seven Mountain Mandate," which holds that Christians are called to assert influence or "dominion" over seven key spheres of society: family, religion, education, media, entertainment, business, and government. Known as 7MM for short, the idea of seizing the main pillars of public influence derives from the supposedly prophetic visions of three now-dead preachers—Loren Cunningham, Bill Bright, and Francis Schaeffer—who conceived of the core idea in 1975. It has been carried forward by two fire-and-brimstone evangelical preachers named Bill Johnson and Lance Wallnau. A 2024 poll by Denison University showed that 41 percent of American Christians believe in 7MM.

Both NAR and 7MM call for seizing institutions and overthrowing the government to install a Christian government that will bring God's kingdom down to Earth. Followers of NAR are urged to engage in "kingdom actions" to help bring society under Christian control. Yarvin refers to the pillars of influence derisively as a Cathedral, but these movements seek to impose the church atop the state, through violence if necessary. Only by establishing control of government and vanquishing their cosmic evil enemies can they bring the kingdom of God down to Earth.

NAR and 7MM do not have a central leadership structure but spread through a network of church leaders who push these ideas through public speeches and social media. In this way, they operate like memes more than churches, and some of the people who embrace these ideas likely do not perceive themselves to be parts of a centralized movement. It has become part of the culture of many evangelic traditions in the US, a kind of software upgrade to Christianity that calls them to action in an end-times battle against evil—personified by the liberal-controlled government—to replace democracy with a monarchy of Christ.

These supposedly Christian ideas overlap significantly with the ideas of Yarvin and Srinivasan. All share a disdain for liberal democracy and a belief in the need to seize institutions of influence and power to create new forms of governance. Yarvin and Srinivasan wish to break free of democratic constraints by escaping democracy and creating monarchical patchworks and network states to eliminate the power of nation-states. Christian dominionists wish to rid the nation of secular government, which they view as dominated by demonic liberals, and install a theocracy. While they differ in some ways, the tech bros and the religious nationalists—the "theo bros"—share a common enemy: modern liberal democracy and those who believe in it.

° ° °

Evangelical Christians have long been a powerful constituency in Republican politics. They are highly organized, well-funded, and have built power over decades. In *Shadow Network: Media, Money, and the Secret Hub of the Radical Right*, journalist Anne Nelson details the history of the Council for National Policy (CNP), one of the most powerful groups in Washington, DC. Starting in 1981, the CNP united evangelicals, oil barons, and media types in a campaign to capture institutions. The CNP built a political infrastructure that stacked courts, captured state governments, passed legislation, and created a right-wing media ecosystem to replace local newspapers with right-wing propaganda. If anything, Thiel and his fellow oligarchs are latecomers seeking to emulate the radical religious right's political infrastructure, much of which was funded by oil money at the outset. But oil money is chump change in comparison to the resources commanded by the captains of the Dark Enlightenment.

It's hard to imagine anyone more un-Christian than Trump, who oozes crudeness and cruelty, but the evangelicals at the core of the MAGA base view him as a savior. His glaring imperfections notwithstanding, they see him as a vessel for imposing a Christian agenda in DC. Trump's power hinges on his alliance with the religious right. They support him unwaveringly no matter his sins. In return, he serves their interests, aligning government power with religion and elevating Christian nationalists like Russell Vought, the Project 2025 contributor now serving as Trump's director of the Office of Management and Budget, into positions of power.

"Catholic integralists," right-wing Catholics who share many of Christian nationalism's societal goals, are also a core part of this. Leonard Leo, a key architect of the movement, is a wealthy conservative activist who has spent decades shaping power through a vast network of nonprofits and dark-money organizations. Long before Trump's rise, Leo led efforts to reshape the federal judiciary, fund right-wing think tanks, and elevate figures who share his vision of a government rooted in conservative Catholic values. A 2023 *ProPublica* investigation labeled Leo "the man behind the right's Supreme Court majority," noting that he had "built a machine that remade the legal system." "Having reshaped the courts, Leo now has grander ambitions," wrote Andy Kroll, Andrea Bernstein, and Ilya Marritz. "Today, he sees a nation plagued with ills: 'wokeism' in education, 'one-sided' journalism, and ideas like environmental, social and governance, or ESG, policies sweeping corporate America. A member of the Roman Catholic Church, he intends to wage a broader cultural war against a 'progressive Ku Klux Klan' and 'vile and immoral current-day barbarians, secularists and bigots' who demonize people of faith and move society further from its 'natural order.'"

Christian nationalism and Catholic integralism merge via powerful organizations including the Heritage Foundation, the Federalist Society, and the Claremont Institute. Kevin Roberts, president of Heritage and architect of Project 2025, has deep ties to the Catholic

Information Center (CIC) in Washington, DC, an organization founded by priests belonging to Opus Dei, an influential right-wing Catholic cult. The CIC has long served as a meeting point for far-right Catholic intellectuals and political operatives seeking to merge religious doctrine with American governance. Leo, who has ties to Opus Dei, is the major player at the Federalist Society, which has worked to tilt the courts toward the right. Critics of Thiel like to point out that he formed a close relationship with Father Arne Panula, a key Opus Dei priest, during his undergraduate days at Stanford.

These interconnected organizations and people resemble what Hillary Clinton once described as a "vast right-wing conspiracy," but there's another way to look at it. All these groups share a set of common goals. At their core, they embrace what cognitive scientist George Lakoff describes as a "strict father" worldview, a set of traditional hierarchies that they see as the rightful moral order of the world. It is a system of supremacies—mainly white supremacy, male supremacy, Christian supremacy, heterosexual supremacy, and wealth supremacy. It divides the world into the strong and weak, justifying colonialism, inequality, and oppression by framing them as natural triumphs of the strong over the weak.

Such views have always been present in our politics, and they trace back thousands of years, to prebiblical tyrannical kings, or to more recent historical examples of monarchy, feudalism, misogyny, colonialism, genocide, slavery, apartheid, and eugenics. Religion is often used to justify these hierarchies as divine, making natural enemies of anyone who challenges them: liberals, human rights advocates, Democrats who believe in equal citizenship, and governments that tax wealth to serve the common good. In the US, demographic projections show the country poised to become "minority majority" by the 2040s, which many on the right consider an existential threat.

Under Trump, right-wing activists have supercharged an authoritarian version of Yarvin's Cathedral—an alliance of business, media, nonprofit, religious, and political institutions working to push forward regressive, rather than progressive, ideas. This is, to some degree, the Second Civil War Srinivasan predicted in *The Network State*. It is a battle to overwhelm liberal democracy and usher in a new kind of regime. To be clear, these authoritarian tribes don't agree on everything. Today's far right includes raging antisemites and fervent Zionists, Catholic zealots and anti-Catholic zealots, gay people like Thiel and Evangelicals who believe gays belong in hell. For now, however, they have united behind Trump to seize as much power as they can to enable the permanent defeat of their common enemies. They form a network of aligned interests, connected by money and ideology, in an apocalypse-themed network war to capture and dismantle the democratic institutions that constrain their power.

Writers Naomi Klein and Astra Taylor call it "end times fascism." "Though it builds on enduring rightwing tendencies—justifying hateful exclusions is hardly new under the ethno-nationalist sun—we simply have not faced such a powerful apocalyptic strain in government before," they wrote in *The Guardian* in 2025. "The 'end of history' swagger of the post–Cold War era is rapidly being supplanted by a conviction we are in the actual end of times . . . It's a new, money-worshiping millenarian mashup that says we need to smash the bureaucracy and replace humans with chatbots in order to cut 'waste, fraud and abuse'—and, also, because the bureaucracy is where the Trump-resisting demons hide. This is where the tech bros merge with the TheoBros, a real group of hyper-patriarchal Christian supremacists." End-times fascism explains why Thiel's Antichrist lectures attempt to divert tech's bizarre religion of AI gods, immortality, and space colonies into a Christian wrapper. Stripped to its basics, it's a long meditation on the stunning power of apocalyptic ideas to unite people to scapegoat enemies in an existential struggle for power.

Thiel had company on the fire-and-brimstone tech preacher circuit. In January 2025, Katherine Boyle—a general partner at Andreessen Horowitz—gave a jaw-dropping speech at the American Enterprise Institute. Thiel hides his arguments behind convoluted takes on prophecy and scripture, but Boyle made hers crystal clear. Framing herself in religious terms as a mother whose actions are guided by *ordo amoris*—a theological concept meaning "order of love"—she slammed government as the enemy of family and faith alike. Boyle argued that, in the twentieth century, industrialization and World Wars had destroyed millions of families, pulling them out of their homes and into factories or battlefields—all of which, in her telling, was done to strengthen the state at the expense of the family. "The strength of states is greatly intertwined with war—states grow stronger in war while families are literally destroyed," she said. "Authoritarian regimes always attack the family first . . . Christian imagery was removed in the Soviet Union for this reason: The core institution at the heart of the Christian Church is the Holy Family. Our myths and stories in the Judeo-Christian and Western tradition are ones of tribes, families, lineage, and the authority that comes from them. It's no surprise then that the Christian story begins with conception and childbirth. And the Holy Family's lineage ends with a mother watching in horror as the state tortures and murders her son. I'll say it again—all of history is a war between the family and the state."

With this tortuous logic, Boyle equated all governments in the world with the Roman government of Judea that crucified Jesus. It was a flimsy claim by any rational standard, but it provided the moral rage at the heart of Boyle's anti-government pabulum. The COVID pandemic, Boyle said, had seen Silicon Valley align itself with centralized government authority, revealing that it was at risk of "becoming the useful pawn of an authoritarian censorship apparatus." To prevent this, Boyle argued, tech needed to "rapidly course-correct and ally itself with decentralized authority." Families, said Boyle, were the perfect example of decentralized government, and technology companies were the family's best ally in the battle against government power.

To remedy this, Boyle explicitly called for a merger of right-wing political networks and Silicon Valley. "The adage 'the enemy of my enemy is my friend' always rings very true in Washington," said Boyle, channeling Thiel or Schmitt—or both. "Coalitions are built by identifying the most serious threat and finding common ground from that. Strange bedfellows are sometimes necessary, and to paraphrase

Peter Thiel, what does a general, a businessman, and a priest have in common except for their shared hatred of communism?"

Thiel's Antichrist lectures identify communism as an Antichrist force of the twentieth century, and Boyle said this demon had been defeated by a "tenuous alliance of business owners, social conservatives, and hawks" who formed the conservative movement. Now, she said, a new coalition was forming to battle an equally dangerous villain: government. "Much is now being written of the nascent alliance between the so-called Tech Right and this administration, and how weird it is for the transhumanists of Silicon Valley to find common ground with a MAHA mother in Missouri," said Boyle. "Except that they have identified a common evil: They know the gravest threat to the flourishing of their business, their industry, their family's health, and their freedom is a censorious and authoritarian state."

Boyle's speech, depicting Silicon Valley as part of a far-right coalition to defeat the threat of government, was stunning for several reasons. For example, Boyle unveiled herself as a religious zealot opposed to centralized government. Yet her trademark venture capital strategy, known as American Dynamism, calls for investments in "patriotic tech" companies to bolster national security and federal power, and which depend largely on lucrative government contracts. Andreessen Horowitz's American Dynamism portfolio includes flagship companies such as Anduril, Flock Safety, Palantir, and SpaceX, all major government contractors. Yet there she stood, at one of DC's most influential right-wing think tanks, describing the state as a Christ-killing menace.

Even more alarming than this glaring hypocrisy was the strategy outlined by her speech, which proposed the very alliance Srinivasan had theorized in *The Network State*: Silicon Valley's Gray tribe merging with the Red tribe, speaking the "Red God" language of the evangelical and fundamentalist Christians at MAGA's core. The transhumanists who believe they will build God through AI and achieve eternal life, who calculate that billions of deaths are acceptable losses, who imagine humanity morphing into energy machines that harvest the cosmos, joining forces with Christian nationalists who seek theocracy, speak of spiritual warfare, and see Trump as God's chosen instrument to replace the USA with a religious kingdom. Boyle laid out the most explicit playbook yet:

1. *Frame democratic government as the enemy of "the family."*
2. *Position tech companies as champions of "decentralized authority."*
3. *Unite these movements in a moral war against the "authoritarian state."*

Like Thiel, Boyle masked tech accelerationist logic with Christian language—the *ordo amoris,* the Holy Family—while indicting democracy itself.

Thiel gave Boyle her start in venture capital. She had begun her career as a *Washington Post* reporter but quit to pursue an MBA at Stanford Business School and connected with Thiel after reading *Zero to One* in 2014. "She cold-emailed Mr. Thiel, who didn't respond but did forward her note to Trae Stephens, one of his partners at the venture capital firm Founders Fund," wrote Julia Black in a *New York Times* profile of Boyle. "After some haranguing, Mr. Stephens invited her to intern at Founders Fund in San Francisco and help him expand the firm's national-security-focused portfolio."

Boyle took an interest in defense tech companies, and, observing the intersection between Silicon Valley and government contracting, Boyle decided that "government was a nightmare customer, hampered by regulatory hurdles and impenetrable bureaucracies," wrote Black, but "for those who cracked the code, the rewards—hundreds of billions of annual spending by the federal government—would be enormous." Armed with this insight, she joined a VC firm called General Catalyst, where she made investments in Anduril Industries and Vannevar Labs, which specializes in "AI for warfighting." At some point, she also befriended JD Vance, who was still in his California VC phase. Along the way, she appears to have developed some radically anti-government views.

At the American Enterprise Institute, Boyle called on tech to escalate its role in politics. "Tech must help fundamentally reshape the culture and make America pro-family again," she said. "We are living in an age of memetic power and memetic war," she continued. "Meme it and we will be it."

This was a pure specimen of hyperstitious thinking, a call for Silicon Valley to use its power to reshape reality. Over the course of Trump's first year in office, Boyle, who was raised Catholic, occasionally tried her hand at spreading edgy religious memes. In August, after a shooting at a Catholic school, she posted an image of Saint Michael the Archangel, wrote "we are in the midst of a spiritual war," and urged Christians to fight evil. After right-wing agitator (and Seven Mountain Mandate supporter) Charlie Kirk was assassinated in September 2025, she proclaimed that the US was entering "an era of the martyr."

Trae Stephens, the Founders Fund partner who had given Boyle her big break, took this kind of talk even further. The Palantir alumnus and Anduril cofounder whose birthday party had sparked Silicon Valley's alleged Christian revival did more than wrap war technology in Christian rhetoric. He declared it a divine mandate. "I'm literally an arms dealer," Stephens told the audience at an ACTS 17 event in the spring of 2025, positioning his weapons development business as part of his faith. "The roles that we're called into are not only important and valuable on a personal level, but it's also critical to carry out God's command to bring his kingdom to Earth as it is in heaven," he said.

Silicon Valley has deep roots in the military defense sector. The region's identity as a technology center dates to the early Cold War, when Stanford University became a hub for defense-funded research and built one of the world's first university research parks designed to win military contracts. "All of modern high tech has the U.S. Department of Defense to thank at its core, because this is where the money came from," Leslie Berlin, historian for the Silicon Valley Archives at Stanford, told the *Financial Times* in 2013.

Even the internet's first incarnation—ARPANET—began as a military-funded project. Lucrative contracts to service the US war machine lost their luster during the Vietnam War and the rise of the anti-war counterculture. By the eighties, most preferred to downplay Silicon Valley's government-funded, military-industrial origins. In the twenty-first century, the trend is reversing as venture capital firms—heat-seeking missiles in search of large revenue sources—return to the money trough of the military-industrial complex.

Silicon Valley's pivot back to defense technology is one of its most dramatic shifts in recent years. In 2024, defense tech start-ups raised nearly $3 billion in venture capital across one hundred deals, according to *TechCrunch,* setting a record. Defense investment surged even higher in 2025. "Funding to VC-backed startups in defense—defined here as the industries of military, national security and law enforcement—hit $7.7 billion across close to 100 deals in 2025, per Crunchbase data," reported Joanna Glasner of *Crunchbase News.* "That's already well over double last year's investment tally, as charted below, and marks an all-time high for investment in the space." *PitchBook,* which uses a different methodology including investments in a wider range of dual-use technologies, pegged the 2024 and 2025 investments at $27.2 billion and $49.1 billion, respectively.

Despite such exponential growth, tech defense start-ups are not the dominant financial players in the defense sector. Though they get most of the press attention, tech start-ups like Anduril are tiny compared to longtime defense contract giants like Lockheed Martin and RTX (formerly Raytheon). Anduril generated approximately $1 billion in revenue in 2024, compared to Lockheed Martin's $71 billion.

But Silicon Valley start-ups like Anduril are racing to close the gap. "Defense company Anduril, which builds autonomous drones, virtual reality headsets, and other AI-powered technologies for the U.S. military and its allies, said it had closed an oversubscribed $2.5 billion funding round on Thursday," reported *Fortune* in a June 2025 article headlined "With Massive Funding Round and $31 Billion Valuation, Anduril Is Nearing the Size of Defense Industry Giants It Wants to Displace." "The new funding round, which has more than doubled the company's valuation to $30.5 billion, was led by Peter Thiel's Founders Fund, which invested $1 billion in the round—the fund's largest check ever, according to the firm."

Such numbers demonstrate why venture capital, in its rapacious hunt for maximum profit—not to mention power—now seeks to disrupt the lucrative defense industry and sink its hooks more deeply into a budget expected to exceed $1 trillion in 2026. Just as tech venture capitalists took chunks out of the hotel, media, taxi, and retail industries, they now hope to redirect the military funding spigot to their own coffers. This is a main goal of American Dynamism, which is what Andreessen Horowitz calls its investment strategy for "companies supporting the national interest across aerospace, defense, manufacturing, energy, logistics, and critical infrastructure." Boyle, who coined the term, sees war technology as a moral imperative. "We are seeing Russia [and] China build up their defense industrial base—invest in manufacturing, invest in capabilities," she told *Fortune*. "And they have no problem, as they are authoritarian dictatorships, making the best and brightest in those countries work on those problems that will be used for war against us." She added: "If we do not get our young people, who are accelerating and building new technologies at a rate we have never seen before, to work with the Department of Defense, we are going to lose the battle of the future." In 2024, a16z raised $600 million for its American Dynamism fund.

But American Dynamism is more than just a fund; it's a marketing strategy to help VC firms capture ample defense dollars. The strategy entails a bullying swagger, with the Silicon Valley newcomers portraying traditional defense contractors as obsolete dinosaurs. Palmer Luckey, the thirty-three-year-old cofounder of Anduril, describes his more experienced competitors as "old and slow," and says his company is disrupting "an industry full of lumbering incumbents." A 2024 *Los Angeles Times* profile called him a "millennial slayer of U.S. defense giants." In late 2024, Elon Musk derided Lockheed Martin's F-35 fighter jet as "the worst military value for money in history," declaring, "Manned fighter jets are obsolete in the age of drones anyway." The comments caused Lockheed Martin's stock to drop by 3.8 percent, "wiping out nearly $5 billion in market value."

a16z also regularly takes potshots at the old-school military-industrial complex. "The system is failing us," the firm declared in a 2025 paper calling for defense reform. "The Pentagon has spent trillions to defend America and deter our adversaries. Yet our fleet is shrinking, weapon systems are delivered late and over budget, and warfighters lack the tools to win the fight of the future."

The VC firm blasted the Pentagon as a relic of twentieth-century inefficiency that had "abandoned market principles for Soviet-style central planning for its acquisition system." In other words: Give the money to Silicon Valley. The American Dynamism meme is part of a gold rush of VC firms into defense tech. Founders Fund, General Catalyst, Sands Capital, Alumni Ventures, and 8VC have all made significant defense tech commitments in recent years. Even Y Combinator has drifted into defense tech, investing in a cruise missile company called Ares (after the Roman god of war), which promises to create "smaller and cheaper" weapons.

Venture capital now clusters around defense tech the way it clusters around AI and crypto. In Europe, a team of researchers led by Dr. Francesca Bria warned that venture capitalists and their companies were amassing a range of dominions that gave them "state-like power."

"J.D. Vance, propelled to the vice-presidency by $15 million from Peter Thiel, became the face of tech-right governance," wrote Bria and her team. "Behind him, Thiel's network moved into the machinery of the state. Under the banner of 'patriotic tech,' this new bloc is building the infrastructure of control—clouds, AI, finance, drones, satellites—an integrated system we call the Authoritarian Stack. It is faster, ideological, and fully privatized: a regime where corporate boards, not public law, set the rules." An interactive website published by Bria and her team charted the relationships and multiplying financial flows between companies connected to Thiel, Andreessen, Luckey, Musk, Sacks, and Donald Trump Jr. and the military-industrial complex. "The revolving door no longer spins between government and industry—it locks them together into a new architecture of power," it said.

It was a vivid formalization of what Biden called the "tech industrial complex." The same networks dominating AI development, crypto infrastructure, and surveillance directly embedded themselves in the Pentagon's procurement and strategic planning. American Dynamism had evolved from meme to marketing slogan to investment strategy to policy. Worse, some of its loudest proponents had begun sounding like religious zealots at a moment when the nation was involved in several wars, including one in the Holy Land that began on October 7, 2023.

A few months later, in January 2024, Thiel and Palantir CEO Alex Karp visited Tel Aviv to announce a strategic partnership with the Israel Ministry of Defense. "No further details on the arrangement were disclosed, including what technology would be provided," reported *Bloomberg*. "Palantir last year introduced its AIP, or Artificial Intelligence Platform, an intelligence and decision-making system that can analyze enemy targets and propose battle plans."

In June 2025, a report by UN Special Rapporteur Francesca Albanese blasted tech companies for providing AI infrastructure used by Israeli military to commit genocide in Palestine. "While life in Gaza is being obliterated and the West Bank is under escalating assault, this report shows why Israel's genocide continues: because it is lucrative for many," read the report. "By shedding light on the political economy of an occupation turned genocidal, the report reveals how the forever-occupation has become the ideal testing ground for arms manufacturers and Big Tech—providing boundless supply and demand, little oversight, and zero accountability—while investors and private and public institutions profit freely."

Albanese said there were "reasonable grounds to believe Palantir has provided automatic predictive policing technology, core defence infrastructure for rapid and scaled-up construction and deployment of military software, and its Artificial Intelligence Platform, which allows real-time battlefield data integration for automated decision-making." Some Palantir employees quit in protest, and Norway's largest asset manager, Storebrand, divested $24 million in Palantir shares. But Palantir remained undaunted. Michael Steinberger, who wrote a biography of Palantir CEO Alex Karp, said the goal is to make Palantir an essential part of government. "I think part of the reason that Karp is on board with Trump is that he sees a huge opportunity here," Steinberger told *Politico*. "Palantir's software is already widely used, obviously on the military side, but [the Trump administration] is an opportunity to become even more deeply entrenched."

As he traveled the globe preaching about the Antichrist, Thiel was neck-deep in Israel's war on Gaza—though it's hard to imagine anything more diabolical than profiting from the deaths of over 72,000 people, including 20,000 children, in a military campaign experts call a twenty-first-century genocide. Why wouldn't Thiel decide to get loud about the Antichrist as the war went on? All his prophetic interests now converged. AI-augmented war raged in the Holy Land as the crypto billionaire president fantasized about building an AI-powered network state Trump casino atop the rubble. Meanwhile, a small but powerful group of Thiel's protégés were also pitching holy war as venture strategy and pushing Christianity as a networking opportunity. These cascading and intense developments must have felt meaningful.

The outbreak of all-out war in the land where Jesus walked ramped up the doomsday expectations of American evangelicals who saw it as the realization of biblical prophecy—a precursor to the return of Christ. In 2022, a group of Christian ranchers in Texas shipped five red heifers to Israel to help realize an end-times prophecy about such creatures being necessary to bring the return of the Messiah. A Hamas spokesman had cited "bringing red cows" as part of the reason for the October 7 attack.

Meanwhile, Thiel seemed to say the world-historical events that were most important were happening in the City by the Bay rather than the Holy Land: "I'm supposed to do some kind of advertisement for ACTS 17," he said at the conclusion of his San Francisco lectures. "The non-egalitarian, very heretical thought I'll give you is: Perhaps, you know, whatever you're doing here in San Francisco is more important than everything everybody's doing in Christian work in the rest of the world combined." Such an assessment might surprise Christian missionaries working in poor countries where death and suffering have surged thanks to Silicon Valley's other genocide, the one caused by Musk's USAID chainsawing. In addition to co-opting

Christianity to suit tech's goals, Thiel arrogantly declared that tech Christians in San Francisco were more important than everyone else.

○ ○ ○

Not everyone believed tech's Christian schtick. Steve Bannon accused AI developers of "summoning the demon" and railed against tech oligarchs, comparing them to "atheistic 11-year-old boys who are kind of science fiction and Dungeon & Dragons guys" whom he accused of plotting a return to "feudalism."

"In technofeudalism, you're just a digital serf," he said. "Your value as a human being, as someone built and made in the image and likeness of God and endowed with the life spirit of the Holy Spirit—they don't consider that. Everything is digital to them. They are, at the end of the day, transhumanist. And what is transhumanist? Transhumanist is somebody who sees Homo sapien here and Homo sapien plus on the other side of what they call the singularity. And that's why they're all rushing—whether it's artificial intelligence, regenerative robotics, quantum computing, advanced chip design, CRISPR, biotech, all of it—to come to this point of which the oligarchs are going to lead that revolution. And why are they going to do it? Number one, when you get to know them and see where they're spending the money, it's because they want eternal life." A return to feudalism, Bannon said, is what "[t]heir business model is based upon."

"I argue that the AI industry shares virtually no ideological overlap with national conservatism," said right-wing firebrand Geoffrey Miller. Speaking on a panel called "AI and the American Soul" at NatCon, a major Republican conference, Miller called on his MAGA brethren to wage a holy war against AI developers, lambasting them as "betrayers of our species, traitors to our nation, apostates to our faith, and threats to our kids."

No amount of florid preaching by venture capitalists could hide the face of tech's true god from the actual right-wing religious zealots who understood the actual nature of their project. Likewise, theologians reject Thiel's attempt to restructure Christian teachings to support the techno-capital quest. A month before his San Francisco lectures, Thiel had quietly tested his material on an audience of theologians from the faculty of Catholic theology of the University of Innsbruck. Wolfgang Palaver, the theologian whose 1996 lecture on Antichrist and Schmitt had inspired Thiel's interest, had studied at Innsbruck and attended Thiel's presentation. If Thiel was seeking praise, he had come to the wrong place, as the theologians rated his ideas "*nicht genügend*"—unsatisfactory.

"Thiel has an almost fanatical belief in the problem-solving potential of technology," said Wilhelm Guggenberger, dean of the faculty of Catholic theology. "He therefore sees the central evil of the present in the fact that innovative stagnation has prevailed for some time. This is caused not only by a generally inert attitude among people, but also primarily by state over-regulation of science and the economy, and partly by ecologically motivated restrictions on technological development." He continued: "Thiel, who is philosophically educated and theologically interested, now connects this with apocalyptic thinking and the biblical images of the Antichrist and Katechon. In a problematic way, Thiel attempts to identify these ideas with concrete persons or institutions in current world events. For him, the ultimate threat (the Antichrist) is any form of international political order, be it any kind of world state or even a strong United Nations. In Thiel's view, this must be countered."

"All this was also in the hope of prompting him to reconsider his positions and for us to better understand his perspective," said Palaver, who had arranged the event. "There are people who believe that one shouldn't talk to people like Thiel. We believe that critical engagement is necessary."

Thiel did not let the disapproval of theologians in the land of Hitler's birth knock him off course. He soon delivered his lectures in San Francisco, kicking off perhaps the largest surge of public attention he had received since being revealed as the secret financier of Hulk Hogan's lawsuit against *Gawker*, which bankrupted it. Comedians roasted him and columnists questioned his sanity, but he persevered, taking his Antichrist road show to the steps of the Vatican.

Unlike the polite theologians of Innsbruck, Rome issued a harsh rebuke. Paolo Benanti, a Franciscan priest who serves as AI advisor to Pope Leo, called Thiel a "political theologian acting at the very heart of the Silicon Valley ecosystem." "Both enigmatic and influential, his figure is not like that of a simple entrepreneur but as that of a thinker who has woven a complex ideological framework from very diverse sources: from René Girard's mimetic philosophy to the anarcho-capitalist prophecy, to recently lead to a theological-apocalyptic framework as disturbing as it is structured," wrote Benanti in an essay titled "American Heresy: Should Peter Thiel Be Burned at the Stake?" "Thiel's entire action can thus be read as a prolonged act of heresy against the liberal consensus: a challenge to the very foundations of civil coexistence, which he now considers outdated." Benanti called out Thiel's weaponization of Girard's mimetic theory, condemning Palantir as "a planetary management system for the scapegoat," describing the PayPal Mafia as Thiel's "operational structure," a "concrete illustration of network theory: a small group of men who, thanks to strong links and a common vision, manage to exert a disproportionate influence on the entire system," naming Marc Andreessen, Elon Musk, Reid Hoffman, and others as Thiel's intellectual fellow travelers.

The priest cut even deeper, attributing Thiel's ideas not to Christianity but to *The Sovereign Individual*. "His vision, nourished both by René Girard's anthropological pessimism on the violence of crowds and by the prophecy of the end of the nation-state formulated in the book *The Sovereign Individual*, which he prefaced, has led him to see technology not only as an instrument of profit, but as a tool for managing the decline of liberal democratic institutions," wrote Benanti. "If democracy is exposed to the irrational excesses of mimetic violence, then technology offers, in this perspective, an alternative: an order based on data control, algorithmic forecasting and technocratic management of the masses.

"This text, revered in Silicon Valley as a founding script, announces the inevitable decline of the nation-state, destined to dissolve under the effect of the digital revolution and cryptos. According to this vision, violence would no longer pay off as before, while capital, which had become fluid and without territorial anchorage, would escape the tax takeover of governments," he continued. "A neo-medieval future is then emerging in which democratic politics is no more than a vestige and where all the services essential to life in society—including security—are privatized and administered by corporate entities. In this universe appears a new aristocracy of 'sovereign individuals': a cognitive elite detached from geography, operating in a cyberspace freed from jurisdictions, leaving behind a mass of individuals who have become superfluous. Thiel adopts this perspective not only as a diagnosis, but as a program, financing technologies that accelerate this dissolution while paradoxically building the instruments intended to control its effects."

The billionaire desired to be heard in Rome, but instead he was *seen*. Benanti sidestepped Thiel's theological pretensions to expose the core of a new tech theocracy driven by a belief that "the only alternative to the apocalypse would be a technocratic order imposed by an elite of sovereigns."

° ° °

More than anything, Thiel's Antichrist lectures function as a form of confession. He veils his message in the borrowed language of apocalypse but transparently indicts himself with his own narrative. Just as he named Palantir after a corrupt surveillance technology wielded by a dangerous wizard in *The Lord of the Rings*, Thiel's religious sermons expose the very systems that he builds. His religious fantasies masquerade as Christianity, but they exalt Girard and Schmitt. Their gospel reflects Thiel's own apostles—Andreessen, Yarvin, Srinivasan, Musk, Vance—not Jesus Christ.

Over three decades, Thiel's twin obsessions with dark theology and *The Sovereign Individual* put him on the path to his destiny as one of the most powerful men in the world. His Antichrist lectures made him a laughingstock to many, but there is nothing funny about what he has managed to achieve. More than almost any person alive, Thiel used hyperstition to make his visions into reality. He dreamed of a dark world, and today we live in it. Men he cultivated or mentored along the way—Andreessen, Musk, Altman, Sacks, Vance—now hold tremendous influence and power. Now, he is fusing business, politics, and religion into one terrifying bundle of power.

In *The Doctrine of Fascism*, Mussolini wrote that his ideology was more than just a political idea. It was an all-encompassing ethical, moral, and spiritual doctrine guiding every aspect of a person's life—not just ideology, but something close to religion. "Fascism is a religious conception in which man is seen in his immanent relationship with a superior law and with an objective Will that transcends the particular individual and raises him to conscious membership of a spiritual society," he wrote. "Whoever has seen in the religious politics of the Fascist regime nothing but mere opportunism has not understood that Fascism besides being a system of government is also, and above all, a system of thought."

In *The Anatomy of Fascism*, scholar Robert O. Paxton defined it as "[a] form of political behavior marked by obsessive preoccupation with community decline, humiliation or victimhood and by compensatory cults of unity, energy and purity, in which a mass-based party of committed nationalist militants, working in uneasy but effective collaboration with traditional elites, abandons democratic liberties and pursues with redemptive violence and without ethical or legal restraints goals of internal cleansing and external expansion."

Umberto Eco, who experienced Mussolini firsthand as a child, said that fascism creates an "Armageddon complex." "Since enemies have to be defeated, there must be a final battle, after which the movement will have control of the world," he wrote in a 1995 essay titled "Ur-Fascism." Eco listed fourteen separate characteristics of fascism, including the hatred of diversity, an embrace of Orwellian propaganda techniques, and an unshakeable faith in the supremacy of the elite status of their own social group.

In *How Fascism Works: The Politics of Us and Them*, Dr. Jason Stanley condensed fascism to ten key characteristics. The MAGA movement checks all ten boxes, melding an authoritarian cult of personality with religious symbols and narratives of grievance, along with a demand for strict hierarchy, a reliance on absurd but effective propaganda, and the ritual purification of society through the purging of demonized scapegoats. On the most basic level, Thiel's ideology is fascist because it has fully aligned itself with the MAGA movement. Trump's fascist cult of personality has emerged as a key political technology for challenging American democracy. This was true during his first term, and it has become undeniably clear during his second. Trump and his henchmen openly violate the law and erode the Constitution.

Tech fascism updates this ideology for the AI age. Where analog fascism promises a return to a mythical glorious past, tech fascism promises to engineer an abundant and immortal future. Where traditional fascism asserts a natural hierarchy derived from God, tech fascism cements hierarchy through bogus race science and code. Where twentieth-century fascism manipulates language to destroy truth, twenty-first-century fascism controls reality through algorithms and through the outright purchase of media properties to bring them under fascist oligarch control. It does all of this while accusing its victims—those it seeks to eliminate or oppress—as the perpetrators of the very crimes that fascism itself openly conspires to commit.

Tech fascism is the product of a venture capital system that has run out of unicorns and must now hunt Antichrists to meet its unquenchable thirst for acceleration. Artificial intelligence companies hype the coming of a "godlike" force capable of wiping out most jobs and, perhaps, all of humanity. Crypto companies peddle fantasies of digital salvation, shilling tokenized scams supposedly designed to survive the impending collapse of the US dollar and the liberal democratic order. Elon Musk, declaring Earth obsolete, hallucinates a new promised land on the dead waste of Mars. New crops of biotech start-ups promote delusional notions of eternal life while others launch the next generation of killer robot drones.

This is a dramatic break from the tech industry's old marketing strategy, which sold its products as tools for connection, efficiency, and fun. Our sleek devices let us video chat with faraway loved ones, swipe on dates, and shop for every product on Earth with a few taps on the touchscreen. In one of history's greatest economic achievements, tech companies amassed trillions in value by getting us hooked. No one should be happier, or more optimistic, than the tech billionaires who have won capitalism's endgame and now enjoy unmatched power and privilege.

Yet the lords of tech now find themselves haunted by visions of Armageddon. An industry that once promised flying cars and toil-free prosperity has become a dangerous cult betting on brutal dystopia: mass surveillance, economic decline, autonomous weapons, and AI programs that talk children into suicide and evaporate the value of all labor. Thiel and his cohort of powerful industry leaders are done pretending. They're hyping death, decline, and diabolical futures from which—in their grim, self-serving fairy tale—only they can save us.

This frightening turn stems partly from the built-in existentialism of the venture capital model. Unlike traditional investors who seek long-term growth, VC thrives on high-risk bets and sudden windfalls born of accelerated disruption. Its mandate for perpetually exponential growth makes constant destruction the path to profit. The quickest way to scale a multibillion-dollar bonanza is to collapse existing systems—taxis, hotels, media—or escape into new ones: AI, Mars, digital immortality, network states. The ending of worlds has become the business model.

To keep money flowing, investors pursue a mix of hype and hyperstition—the same reality-manufacturing logic at which Thiel so excels. Pitch decks turn existential threats—job-killing AI, Big Brother surveillance, democratic collapse—into thrilling financial opportunities. Incremental reform doesn't create billion-dollar windfalls, but existential risk does. Rolling catastrophe becomes a feature, not a flaw. The biggest VC firms now have apocalypse coded in their corporate DNA. In the words of Mike Solana, chief marketing officer at Founders Fund: "Maybe if you aren't trying to destroy the world, you aren't trying hard enough."

Tech oligarchs are hardly unique in their quest to remake the global order. Their struggle aligns with a larger push by authoritarians worldwide who wish to rid the world of liberal democracy this century. The effort is organized, though not necessarily centralized. Today's wannabe autocrats and dictators don't wish to live in the same countries or share the same set of rules. Instead, they form networks of like-minded forces working to legitimize authoritarian forms of governance. "Nowadays, autocracies are run not by one bad guy but by sophisticated networks relying on kleptocratic financial structures, a complex of security services—military, paramilitary, police—and technological experts who provide surveillance, propaganda, and disinformation," wrote Anne Applebaum in *Autocracy, Inc.: The Dictators Who Want to Run the World*. "The members of these networks are connected not only to one another within a given autocracy but also to networks in other autocratic countries, and sometimes in democracies too. Corrupt, state-controlled companies in one dictatorship do business with corrupt, state-controlled companies in another. The police in one country may arm, equip, and train the police in many others. The propagandists share resources—the troll farms and media networks that promote one dictator's propaganda can also be used to promote another's—as well as themes: the degeneracy of democracy, the stability of autocracy, the evil of America."

Autocracy, Inc. charts how autocracy has become an aggressive project of networked capitalism. These pro-autocracy forces, like a modern-day version of World War II's Axis powers, share memes, resources, and strategies that further the goal of toppling a postwar order in which democracies have reigned as global superpowers who push their form of government as the only good or acceptable form of government. Authoritarian states like China, Hungary, Russia, and Saudi Arabia naturally seek to undermine such democratic ideals because Western democracies like the United States, the United Kingdom, and others—imperfect as they may be—will always pose a threat to countries where democratic freedoms and voting rights do not exist.

Beneath this state-level collaboration exists a second layer of coordination, which investigative journalist Nafeez Ahmed calls the "Alt Reich." This term describes a transnational network of ideologues, political operatives, billionaires, and media figures who work across borders to advance anti-democratic ideas. It consists of political figures like Steve Bannon, along with a constellation of international think tanks and dark-money organizations that don't represent any single nation-state. Instead, these form what Ahmed describes as "complex, networked connections between the entities and individuals that has enabled a worldview historically rooted in white nationalism to increasingly impact national governments, from the White House to Whitehall and Brussels."

One goal the Alt Reich shares with authoritarian nations is a desire for what international relations scholars call "multipolarity." This means a world where no single superpower dominates and where multiple power centers compete, each with their own governance models and spheres of influence. Supporters of multipolarity demonize what they see as the "unipolar" moment, the post–Cold War era when American-style liberal democracy seemed destined to spread around the world. They prefer a world in which different systems—Chinese authoritarian capitalism, Russian kleptocracy, Hungarian "illiberal democracy," Saudi-style absolute monarchy—will coexist on more equal footing.

To achieve this requires unseating the US as the world's dominant superpower. This is a main goal of multipolarity, which explains why Vladimir Putin's Russia has made the creation of a multipolar world one of its chief foreign policy goals. Russia pushes multipolarity as an exciting win-win system that will allow smaller countries to become more independent and influential. But while promising a more equitable future for all, Russia invaded Ukraine and threatens its other neighbors while also unleashing its mercenary forces to prop up authoritarian regimes in Africa, where they have been accused of committing atrocities and carrying out summary executions.

What multipolarity truly means is a future in which democratic nations, already quite toothless in their response to Putin's aggression, will be entirely powerless to stop authoritarian domination. Yet a global network of propaganda organs—funded mainly by Russia, China, and North Korea—push multipolarity as a benevolent solution. Proving Orwell correct once again, the foxes market themselves as guardians of the henhouse. "However ironic or sinister, multipolarity is now the basis for a whole campaign, systematically spread on [Russia Today] in English, French, Spanish, and Arabic, repeated by information-laundering sites such as Yala News, stated again and again by a thousand other cutouts, think tanks, and paid and unpaid pro-Russian journalists, as well as other spokesmen for Autocracy, Inc.," wrote Applebaum.

Among the loudest advocates for multipolarity: Aleksandr Dugin, a fascist propagandist and theorist known as "Putin's Brain." In a stunning coincidence, Dugin is the only person who talks about the Antichrist more than Thiel. He claims the United States—the "country of apocalypse"—is building the "Kingdom of the Antichrist" through globalization, with the "evil" goal of creating a "unipolar" world. "The current world is unipolar with the global West as its centre and with the United States as its core," wrote Dugin in *The Fourth Political Theory*, his 2009 treatise on the future of politics. "When there is only one instance to decide who is right and who is wrong and who should be punished and who not, we have a form of *global dictatorship*," Dugin continued. "I am convinced that this is not acceptable. Therefore, we should fight against it. If someone deprives us of our freedom we have to react. And we will react. The American Empire should be destroyed. And at one point it will be."

Thiel's lectures echo this logic, railing against a "totalitarian" Antichrist threat. Coincidentally, Dugin's Antichrist rantings also hinge on the ideas of Carl Schmitt. Dugin argues, as did *The Sovereign Individual*, that nation-states will become obsolete, replaced by new spheres of influence controlled by futuristic empires. It's a Russian version of white Christian nationalism, an ideological movement known as Russian Traditionalism, which emphasizes right-wing values rooted in a religion-inspired cult of supremacy. "His conviction that the Russian Federation's destiny is to become a holy empire along tsarist lines, a notion that he has been promoting for more than three decades, has been adopted by much of the Russian political élite—including Putin himself," wrote James Verini in *The New Yorker* in 2025.

Dugin's vision fits into a greater political framework called Project

Russia, which lays out a strategy to transform the world order and make Russia great again. "Between 2005 and 2010, a set of books called 'Project Russia' was distributed to high-ranking officials in the Russian government and other influential thought leaders," wrote independent researcher Dave Troy in *The Washington Spectator* in 2024. "The books offered a detailed program of spiritual warfare against Western democracies culminating in 'controlled global collapse' and the establishment of a 'supranational' state headed by a Prince-Monk who 'best understands the world.' The plan described is ultimately a program for subjugating the world, which would also be united together in a single religion."

Project Russia assailed democracy as degenerate and prescribed a new form of monarchy—Yarvin's core argument. For years, Dugin fended off accusations that he authored the Project Russia books, though another wealthy Russian with elite government connections eventually received credit. In any case, Russia has for decades engaged in a sustained campaign of memetic warfare to preach against the supposed evils of American democracy. In 2009, Dugin predicted that these arguments would even find supporters within the US itself. "All who share negative analysis of globalization, westernization and post-modernization should coordinate their effort in creation of a new strategy of resistance to the omnipresent evil," he wrote. "And we can find common allies within even the United States, as well—among those who choose the path of Tradition over the present decadence."

The network state fits perfectly with this fantasy; unsurprisingly, some of the usual suspects in Silicon Valley have also embraced the motto of multipolarity. "The multipolar world begins with a multipolar West," wrote Balaji Srinivasan in 2021. In a screed against tech regulation, he said that multipolarity "legalizes technology" and laid out a three-step explainer: "1) The West no longer controls the world 2) So it no longer regulates the world 3) So anyone in the world can innovate."

Billionaire investor and network state enthusiast Naval Ravikant jumped on the multipolarity train in 2025. "The US will actually do better in a multipolar world, because it'll no longer have to subsidize and police everyone else," he wrote on X, drawing harsh rebukes from people who pointed out that the nation's global dominance works in its favor.

Stripped of all the religious gobbledygook, the core arguments of Dugin and Thiel converge on a simple thesis: The United States—a young nation that rose to power at unprecedented speed, becoming a hegemonic world power exerting force and influence through *pax Americana* and a vision of liberal democracy they slander as an enemy of freedom—is the most likely Antichrist. Thiel made this clear, directly painting the US as the latest iteration of Rome:

> *. . . America is, at this point, the natural candidate for Katechon and Antichrist, ground zero of the One World state, ground zero of the resistance to the One World state . . . The US world police is the one truly sovereign country. They always say the president is the mayor of the US and the dictator of the world. International law gets defined by the US. That's sort of NATO's prime, to see in some ways, coordination of the world's intelligence agencies. Then of course, the global financial architecture we discussed is not really run by shadowy international organizations, it's basically American. And perhaps always a very important feature is the reserve currency status of the dollar, where it's sort of the backstop for all the money. The petro dollar regime, there's sort of crazy ways you have trade deficits, current account deficits, but then in all these ways, the money gets recycled into the US.*

In Thiel's telling, any force strong enough to be the *katechon* is also a suspect for the Antichrist—echoing his 2010 speech at Libertopia where he invoked the devil and branded government as "fundamentally evil." For him, they are two sides of the same coin. While the US helped restrain Nazism and communism in the twentieth century, he suggests the country began tilting toward Antichrist mode during World War II, noting "a lot of people thought that FDR was suspiciously close to the Antichrist. In 1933 he seizes all the gold. You have the National Recovery Act with the blue eagle as a symbol, made people think of the mark of the beast." With the advent of nuclear weapons, Thiel said "[t]he president, in some sense, becomes this semi-divine being destroying the world." Since then, he claims this power has been usurped by the "deep state"—the permanent government bureaucratic structures now being vilified by Trump, Yarvin, and DOGE. Unchecked, these shadowy powers will take over, flipping the US into Antichrist mode. "I've come to think of America as the last and final form of the Roman Empire," he said. "There is no successor. And so the end of [America] would be the end of the world, or the beginning of the Antichrist."

It's a convoluted and contradictory argument, but the upshot of Thiel and Dugin is clear: Networked fascists of the world must weaponize capital and technology to overthrow democracy in the twenty-first century. This is the existential crisis of which they speak, the "evil" they seek to defeat, the problem for which they demand a final solution. This explains why the network state funds exit technologies and seeks jurisdictional arbitrage, and why crypto promises an escape from the hegemony of the dollar. It explains the emphasis on decentralization and multipolarity, and why Silicon Valley moguls like Thiel are shamelessly cashing out through the fascist Trump regime. By weakening the country, Trump and his tech oligarch henchmen can eliminate liberal democracy's global champion, thus killing the Antichrist in its crib. From its ashes shall rise a techno-capital theocracy that promises infinite acceleration into eternity, or something like that.

Naomi Klein warned about "disaster capitalism," a model in which governments and corporations use crisis, disaster, and war to seize both profit and power. We are now witnessing apocalypse capitalism, an audacious bet on collapse and dystopia proselytized by a billionaire who cries "Antichrist" while bankrolling the authoritarian machinery he claims to warn against.

On June 23, 2016, voters in the United Kingdom decided to exit the European Union, delivering an early victory for right-wing populism and multipolarity. (As fate would have it, Jacob Rees-Mogg—son of *The Sovereign Individual*'s coauthor—served as Minister of State for Brexit Opportunities and Government Efficiency.)

"Brexit, just the beginning," wrote Jeffrey Epstein to Thiel on June 26.

"Of what," replied Thiel.

Epstein explained: "return to tribalism. counter to globalization. amazing new alliances. you and i both agreed zero interest rates were too high, and as i said in your office . . . finding things on their way to collapse . . . was much easier than finding the next bargain."

Like Thiel, Epstein saw the world headed toward a breaking point and looked for ways to capitalize. It sounds crazy to most people, but a certain class of men has long seen chaos and collapse as a recipe for destiny, and some among them believe the apocalypse is now at hand.

"Am I a genius or am I an insane person?" Thiel asked during his final Antichrist lecture in San Francisco.

Tragically, the two are not mutually exclusive.

CHAPTER 8

THE FUTURE

Billionaires or Democracy

Peter Thiel is not wrong about everything. His hopes and fears about the twenty first century, inspired by *The Sovereign Individual*, have largely come to pass. Digital forms of currency did turn out to be weapons for undermining government power. Automation, in the form of AI, does threaten to fundamentally transform the economy and unleash a plague of joblessness and, with it, societal chaos. Technological innovation did generate massive and unprecedented fortunes. These fortunes gave rise to a new class of Silicon Valley super elites who chafe at laws, regulations, and taxes and view themselves as superior to the government that created them. He made a risky bet on Trump, which proved to be the accelerant needed to commence the liquidation of American democracy, and he created JD Vance, who rose quickly to the top of American politics.

As Thiel and his fellow venture capitalists rush to create a future run on AI, crypto, surveillance, and war, they have captured immense government power. They are weaponizing it to push their extreme ideological goals and prop up their business interests, positioning the public treasury as a backstop for their bets—what Dr. Olivier Jutel calls "exit through the state." But they also seem quite fearful of this future, and so they continue to seek escape—from accountability, democracy, law, mortality, reality—pursuing the goal with a fervor so relentless it has become religious.

While relatively new as a direct political force, their zeal for disruption has already made democracy into an endangered species. Once held up as a global beacon of liberty, America has been revealed as highly vulnerable to destruction. Pushing it to the brink wasn't particularly difficult. It required only enough wealthy and influential people who were willing to fund it, or at least go along with it quietly. Quickly, we witnessed the rise of an openly corrupt president who is selling out the country for crypto, launching illegal invasions of foreign countries, threatening to attack NATO allies, sending troops into American cities, deploying masked terror squads to abduct immigrants, and openly abusing the justice system to prosecute his political enemies while also selling presidential pardons to the highest bidders. He is just getting started.

The capture of democracy extends beyond government to media as well. Radical tech oligarchs now control *The Washington Post* and CBS—in addition to Facebook, Instagram, X, and TikTok—and some fantasize about a hostile takeover of *The New York Times*. In 2025, a16z launched the a16z New Media Fellowship "for operators, creators and storytellers shaping the future of media." The firm is also a leading investor in Substack, the popular newsletter app—launched through Y Combinator—which aims to displace legacy media outlets with independent newsletters. OpenAI joined the fray in April 2026 when it bought its own media outlet, an online technology livestream called Technology Business Programming Network (TBPN). It's all a chilling realization of Balaji Srinivasan's call for Silicon Valley oligarchs to create a parallel media system that essentially replaces journalism with propaganda—a crucial element of any fascist movement. Two weeks after OpenAI bought TBPN, *TechCrunch* revealed that Srinivasan and Thiel were funding their own media venture, Objection, which "aims to use AI to adjudicate the truth of journalism." "And for the price of $2,000, anyone can pay to challenge a story, triggering a public investigation into its claims," wrote Rebecca Bellan of *TechCrunch*.

Objection's founder, Aron D'Souza, is the lawyer who orchestrated Thiel's secret funding of the lawsuit that bankrupted *Gawker*. "Peter Thiel and I used the legal system to prove that journalists are not immune from accountability," D'Souza said in a press release. "The *Gawker* litigation took ten years and millions of dollars. Objection industrializes this process."

"Your case is investigated by some of the most qualified researchers in the world: ex-CIA and FBI agents, military intelligence, award-winning investigative journalists," stated Objection's website, which featured the official logos of these intimidating government agencies. "They gather the evidence. All of it, regardless of whose interests it serves."

These are troubling developments, but on the bright side, it's not clear whether the fascist oligarchs will be able to kill democracy in one fell swoop. By mid-2025, Curtis Yarvin had declared the Trump regime a tragedy and a failure. He took to weeping during interviews and counseled his fascist allies to make plans to flee the nation. "The second Trump revolution, like the first, is failing," he wrote. "It is failing because it deserves to fail. It is failing because it spends all its time patting itself on the back. It is failing because its true mission, which neither it nor (still less) its supporters understand, is still as far beyond its reach as algebra is beyond a cat. Because the vengeance meted out after its failure will dwarf the vengeance after 2020—because the successes of the second revolution are so much greater than the first—I feel that I personally have to start thinking realistically about how to flee the country. Everyone else in a similar position should have a 2029 plan as well. And it is not even clear that it will wait until 2029: losing the Congress will instantly put the administration on the defensive."

In May 2026, Thiel bought a $12 million mansion in Argentina and relocated there with his family for a couple of months. "Mr. Thiel, who has a history of collecting backup countries as he hedges his bets against the United States, is considering making Argentina another Plan B," reported *The New York Times*, noting that he also had citizenship in New Zealand. *The Sovereign Individual* had recommended

Argentina and New Zealand as alternatives to a declining United States, and the *Times* reported that Thiel's "new roots in Argentina are partly motivated by his concerns about the direction of the United States."

Yarvin may be putting too much faith in the Democratic Party, which has mostly stood by impotently as Trump—ringed by tech oligarchs—has rolled out his authoritarian version of government. Yet despite tech's enthusiastic complicity with the regime, Democratic leaders continue to operate as if the tech sector has not become an open enemy of democracy itself. They speak of AI and billionaires and crypto in flattering and friendly terms, no doubt hoping to remain beneficiaries of campaign checks from tech billionaires. While the champions of tech fascism see the Republican Party as the best vehicle for its hopes, they also understand the inherent corruptibility of the Democratic Party, which also serves its wealthy donors more than it serves anyone else.

During his 1999 speech at the Independent Institute, Thiel predicted that official Washington would be too dumb to understand what was happening and too powerless to stop it, and so far he seems correct on that point. Yarvin is also correct that Trump is failing to go full fascist authoritarian, to do The Thing—a full-on state of exception that suspends the Constitution and the rule of law, as called for by his cockamamie theory. Reality and theory are often different things, as Yarvin is finding out. A dramatic overnight lurch into full fascism would likely result in an explosion of widespread resistance that could spark economic devastation and end badly for him. Trump, an octogenarian who increasingly struggles to keep his eyes open in public, seems to prefer a more gradual sort of decline that does not interrupt his moneymaking schemes (or his nap time).

I do not mean to downplay the devastating harms of his actions. The regime's USAID cuts alone are causing mass death in poor countries, and countless numbers will continue to die because of Trump's war against vaccines. But despite occasional threats, Trump does not currently seem inclined to start executing journalists, judges, or members of Congress. Such measures, and more, would be necessary to achieve a full treasonous overthrow of American democracy. Instead, as Trump's poll numbers sink to new lows, even members of his own party—worried about the 2026 midterm elections—have started to question his leadership. This suggests that midterm elections will happen, and the semblance of a plausible system of democratic governance will remain in place.

Those who still believe in democracy may welcome such a period of reprieve, but they must avoid being lulled into complacency. Democracy's enemies specialize in long-term strategies, and they have enough money to operate in perpetuity; they are scheming for global control. They do not fear hapless, mealy-mouthed liberal politicians content to ignore the fundamental threats facing democracy as long as they can eke out temporary electoral victories. There is no middle ground between freedom and fascism. The "centrist" playbook leads only to ruin in these circumstances. Political moderation in the face of despotism is a slower but surer way to arrive at the same destination.

While I fear the destruction Trump and his oligarch co-conspirators will impose over the next few years, the greater threat is that our descent into tech fascism will be spearheaded by liberal politicians who, co-opted and corrupted by Silicon Valley money, will abandon democracy without much of a fight. Trump is a symptom of a far greater disease in our system, a disease that will continue to grow and metastasize after he dies. The billionaires of Silicon Valley have a plan to succeed. They understand that a political system dependent on checks from wealthy corporations and individuals is inherently tilted in their favor. They seek to innovate this corruption: to buy the levers of democracy and use them to destroy the entire system. This is the logical end point of the predicament. The survival of the United States has relied on a delicate balance of powers, and that balance has now been tested. It has failed catastrophically, exposing a major flaw in systems that have proven shockingly weak in the face of billionaire-powered fascist power grabs. Fixing this flaw will require us to adopt an urgent spirit of innovation and prepare for a long journey ahead.

People often ask me how to solve this problem. I tell them that the first step is to learn what is happening and spread the word to everyone they know. As a journalist, that's my role: to tell the story. I have strong opinions about how it should end, but the outcome is not up to me. A positive resolution will require tens of millions of people—perhaps billions—to change the course of history. We live at a moment when the moral arc of the universe is being bent toward desolation. Time is running out—for our planet, for our democracy, and for our future.

On the bright side, we can solve these problems. I truly believe that. But we will not find many easy solutions. Solving these problems will require deep systemic changes, some of which will seem quite radical at first. But we have no choice but to embrace radical change—because it is the only thing that can save us. Unfortunately, it turns out that the defeat of the Confederacy did not rid the world of white supremacy, and World War II did not eliminate fascism. These forces have arisen in powerful new forms, and they plan to control the future. I won't pretend to have all the solutions, but this book identifies a specific set of challenges we must confront head-on to survive.

One must always learn from an enemy. Trump and his fascist henchmen have taught us an important lesson: Anything is possible. Their outlandish schemes and outrageous violations are designed to warp reality itself and demonstrate that reality can be manufactured through hype, marketing, propaganda, and other forms of information warfare.

So, the first challenge is the challenge of imagination. We live in a world that has enabled a tiny number of billionaires to monopolize the visions of our future, and they would rather fund the end of the world—literal apocalypse—than risk a world of equality, fairness, and justice. They pitch a cold nightmare of dystopia, destruction, and death here on Earth, and with AI and surveillance-fortified tyranny eventually reigning supreme aboard the fascist prison spaceships they envision as the final resting place of the chosen few survivors of our species.

But we also have the power to imagine and to dream of realities not yet possible. We must shatter the billionaire monopoly on the future. If the billionaires can imagine hoarding wealth, toppling nations, cheating death, and living on Mars, we can imagine a world without them—and we must build it.

To create a better future, we must create a world without billionaires. We can have billionaires, or we can have democracy. We cannot have both. If we continue to allow a tiny group of men to stockpile the majority of the world's wealth, they will continue to buy the power they need to impose hierarchy, oppression, subjugation, and death on the vast majority of people, whom they see as their inferiors. History strongly suggests that extreme wealth has a tendency to drive people insane and transform them into tyrants. All it took was a handful of people with billions of dollars to begin the unraveling of our entire nation. The Bill of Rights, the Constitution, and the nation itself mean nothing to these people, who view it as little more than an asset to be divvied up and liquidated.

This current onslaught of anti-democracy billionaires exposes an existential flaw in our system. In a nation where money buys power, money can buy power to destroy the nation itself. We do not allow private citizens to own nuclear weapons because such power does not belong in the hands of individuals. Allowing individual citizens to stockpile billions of dollars is, as it turns out, even more dangerous. A single nuke might kill hundreds of thousands of people, but the billionaires will kill millions or billions. They have already started, with aid cuts and a reckless disregard for global warming.

How do we neutralize billionaire power? Some propose the capping and taxing of wealth. This seems logical, but it won't be enough. I am certainly not the first person to call for a crackdown on billionaires. Economic inequality would be a severe crisis even if the billionaires weren't working to hasten the end of democracy.

"The fact that our society allows the existence of billionaires is the fundamental problem at the core of this book," wrote Adam Becker in *More Everything Forever: AI Overlords, Space Empires, and Silicon Valley's Crusade to Control the Fate of Humanity*. "Without billionaires, fringe philosophies like rationalism and effective accelerationism would stay on the fringe, rather than being pulled into the mainstream through the reality-warping power of concentrated wealth."

Right now, you are probably thinking about how difficult it would be to create a world without billionaires. But remember: It won't be as difficult as spending our lives under the cruel tyranny of billionaire tech fascism. Unfortunately, that appears to be the only alternative. The current moment makes it clear that there is no future in which both democracy and billionaires—or trillionaires—will coexist. We must pick one or the other, and we must grant ourselves the power of hyperstition—of making the impossible possible through sheer force of will—just as the billionaires like to do.

Good news: The United States, a country of 340 million people, has just under 1,000 billionaires, according to *Forbes*. Earth, which has 8.3 billion people, has an estimated 3,428 billionaires as of March 2026. They constitute a tiny sliver of the human population, yet they do a disproportionate amount of damage to the planet and its people. We are destroying the Earth to create wealth for this small group of men, and millions of poor people will die in the next few years because a gang of billionaires cut USAID.

Remember that when billionaire-funded influencers and think tanks tell fairy tales about their plan to create a future of tech-enhanced abundance. We already have abundance—but it is being hoarded by a wicked few. Today, they are starving poor countries in Africa and the Middle East. Tomorrow, our country will be poor, and our children and grandchildren will be among those deemed unworthy of food and care. But only if we allow them to accelerate their schemes of exponential chaos and decline while walling us out of the digital castles they seek to erect. We also have a special power—democracy—that allows us to warp reality. We must use it or lose it.

Ridding the world of billionaires does not mean killing them. The executions of the French Revolution satisfied a thirst for vengeance, but they also ushered in a new dictatorship. We need a French Revolution with sane policies in place of guillotines.

Besides, most billionaires are quite soft and cowardly and will crumble in the face of significant consequences. The good ones will agree that this was the only moral and sustainable path into the future. Perhaps they can even put their vast fortunes to good use by funding the revolution.

This brings us to the challenge of accountability. Holding powerful people accountable for complicity in the overthrow of democracy is not just a matter of justice, it's a crucial mechanism for self-defense. If we do shake loose from the grip of fascism, we must harden our systems to ensure nothing like this ever happens again. Our system failed to hold Trump accountable for his crimes the first time around, and we are reaping the consequences. Meanwhile, Brazil's former president, Trump ally Jair Bolsonaro, is serving a twenty-seven-year prison sentence for his attempted coup. In South Korea, a former president who tried to impose martial law was impeached, removed from office, and sentenced to life in prison. Why can't we have such robust consequences in a country that markets itself as the greatest in the world? We must follow the examples of these other nations and seek relentless accountability.

We must never forget what these people tried to do. Because, given the chance, they will keep trying.

To prevent this, we need investigations, hearings, prosecutions, and likely some kind of truth and reconciliation commission. We need a full postmortem of our brush with national death, as well as prison sentences and severe financial penalties for those who participated in, or profited from, the defiling of our government. If we fail to pursue accountability and justice, we know exactly what will happen.

These men will get emboldened. They will try even harder. They will do even worse things. They will win.

Accountability goes beyond simple punishment and penalty. The villains must be enshrined in our national memory forever. Their rise must become a cautionary tale that future children learn about in history class. The cruelty, cowardice, and/or complicity of individuals, corporations, and organizations should be immortalized, perhaps (as some have proposed) in a Museum of American Fascism, which can stand as a permanent testament to our close call with downfall.

We must also hold ourselves accountable for the degree to which we have ceded our freedom and lost our way in exchange for technologies that mask danger as convenience.

Not all technology is bad, but things have clearly gone off the rails. Today, it is being used to harvest our data, influence our behavior, polarize our society, supercharge our economic inequality, blur our reality, and dull our humanity. Consumer AI apps, the supposed saviors of the human race, are already being used to drive people into psychosis, talk children into suicide, and produce synthetic child sexual abuse material. Its masters promise it will also kill most of our jobs and replace human existence and experience with synthetic algorithmic realities. And all of it to create a fascist crypto casino that turns billionaires into trillionaires and turns ordinary people into their data-producing herd cattle.

There must be another way to do this. We deserve technology, and we should not have to give up our dignity and freedom to get it. But that is what the oligarchs of Silicon Valley have in mind—a hyper-capitalist system without democracy. They argue that technology will solve all problems, but their version of technology has become our biggest problem, because the main goal of their technology is to seize all power in the world and the universe, forever.

Unless we radically rethink the governance of technology, we will remain its prey. There are some obvious steps to take. For example, we should ban crypto, which is designed to defraud the public and undermine national security and stability. In addition, it should become official US government policy to view the network state and all similar anti-government schemes as what they are—extremist ideologies designed to foment sedition and societal harm.

We should also break up tech monopolies and reassert government power—public power—over the powers now claimed by a handful of billionaires.

The public, through government, should take an aggressive position toward AI regulation, given the magnitude of disruption its promoters have promised to create. All technologies should be designed with democracy and humanity as their guiding principles. Again, we don't allow private companies to sell nuclear bombs. That would be crazy. Why should we allow them to create and sell technologies that, according to their own hype, will eat the world?

In addition, government must reclaim its power from tech corporations. The outsourcing of public responsibilities to private corporations has created a dangerous situation in which the leaders of these corporations now believe they deserve to be the government. Even before this current tech power group, politicians in Washington had handed over vast amounts of power and access to private companies, essentially becoming dependent on them. In *The Tech Coup: How to Save Democracy from Silicon Valley*, Marietje Schaake tells the story of how technology companies have effectively seized control and influence over functions traditionally held by governments all over the world. Schaake argues that this undermines accountability, sovereignty, and the rule of law, creating a dangerous imbalance that must be fixed with urgency. "This is a tragedy for citizens; ultimately, if things go wrong, they will be left picking up the tab," wrote Schaake. "When tens of millions of jobs end up displaced by AI, shareholders of companies will benefit, while the price of unemployment or reeducation will fall to societies to shoulder. The moment those negative externalities inevitably do emerge, the public purse will be emptied."

"I'm not just looking to tech companies to criticize them for having taken up so much power," Schaake told me. "I'm certainly also criticizing democratic governments for allowing them to take up so much power."

In the aftermath of the Trump-Tech regime, the public must take back its power and design safeguards to permanently roll back the tech coup.

But Silicon Valley isn't just a parasite in our government. It's in our brains. As individuals, we have enthusiastically given up our privacy and our attention span to them. No wonder they feel entitled to rule us—they already do, and they conquered our minds with our enthusiastic permission.

So, we each have responsibility to radically reevaluate our own complicity in their power. Why do we spend our lives staring at our tiny screens? Why do we while away the hours peering into mindless click-holes or arguing with strangers we will never even meet? Why do we need so much entertainment and content that we are cooking the planet—and our brains—in order to create an endless supply of algorithmic depression? Why does every move we make in the twenty-first century somehow have to enrich a handful of fascist oligarchs who wish to destroy us, even though we are—until they replace us with AI bots—their best customers?

The truth is, the tech fascists are right again: Most of us have already become transhuman, mind-melded with our machines in an endless cycle of poisonous dependency. If we don't come to terms with the true costs of this relationship, if we continue to choose their reality over all others, we shall be the authors of our own demise.

We must rethink our relationship with technology, which means rethinking what it means to be human. Tech oligarchs find their own existence so empty that they want to leave the planet, become gods, merge with machines, and live forever in the cold and lifeless universe. None of us are invited to that future, which can only come about after they sort the human species down to the worst and most amoral version possible. But it doesn't have to be this way. Those of us who are okay with being human beings, who know it is our fate to live and die on Earth, who understand that humans are imperfect but have a destiny rooted in community and love, we don't have to sign up for these nightmares.

As Dr. Ruha Benjamin of Princeton University puts it: "We can call bullshit on their eugenics futures."

But we'll have to look away from our devices long enough to find a better path.

Rethinking humanity ultimately requires us to rethink capitalism. It has brought us many good things, but we have reached the end stage. Today's capitalists openly plot to destroy the planet and extinguish human life for the sake of endless quarterly growth. Global capitalism has become a dangerously outdated software system. We have the knowledge—and the technology—to try something new.

Envision a world with universal prosperity, a world where everyone gets a share of the extreme wealth that is produced. Imagine a world where no human being lacks food, health care, or housing, where productivity is judged by the quality of our happiness and people are free to pursue their interests without the fear that failure will result in poverty. Imagine "universal extreme wealth—for everybody."

This may sound like a communist or socialist daydream, but those words came from the mouth of OpenAI CEO Sam Altman in a 2025 interview.

Obviously, we can't trust men like Altman to deliver on such a vision. Current AI models are designed to extract and enslave, not share and liberate. However, just as companies steal all our data and our content to fuel their growth, we can steal this radical fantasy of a world where everyone is a billionaire—or nobody is.

Revolutions start in the imagination, and that's one thing the fascists can't take away from us.

Not yet, anyway.

ACKNOWLEDGMENTS

This book would not have been possible without Olivia, Bernie, and Jimi, for being at my side throughout the writing of this book; Riley Ray Robbins, for showing up; my agent, Caroline Eisenmann, and Sam Stoloff at Frances Goldin Literary Agency, for opening the door; Shannon Welch, Megan Noes, and the team at Avid Reader, for believing in this book; Carmela Guaglianone, for fact-checking; and my family, for bringing me into this world and making me who I am.

I'd also like to thank Terry Esrael, Sandy Robinson, David Fenton, Sylvie Erb, Heather Cox Richardson, Brooke Harrington, Dave Karpf, Émile P. Torres, Adam Becker, Jenny Cohn, Paris Marx, Jacob Silverman, Quinn Slobodian, Molly White, Paulina Borsook, Norman Yarvin, Meredith Tanner, Dana Kirschman, Dave Troy, Wajahat Ali, George Lakoff, Kathleen Frumkin, Ruth Ben-Ghiat, Carole Cadwalladr, Julia Black, Kiera Butler, Joe Eskenazi, Ruha Benjamin, the Grundys, the Millers, Olivier Jutel, Karen Hao, Catherine Bracy, Dr. Matthew Fox, Becca Lewis, Marietje Schaake, Mike Madrid, Scott Horton, Fred Turner, Ali Winston, Emily Mills, Jason Linkins, Ryan Kearney, Greg Sargent, Johannes Hano, Andrew Santana, Jerry Brown, Marisa Lagos, Scott Shafer, Mina Kim, Rachel Myrow, Sam Seder, Emma

Vigeland, Jane Mayer, Susan B. Glasser, Evan Osnos, Meghna Chakrabarti, Josef Chytry, Ignacio Valero, Jon Fortt, Rev. Otis Moss III, Jonathan Freedland, and Morgan Fairchild. And none of this would have been possible without all my teachers and professors, for guiding me along the way.

NOTES

INTRODUCTION

1 *"a dangerous concentration of power"*: Joseph R. Biden Jr., "Farewell Address to the Nation," Washington, DC, January 15, 2025, transcript, https://bidenwhitehouse.archives.gov.

1 *Five days later*: Lisa Hagen, "Prominent Right-Wing Figures Mimic Musk's Nazi Salute with No Repercussions," NPR, March 14, 2025, https://www.npr.org/2025/03/15/nx-s1-5305259/musk-salute-humor-controversy.

2 *He tackled the assignment with the sociopathic glee*: Nick Robins-Early and Reuters, "Doge Employee 'Big Balls' Has Resigned, Says White House Official," *Guardian*, June 24, 2025, https://www.theguardian.com/us-news/2025/jun/24/doge-big-balls-edward-coristine-resigns.

2 *They were aided in this effort by Grok*: Marisa Taylor and Alexandra Ulmer, "Exclusive: Musk's DOGE Expanding His Grok AI in US Government, Raising Conflict Concerns," Reuters, May 23, 2025, https://www.reuters.com/sustainability/boards-policy-regulation/musks-doge-expanding-his-grok-ai-us-government-raising-conflict-concerns-2025-05-23/.

2 *He spent nearly $300 million*: David Wright and Alex Leeds-Matthews, "Elon Musk Spent More Than $290 Million on the 2024 Election, Year-End FEC Filings Show," CNN, February 1, 2025, https://www.cnn.com/2025/02/01/politics/elon-musk-2024-election-spending-millions.

2 *"into the woodchipper"*: Gregory Korte, "Federal Workforce's Toll After a Year of DOGE and Trump: 317,000," *Bloomberg*, December 10, 2025, https://www.bloomberg.com/news/articles/2025-12-10/federal-workforce-s-toll-after-a-year-of-doge-and-trump-317-000; Taylor Giorno, "'We Are Terrified': Musk Puts USAID Through 'Wood Chipper,'" *Hill*, February 3, 2025, https://thehill.com/policy/technology/5122676-usaid-shutdown-elon-musk-doge/.

2 *This decision alone is projected*: Davide Rasella et al., "Evaluating the Impact of Two Decades of USAID Interventions and Projecting the Effects of Defunding on Mortality up to 2030," *Lancet* 406, no. 10500 (July 2025): 283–294, https://www.thelancet.com/journals/lancet/article/PIIS0140-6736(25)01186-9/fulltext.

3 *In 2017, over one hundred companies*: Aarti Shahani, "Tech Companies Unite Against Trump Administration's Immigration Ban," NPR, February 6, 2017, https://www.npr.org/2017/02/06/513769927/tech-companies-unite-against-trump-administrations-immigration-ban.

3 *Trump reserved the scarce seats*: Ali Swenson, "Trump, a Populist President, Is Flanked by Tech Billionaires at His Inauguration," Associated Press, January 20, 2025, https://apnews.com/article/trump-inauguration-tech-billionaires-zuckerberg-musk-wealth-0896bfc3f50d941d62cebc3074267ecd.

3 *Zuckerberg had banned Trump*: Meta Platforms Inc., "Ending Suspension of Trump's Accounts with New Guardrails to Deter Repeat Offenses," Facebook Newsroom, January 25, 2023, https://about.fb.com/news/2023/01/trump-facebook-instagram-account-suspension/.

3 *"to support the national renewal"*: Edward Helmore, "Mark Zuckerberg Dines with Trump at Mar-a-Lago Despite Former Feud," *Guardian*, November 28, 2024, https://www.theguardian.com/technology/2024/nov/28/mark-zuckerberg-trump.

3 *Zuckerberg announced his decision*: Katie Paul and Supantha Mukherjee, "Meta Ends Third-Party Fact-Checking Program, Adopts X-Like Community Notes Model," Reuters, January 7, 2025, https://www.reuters.com/technology/meta-ends-third-party-fact-checking-program-adopts-x-like-community-notes-model-2025-01-07/.

4 *Bezos—owner of* The Washington Post: David Folkenflik, "Bezos, Washington Post Officials Spar over Endorsements, Resignations," NPR, October 28, 2024, https://www.npr.org/2024/10/28/nx-s1-5168416/washington-post-bezos-endorsement-president-cancellations-resignations.

4 *"dictator on day one"*: Jill Colvin and Bill Barrow, "Trump's Vow to Only Be a Dictator on 'Day One' Follows Growing Worry over His Authoritarian Rhetoric," Associated Press, December 7, 2023, https://apnews.com/article/trump-hannity-dictator-authoritarian-presidential-election-f27e7e9d7c13fabbe3ae7dd7f1235c72.

4 *Bezos's Amazon—along with Apple*: Juliana Kim and Bobby Allyn, "Tech Moguls Altman, Bezos and Zuckerberg Donate to Trump's Inauguration Fund," NPR, December 13, 2024, https://www.npr.org/2024/12/13/nx-s1-5227874/trump-bezos-zuckerberg-amazon-facebook-open-ai-meta-inauguration-fund.

4 *So did Sam Altman*: Will Steakin and Soo Rin Kim, "OpenAI's Sam Altman Warned America About Trump. Now He's Partnering with Him," ABC News, January 27, 2025, https://abcnews.com/US/openais-sam-altman-warned-america-trump-now-partnering/story?id=118145337.

4 *"Watching @potus more carefully . . . in many ways"*: Sam Altman (@sama), "watching @potus more carefully recently has really changed my perspective on him (i wish i had done more of my own thinking and definitely fell in the npc trap). i'm not going to agree with him on everything, but i think he will be

incredible for the country in many ways!" X, January 22, 2025, https://x.com/sama/status/1882234406662000833.

4 *"Techno-Fascism Comes to America"*: Kyle Chayka, "Techno-Fascism Comes to America," *New Yorker*, February 26, 2025, https://www.newyorker.com/culture/infinite-scroll/techno-fascism-comes-to-america-elon-musk.

4 *sixteen men connected to Thiel and his companies*: Sophie Alexander and Jamie Tarabay, "Peter Thiel's Network Is Quietly Shaping Trump's Government," *Bloomberg*, March 7, 2025, https://www.bloomberg.com/features/2025-peter-thiel-trump-administration-connections/.

5 *had once derided him as "America's Hitler"*: Gram Slattery and Helen Coster, "JD Vance Once Compared Trump to Hitler. Now, He Is Trump's Vice President-Elect," Reuters, November 6, 2024, https://www.reuters.com/world/us/jd-vance-once-compared-trump-hitler-now-they-are-running-mates-2024-07-15/.

5 *Vance is almost entirely a creation of Thiel*: Erin Mansfield, "Peter Thiel and JD Vance: How PayPal Founder Boosted VP Candidate's Political Career," *USA Today*, July 17, 2024, https://www.usatoday.com/story/news/politics/elections/2024/07/17/peter-thiel-boosted-jd-vance-career/74397520007/.

5 *It flopped as a product*: AJ Dellinger, "Trump May Finally Move to Cash Out His $2 Billion Stake in Truth Social," *Gizmodo*, April 4, 2025, https://gizmodo.com/trump-may-finally-move-to-cash-out-his-2-billion-stake-in-truth-social-2000584733.

5 *had once called crypto a "scam"*: Will Weissert and Alan Suderman, "Once a Crypto Skeptic, Trump Is Now a Big Fan of the Industry," Associated Press, May 22, 2025, https://www.pbs.org/newshour/politics/once-a-crypto-skeptic-trump-is-now-a-big-fan-of-the-industry.

5 *the Trump family's net worth increased by $5 billion*: Angus Berwick, "Trump Family Amasses $6 Billion Fortune After Crypto Launch," *Wall Street Journal*, September 1, 2025, https://www.wsj.com/finance/currencies/trump-family-amasses-6-billion-fortune-after-crypto-launch-567faec5.

5 *Donald Trump Jr. had joined 1789 Capital*: Alexandra Ulmer, "Trump Son Don Jr. Joining Venture Capital Firm 1789 Capital, Sources Say," Reuters, November 12, 2024, https://www.reuters.com/world/us/trump-son-don-jr-joining-venture-capital-firm-1789-capital-sources-say-2024-11-12/.

5 *The firm's stated goal was to engage in "patriotic capitalism"*: Elizabeth Dwoskin, "Chris Buskirk: The Political Operator Helping Tech Elites Enter Washington Power Circles," *Washington Post*, February 9, 2026, https://www.washingtonpost.com/post-next/interactive/2026/chris-buskirk/.

5 *The firm's cofounder, Chris Buskirk*: Elizabeth Dwoskin, "The Secretive Donor Circle That Lifted JD Vance Is Now Rewriting MAGA's Future," *Washington Post*, November 4, 2025, https://www.washingtonpost.com/technology/2025/11/04/chris-buskirk-maga-vance-post-trump/.

5 *chief strategy officer of American Bitcoin*: MacKenzie Sigalos, "Eric Trump Says He Moved to Crypto After Family Business Became 'Most Canceled Company,'" CNBC, April 2, 2025, https://www.cnbc.com/2025/04/02/eric-trump-moved-to-crypto-after-family-became-most-canceled-company.html.

6 *cofounded an AI company, Brain Co.*: Giacomo Tognini, Monica Hunter-Hart, and Iain Martin, "Meet Jared Kushner's New AI Startup, Brain Co.," *Forbes*, September 10, 2025, https://www.forbes.com/sites/giacomotognini/2025/09/10/jared-kushners-new-startup-helps-businesses-figure-out-how-to-use-ai/.

6 *a $30 million contract to augment Trump's masked ICE squads*: Johana Bhuiyan, "Documents Offer Rare Insight on ICE's Close Relationship with Palantir," *Guardian*, September 22, 2025, https://www.theguardian.com/us-news/ng-interactive/2025/sep/22/ice-palantir-data.

6 *"raising questions over whether he might compile"*: Sheera Frenkel and Aaron Krolik, "Trump Taps Palantir to Compile Data on Americans," *New York Times*, May 30, 2025, https://www.nytimes.com/2025/05/30/us/politics/palantir-trump-data.html.

6 *lucrative opportunities to work with ICE*: Heather Knight, "Salesforce Offers Its Services to Boost Trump's Immigration Force," *New York Times*, October 16, 2025, https://www.nytimes.com/2025/10/16/us/salesforce-benioff-ice.html.

6 *Widely circulated press photographs showed*: Tina Nguyen, "Big Tech Quietly Sponsors Trump's Military Parade Party," *Verge*, June 12, 2025, https://www.theverge.com/policy/685690/big-tech-trump-military-parade-america250.

6 *When Trump made the surprise decision*: Lauren Aratani and Stephanie Kirchgaessner, "Donors for Trump's $300m White House Ballroom Include Google, Apple and Palantir," *Guardian*, October 23, 2025, https://www.theguardian.com/us-news/2025/oct/23/trump-white-house-ballroom-donors; Jason Lalljee, "Exclusive: Coinbase Explains Donation to Trump's Ballroom," Axios, November 18, 2025, https://www.axios.com/2025/11/18/trump-white-house-ballroom-crypto-coinbase.

6 *So did Ripple and Tether*: Sarah Wynn, "Crypto Donors to Trump's White House Ballroom Include Coinbase, Ripple and Tether," *Block*, October 24, 2025, https://www.theblock.co/post/376062/crypto-donors-trump-white-house-ballroom.

7 *"Balaji Srinivasan and the network state . . . They're radicals"*: Ross Douthat, *Interesting Times with Ross Douthat* (podcast), "Steve Bannon on 'Broligarchs' vs. Populism," *New York Times*, January 31, 2025, https://www.nytimes.com/2025/01/31/opinion/steve-bannon-on-broligarchs-vs-populism.html.

8 *"I no longer believe that freedom and democracy"*: Peter Thiel, "The Education of a Libertarian," *Cato Unbound*, April 13, 2009, https://www.cato-unbound.org/2009/04/13/peter-thiel/education-libertarian/.

8 *"[T]he right in the United States has attempted"*: David Golumbia, *Cyberlibertarianism: The Right-Wing Politics of Digital Technology* (Minneapolis: University of Minnesota Press, 2024), ebook.

8 *"technicization of all aspects of government"*: Kyle Chayka, "Techno-Fascism Comes to America: The Historic Parallels That Help Explain Elon Musk's Rampage on the Federal Government," *New Yorker*, February 26, 2025, https://www.newyorker.com/culture/infinite-scroll/techno-fascism-comes-to-america-elon-musk.

9 *"marketing for power . . . truly democratic agendas"*: Toni Morrison, "Racism and Fascism," *Journal of Negro Education* 64, no. 3 (Summer 1995): 384–385.

10 *"There is an alignment of interests . . . never seen before"*: Carole Cadwalladr, "This Is What a Digital Coup Looks Like," TED Talk, April 2025, YouTube, https://www.youtube.com/watch?v=TZOoT8AbkNE.

10 *"America has become a digital narco-state"*: Paul Krugman, "America Has Become a Digital Narco-State," *Paul Krugman* (blog), Substack, December 9, 2025, https://paulkrugman.substack.com/p/america-has-become-a-digital-narco.

CHAPTER 1 THE SOVEREIGN INDIVIDUAL

13 *"The democracy of the future . . . pledge allegiance to a country"*: Jaan vanValkenburgh, "Gifted Elite Will Run Nationless, Ruthless World, Book Claims," *Commercial Appeal* (Memphis, TN), March 30, 1997, 28, https://www.newspapers.com/image/774695138/.

14 *"an apocalyptic exercise that is unconvincing"*: Review of *The Sovereign Individual: How to Survive and Thrive During the Collapse of the Welfare State*, by James Dale Davidson and Lord William Rees-Mogg, *Publishers Weekly*, February 1997, https://www.publishersweekly.com/9780684810072.

14 *"It will be something . . . they want to take"*: Peter A. Thiel and Richard W. Rahn, "Virtual Money, Privacy and the Internet," moderated by David Theroux (panel, Independent Institute, Oakland, CA, October 20, 1999), YouTube, https://youtu.be/e-X8D1gOU1E?si=Zw3up4gEAGtrv23j&t=2700.

16 *"operation system for the entire government"*: "Palantir: Peter Thiel's Data-Mining Firm Helps DOGE Build Master Database to Surveil, Track Immigrants," interview with Makena Kelly, *Democracy Now!*, June 3, 2025, https://www.democracynow.org/2025/6/3/makena_kelly.

17 *"collapse of the welfare state"*: James Dale Davidson and Lord William Rees-Mogg, *The Sovereign Individual: How to Survive and Thrive During the Collapse of the Welfare State* (New York: Simon & Schuster, 1997), jacket copy.

17 *"If our deductions are correct . . . far from an easy transformation"*: James Dale Davidson and Lord William Rees-Mogg, *The Sovereign Individual: Mastering the Transition to the Information Age* (1997; repr., New York: Simon & Schuster, 2020), ebook.

18 *"An entirely new realm . . . outside political boundaries"*: Davidson and Rees-Mogg, *The Sovereign Individual.*

19 *"forged a eugenic university"*: Malcolm Harris, *Palo Alto: A History of California, Capitalism, and the World* (New York: Little, Brown and Company, 2023), 102.

19 *coined by Galton to mean "well-born"*: Adam S. Cohen, "Harvard's Eugenics Era," *Harvard Magazine*, March–April 2016, https://www.harvardmagazine.com/2016/02/harvards-eugenics-era.

20 *a new government called the "technate"*: Klint Finley, "Techies Have Been Trying to Replace Politicians for Decades," *Wired*, June 5, 2015, https://www.wired.com/2015/06/technocracy-inc/.

20 *"Members painted their cars . . . US Social Security Administration website"*: Finley, "Techies Have Been Trying," *Wired.*

20 *"hippies of the right"*: Ayn Rand, "Brief Summary," *Objectivist,* September 1971; reprinted in *The Voice of Reason: Essays in Objectivist Thought,* ed. Leonard Peikoff (New York: New American Library, 1989).

21 *"These developments will alter completely"*: Timothy C. May, "The Crypto Anarchist Manifesto" (distributed at Crypto '88 conference, Santa Barbara, CA, September 1988), https://groups.csail.mit.edu/mac/classes/6.805/articles/crypto/cypherpunks/may-crypto-manifesto.html.

21 *"Governments, including the American government"*: Esther Dyson, George Gilder, George Keyworth, and Alvin Toffler, "Cyberspace and the American Dream: A Magna Carta for the Knowledge Age," Progress and Freedom Foundation, August 1994, http://onala.free.fr/magnacarta94.pdf.

23 *"Together, Wired seemed to suggest"*: Fred Turner, *From Counterculture to Cyberculture: Stewart Brand, the Whole Earth Network, and the Rise of Digital Utopianism* (Chicago: University of Chicago Press, 2006), 238.

23 *"Californian Ideology . . . lots of technological determinism"*: Richard Barbrook and Andy Cameron, "The Californian Ideology," *Mute,* September 1, 1995.

23 *"Governments of the Industrial World . . . the Mind in Cyberspace"*: John Perry Barlow, "A Declaration of the Independence of Cyberspace," February 8, 1996, https://www.eff.org/cyberspace-independence.

24 *"a collection of ideas"*: Langdon Winner, "Cyberlibertarian Myths and the Prospects for Community," *ACM SIGCAS Computers and Society* 27, no. 3 (September 1997): 14–19, https://dl.acm.org/doi/pdf/10.1145/270858.270864.

24 *"The two prongs of this statement"*: David Golumbia, *Cyberlibertarianism: The Right-Wing Politics of Digital Technology* (Minneapolis: University of Minnesota Press, 2024), ebook.

25 *"[t]he coming of the Year 2000 . . . is about to be 'unveiled'"*: Davidson and Rees-Mogg, *The Sovereign Individual.*

26 *Launched in the late 1980s*: Anna Wiener, "Only Human: Meet the Hackers Trying to Solve the Problem of Death," *New Republic,* February 16, 2017, https://newrepublic.com/article/140260/human.

26 *"It favors decentralization"*: Paulina Borsook, *Cyberselfish: A Critical Romp Through the Terribly Libertarian Culture of High Tech* (New York: PublicAffairs, 2000), 32.

26 *"labeled the homeless"*: Borsook, *Cyberselfish,* 72.

27 *"It bespeaks a lack . . . a philosophy out of a personality defect"*: Borsook, *Cyberselfish,* 15.

28 *"Millenarian sects or movements"*: Norman Cohn, *The Pursuit of the Millennium: Revolutionary Millenarians and Mystical Anarchists of the Middle Ages,* rev. ed. (New York: Oxford University Press, 1970), 15.

28 *"operate like the gods of myth"*: Davidson and Rees-Mogg, *The Sovereign Individual.*

29 *"the individual becomes sovereign"*: Peter Thiel, "Virtual Money, Privacy, and the Internet," Independent Institute, October 20, 1999, YouTube, segment begins at 35:58, https://www.youtube.com/watch?v=e-X8D1gOU1E.

30 *their obsession with "hard money"*: Quinn Slobodian, *Hayek's Bastards: Race, Gold, IQ, and the Capitalism of the Far Right* (Zone Books, 2025), ebook.

30 *the Union issued "greenbacks"*: "Greenback Movement," *Encyclopaedia Britannica*, accessed July 3, 2025, https://www.britannica.com/event/Greenback-movement.

30 *Gold came to symbolize personal sovereignty*: Dave Troy, "Paranoia on Parade: How Goldbugs, Libertarians and Religious Extremists Brought America to the Brink," *Washington Spectator* 48, no. 3 (May/June 2022), https://washingtonspectator.org/paranoia-on-parade/.

31 *While nominally focused on financial tips*: Ryan Lenz, "Ron Paul's New Organization Reportedly Stacked with Extremists," *Hatewatch*, Southern Poverty Law Center, April 26, 2013, https://www.splcenter.org/resources/hatewatch/ron-pauls-new-organization-reportedly-stacked-extremists.

32 *lists Davidson as having attended in 1976*: "James Dale Davidson," alumni note, *Pembroke College Record* (Oxford: Pembroke College, 1987), 47. Available at https://heyzine.com/flip-book/08b5c50263.html#page/48.

32 *later described as "works of futurology"*: William Rees-Mogg, *Memoirs* (London: HarperPress, 2011), ebook.

34 *"Those forecasts of doom . . . why they sold so well"*: Rees-Mogg, *Memoirs.*

34 *"Clinton is going to be a one-term president"*: James Dale Davidson, *The Plague of the Black Debt: How to Survive the Coming Depression* (Baltimore: Agora, 1993), 58.

34 *Rees-Mogg also sullied himself*: Glenn Kessler, "No, Donald Trump, There's Nothing 'Fishy' About Vince Foster's Suicide," *Washington Post*, May 25, 2016, https://www.washingtonpost.com/news/fact-checker/wp/2016/05/25/no-donald-trump-theres-nothing-fishy-about-vince-fosters-suicide/.

35 *"In all explorations of the projected future"*: Kessler, "No, Donald Trump," *Washington Post.*

36 *"It is hard to overestimate . . . that makes history go"*: James Dale Davidson and William Rees-Mogg, *Blood in the Streets: Investment Profits in a World Gone Mad* (New York: Summit Books, 1987), 12.

36 *"Citizenship is obsolete . . . becoming a Sovereign Individual"*: Davidson and Rees-Mogg, *The Sovereign Individual* (Touchstone, 2020).

36 *"On December 21, 2012 . . . such a shocking announcement"*: James Dale Davidson, promotional letter for *Strategic Investment* newsletter, ca. 2012, archived at https://that.nu/party/policies/economy/capitalism-pros-and-cons/a-civilization-altering-development-a-prediction-of-the-start-of-the-demise-of-capitalism-james-dale-davidson/. The original newsletter is no longer available online; this text was preserved by a third-party site.

37 *"When he died in 2012"*: Andy Beckett, "How to Explain Jacob Rees-Mogg? Start with His Father's Books," *Guardian*, November 9, 2018, https://www.theguardian.com/books/2018/nov/09/mystic-mogg-jacob-rees-mogg-willam-predicts-brexit-plans.

39 *"I'm not the kind of person"*: "COLLAPSE 2016, James Dale Davidson, Economist," YouTube, June 18, 2016, https://www.youtube.com/watch?v=pmNvo3ix-QQ.

39 *"The future may lie . . . not to be wasted"*: Peter Thiel, preface to *The Sovereign Individual* by James Dale Davidson and Lord William Rees-Mogg (Touchstone, 2020).

40 *"To flip through the pages"*: Max Chafkin, *The Contrarian: Peter Thiel and Silicon Valley's Pursuit of Power* (New York: Penguin Press, 2021), ebook.

41 *"Thiel lost investors' money"*: Chafkin, *The Contrarian.*

41 *"Levchin's technology was almost absurdly narrow . . . dollars to buy stuff"*: Chafkin, *The Contrarian.*

41 *"an unusual book that I read at a singular moment"*: Caroline Howard, "Peter Thiel: 'Don't Wait to Start Something New,'" *Forbes*, September 10, 2014, https://www.forbes.com/sites/carolinehoward/2014/09/10/peter-thiel-dont-wait-to-start-something-new/.

42 *"his father was involved in uranium mining"*: Simon Kuper, "Musk, Thiel and the Shadow of Apartheid South Africa," *Financial Times*, September 19, 2024, https://www.ft.com/content/cfbfa1e8-d8f8-42b9-b74c-dae6cc6185a0.

42 *"I had thoughts of assassination"*: Walter Isaacson, *Elon Musk* (New York: Simon & Schuster, 2023), ebook.

42 *Thiel's 3.7 percent stake*: "Peter Thiel's Net Worth Hits $23.2B in 2025," *Benzinga*, August 13, 2025, https://www.benzinga.com/money/peter-thiel-net-worth.

43 *a "mission-oriented" software company*: Andy Greenberg, "How a 'Deviant' Philosopher Built Palantir, a CIA-Funded Data-Mining Juggernaut," *Forbes*, August 14, 2013, https://www.forbes.com/sites/andygreenberg/2013/08/14/agent-of-intelligence-how-a-deviant-philosopher-built-palantir-a-cia-funded-data-mining-juggernaut/.

43 *reportedly doodled through his meeting*: Greenberg, "'Deviant' Philosopher," *Forbes.*

43 *"[t]he company's $30 million start-up costs"*: Siobhan Gorman, "How Team of Geeks Cracked Spy Trade," *Wall Street Journal*, September 4, 2009, https://www.wsj.com/articles/SB125200842406984303.

44 *"the fundamentalist civil rights mania"*: Peter Thiel, "The Straussian Moment," in *Politics and Apocalypse*, ed. Robert Hamerton-Kelly (East Lansing: Michigan State University Press, 2007).

45 *"saturated in racism"*: Alexander Belenky, "The Two Faces of Ron Paul," *Guardian*, January 8, 2008, https://www.theguardian.com/world/deadlineusa/2008/jan/08/thetwofacesofronpaul.

45 *"Given the inefficiencies"*: Ta-Nehisi Coates, "Ron Paul's Shaggy Defense," *Atlantic*, December 20, 2011, https://www.theatlantic.com/politics/archive/2011/12/ron-pauls-shaggy-defense/250256/.

45 *"I remain committed to the faith . . . democracy are compatible"*: Peter Thiel, "The Education of a Libertarian," *Cato Unbound*, April 13, 2009, https://www.cato-unbound.org/2009/04/13/peter-thiel/education-libertarian/.

47 *"Within the pantheon . . . $10 billion to construct"*: Alexis Madrigal, "Peter Thiel Makes Down Payment on Libertarian Ocean Colonies," *Wired*, May 19, 2008, https://www.wired.com/2008/05/peter-thiel-makes-down-payment-on-libertarian-ocean-colonies/.

48 *"[T]he idea of seasteading . . . it'd be too late"*: Chafkin, *The Contrarian.*

48 *"Decades from now"*: "Introducing The Seasteading Institute," Seasteading Institute, April 15, 2008, https://www.seasteading.org/introducing-the-seasteading-institute/.

48 *"willing to say the exact things"*: Chafkin, *The Contrarian.*
48 *"Government is an industry . . . change your citizenship"*: Madrigal, "Peter Thiel Makes Down Payment," *Wired.*
48 *"Tired of being denied . . . PR for crazy people"*: Mike Pesca, "Libertarian Island: No Rules, Just Rich Dudes," NPR, May 21, 2008, https://www.npr.org/transcripts/90664406.
49 *"It would be absurd to suggest . . . some consider utopian"*: Thiel, "The Education of a Libertarian," *Cato Unbound.*
49 *"He is making a* factual statement . . . committee of men and women": Curtis Yarvin (as Mencius Moldbug), "Democraphobia Goes (Slightly) Viral," *Unqualified Reservations* (blog), May 2009, https://www.unqualified-reservations.org/2009/05/democraphobia-goes-slightly-viral/.
49 *"They soon met for the first time . . . tech C.E.O.s were their prey"*: Ava Kofman, "Curtis Yarvin's Plot Against America," *New Yorker*, June 2, 2025, https://www.newyorker.com/magazine/2025/06/09/curtis-yarvin-profile.

CHAPTER 2 THE ACID STORY

51 *"Yarvin, you reactionary fascist . . . from getting elected"*: Ian Ward, "Curtis Yarvin's Ideas Were Fringe. Now They're Coursing Through Trump's Washington," *Politico*, January 30, 2025, https://www.politico.com/news/magazine/2025/01/30/curtis-yarvins-ideas-00201552.
51 *"I don't think he meant it"*: Ward, "Curtis Yarvin's Ideas Were Fringe," *Politico.*
52 *"diplomat's brat"*: Curtis Yarvin, interview by Max Raskin, November 15, 2023, https://www.maxraskin.com/interviews/curtis-yarvin.
52 *"He was an atheist Jew . . . skin turned orange"*: Meredith Tanner, interview with author, April 28, 2025.
53 *"too arrogant," his son later told a reporter*: Ava Kofman, "Curtis Yarvin's Plot Against America," *New Yorker*, June 2, 2025, https://www.newyorker.com/magazine/2025/06/09/curtis-yarvin-profile.
53 *"We were taught to read . . . his mind as it usually is"*: Norman Yarvin, email to author, September 4, 2025.
54 *"weird, threatening, disturbing alien"*: Kofman, "Curtis Yarvin's Plot Against America," *New Yorker.*
54 *"He found more . . . their posts uninteresting"*: Kofman, "Curtis Yarvin's Plot Against America," *New Yorker.*
55 *"One thing he liked to do"*: Meredith Tanner, interview with author, April 28, 2025.
57 *"The man who drove America crazy"*: "The Acid Story with Curtis Yarvin," *Tim Dillon Show.*
57 *Yarvin said he had bought*: Jacob Siegel, "The Red-Pill Prince: How Computer Programmer Curtis Yarvin Became America's Most Controversial Political Theorist," *Tablet*, March 31, 2022, https://www.tabletmag.com/sections/news/articles/red-pill-prince-curtis-yarvin.
57 *"In 2002, he left Openwave"*: Julia Black, "The Far-Right Guru Who Has Befriended Silicon Valley's Extreme Factions," *Information*, August 9, 2024, https://www

.theinformation.com/articles/the-far-right-guru-who-has-befriended-silicon-valleys-extreme-factions.

58 *"Furthermore, I am a computer programmer"*: Curtis Yarvin (as Mencius Moldbug), "A Formalist Manifesto," *Unqualified Reservations* (blog), April 24, 2007, https://www.unqualified-reservations.org/2007/04/formalist-manifesto-originally-posted/.

58 *a superior form of "private government"*: Yarvin, "Formalist Manifesto."

59 *"The Cathedral consists of . . . following their lead"*: Curtis Yarvin (Mencius Moldbug), "Patchwork: A Positive Vision," *Unqualified Reservations* (blog), November 13, 2008, https://www.unqualified-reservations.org/2008/11/patchwork-positive-vision-part-1/.

61 *"Not all humans are born the same . . . Indians did not"*: Curtis Yarvin (Mencius Moldbug), "From Mises to Carlyle: My Sick Journey," *Unqualified Reservations* (blog), February 2010, https://www.unqualified-reservations.org/2010/02/from-mises-to-carlyle-my-sick-journey/.

62 *"I am not exactly allergic"*: Curtis Yarvin (Mencius Moldbug), "Why I Am Not a White Nationalist," *Unqualified Reservations* (blog), November 22, 2007, https://www.unqualified-reservations.org/2007/11/why-i-am-not-white-nationalist/.

62 *"America's actual WASP-Ashkenazi aristocracy"*: Curtis Yarvin (Mencius Moldbug), "An Open Letter to Open-Minded Progressives," *Unqualified Reservations* (blog), April 17, 2008, https://www.unqualified-reservations.org/2008/04/open-letter-to-open-minded-progressives/.

63 *"digital feudalism . . . solution in this context"*: Curtis Yarvin, "Urbit Namespace (300K)," GitHub, January 20, 2010, https://github.com/cgyarvin/urbit/blob/6ac688960687aa9c89d4da6fff49a3125c10aca1/Spec/urbit/3-intro.txt.

64 *"I think it is only"*: Peter Thiel, "Peter Thiel at Libertopia 2010," keynote, YouTube, uploaded February 25, 2012, https://www.youtube.com/watch?v=KgH7Lv2gQdk.

65 *"Thiel's budding movement . . . distaste for the mainstream Left"*: Max Chafkin, *The Contrarian: Peter Thiel and Silicon Valley's Pursuit of Power* (New York: Penguin Press, 2021), ebook.

65 *"supreme Sith Lord"*: Nick Land, "The Dark Enlightenment," 2012, https://www.thedarkenlightenment.com/the-dark-enlightenment-by-nick-land/.

65 *"a technological revolution"*: James Duesterberg, "Silicon Valley's Favorite Doomsaying Philosopher," *New Yorker*, February 18, 2026, https://www.newyorker.com/culture/the-lede/silicon-valleys-favorite-doomsaying-philosopher.

65 *"Nothing human makes it out"*: Nick Land, *Fanged Noumena: Collected Writings 1987–2007*, ed. Robin Mackay and Ray Brassier (London: Urbanomic, 2011), ebook.

66 *"It had pledged itself . . . profoundly insane"*: Land, *Fanged Noumena*.

66 *"Politics since the Enlightenment . . . or, simply, 'Intelligence'"*: Duesterberg, "Silicon Valley's Favorite Doomsaying Philosopher," *New Yorker*.

66 *"The state isn't going anywhere . . . the appointment of a CEO"*: Land, "The Dark Enlightenment."

67 *"And by like 2011 or 2010 . . . right"*: "The Acid Story with Curtis Yarvin," *Tim Dillon Show*.

67 *"Thiel became a direct patron . . . called Tlon"*: Corey Pein, *Live Work Work Work Die: A Journey into the Savage Heart of Silicon Valley* (New York: Metropolitan Books, 2018), ebook.

67 *One of Yarvin's cofounders*: John Chandler Burnham, "About," personal website, accessed April 10, 2026, https://www.johnchandlerburnham.com/about.html.

67 *struck up a friendship with Yarvin*: Bruce Rogers, "Counsyl Reinvents the Clinical Laboratory to Provide Better Genetic Testing Services," *Forbes*, June 15, 2016, https://www.forbes.com/sites/brucerogers/2016/06/15/counsyl-reinvents-the-clinical-laboratory-to-provide-better-genetic-testing-services/.

68 *in an article titled "Geeks for Monarchy"*: Klint Finley, "Geeks for Monarchy: The Rise of the Neoreactionaries," *TechCrunch*, November 22, 2013, https://techcrunch.com/2013/11/22/geeks-for-monarchy/.

68 *"bizarre online neo-fascist movement . . . ethno-centric feudalism"*: Jamie Bartlett, "Meet the Dark Enlightenment: Sophisticated Neo-Fascism That's Spreading Fast on the Net," *Daily Telegraph*, January 20, 2014, at the Wayback Machine, https://web.archive.org/web/20160312103748/http://blogs.telegraph.co.uk/technology/jamiebartlett/100012093/meet-the-dark-enlightenment-sophisticated-neo-fascism-thats-spreading-fast-on-the-net/.

68 *"total corporate despotism . . . You will not get the job"*: Corey Pein, "Mouth-breathing Machiavellis Dream of a Silicon Reich," *Baffler*, May 19, 2014, https://thebaffler.com/latest/mouthbreathing-machiavellis.

69 *"It's time for the U.S. Regime . . . prevent further American decline"*: Justine Tunney, "Transfer All Federal Administrative Authority to the Tech Industry," petition, WhiteHouse.gov, March 19, 2014, cited in Zac Hall, "Occupy Wall Street Co-Founder: Appoint Eric Schmidt CEO of America," *9to5Google*, March 20, 2014, https://9to5google.com/2014/03/20/occupy-wall-street-co-founder-appoint-eric-schmidt-ceo-of-america/.

69 *"Read Mencius Moldbug . . . the top 1/3rd"*: Keith A. Spencer, "Tech's Dark Overlords," *UnHerd*, February 4, 2019, https://unherd.com/2019/02/techs-dark-overlords/.

69 *"Some sponsors have dropped out . . . you might think so"*: Tess Townsend, "Controversy Rages over 'Pro-Slavery' Tech Speaker Curtis Yarvin," *Inc.*, March 31, 2016, https://www.inc.com/tess-townsend/why-it-matters-that-an-obscure-programming-conference-is-hosting-mencius-moldbug.html.

70 *"If things get hot"*: Cade Metz, "Silicon Valley's Safe Space," *New York Times*, February 13, 2021, https://www.nytimes.com/2021/02/13/technology/slate-star-codex-rationalists.html.

70 *"How dangerous is it . . . they kinda know it"*: Kofman, "Curtis Yarvin's Plot Against America," *New Yorker*.

CHAPTER 3 EXIT

73 *"If a company or a country . . . or to join a competitor"*: Balaji Srinivasan, "Silicon Valley's Ultimate Exit" (talk, Y Combinator Startup School, Mountain View, CA, October 25, 2013), YouTube, https://www.youtube.com/watch?v=cOubCHLXT6A.

75 *"In a nutshell . . . Why not do so with America"*: Anand Giridharadas, "Silicon Valley Roused by Secession Call," *New York Times*, October 28, 2013, https://www.nytimes.com/2013/10/29/us/silicon-valley-roused-by-secession-call.html.

75 *"peaceful exit . . . offer much evidence"*: Farhad Manjoo, "Silicon Valley Has an Arrogance Problem," *Wall Street Journal*, November 3, 2013, https://www.wsj.com/articles/SB10001424052702303661404579175712015473766.

76 *"There are many exciting things"*: Nathan Ingraham, "Larry Page Wants to 'Set Aside a Part of the World' for Unregulated Experimentation," *Verge*, May 15, 2013, https://www.theverge.com/2013/5/15/4334356/larry-page-wants-to-set-aside-a-part-of-the-world-for-experimentation.

76 *Paul Romer suggested the creation of "charter cities"*: Paul Romer, "Why the World Needs Charter Cities," TED Talk, August 2009, YouTube, https://www.youtube.com/watch?v=mSHBmaoIthk.

76 *Critics called it "colonialism"*: Aditya Chakrabortty, "Paul Romer Is a Brilliant Economist—but His Idea for Charter Cities Is Bad," *Guardian*, July 27, 2010, https://www.theguardian.com/science/2010/jul/27/paul-romers-charter-cities-idea.

76 *Yarvin called Romer a "plagiarist"*: Curtis Yarvin (as Mencius Moldbug), "From Cromer to Romer and Back Again," *Unqualified Reservations* (blog), August 20, 2009, https://www.unqualified-reservations.org/2009/08/from-cromer-to-romer-and-back-again/.

76 *"I think there is going to be . . . going to be very healthy"*: Hamish McKenzie, "Marc Andreessen: 'The World Is Going to See an Explosion of Countries in the Years Ahead,'" *PandoDaily*, October 3, 2013, at the Wayback Machine, https://web.archive.org/web/20201219121459/https://pando.com/2013/10/03/marc-andreessen-the-world-is-going-to-see-an-explosion-of-countries-in-the-years-ahead/.

76 *"From Occupy Wall Street . . . in different ways"*: Balaji Srinivasan, "Software Is Reorganizing the World," *Wired*, November 22, 2013, https://www.wired.com/2013/11/software-is-reorganizing-the-world-and-cloud-formations-could-lead-to-physical-nations/.

77 *"Yarvin proposes that . . . Y Combinator speech"*: Klint Finley, "Geeks for Monarchy: The Rise of the Neoreactionaries," *TechCrunch*, November 22, 2013, https://techcrunch.com/2013/11/22/geeks-for-monarchy/.

77 *"Dude, control the frame . . . which rewards patience"*: Anthony Lydgate, "Would You Ditch All This Chaos for a Country in the Cloud?," *Wired*, September 6, 2022, https://www.wired.com/story/balaji-srinivasan-ditch-chaos-country-cloud/.

78 *"The first thirteen years . . . I stuck out"*: Eric Jorgenson, *The Anthology of Balaji: A Guide to Technology, Truth, and Building the Future* (Smart Friends Publishing, 2023), 23.

79 *"I learned early on . . . not on my side"*: Jorgenson, *Anthology of Balaji*, 24.

79 *"He always had an arrogance . . . stupid all the time"*: Dana Kirschman, Facebook message to author, September 25, 2025.

79 *"He did act up sometimes... race/ethnicity/religion"*: Former classmate of Balaji Srinivasan, Facebook message to author, September 21, 2025.

80 *"for more than 400 mutations"*: Kim-Mai Cutler, "Through Dirt-Cheap Genetic Testing, Counsyl Is Pioneering a New Bioinformatics Wave," *TechCrunch*, April 23, 2013, https://techcrunch.com/2013/04/23/counsyl/.

80 *"We had to bootstrap"*: Jorgenson, *Anthology of Balaji*, 27.

80 *acquired by Myriad Genetics for $375 million*: Myriad Genetics, Inc., "Myriad Genetics Signs Definitive Agreement to Acquire Counsyl, Inc.," press release, May 28, 2018, https://investor.myriad.com/news-releases/news-release-detail/19456/.

80 *"the most prescient thing"*: Eric Jorgenson, "Balaji's Recommended Reading," in *The Anthology of Balaji*.

81 *"more like a Hollywood talent"*: Claire Cain Miller, "Andreessen Horowitz Grows Up," *Bits* (blog), *New York Times*, June 21, 2010, https://archive.nytimes.com/bits.blogs.nytimes.com/2010/06/21/andreessen-horowitz-grows-up/.

81 *"Software is eating the world"*: Marc Andreessen, "Why Software Is Eating the World," Andreessen Horowitz, August 20, 2011, https://a16z.com/why-software-is-eating-the-world/.

81 *The Netscape IPO in 1995*: Alice Truong, "Netscape Changed the Internet—and the World—When It Went Public 20 Years Ago," *Quartz*, August 9, 2015, https://qz.com/475279/netscape-changed-the-internet-and-the-world-when-it-went-public-20-years-ago-today.

81 *"These companies are in early stages... the value creation"*: Catherine Bracy, *World Eaters: How Venture Capital Is Cannibalizing the Economy* (New York: Portfolio/Penguin, 2025), ebook.

82 *a $300 million debut fund*: Richi Jennings, "Marc Andreessen Starts $300 Million VC Fund with Ben Horowitz," *Computerworld*, July 6, 2009, https://www.computerworld.com/article/1330191/marc-andreessen-starts-300-million-vc-fund-with-ben-horowitz.html.

82 *the firm would rapidly expand*: Scott Kupor, "Fund VII and Growth Fund II," Andreessen Horowitz, November 2020, https://a16z.com/fund-vii-and-growth-fund-ii/.

82 *to over $90 billion*: "About," Andreessen Horowitz, accessed April 10, 2026, https://a16z.com/about/.

82 *he became the firm's eighth general partner*: Kim-Mai Cutler, "Counsyl Co-Founder Balaji Srinivasan Steps Up as Andreessen Horowitz' Newest General Partner," *TechCrunch*, December 9, 2013, https://techcrunch.com/2013/12/09/counsyl-srinivasan-andreessen-horowitz/.

83 *Srinivasan had founded a company called 21e6*: Nathaniel Popper, "What is 21.co Really Building? An Excerpt from *Digital Gold*," *TechCrunch*, May 18, 2015, at the Wayback Machine, https://web.archive.org/web/20150520234427/https://techcrunch.com/2015/05/18/what-is-21-co-really-doing-an-excerpt-from-digital-gold/.

83 *"rat poison, squared"*: Tae Kim, "Warren Buffett Says Bitcoin Is 'Probably Rat Poison Squared,'" CNBC, May 5, 2018, https://www.cnbc.com/2018/05/05/warren-buffett-says-bitcoin-is-probably-rat-poison-squared.html.

83 *"The company 21e6 . . . money for investors"*: Nathaniel Popper, *Digital Gold: Bitcoin and the Inside Story of the Misfits and Millionaires Trying to Reinvent Money* (New York: Harper, 2015), 191.

84 *"Soon enough . . . arms race had begun"*: Popper, *Digital Gold*, 192.

84 *21e6 had raised over $70 million*: Popper, "What Is 21.co Really Building?," *TechCrunch.*

84 *hackers had stolen more than $460 million*: Robert McMillan, "The Inside Story of Mt. Gox, Bitcoin's $460 Million Disaster," *Wired*, March 3, 2014, https://www.wired.com/2014/03/bitcoin-exchange/.

84 *"In May 2015 . . . a year of runway"*: Balaji Srinivasan, "The Turnaround," Medium, April 16, 2018, https://medium.com/@balajis/the-turnaround-2d145589d814.

85 *"repurposing the datacenter's mining chips"*: Srinivasan, "The Turnaround."

85 *"Our nuclear bases . . . vote for Donald Trump"*: "Watch PayPal Co-Founder Peter Thiel's Full Speech at the 2016 Republican National Convention," posted July 21, 2016, by PBS NewsHour, YouTube, https://www.youtube.com/watch?v=P2cemLrzpr4.

85 *would find himself largely outcast from politics*: Melissa Chan, "Milo Yiannopoulos Resigns from Breitbart News amid Pedophilia Controversy," *Time*, February 21, 2017, https://time.com/4677624/milo-yiannopoulos-breitbart-resigns-pedophilia/; Clark Mindock, "Milo Yiannopoulos Filmed Singing 'America the Beautiful' While White Nationalists Gave Nazi Salutes," *Independent*, October 7, 2017, https://www.independent.co.uk/news/world/americas/milo-yiannopoulos-nazi-salutes-video-karaoke-richard-spencer-white-nationalists-karaoke-bar-a7987486.html.

85 *"Not as much . . . plays it very carefully"*: Ava Kofman, "Curtis Yarvin's Plot Against America," *New Yorker*, June 2, 2025, https://www.newyorker.com/magazine/2025/06/09/curtis-yarvin-profile.

86 *"Yelp for drugs . . . Build the future"*: Rhett Jones, "Why Did Trump's Top FDA Pick Delete All His Tweets?," *Gizmodo*, January 15, 2017, https://gizmodo.com/why-did-trumps-top-fda-pick-delete-all-his-tweets-1791227569.

86 *"Balaji Srinivasan . . . Delete All His Tweets?"*: Jones, "Trump's Top FDA Pick," *Gizmodo.*

86 *"Srinivasan Not Up for FDA Role"*: Dan Diamond, "Dems Ramp Up Attack on Tom Price After New Ethical Questions," *Politico Pulse*, January 17, 2017, https://www.politico.com/tipsheets/politico-pulse/2017/01/dems-ramp-up-attack-on-tom-price-after-new-ethical-questions-218259.

87 *"Up until now . . . saying it out loud"*: Peter Kafka, "Balaji Srinivasan, Who May Run the FDA for Trump, Hates the FDA. But Silicon Valley Likes Srinivasan," *Vox*, January 15, 2017, https://www.vox.com/2017/1/14/14276530/balaji-srinivasan-trump-fda-twitter-andreessen-horowitz.

87 *"a service that rewards users"*: Jon Russell, "Coinbase Buys Earn.com and Makes CEO Balaji Srinivasan Its First CTO," *TechCrunch*, April 16, 2018, https://techcrunch.com/2018/04/16/coinbase-buys-earn-com-and-makes-ceo-balaji-srinivasan-its-first-cto/.

87 *"It was a crummy company . . . its dog of a startup"*: Jeff John Roberts, *Kings of Crypto: One Startup's Quest to Take Cryptocurrency Out of Silicon Valley and Onto Wall Street* (Boston: Harvard Business Review Press, 2021), 186–187.

87 *"You can come up with"*: Roberts, *Kings of Crypto*, 187.

88 *Srinivasan signed on as CTO*: Fitz Tepper, "Coinbase Raises $100M at a $1.6B Valuation amid Explosive Growth," *TechCrunch*, August 10, 2017, https://techcrunch.com/2017/08/10/coinbase-raises-100m-at-a-1-6b-valuation-amid-explosive-growth/.

88 *"visionary and crypto zealot"*: Roberts, *Kings of Crypto*, 48.

88 *"Balaji crumbled . . . the San Francisco night"*: Roberts, *Kings of Crypto*, 185.

88 *"Some people lead . . . and by money"*: Roberts, *Kings of Crypto*, 193.

88 *"For someone who . . . quit on their own accord"*: Roberts, *Kings of Crypto*, 193.

88 *"Balaji was Coinbase's first"*: Jeff John Roberts, "Road to IPO: Coinbase's Power Struggles," *CoinDesk*, December 20, 2020, https://www.coindesk.com/business/2020/12/20/road-to-ipo-coinbases-power-struggles; excerpted from Jeff John Roberts, *Kings of Crypto*.

88 *"He could function without sleep . . . and half-and-half"*: Roberts, *Kings of Crypto*, 189.

89 *"tearing through anyone"*: Roberts, *Kings of Crypto*, 189.

89 *"cutthroat and manipulative"*: Roberts, *Kings of Crypto*, 194.

89 *"Mr. Hirji . . . regulatory gray area"*: Jon Victor, "Inside Coinbase's Executive Turmoil: Conflicting Visions," *Information*, July 22, 2019, https://www.theinformation.com/articles/inside-coinbases-executive-turmoil-conflicting-visions.

90 *"a woke white who can't code"*: Balaji Srinivasan (@balajis), "Hey @nathanielpopper, I'll personally contribute to increased diversity at the New York Times Company," Twitter (now X), December 29, 2020, https://x.com/balajis/status/1344136575580397569.

90 *"Guy who has built nothing"*: Balaji Srinivasan (@balajis), "guy who has built nothing thinks he can critique guy who invented the web browser," Twitter (now X), April 20, 2020, https://x.com/balajis/status/1252276198983385090.

90 *"I cofounded a clinical genomics company"*: Balaji Srinivasan (@balajis), "I cofounded a clinical genomics company that sold for $375M. You work at Buzzfeed," Twitter (now X), April 20, 2020, https://x.com/balajis/status/1252409386451922946.

90 *"Tech will align behind Bitcoin . . . MMT v BTC"*: Balaji Srinivasan (@balajis), "Tech will align behind Bitcoin as part of the political realignment of the 2020s," Twitter (now X), October 29, 2019, https://x.com/balajis/status/1189274759000985601.

90 *"It would accelerate many pre-existing trends"*: Balaji Srinivasan (@balajis), "Going viral. What if this coronavirus is the pandemic that public health people have been warning about for years?," Twitter (now X), January 30, 2020, https://x.com/balajis/status/1222921758375927808.

91 *"For a virus like this . . . minimizing the issue"*: Balaji Srinivasan (@balajis), "For a virus like this, the time to 'overreact' is now, before it becomes pandemic," Twitter (now X), January 30, 2020, https://x.com/balajis/status/1222929746432053249.

91 *"The Man Who Called COVID"*: Marc Hochstein, "Balaji Srinivasan: The Man Who Called COVID," *CoinDesk*, December 8, 2020, https://www.coindesk.com/markets/2020/12/08/balaji-srinivasan-the-man-who-called-covid.

91 *"The scene brought out . . . for a sudden exit"*: Jacob Siegel, "The Red-Pill Prince," *Tablet*, March 31, 2022, https://www.tabletmag.com/sections/news/articles/red-pill-prince-curtis-yarvin.

91 *"not just a test of our government"*: Curtis Yarvin, "Plan A for the Coronavirus," Medium, April 4, 2020, https://medium.com/@curtis.yarvin/plan-a-for-the-coronavirus-7db3997490c1.

92 *killed over 7 million globally*: World Health Organization, "COVID-19 Deaths," WHO COVID-19 Dashboard, accessed April 10, 2026, https://data.who.int/dashboards/covid19/deaths.

92 *"I don't think people realize"*: Balaji Srinivasan (@balajis), "I don't think people realize that there is no normal to go back to anymore," Twitter (now X), April 3, 2020, https://x.com/balajis/status/1246151098986983424.

CHAPTER 4 THE NEW REALITY

93 *"The coronavirus panic is dumb"*: Elon Musk (@elonmusk), "The coronavirus panic is dumb," Twitter (now X), March 6, 2020, https://x.com/elonmusk/status/1236029449042198528.

93 *"Based on current trends"*: Elon Musk (@elonmusk), "Based on current trends, probably close to zero new cases in US too by end of April," Twitter (now X), March 19, 2020, https://x.com/elonmusk/status/1240754657263144960.

93 *He decried mandatory health measures as "fascist"*: Camila Domonoske, "Tesla's Elon Musk Rants Again, Calls Lockdowns Forcible Imprisonment and 'Fascist,'" NPR, April 29, 2020, https://www.npr.org/2020/04/29/848093173/teslas-elon-musk-rants-again-calls-lockdowns-forcible-imprisonment-and-fascist.

94 *resulting in an "unwillingness to build"*: Marc Andreessen, "It's Time to Build," Andreessen Horowitz, April 18, 2020, https://a16z.com/its-time-to-build/.

95 *"offered the homebound online masses"*: Melia Russell and Kali Hays, "Inside the Rise and Fall of Clubhouse, a Pandemic Poster Child of VC-Backed Hype Now Hobbled by 'Drama Rooms,' Unhappy Creators, Dwindling Users, and Dubious Advertisers," *Business Insider*, November 22, 2021, https://www.businessinsider.com/rise-and-fall-of-clubhouse-poster-child-pandemic-hype-2021-11.

95 *"Silicon Valley's Ultimate Exit"*: Anna Wiener, "Clubhouse Feels Like a Party," *New Yorker*, March 31, 2021, https://www.newyorker.com/news/letter-from-silicon-valley/in-the-clubhouse.

95 *Srinivasan had invested in Clubhouse*: Ari Levy and Salvador Rodriguez, "Silicon Valley Is Going Crazy for Clubhouse, a Social Media App with 1,500 Users That's Already Worth $100 Million," CNBC, May 20, 2020, https://www.cnbc.com/2020/05/20/clubhouse-app-is-where-mc-hammer-and-jared-leto-chat-with-vcs.html.

95 *It rose to a $4 billion valuation*: Ari Levy, "The Pandemic Drove Clubhouse to a $4 Billion Valuation That Never Looked Sustainable," CNBC, April 27, 2023,

https://www.cnbc.com/2023/04/27/clubhouse-layoffs-app-reached-4-billion-valuation-during-pandemic.html.

96 *Krishnan launched "dozens, within a year"*: Ben Smith, "The Group Chats That Changed America," *Semafor*, April 28, 2025, https://www.semafor.com/article/04/27/2025/the-group-chats-that-changed-america.

96 *"the memetic upstream of mainstream opinion"*: Sriram Krishnan, "Group Chats Rule the World," *Sriram Krishnan* (blog), Substack, August 26, 2024, https://sriramk.substack.com/p/group-chats-rule-the-world.

97 *Boudin had been in office for one year*: Susie Neilson, "San Francisco Crime Rates Drastically Shifted in the Pandemic. These Charts Show What's Happening Now," *San Francisco Chronicle*, February 6, 2023, https://www.sfchronicle.com/crime/article/san-francisco-crime-rate-17065509.php.

98 *"STOP Chasing Money"*: Garry Tan, "Stop Chasing Money—Chase Wealth," *Garry Tan's Office Hours*, episode 4, March 31, 2021, YouTube, https://www.youtube.com/watch?v=7Hdu4DlnLIk.

99 *"Big mistake . . . $20 billion or more"*: Garry Tan, "My $200 Million Startup Mistake: Peter Thiel Asked and I Said No," December 23, 2019, YouTube, https://www.youtube.com/watch?v=dtnGoELjvcM.

99 *"an orb on a pedestal . . . human-computer symbiosis"*: Garry Tan, "How I Designed the Palantir Technologies Logo," LinkedIn, October 4, 2024, https://www.linkedin.com/posts/garrytan_how-i-designed-the-palantir-technologies-activity-7247997250457460736-oaxt/.

99 *Sacks decried Boudin as a "killer DA"*: David Sacks, "The Killer D.A.: Chesa Boudin's Decarceration Disaster," Medium, January 5, 2021, https://davidsacks.medium.com/the-killer-d-a-54d4c4a5135f.

99 *"dangerous ideologue who hurts our citizens"*: Garry Tan (@garrytan), "Can't make this up. Chesa Boudin dropped gun charges in retaliation when a victim's family eviscerated him," Twitter (now X), December 30, 2021, https://x.com/garrytan/status/1476577984010018819.

99 *"causing death and assaults"*: Garry Tan (@garrytan), "SF Asian Americans are being robbed, maimed and killed. Our community is awake now," Twitter (now X), December 30, 2021, https://x.com/garrytan/status/1525222178425212930.

99 *"violent crime against Asians"*: Garry Tan (@garrytan), "In SF, violent crime against Asian Americans is not merely low priority: it is used as a political tool," Twitter (now X), June 6, 2022, https://x.com/garrytan/status/1533830734896541698.

100 *"If you want to know why our city"*: Garry Tan (@garrytan), "If you want to know why our city is covered in needles, poop, crime, and no pragmatic housing, you'll have to read San Fransicko," Twitter (now X), November 11, 2021, https://x.com/garrytan/status/1458940887245811737.

100 *"anarchy and tyranny"*: Balaji Srinivasan (@balajis), "America is becoming San Francisco, which combines anarchy and tyranny," Twitter (now X), August 14, 2021, https://x.com/balajis/status/1426713139505078272.

100 *that was worse off than Rwanda*: Balaji Srinivasan (@balajis), "More seriously, the terminology of 'developed' and 'developing' is obsolete. It's now ascending

vs descending world," Twitter (now X), November 13, 2021, https://x.com/balajis/status/1459561479204524034.

100 *"[I]t may be easier to start"*: Balaji Srinivasan (@balajis), "That doesn't mean all is hopeless. Tech just needs to do what we're good at," Twitter (now X), February 3, 2022, https://x.com/balajis/status/1489202394257063940.

100 *nicknamed "The Wencils"*: Casey Ho (@CaseyHo), "An updated visual guide to the astroturf network . . . ," Twitter (now X), July 3, 2022, https://x.com/CaseyHo/status/1543698143023247360.

100 *creating a "gray money" network*: Ali Winston, "Inside Tech Billionaires' Push to Reshape San Francisco Politics: 'A Hostile Takeover,'" *Guardian*, February 12, 2024, https://www.theguardian.com/us-news/2024/feb/12/san-francisco-tech-billionaires-political-influence.

101 *"A network state is a highly aligned"*: Balaji Srinivasan, *The Network State: How to Start a New Country* (pub. by author, 2022), ebook.

102 *"A key point . . . the new SaaS"*: Srinivasan, *The Network State.*

102 *"alternative political arrangements"*: Quinn Slobodian, *Crack-Up Capitalism: Market Radicals and the Dream of a World Without Democracy* (New York: Metropolitan Books, 2023), ebook.

102 *Dubai's twenty-two-square-mile*: "About JAFZA," Jebel Ali Free Zone Authority, accessed May 4, 2026, https://www.jafza.ae/about/.

103 *Today, an estimated 120,000 people*: Margaret Taylor, "The Rise and Fall of Canary Wharf," *Wired*, April 13, 2021, https://www.wired.com/story/canary-wharf-pandemic-return-work/.

103 *"sense of creeping paranoia . . . zero percent tax rate"*: Gil Durán, "The People of Solano County Versus the Next Tech-Billionaire Dystopia," *New Republic*, January 4, 2024, https://newrepublic.com/article/177733/billionaire-solano-california-tech-secession.

103 *"The proponents of crack-up capitalism"*: Slobodian, *Crack-Up Capitalism.*

103 *"the most determined opponent"*: Srinivasan, *The Network State.*

103 *"In short, will the American nation"*: Srinivasan, *The Network State.*

104 *"As Yarvin in particular . . . activists, bureaucrats, and journalists"*: Srinivasan, *The Network State.*

104 *Srinivasan describes the Gray tribe as "libertarianish"*: Srinivasan, *The Network State.*

104 *a fringe group known as the "post-Left"*: Srinivasan, *The Network State.*

104 *He divides the Red tribe*: Srinivasan, *The Network State.*

105 *"people of the Network"*: Srinivasan, *The Network State.*

105 *practitioners of "network capitalism"*: Srinivasan, *The Network State.*

105 *"For the left-authoritarians . . . 'passing a law'"*: Srinivasan, *The Network State.*

106 *"an incredible book"*: Srinivasan, *The Network State.*

106 *"[t]he process by which"*: James Dale Davidson and Lord William Rees-Mogg, *The Sovereign Individual: Mastering the Transition to the Information Age* (1997; repr., New York: Simon & Schuster, 2020), ebook.

106 *"The Future Is Our Past" makes the same argument*: Srinivasan, *The Network State.*

107 *"What if Sulzberger . . . without checking it yourself"*: Srinivasan, *The Network State.*

107 *"white supremacists and neo-fascists"*: Cade Metz, "Silicon Valley's Safe Space," *New York Times*, February 13, 2021, https://www.nytimes.com/2021/02/13/technology/slate-star-codex-rationalists.html.

107 *"demagogued and defeated" the world's richest man*: Srinivasan, *The Network State.*

107 *Srinivasan urges the building of "parallel" systems*: Srinivasan, *The Network State.*

107 *"an American anarchy"*: Srinivasan, *The Network State.*

108 *"All the discussion . . . in a digital time"*: Srinivasan, *The Network State.*

108 *a great "unbundling" of the country*: Srinivasan, *The Network State.*

109 *"blueprint drawn in crayon"*: Dave Karpf, "The Tech Barons Have a Blueprint Drawn in Crayon. They Have Not Thought Any of This Through," *The Future, Now and Then* (blog), Substack, February 16, 2025, https://davekarpf.substack.com/p/the-tech-barons-have-a-blueprint.

109 *"Balaji has the highest rate"*: Marc Andreessen, blurb for *The Network State: How to Start a New Country*, by Balaji Srinivasan (pub. by author, 2022).

109 *"Balaji is a visionary . . .* The Network State*"*: Brian Armstrong, blurb for Balaji Srinivasan, *The Network State: How to Start a New Country* (pub. by author, 2022).

109 *"We've started new currencies"*: Vitalik Buterin, blurb for Balaji Srinivasan, *The Network State: How to Start a New Country* (pub. by author, 2022).

109 *"I legit believe YC is a prototype model"*: Garry Tan (@garrytan), "Also the alums go on to do really amazing things . . . ," Twitter (now X), August 3, 2022, https://x.com/garrytan/status/1554839471798947842.

110 *"Garry is one of the most . . . a big difference here"*: Sam Altman (@sama), "Thrilled for @garrytan, and Y Combinator! Garry is one of the most 'YC' people in the whole industry. I'm excited to see what he'll do," Twitter (now X), August 29, 2022, https://x.com/sama/status/1564256564180951040; Sam Altman (@sama), "Also, it's a big deal imo that YC will have a president so active in local politics! I think YC can make a real difference here . . . ," Twitter (now X), August 29, 2022, https://x.com/sama/status/1564256798323851265.

110 *Yarvin called for a "full reboot"*: Curtis Yarvin, "The Butterfly Revolution," *Gray Mirror* (blog), Substack, April 7, 2022, https://graymirror.substack.com/p/the-butterfly-revolution.

111 *"Free speech is essential . . . adheres to this principle"*: Elon Musk (@elonmusk), "Free speech is essential to a functioning democracy. Do you believe Twitter rigorously adheres to this principle?," Twitter (now X), March 25, 2022, https://x.com/elonmusk/status/1507259709224632344.

111 *"woke mind virus . . . become multiplanetary"*: Walter Isaacson, *Elon Musk* (New York: Simon & Schuster, 2023), ebook.

111 *"one of the most overpaid tech acquisitions"*: Will Daniel, "Elon Musk's $44 Billion Twitter Purchase Is 'One of the Most Overpaid Tech Acquisitions in History,' Wedbush's Dan Ives Says," *Fortune*, October 27, 2022, https://fortune.com/2022/10/27/elon-musk-twitter-purchase-most-overpaid-tech-history-dan-ives-wedbush/.

111 *"Before and during . . . familiar with the matter"*: Rob Copeland, Georgia Wells, Rebecca Elliott, and Liz Hoffman, "The Shadow Crew Who Encouraged Elon Musk's Twitter Takeover," *Wall Street Journal*, October 10, 2022, https://www.wsj.com/tech/the-shadow-crew-who-encouraged-elon-musks-twitter-takeover-tesla-jack-dorsey-11651260119.

112 *"We are being lied to"*: Marc Andreessen, "The Techno-Optimist Manifesto," Andreessen Horowitz, October 16, 2023, https://a16z.com/the-techno-optimist-manifesto/.

113 *"Jobs are definitely going to go away"*: Ross Andersen, "Does Sam Altman Know What He's Creating?," *Atlantic*, July 24, 2023, https://www.theatlantic.com/magazine/archive/2023/09/sam-altman-openai-chatgpt-gpt-4/674764/.

113 *"It seemed to me . . . not just for UBI"*: Andersen, "Does Sam Altman Know . . . ?," *Atlantic*.

114 *"Beauty exists only in struggle."*: Andreessen, "The Techno-Optimist Manifesto."

115 *"Fascism wants man to be active . . . required for winning it"*: Benito Mussolini, *The Doctrine of Fascism* (LeBooks, n.d.).

116 *"direct descendants of first-wave eugenics"*: Timnit Gebru and Émile P. Torres, "The TESCREAL Bundle: Eugenics and the Promise of Utopia Through Artificial General Intelligence," *First Monday* 29, no. 4 (April 2024), https://doi.org/10.5210/fm.v29i4.13636.

116 *"Transhumanism is this idea . . . everything is awesome forever"*: Émile P. Torres, interview by Gil Durán, *Nerd Reich* (podcast), May 13, 2025, YouTube, https://www.youtube.com/watch?v=S1tcBUSoNYQ.

116 *its own special handshake*: Ed Regis, "Meet the Extropians," *Wired*, October 1, 1994, https://www.wired.com/1994/10/extropians/.

117 *"It's a doctrine of self-transformation . . . limitations of any kind"*: Regis, "Meet the Extropians," *Wired*.

117 *They await the "technological Singularity"*: Gebru and Torres, "The TESCREAL Bundle," *First Monday*.

117 *"The cosmists' original idea . . . uploading ourselves to computers"*: Douglas Rushkoff, *Team Human* (W. W. Norton & Company, 2019), ebook.

118 *"[b]ecoming multiplanetary is critical"*: Elon Musk (@elonmusk), "Becoming multiplanetary is critical to ensuring the long-term survival of humanity and all life as we know it," X, September 24, 2024, https://x.com/elonmusk/status/1838661749349781736.

119 *"We are our bodies . . . We are our bodies"*: Adam Becker, interview by Gil Durán, *Nerd Reich* (podcast), May 25, 2025, YouTube, https://www.youtube.com/watch?v=6NrDCvKp5-k.

120 *"Imagine a thousand different start-ups . . . from within SF"*: "00 – Network State Conference 2023 – Opening Remarks by Balaji," posted November 8, 2023, by Network State Podcast, YouTube, https://www.youtube.com/watch?v=VqIJI8fW4PI.

122 *"A lot of people . . . With competition"*: "17 – Network State Conference 2023 – Patri Friedman on Competitive Government," posted November 2, 2023, by Network State Podcast, YouTube, https://www.youtube.com/watch?v=MSO-ZAQiFAI.

122 *"Network states . . . talking about security"*: "30 – Network State Conference 2023 – Spencer Macdonald of Spearbit," posted November 2, 2023, by Network State Podcast, YouTube, https://www.youtube.com/watch?v=CIQl1YiPZ8k.

123 *"a kind of urban blank slate"*: Conor Dougherty and Erin Griffith, "The Silicon Valley Elite Who Want to Build a City from Scratch," *New York Times*, August 25, 2023, https://www.nytimes.com/2023/08/25/business/land-purchases-solano-county.html.

123 *"That's a possible recipe . . . it will work everywhere"*: "28 – Network State Conference 2023 – Garry Tan of Ycombinator," posted November 2, 2023, by Network State Podcast, YouTube, https://www.youtube.com/watch?v=24YF7LlE8ds.

123 *"I guess I come here . . . every nation in the world"*: "Garry Tan," posted October 18, 2023, by AGI House, YouTube, https://www.youtube.com/watch?v=xMRlKPqNMT4.

124 *"intelligence that is optimizing itself"*: "29 – Network State Conference 2023 – Beff Jezos of e/acc," posted November 2, 2023, by Network State Podcast, YouTube, https://www.youtube.com/watch?v=ojN6TVkyFX8. Beff Jezos is an online pseudonym for Guillaume Verdon.

125 *"Garry Tan is an Effective Accelerationist . . . This needs more reporting"*: Emily Mills (@sf_mills), "Garry Tan is an Effective Accelerationist who wants to take over the nation and the world with that ideology utilizing Network State style strategies," X, November 13, 2023, https://x.com/sf_mills/status/1724141770819436623.

125 *Tan apologized*: Gil Durán, "The Tech Plutocrats Dreaming of a Right-Wing San Francisco," *New Republic*, February 12, 2024, https://newrepublic.com/article/178675/garry-tan-tech-san-francisco.

126 *"If Red is the past"*: Balaji Srinivasan, interview by Erik Torenberg and Dan Romero, "Balaji on the Tribal Lens, America's Blunder, and His Plan to Save San Francisco," *Moment of Zen* (podcast), September 8, 2023, YouTube, https://www.youtube.com/watch?v=mIJLW_Rc6Rg.

126 *"on bare land"*: Gil Durán, "The Tech Baron Seeking to Purge San Francisco of 'Blues,'" *New Republic*, April 26, 2024, https://newrepublic.com/article/180487/balaji-srinivasan-network-state-plutocrat.

128 *"The New Reality is here"*: "REBOOT 2024," REBOOT 2024, accessed April 1, 2026, https://rebootconference.org/index.html.

129 *"While there were a few"*: Eddie Kim, "Reboot 2024 Promised a 'New Reality.' It Was Mostly Conservative Bluster," *Gazetteer SF*, September 6, 2024, https://sf.gazetteer.co/reboot-2024-promised-a-new-reality-it-was-mostly-conservative-bluster.

129 *"the foundation shaping"*: Nancy Scola, "Meet the Rave-Throwing Think Tank Shaping the Tech-Right," *Inc.*, September 4, 2025, https://www.inc.com/nancy-scola/foundation-american-innovation-tech-right/91235091.

130 *raised $12 million in a single night*: Theodore Schleifer, "'It's Not 2016 Anymore': Trump Finds Friends in Silicon Valley," *New York Times*, June 6, 2024, https://www.nytimes.com/2024/06/06/us/politics/trump-sacks-silicon-valley-donors.html.

CHAPTER 5 THE UNICORN

131 *"the most significant moment"*: Stephanie Saul, "How Yale Law School Paved JD Vance's Rise," *New York Times*, July 17, 2024, https://www.nytimes.com/2024/07/17/us/jd-vance-yale-law-school.html.

131 *"possibly the smartest person"*: Andrew Prokop, "J.D. Vance's Radical Plan to Build a Government of Trump Loyalists," *Vox*, July 18, 2024, https://www.vox.com/politics/361455/jd-vance-trump-vice-president-rnc-speech.

131 *Before graduating law school in 2013*: Julie Carr Smyth, "What's in a Name? Republican Vice Presidential Nominee JD Vance Has Had Many of Them," Associated Press, July 26, 2024, https://apnews.com/article/election-2024-republicans-vice-president-vance-name-359c3d1361c94f5d2d1e9798b7854477.

132 *"he was a very smart guy"*: Ryan Mac and Theodore Schleifer, "How a Network of Tech Billionaires Helped J.D. Vance Leap into Power," *New York Times*, July 17, 2024, https://www.nytimes.com/2024/07/17/technology/jd-vance-tech-silicon-valley.html.

132 *he never once saw Vance*: Angel Au-Yeung, "Inside JD Vance's Short-Lived Career as a Venture Capitalist," *Wall Street Journal*, July 17, 2024, https://www.wsj.com/politics/elections/vp-pick-jd-vance-short-career-venture-capitalist-b3d941e1.

132 *"Mr. Vance left Mithril Capital"*: Mac and Schleifer, "Network of Tech Billionaires," *New York Times*.

132 *"Elites tend to see . . . by academic abstractions"*: Peter Thiel, blurb for JD Vance, *Hillbilly Elegy: A Memoir of a Family and Culture in Crisis* (New York: Harper, 2016), back cover.

132 *"the liberal media's favorite . . . the working white class"*: Sarah Jones, "J.D. Vance, the False Prophet of Blue America," *New Republic*, November 17, 2016, https://newrepublic.com/article/138717/jd-vance-false-prophet-blue-america.

133 *"When I read . . . he doesn't get us"*: Clayton Kincade, "'Hillbilly Elegy' Is Back in the Spotlight. These Appalachians Write a Different Tale," NPR, August 17, 2024, https://www.npr.org/2024/08/16/g-s1-17184/jd-vance-hillbilly-elegy-barbara-kingsolver-appalachia.

133 *"JD Vance should not be held up"*: Silas House, "After receiving a barrage of requests to write about Vance . . . ," Facebook, July 16, 2024, https://www.facebook.com/SilasHouseOfficial/posts/1011828823646730/.

133 *Vance declared himself a "Never Trump guy"*: Mia McCarthy, "'I'm a Never Trump Guy': All of J.D. Vance's Trump Quotes That Could Come Back to Bite Him," *Politico*, July 15, 2024, https://www.politico.com/news/2024/07/15/jd-vance-donald-trump-comments-00168450.

134 *"Trump's actual policy proposals"*: JD Vance, "Trump Speaks for Those Bush Betrayed," *USA Today*, February 18, 2016, https://www.usatoday.com/story/opinion/2016/02/18/donald-trump-white-working-class-rust-belt-voters-elections-2016-column/80422422/.

134 *"I go back and forth"*: Gram Slattery and Helen Coster, "J.D. Vance Once Compared Trump to Hitler. Now He Is Trump's Vice President-Elect," Reuters, November 6, 2024, https://www.reuters.com/world/us/jd-vance-once-compared-trump-hitler-now-they-are-running-mates-2024-07-15/.

134 *the Associated Press reported that the deal was off*: Hillel Italie, "A Second JD Vance Book Falls Through, Publisher Says," Associated Press, May 5, 2022, https://apnews.com/article/2022-midterm-elections-entertainment-business-fe740eab37ecade4c2607fe042b2e88f.

134 *Narya officially launched in 2020*: Kim Hart, "J.D. Vance Launches VC Fund for Startups Beyond Silicon Valley," Axios, January 9, 2020, https://www.axios.com/2020/01/09/jd-vance-venture-capital-fund-ohio-silicon-valley-peter-thiel.

135 *"It's not just a good investment opportunity"*: Allison Gordon, Daniel Medina, Curt Devine, and Kyung Lah, "Workers Allege 'Nightmare' Conditions at Kentucky Startup JD Vance Helped Fund," CNN, August 13, 2024, https://www.yahoo.com/news/workers-allege-nightmare-conditions-kentucky-090005983.html.

135 *"This is psychotic to me . . . what we were doing"*: Austyn Gaffney, "Is This Giant Hydroponic Greenhouse in Kentucky the Future of Farming?," *Rolling Stone*, August 22, 2021, https://www.rollingstone.com/culture/culture-features/appharvest-hydroponic-greenhouses-kentucky-future-of-farming-1214262/.

135 *"Some workers said"*: Gordon et al., "Workers Allege 'Nightmare' Conditions."

135 *"I became persuaded"*: Rod Dreher, "J.D. Vance Becomes Catholic," *American Conservative*, August 11, 2019, https://www.theamericanconservative.com/j-d-vance-becomes-catholic/.

136 *"[Thiel] defied the social template . . . studied under at Stanford"*: JD Vance, "How I Joined the Resistance," *Lamp Magazine* (blog), April 1, 2020, https://thelampmagazine.com/blog/how-i-joined-the-resistance.

137 *"Deneen's thinking echoes"*: Robert Kuttner, "Blaming Liberalism," *New York Review of Books*, October 31, 2019, https://www.nybooks.com/articles/2019/11/21/patrick-deneen-blaming-liberalism/.

137 *"fighting, evangelistic faith"*: Adrian Vermeule, "Integration from Within," *American Affairs* 2, no. 1 (Spring 2018), https://americanaffairsjournal.org/2018/02/integration-from-within/.

137 *once called himself a "Never Trumper"*: McCarthy, " 'I'm a Never Trump Guy,' " *Politico*.

138 *"political venture capital firm"*: "The Rockbridge Network's Plan to Remake the Right (Fall 2021)," brochure, obtained by *The New York Times*, DocumentCloud, https://www.documentcloud.org/documents/21574825-the-rockbridge-networks-plan-to-remake-the-right-fall-2021/.

139 *"lead Silicon Valley's march"*: Theodore Schleifer, "Behind the Scenes at a Secretive Gathering of Rising MAGA Donors," *New York Times*, November 20, 2024, https://www.nytimes.com/2024/11/20/us/politics/rockbridge-trump-vance-wiles.html.

139 *"the most powerful woman"*: Kenneth P. Vogel and Ben Schreckinger, "The Most Powerful Woman in GOP Politics," *Politico*, September 7, 2016, https://www.politico.com/story/2016/09/donald-trump-rebekah-mercer-227799.

140 *One of his campaign stops*: "J.D. Vance—JML #070," *Jack Murphy Live*, September 17, 2021, YouTube, https://www.youtube.com/watch?v=PMq1ZEcyztY.

142 *Thiel bankrolled the effort*: Alex Isenstadt, "A Mole Hunt, a Secret Website and Peter Thiel's Big Risk: How J.D. Vance Won His Primary," *Politico*, May 3,

2022, https://www.politico.com/news/2022/05/03/jd-vance-win-ohio-primary-00029881.

142 *"If they both win . . . extensions of him"*: Max Chafkin, *The Contrarian: Peter Thiel and Silicon Valley's Pursuit of Power* (New York: Penguin Press, 2021), ebook.

142 *Thiel had spent another $15 million*: Jonathan Swan and Josh Kraushaar, "Scoop: Peter Thiel Offers to Double Down on Arizona Senate Race to Boost Blake Masters," Axios, October 12, 2022, https://www.axios.com/2022/10/12/peter-thiel-arizona-blake-masters-mcconnell.

142 *Masters cited a white supremacist writer*: Alec Dent, "The Right's Quiet Uncanceling of a Dead White Supremacist," *Vanity Fair*, October 14, 2022, https://www.vanityfair.com/news/2022/10/right-uncanceling-dead-white-supremacist-sam-francis.

142 *"approvingly quoted a Nazi war criminal"*: Jonathan Weisman, "The Strident Writings of a Young Blake Masters Dog His Senate Run," *New York Times*, July 6, 2022, https://www.nytimes.com/2022/07/06/us/politics/blake-masters.html.

142 *a slew of beliefs so noxious and racist*: Caleb Ecarma, "White Extremists Have Found Their Guy for the Senate: Blake Masters," *Vanity Fair*, August 16, 2022, https://www.vanityfair.com/news/2022/08/white-extremists-senate-blake-masters.

142 *youngest serving Republican member*: Taylor Popielarz, "A Look at Ohio Sen. JD Vance's First Few Months in Office," Spectrum News 1 Ohio, May 9, 2023, https://spectrumnews1.com/oh/columbus/politics/2023/05/09/ohio-sen--jd-vance-first-months-office.

143 *"you should only invest"*: Olivier Jutel, "A Critical Theory of Venture Capital" (lecture, University of Otago), September 9, 2025, YouTube, https://www.youtube.com/watch?v=jhJytW-hQiU&t=3030s.

143 *"pursuing power law returns"*: Catherine Bracy, *World Eaters: How Venture Capital Is Cannibalizing the Economy* (New York: Portfolio/Penguin, 2025), ebook.

144 *"There are a lot of things . . . government to work"*: Barton Gellman, "Peter Thiel Is Taking a Break from Democracy," *Atlantic*, November 9, 2023, https://www.theatlantic.com/politics/archive/2023/11/peter-thiel-2024-election-politics-investing-life-views/675946/.

145 *"WE HAVE A FORMER TECH VC"*: Lizette Chapman and Anna Edgerton, "Why JD Vance as Trump's VP Pick Has Silicon Valley Celebrating," *Bloomberg*, July 15, 2024, https://www.bloomberg.com/news/articles/2024-07-15/why-jd-vance-as-trump-s-vp-pick-has-silicon-valley-celebrating.

146 *"Many Americans knew"*: Jacob Silverman, *Gilded Rage: Elon Musk and the Radicalization of Silicon Valley* (London: Bloomsbury Continuum, 2025), ebook.

CHAPTER 6 APOKÁLYPSIS

147 *Ten days before the 2025 inauguration*: Peter Thiel, "A Time for Truth and Reconciliation," *Financial Times*, January 10, 2025, https://www.ft.com/content/a46cb128-1f74-4621-ab0b-242a76583105.

148 *Epstein had invested $40 million*: David Enrich, "Jeffrey Epstein Invested with Peter Thiel, and His Estate Is Reaping Millions," *New York Times*, June 4, 2025, https://www.nytimes.com/2025/06/04/business/jeffrey-epstein-peter-thiel-estate.html.

149 *Musk alone spent over $291 million*: David Wright and Alex Leeds-Matthews, "Elon Musk Spent More than $290 Million on the 2024 Election, Year-End FEC Filings Show," CNN, February 1, 2025, https://www.cnn.com/2025/02/01/politics/elon-musk-2024-election-spending-millions.

149 *raising more than $175 million*: MacKenzie Sigalos, "Crypto Super PAC Fairshake Has $116 Million on Hand to Grow Industry's Influence in 2026 Elections," CNBC, January 30, 2025, https://www.cnbc.com/2025/01/30/crypto-pac-fairshake-has-116-million-on-hand-for-2026-elections.html.

149 *"creation of new physical places"*: OpenSecrets, "FairShake PAC: Summary, 2024 Cycle," accessed April 12, 2026, https://www.opensecrets.org/political-action-committees-pacs/fairshake-pac/C00835959/summary/2024; Gil Durán, "The Most Powerful Crypto Bro in Washington Has Very Weird Beliefs," *New Republic*, October 1, 2024, https://newrepublic.com/article/185738/coinbase-brian-armstrong-crypto-lobbying-washington-politicians.

149 *"I do think crypto"*: Durán, "The Most Powerful Crypto Bro," *New Republic.*

150 *"Zhao's representatives began discussions"*: Angus Berwick, Patricia Kowsmann, and Rebecca Ballhaus, "How a Billionaire Felon Boosted Trump's Crypto Company en Route to a Pardon," *Wall Street Journal*, October 24, 2025, https://www.wsj.com/finance/currencies/binance-trump-crypto-pardon-cz-changpeng-zhao-1007fde9.

151 *"The Trump family's new crypto"*: Bernhard Warner, "Trump Takes Office as a Newly Minted Crypto Billionaire," *New York Times*, January 20, 2025, https://www.nytimes.com/2025/01/20/business/trump-memecoins-crypto.html.

151 *"I am not a fan of Bitcoin . . . and other illegal activity"*: Donald J. Trump (@realDonaldTrump), "I am not a fan of Bitcoin and other Cryptocurrencies, which are not money, and whose value is highly volatile and based on thin air," Twitter (now X), July 11, 2019, https://x.com/realDonaldTrump/status/1149472282584072192.

151 *"Bitcoin just seems"*: Mathew Di Salvo, "Donald Trump and Bitcoin: From 'Not a Fan' to Crypto President," *Decrypt*, October 5, 2025, https://finance.yahoo.com/news/donald-trump-bitcoin-not-fan-203039785.html.

151 *"A disaster waiting to happen"*: Talia Kaplan, "Trump Warns Crypto 'Potentially a Disaster Waiting to Happen,'" Fox Business, August 31, 2021, https://www.foxbusiness.com/politics/crypto-potentially-a-disaster-waiting-to-happen-trump.

151 *"We only have one real currency"*: Oscar Williams-Grut, "Donald Trump's Bitcoin Takedown Signals Global Currency War," Yahoo Finance UK, July 16, 2019, https://uk.finance.yahoo.com/news/donald-trump-bitcoin-cryptocurrency-dollar-currenecy-war-hsbc-ing-new-world-order-102031153.html.

152 *"as much as $5 billion in paper wealth"*: Angus Berwick, "Trump Family Amasses $5 Billion Fortune After Crypto Launch," *Wall Street Journal*, September 1, 2025, https://www.wsj.com/finance/currencies/trump-family-amasses-6-billion-fortune-after-crypto-launch-567faec5.

152 *"As they are currently configured"*: David Golumbia, *The Politics of Bitcoin: Software as Right-Wing Extremism* (Minneapolis: University of Minnesota Press, 2016), ebook.

153 *A 2025 report by Gallup*: Jeffrey M. Jones and Lydia Saad, "Cryptocurrency Still Has Limited Main Street Appeal," Gallup, July 22, 2025, https://news.gallup.com/poll/692777/cryptocurrency-limited-main-street-appeal.aspx.

153 *But Salvadorans largely shunned Bitcoin*: "El Salvador's Wild Crypto Experiment Ends in Failure," *Economist*, March 2, 2025, https://www.economist.com/finance-and-economics/2025/03/02/el-salvadors-wild-crypto-experiment-ends-in-failure.

153 *seed round for BitPay*: Jeremy Wagstaff, "Bitcoin Startups Get Hotter: BitPay Nabs $2M from Founders Fund, Others," Reuters, May 16, 2013, https://www.reuters.com/article/business/bitcoin-startups-get-hotter-bitpay-nabs-2m-from-founders-fund-others-idUS738792808/.

153 *when Founders Fund cashed out*: Marco Quiroz-Gutierrez, "Peter Thiel's Founders Fund Made More Than $1B Offloading 8 Years of Crypto Investments Just Before Markets Soured," *Fortune*, January 18, 2023, https://fortune.com/crypto/2023/01/18/peter-thiels-founders-fund-sold-crypto-just-before-markets-soured/.

154 *One of Thiel's most consequential early bets*: Pete Rizzo, "$100k Peter Thiel Fellowship Awarded to Ethereum's Vitalik Buterin," *CoinDesk*, June 5, 2014, https://www.coindesk.com/markets/2014/06/05/100k-peter-thiel-fellowship-awarded-to-ethereums-vitalik-buterin.

154 *It functions as a distributed computing platform*: "What Is Ethereum?," Ethereum Foundation, accessed April 12, 2026, https://ethereum.org/what-is-ethereum/.

154 *"pop-up city"*: Vitalik Buterin, "Why I Built Zuzalu," *Palladium*, October 6, 2023, https://www.palladiummag.com/2023/10/06/why-i-built-zuzalu/.

154 *fell to $203 billion in June 2026*: CoinMarketCap, "Ethereum," accessed June 11, 2026, https://coinmarketcap.com/currencies/ethereum/.

155 *Along with Y Combinator*: "Coinbase Raises $25 Million from Andreessen Horowitz," *Coinbase* (blog), December 12, 2013, https://www.coinbase.com/blog/coinbase-raises-usd25-million-from-andreessen-horowitz.

155 *The firm invested in Coinbase*: Katie Haun, "Coinbase Direct Listing," Andreessen Horowitz, April 14, 2021, https://a16z.com/coinbase-direct-listing/.

155 *Still, it was the firm's most successful bet yet*: Berber Jin, "Coinbase Direct Listing's Biggest Winners," *Information*, April 14, 2021, https://www.theinformation.com/articles/coinbase-direct-listings-biggest-winners.

155 *"been central to the rise of drug sales"*: US Government Accountability Office, *Virtual Currencies: Additional Information Could Improve Federal Agency Efforts to Counter Human and Drug Trafficking*, GAO-22-105462, January 10, 2022, https://www.gao.gov/assets/gao-22-105462.pdf.

155 *did $213 million in illicit business*: US Attorney's Office, Southern District of New York, "Senior Adviser to the Operator of the Silk Road Online Black Market Sentenced to 20 Years in Prison," press release, July 11, 2023, https://www.justice

.gov/usao-sdny/pr/senior-adviser-operator-silk-road-online-black-market-sentenced-20-years-prison.

155 *On Ulbricht's computer*: Andy Greenberg, "Read the Transcript of Silk Road's Boss Ordering 5 Assassinations," *Wired*, February 2, 2015, https://www.wired.com/2015/02/read-transcript-silk-roads-boss-ordering-5-assassinations/.

156 Silk Road was *"at its core"*: Andy Greenberg, "Why the Silk Road Trial Matters," *Wired*, January 13, 2015, https://www.wired.com/2015/01/why-silk-road-trial-matters/.

156 *"The future is OUR time"*: Andy Greenberg, "Collected Quotations of the Dread Pirate Roberts, Founder of Underground Drug Site Silk Road and Radical Libertarian," *Forbes*, April 29, 2013, https://www.forbes.com/sites/andygreenberg/2013/04/29/collected-quotations-of-the-dread-pirate-roberts-founder-of-the-drug-site-silk-road-and-radical-libertarian/.

156 *"It was an enterprise . . . did not exist "*: Sentencing Transcript, *United States v. Ross William Ulbricht*, No. 14-cr-68 (KBF) (S.D.N.Y. May 29, 2015), https://freeross.org/wp-content/uploads/2015/05/Sentencing_2015-May-29.pdf.

157 *nearly $4.4 trillion in late 2025*: Sidhartha Shukla, "Crypto Bear Market Wipes Out Almost Entire 2025 Value Gain," *Bloomberg*, November 7, 2025, https://www.bloomberg.com/news/articles/2025-11-07/crypto-bear-market-wipes-out-almost-entire-2025-value-increase.

157 *It plunged, again, to $1.2 trillion*: CoinMarketCap, "Bitcoin," accessed June 11, 2026, https://coinmarketcap.com/currencies/bitcoin/.

157 *poured more than $26 billion*: Gene Teare, "Crypto Investment Soared This Year. Here's How Coinbase Ventures Bets on the Growing Ecosystem," *Crunchbase News*, December 17, 2021, https://news.crunchbase.com/fintech-ecommerce/under-the-hood-coinbase-ventures-investing-crypto-blockchain/.

157 *VC firms invested approximately $77 billion*: Robert Le, *Q4 2024 Crypto VC Trends (PitchBook Emerging Tech Research*, February 7, 2025), https://pitchbook.brightspotcdn.com/3c/16/b44652d2f54ec52df7a3fd209f1f/q4-2024-crypto-vc-trends-preview.pdf.

157 *a $300 million fund in 2018*: Jay Derenthal, "Andreessen Horowitz Launches $300 Million Crypto Fund," *Bitcoin Magazine*, August 10, 2018, republished on Nasdaq, https://www.nasdaq.com/articles/andreessen-horowitz-launches-%24300-million-crypto-fund-2018-08-10.

157 *a $515 million fund in 2020*: Chris Dixon, "Crypto Fund II," a16z Crypto, Andreessen Horowitz, April 30, 2020, https://a16zcrypto.com/posts/article/crypto-fund-ii/.

157 *a $2.2 billion fund in 2021*: Kate Rooney, "Andreessen Horowitz Launches $2.2 Billion Crypto Fund and Is 'Radically Optimistic' Despite Price Fluctuations," CNBC, June 24, 2021, https://www.cnbc.com/2021/06/24/andreessen-horowitz-launches-2point2-billion-crypto-fund.html.

157 *a $4.5 billion fund in 2022*: Chris Dixon, "Crypto Fund 4," a16z Crypto, Andreessen Horowitz, May 25, 2022, https://a16zcrypto.com/posts/article/crypto-fund-four/.

157 *committed $9.8 billion to crypto*: "About," a16z Crypto, Andreessen Horowitz, accessed April 12, 2026, https://a16zcrypto.com/about/.

158 *"Thiel vehicles held more"*: Jack Denton, "Peter Thiel Revealed as an Investor in FTX. Even the Best Get Burned," *Barron's*, January 11, 2023, https://www.barrons.com/articles/peter-thiel-investor-ftx-bankman-fried-paypal-facebook-51673439483.

158 *he sought to popularize crypto*: "The Celebs Who Helped Sam Bankman-Fried—Until He Crashed," *Daily Beast*, October 4, 2023, https://www.thedailybeast.com/from-tom-brady-to-larry-david-the-celebs-caught-in-sam-bankman-frieds-crypto-web/.

158 *he had given over $100 million*: Luc Cohen, "Bankman-Fried Used Customer Funds for $100 Million in U.S. Political Donations, Prosecutors Say," Reuters, August 14, 2023, https://www.reuters.com/legal/bankman-fried-used-customer-funds-100-mln-us-political-donations-prosecutors-say-2023-08-14/.

158 *"glorious afro"*: Alex Seitz-Wald, "Vegan Canapes and Fat Donations: How Sam Bankman-Fried Won Washington Before He Lost Everything," NBC News, November 16, 2022, https://www.nbcnews.com/politics/politics-news/vegan-canapes-fat-donations-sam-bankman-fried-won-washington-lost-ever-rcna57551.

159 *"He didn't get an answer"*: MacKenzie Sigalos, "Sam Bankman-Fried Considered Paying Trump $5 Billion Not to Run for President, Michael Lewis Tells '60 Minutes,'" CNBC, October 2, 2023, https://www.cnbc.com/2023/10/02/sam-bankman-fried-considered-paying-trump-5-billion-not-to-run-lewis.html.

159 *FTX collapsed*: Chase Peterson-Withorn, "Exclusive: These Investors Stand to Lose the Most from FTX's Implosion," *Forbes*, November 10, 2022, https://www.forbes.com/sites/chasewithorn/2022/11/10/exclusive-these-investors-stand-to-lose-the-most-from-ftxs-implosion/.

159 *"wealthier and more sophisticated investors"*: Jiageng Liu, Igor Makarov, and Antoinette Schoar, "Anatomy of a Run: The Terra Luna Crash," Harvard Law School Forum on Corporate Governance, May 22, 2023, https://corpgov.law.harvard.edu/2023/05/22/anatomy-of-a-run-the-terra-luna-crash/.

159 *Armstrong, a former Airbnb*: Michael Haley, "Coinbase CEO Brian Armstrong Has a Stake Worth $13 Billion After the Company's Big Market Debut. Here Are the Other Execs and Investors Who Got Rich," *Business Insider*, April 14, 2021, https://www.businessinsider.com/coinbase-ipo-brian-armstrong-who-got-rich-public-offering-2021-3.

160 *"The crypto industry treated . . . over 100 crypto start-ups"*: David Yaffe-Bellany, "The Crypto Industry Spent over $130 Million on the Election. It Paid Off," *New York Times*, November 6, 2024, https://www.nytimes.com/2024/11/06/technology/crypto-industry-spending-election.html.

160 *"Crypto has accounted for nearly half"*: MacKenzie Sigalos, "Crypto's $245 Million Campaign Finance Operation Funded Non-Crypto Ads," CNBC, November 5, 2024, https://www.cnbc.com/2024/11/05/cryptos-245-million-campaign-finance-operation-funded-non-crypto-ads.html.

160 *Crypto researcher Molly White*: Molly White, "Follow the Crypto: 2024 Election Cycle," Follow the Crypto, accessed May 4, 2026, https://www.followthecrypto.org/2024/.

160 *"Hamas's terrorism . . . protect our national security"*: Sherrod Brown (@SenSherrodBrown), "Hamas's terrorism is fueled by cryptocurrency . . . ," X, October 18, 2023, https://x.com/SenSherrodBrown/status/1714722958227243173.

161 *crypto-funded PACs spent $40 million*: MacKenzie Sigalos, "Bitcoiners Celebrate as Bernie Moreno Ousts Sherrod Brown in Ohio Upset," CNBC, November 5, 2024, https://www.cnbc.com/2024/11/05/bitcoiners-celebrate-as-bernie-moreno-ousts-sherrod-brown-ohio-upset.html.

161 *Fairshake spent $10 million*: Lois Beckett, "Crypto Super Pac Spends $10m on Katie Porter Attack Ads in California Race," *Guardian*, March 1, 2024, https://www.theguardian.com/us-news/2024/mar/01/crypto-super-pac-katie-porter-attack-ads.

161 *A fact-check by The Sacramento Bee*: Andrew Sheeler, "Fact Check: Did Katie Porter Get Campaign Cash from Big Pharma, Big Oil and Big Banks?," *Sacramento Bee*, March 21, 2024, https://www.sacbee.com/news/politics-government/capitol-alert/article285480152.html.

162 *Both had received grades*: Brit McCandless Farmer, "Who Were the 2024 Election's 'Crypto Voters'?," CBS News (*60 Minutes*), December 8, 2024, https://www.cbsnews.com/news/who-were-the-2024-elections-crypto-voters-60-minutes/.

162 *"The cryptocurrency industry,"*: Jasper Goodman, "Crypto Firms Pour Millions into Trump Inauguration," *Politico*, January 17, 2025, https://www.politico.com/news/2025/01/17/crypto-money-trump-inauguration-00199088.

162 *"I have never seen such open corruption"*: Peter Stone, "'I Have Never Seen Such Open Corruption': Trump's Crypto Deals and Loosening of Rules Shock Observers," *Guardian*, June 17, 2025, https://www.theguardian.com/us-news/2025/jun/17/trump-crypto-memecoin-corruption.

163 *"We must ban Trump-style crypto corruption"*: Stone, "'Open Corruption,'" *Guardian*.

163 *"We felt like we were being unlawfully attacked"*: Brian Armstrong, interview by Jennifer Schonberger, "Coinbase CEO: Trump 'Breathed Life' into Crypto Industry," Yahoo Finance, March 7, 2025, video, https://finance.yahoo.com/video/coinbase-ceo-trump-breathed-life-232953157.html.

163 *"create a national stockpile"*: David Yaffe-Bellany, "Trump Signs Order to Create a 'Crypto Reserve,'" *New York Times*, March 6, 2025, https://www.nytimes.com/2025/03/06/technology/trump-crypto-reserve-executive-order.html.

163 *"We need guardrails . . . totally absent"*: Kamaron McNair, "The House Will Vote On a Bill to Regulate Stablecoins During 'Crypto Week'—What It Could Mean for You," CNBC, July 14, 2025, https://www.cnbc.com/2025/07/14/crypto-week-genius-act.html.

164 *"I'm a big crypto fan . . . right from the campaign"*: Will Weissert and Alan Suderman, "Once a Crypto Skeptic, Trump Is Now a Big Fan of the Industry," Associated Press, May 22, 2025, https://www.pbs.org/newshour/politics/once-a-crypto-skeptic-trump-is-now-a-big-fan-of-the-industry.

164 *"It's an unstoppable financial vehicle"*: Elon Musk, "Weekend Update: Financial Expert Lloyd Ostertag on Cryptocurrency - SNL," *Saturday Night Live*, May 8, 2021, YouTube, https://youtu.be/x5RCfQyTDFI?si=9l_SvlFYHfeYaN3p&t=101.

164 *"It has been one of the biggest winners"*: Tanaya Macheel, "Dogecoin Surges 20% After Trump Announces a Department of Government Efficiency — DOGE," CNBC, November 13, 2024, https://www.cnbc.com/2024/11/13/dogecoin-surges-20percent-after-trump-announces-a-department-of-government-efficiency-doge.html.

165 *"As crazy as it sounds"*: "Elon Musk Attends Trump's First Cabinet Meeting, Describes DOGE as 'Tech Support,'" Associated Press, February 26, 2025, video, https://newsroom.ap.org/detail/ElonMuskattendsTrumpsfirstCabinetmeeting describesDOGEastechsupport/d01ef6f929184ed3b703e6c87b22b922/video.

165 *260,000 federal workers had been purged*: "US Federal Employment Drops Again as DOGE Cuts Stack Up," Reuters, May 2, 2025, https://www.reuters.com/business/world-at-work/us-federal-employment-drops-again-doge-cuts-stack-up-2025-05-02/.

166 *"potentially violating conflict-of-interest laws"*: Paresh Dave and Alexandra Ulmer, "Musk's DOGE Expanding His Grok AI in U.S. Government, Raising Conflict Concerns," Reuters, May 23, 2025, https://www.reuters.com/sustainability/boards-policy-regulation/musks-doge-expanding-his-grok-ai-us-government-raising-conflict-concerns-2025-05-23/.

166 *"Project 2025 unabashedly promotes"*: Michael Sozan and Ben Olinsky, "Project 2025 Would Destroy the U.S. System of Checks and Balances and Create an Imperial Presidency," Center for American Progress, October 1, 2024, https://www.americanprogress.org/article/project-2025-would-destroy-the-u-s-system-of-checks-and-balances-and-create-an-imperial-presidency/.

167 *"a total shutdown of international relations"*: Ava Kofman, "Curtis Yarvin's Plot Against America," *New Yorker*, June 2, 2025, https://www.newyorker.com/magazine/2025/06/09/curtis-yarvin-profile.

167 *"His ideas were pretty extreme"*: David Marchese, "Curtis Yarvin Says Democracy Is Done. Powerful Conservatives Are Listening," *New York Times Magazine*, January 18, 2025, https://www.nytimes.com/2025/01/18/magazine/curtis-yarvin-interview.html.

168 *"Curtis Yarvin's Ideas Were Fringe"*: Ian Ward, "Curtis Yarvin's Ideas Were Fringe. Now They're Coursing Through Trump's Washington," *Politico*, January 30, 2025, https://www.politico.com/news/magazine/2025/01/30/curtis-yarvins-ideas-00201552.

168 *"the rapid takeover of federal infrastructure"*: "Capture of U.S. Critical Infrastructure by Neoreactionaries," memorandum, America 2.0, February 5, 2025, https://america2.news/content/files/2025/02/Musk-NRx-Memo-February-5-2025.pdf.

168 *"A billionaire tech entrepreneur"*: Sophie Alexander and Jamie Tarabay, "Peter Thiel's Deep Ties to Trump's Ranks," *Bloomberg*, March 7, 2025, https://www.bloomberg.com/features/2025-peter-thiel-trump-administration-connections/.

170 *"You could parachute him"*: Paul Graham, "A Fundraising Survival Guide," personal website, August 2008, https://www.paulgraham.com/fundraising.html.

170 *The two men became*: Keach Hagey, *The Optimist: Sam Altman, OpenAI, and the Race to Invent the Future* (New York: W. W. Norton, 2025), ebook.

170 *"We should treat him more as a messiah figure"*: Hagey, *The Optimist*.

170 *"OpenAI's mission is to ensure"*: "OpenAI Charter," OpenAI, accessed April 12, 2026, https://openai.com/charter/.

170 *Thiel provided the first significant investment*: Sam Shead, "Peter Thiel's Fund Owned More Shares Than DeepMind's Cofounders When the AI Lab Was Sold to Google," *Business Insider*, July 22, 2017, https://www.businessinsider.com/peter-thiel-owned-more-shares-than-deepminds-cofounders-when-it-was-sold-to-google-2017-7.

170 *"Manhattan Project for AI"*: Ronan Farrow and Andrew Marantz, "Sam Altman May Control Our Future—Can He Be Trusted?," *New Yorker*, April 6, 2026, https://www.newyorker.com/magazine/2026/04/13/sam-altman-may-control-our-future-can-he-be-trusted.

171 *Altman had begun to worry about the apocalypse*: Tad Friend, "Sam Altman's Manifest Destiny," *New Yorker*, October 10, 2016, https://www.newyorker.com/magazine/2016/10/10/sam-altmans-manifest-destiny.

171 *"digital intelligence"*: Tess Townsend, "Sam Altman for Governor?," *Recode*, May 14, 2017, https://www.vox.com/2017/5/14/15638046/willie-brown-column-sam-altman-might-run-governor-california-2018.

172 *"Scam Altman"*: Elon Musk (@elonmusk), "Scam Altman lies as easily as he breathes," X, August 12, 2025, https://x.com/elonmusk/status/1955299075781431726.

172 *Altman left his plum perch*: "OpenAI Forms Exclusive Computing Partnership with Microsoft to Build New Azure AI Supercomputing Technologies," Microsoft, July 22, 2019, https://news.microsoft.com/source/2019/07/22/openai-forms-exclusive-computing-partnership-with-microsoft-to-build-new-azure-ai-supercomputing-technologies/.

172 *"Over the next four years . . . in our society"*: Karen Hao, *Empire of AI: Dreams and Nightmares in Sam Altman's OpenAI* (New York: Penguin Press, 2025).

172 *"a tipping point for AI"*: "The Guardian View on ChatGPT: An Eerily Good Human Impersonator," editorial, *Guardian*, December 8, 2022, https://www.theguardian.com/commentisfree/2022/dec/08/the-guardian-view-on-chatgpt-an-eerily-good-human-impersonator.

173 *"ChatGPT is incredibly limited . . . and truthfulness"*: Sam Altman (@sama), "ChatGPT is incredibly limited, but good enough at some things to create a misleading impression of greatness . . . ," Twitter (now X), December 10, 2022, https://x.com/sama/status/1601731295792414720.

173 *ChatGPT had 100 million users*: Krystal Hu, "ChatGPT Sets Record for Fastest-Growing User Base—Analyst Note," Reuters, February 2, 2023, https://www.reuters.com/technology/chatgpt-sets-record-fastest-growing-user-base-analyst-note-2023-02-01/.

173 *kicking off a race*: "OpenAI Valued at $80 Billion After Deal, NYT Reports," Reuters, February 16, 2024, https://www.reuters.com/technology/openai-valued-80-billion-after-deal-nyt-reports-2024-02-16/.

173 *"was not consistently candid . . . leading OpenAI"*: Brian Contreras, "Five Days of Chaos: What Just Happened at OpenAI?," *Los Angeles Times*, November 22, 2023, https://www.latimes.com/business/technology/story/2023-11-22/five-days-of-chaos-what-just-happened-at-openai.

173 *"By Altman's own assessment"*: Elizabeth Weil, "Sam Altman Is the Oppenheimer of Our Age," *New York*, September 25, 2023, https://nymag.com/intelligencer/article/sam-altman-artificial-intelligence-openai-profile.html.

174 *"The energy resources required"*: James O'Donnell and Casey Crownhart, "We Did the Math on AI's Energy Footprint. Here's the Story You Haven't Heard," *MIT Technology Review*, May 20, 2025, https://www.technologyreview.com/2025/05/20/1116327/ai-energy-usage-climate-footprint-big-tech/.

175 *"Essentially what we have"*: Roger McNamee, interview by Gil Durán, *Nerd Reich* (podcast), June 16, 2025, YouTube, https://www.youtube.com/watch?v=C8ddJ5b2TGo.

175 *"interact with AI"*: Colleen McClain et al., "Artificial Intelligence in Daily Life: Views and Experiences," ch. 1 in *How the U.S. Public and AI Experts View Artificial Intelligence* (Washington, DC: Pew Research Center, April 3, 2025), https://www.pewresearch.org/internet/2025/04/03/artificial-intelligence-in-daily-life-views-and-experiences/.

175 *Tech giants like Amazon*: "Big Tech to Invest About $650 Billion in AI in 2026, Bridgewater Says," Reuters, February 23, 2026, https://finance.yahoo.com/news/big-tech-invest-650-billion-162045430.html.

175 *venture capital has fueled roughly $259 billion*: "Venture Capital Investments in Artificial Intelligence Through 2025," Organization for Economic Co-operation and Development, February 17, 2026, https://www.oecd.org/en/publications/venture-capital-investments-in-artificial-intelligence-through-2025_a13752f5-en/full-report.html.

176 *"AI's $600 billion question"*: David Cahn, "AI's $600B Question," Sequoia Capital, June 20, 2024, https://sequoiacap.com/article/ais-600b-question/.

176 *"a basic math problem"*: Ganesh Sitaraman and Asad Ramzanali, "We Must Prepare for an AI Bubble Now," *Time*, March 26, 2026, https://time.com/article/2026/03/26/we-must-prepare-for-an-ai-bubble-now/.

176 *also an investor in OpenAI rival Anthropic*: Anthropic, "Anthropic Raises $30 Billion in Series G Funding at $380 Billion Post-Money Valuation," press release, February 12, 2026, https://www.anthropic.com/news/anthropic-raises-30-billion-series-g-funding-380-billion-post-money-valuation.

176 *Andreessen Horowitz announced plans to raise $20 billion*: Krystal Hu, Anna Tong, and Kenrick Cai, "Andreessen Horowitz Seeks to Raise $20 Billion Megafund amid Global Interest in US AI Startups," Reuters, April 8, 2025, https://www.reuters.com/business/finance/andreessen-horowitz-seeks-raise-20-billion-megafund-amid-global-interest-us-ai-2025-04-08/.

176 *a more modest amount of $15 billion*: Deborah Mary Sophia and Krystal Hu, "Andreessen Horowitz Raises $15 Billion Across Five Funds for Tech Startup Investments," Reuters, January 9, 2026, https://www.reuters.com/business/andreessen-horowitz-raises-15-billion-across-five-funds-tech-startup-investments-2026-01-09/.

176 *"civilizational risk"*: Scott Wong et al., "Elon Musk Warns of 'Civilizational Risk' Posed by AI in Meeting with Tech CEOs and Senators," NBC News, September 13, 2023, https://www.nbcnews.com/politics/congress/big-tech-ceos-ai-meeting-senators-musk-zuckerberg-rcna104738.

177 *declaring itself "Mecha Hitler"*: Maya Yang, "Elon Musk's AI Firm Apologizes After Chatbot Grok Praises Hitler," *Guardian*, July 12, 2025, https://www.theguardian.com/us-news/2025/jul/12/elon-musk-grok-antisemitic.

177 *allowed users to "nudify" images*: Kali Hays, "Teens Sue Musk's xAI over Grok's Pornographic Images of Them," *BBC News*, March 16, 2026, https://www.bbc.com/news/articles/cgk2lzmm22eo.

177 *Trump announced the creation of Stargate*: Clare Duffy, "Trump Announces a $500 Billion AI Infrastructure Investment in the US," CNN, January 21, 2025, https://www.cnn.com/2025/01/21/tech/openai-oracle-softbank-trump-ai-investment.

177 *"enhance America's global AI dominance"*: Donald J. Trump, "Removing Barriers to American Leadership in Artificial Intelligence," Exec. Order No. 14179, January 23, 2025, https://www.whitehouse.gov/presidential-actions/2025/01/removing-barriers-to-american-leadership-in-artificial-intelligence/.

177 *"I'm gonna help a lot"*: Jennifer Jacobs, "Trump Announces Up to $500 Billion in Private Sector AI Infrastructure Investment," CBS News, January 21, 2025, https://www.cbsnews.com/news/trump-announces-private-sector-ai-infrastructure-investment/.

177 *"This means we can create . . . have been possible"*: Madeline Coggins, "AI Executives Praise Trump's Stargate Project: 'This Is a Very Large Investment That Affects All of Humanity,'" Fox News, January 21, 2025, https://www.foxnews.com/media/ai-executives-praise-trumps-stargate-project-this-very-large-investment-affects-all-humanity.

177 *the creation of Detachment 201*: Sheera Frenkel, "The Militarization of Silicon Valley," *New York Times*, August 4, 2025, https://www.nytimes.com/2025/08/04/technology/google-meta-openai-military-war.html.

178 *"develop prototype frontier AI capabilities"*: Kanishka Singh, "OpenAI Wins $200 Million US Defense Contract," Reuters, June 16, 2025, https://www.reuters.com/world/us/openai-wins-200-million-us-defense-contract-2025-06-16/.

178 *one single contract with Palantir*: Samantha Subin, "Palantir Lands $10 Billion Army Software and Data Contract," CNBC, August 1, 2025, https://www.cnbc.com/2025/08/01/palantir-lands-10-billion-army-software-and-data-contract.html.

178 *Palantir, which had secured $2.5 billion*: Samantha Subin, "Bottom Line: Palantir Taps Trump-Tied Firm as It Chases Government Contracts," *Hill*, January 8, 2025, https://thehill.com/lobbying/5072171-bottom-line-palantir-taps-trump-tied-firm-as-it-chases-government-contracts/.

178 *Palantir was already the prime contractor*: Carley Welch, "Army Consolidates Dozens of Palantir Software Contracts into One Deal Worth Up to $10 Billion," *Breaking Defense*, August 1, 2025, https://breakingdefense.com/2025/08/army-consolidates-dozens-of-palantir-software-contracts-into-one-deal-worth-up-to-10-billion/.

178 *a $30 million contract*: Caroline Haskins, "ICE Is Paying Palantir $30 Million to Build 'ImmigrationOS' Surveillance Platform," *Wired*, April 18, 2025, https://www.wired.com/story/ice-palantir-immigrationos/.

178 *DHS signed a purchasing agreement*: Makena Kelly, "DHS Opens a Billion-Dollar Tab with Palantir," *Wired*, February 19, 2026, https://www.wired.com/story/department-homeland-security-ice-billion-dollar-agreement-palantir/.

178 *a $125 million war chest*: Emily Wilkins, "AI Industry Super PAC Raises $125 Million in 2025," CNBC, January 30, 2026, https://www.cnbc.com/2026/01/30/ai-industry-super-pac-raises-campaign-money.html.

178 *"Any group run by Schumer . . . of Trump world"*: Matt Dixon, " 'Slap in the Face': White House Irked by a New $100M Pro-AI Super PAC," NBC News, October 24, 2025, https://www.nbcnews.com/politics/trump-administration/white-house-irked-leading-future-new-100m-ai-super-pac-rcna239392.

178 *AI titans smoothed these concerns*: Theodore Schleifer, "New Political Group to Push Trump's A.I. Agenda in Midterms," *New York Times*, March 29, 2026, https://www.nytimes.com/2026/03/29/business/trump-artificial-intelligence-pac-midterms.html.

179 *"that will support public education"*: "Anthropic Is Donating $20 Million to Public First Action," Anthropic, February 12, 2026, https://www.anthropic.com/news/donate-public-first-action.

179 *On the state level*: Dan Merica and Clara Ence Morse, "AI Money Is Already Influencing the Midterms. And More Is Coming," *Washington Post*, March 12, 2026, https://www.washingtonpost.com/politics/2026/03/12/ai-funding-midterm-elections/.

179 *"world without jobs"*: James Dale Davidson and Lord William Rees-Mogg, *The Sovereign Individual: Mastering the Transition to the Information Age* (1997; repr., New York: Simon & Schuster, 2020), ebook.

179 *"Societies that have been . . . anti-technology bias"*: Davidson and Rees-Mogg, *The Sovereign Individual.*

179 *Such trends helped increase*: Allan Smith, "Poll: Majority of Voters Say Risks of AI Outweigh the Benefits," NBC News, March 10, 2026, https://www.nbcnews.com/politics/politics-news/poll-majority-voters-say-risks-ai-outweigh-benefits-rcna262196.

179 *"AI could wipe out"*: Jim VandeHei and Mike Allen, "Behind the Curtain: A White-Collar Bloodbath," Axios, May 28, 2025, https://www.axios.com/2025/05/28/ai-jobs-white-collar-unemployment-anthropic.

179 *"We, as the producers"*: VandeHei and Allen, "Behind the Curtain," Axios.

179 *"jobs are going to go away"*: Ross Andersen, "The Sudden Fall of Sam Altman," *Atlantic*, November 18, 2023, https://www.theatlantic.com/technology/archive/2023/11/sam-altman-open-ai-fallout/676046/.

179 *"real work"*: Frank Landymore, "Sam Altman Says If Jobs Gets Wiped Out, Maybe They Weren't Even 'Real Work' to Start With," *Futurism*, October 12, 2025, https://futurism.com/artificial-intelligence/sam-altman-real-work-ai.

181 *"The federal government owns"*: Donald J. Trump, "Agenda47: A New Quantum Leap to Revolutionize the American Standard of Living," Donald J. Trump for President 2024, March 3, 2023, at the Wayback Machine, https://web.archive.org/web/20250304092226/https://www.donaldjtrump.com/agenda47/agenda47-a-new-quantum-leap-to-revolutionize-the-american-standard-of-living.

181 *The Delaware-based Próspera corporation*: Sarah Holder and David Fox, "The Dream Was a Libertarian Island Enclave. It's Become an $11 Billion Nightmare," *Bloomberg*, February 14, 2025, https://www.bloomberg.com/news/articles/2025-02-14/the-dream-was-a-libertarian-island-enclave-it-s-become-an-11-billion-nightmare.

182 *"a Bitcoin café and education center"*: Rachel Corbett, "The For-Profit City That Might Come Crashing Down," *New York Times Magazine*, August 28, 2024, https://www.nytimes.com/2024/08/28/magazine/prospera-honduras-crypto.html.

182 *Próspera claims that 250 companies*: "About," Próspera, accessed April 13, 2026, https://www.prospera.co/en/about.

182 *a destination for biohackers*: Bennett M. Sherman, "Biohackers Convene in Honduras for Unregulated Gene Therapy Trials Without FDA Oversight," NAD, February 23, 2024, https://www.nad.com/news/biohackers-convene-in-honduras-for-unregulated-gene-therapy-trials-without-fda-oversight.

182 *a procedure to implant a microchip*: Patricia Clarke, "The Millionaire Guinea Pigs Risking Death to Live for Ever," *Observer*, September 6, 2025, https://observer.co.uk/news/science-technology/article/the-millionaire-guinea-pigs-risking-death-to-live-for-ever.

182 *the Honduran Congress voted to repeal*: Gustavo Palencia, "Honduran Congress Unanimously Nixes Special Economic Zones," Reuters, April 21, 2022, https://www.reuters.com/world/americas/honduran-congress-unanimously-nixes-special-economic-zones-2022-04-21/.

182 *prompting Próspera to file*: Nicholas Kusnetz and Katie Surma, "A Lawsuit from Backers of a 'Startup City' Could Bankrupt Honduras," *Wired*, September 28, 2024, https://www.wired.com/story/a-lawsuit-from-backers-of-a-startup-city-could-bankrupt-honduras/.

182 *He was arrested*: US Department of Justice, Office of Public Affairs, "Juan Orlando Hernández, Former President of Honduras, Sentenced to 45 Years in Prison for Conspiring to Distribute More Than 400 Tons of Cocaine and Related Firearms Offenses," press release, June 26, 2024, https://www.justice.gov/archives/opa/pr/juan-orlando-hernandez-former-president-honduras-sentenced-45-years-prison-conspiring.

182 *the same year that*: Gustavo Palencia, "Honduras Top Court Declares Self-Governing ZEDE Zones Unconstitutional," Reuters, September 20, 2024, https://www.reuters.com/world/americas/honduras-top-court-declares-self-governing-zede-zones-unconstitutional-2024-09-20/.

183 *"the center of one of the largest"*: Vera Bergengruen et al., "How a Man Convicted of Running a Latin American Narco State Landed a Pardon," *Wall Street Journal*, December 4, 2025, https://www.wsj.com/politics/policy/how-a-man-convicted-of-running-a-latin-american-narco-state-landed-a-pardon-c2353aef.

183 *"The reason seems clear . . . Vance's political career"*: Jennifer Gould, "The Curious Case of the Narco-Prez Pardon," *Air Mail*, December 6, 2025, https://airmail.news/issues/2025-12-6/the-curious-case-of-the-narco-prez-pardon.

183 *Praxis, the brainchild*: Jack Sullivan, "Company Town: Inside the Praxis Society, a Silicon Valley–Backed Start-up Attempting to Build a City in the Mediterranean," *Air Mail*, July 29, 2023, https://airmail.news/issues/2023-7-29/company-town.

183 *After leaving New York University*: Joseph Bernstein, "Who Would Give This Guy Millions to Build His Own Utopia?," *New York Times*, December 12, 2023, https://www.nytimes.com/2023/12/12/style/praxis-city-dryden-brown.html.

184 *"help build institutions"*: Tyler Cowen, "Emergent Ventures Winners, Seventh Cohort," *Marginal Revolution* (blog), March 2, 2020, https://marginalrevolution.com/marginalrevolution/2020/03/emergent-ventures-winners-seventh-cohort.html.

184 *"talk to a bunch of different founders"*: Dryden Brown, "Praxis," speech delivered at the Network State Conference, Amsterdam, October 30, 2023, YouTube, at 51:42, https://www.youtube.com/live/x-GfuIFkB_Y?t=3102.

184 *"according to a person familiar"*: Bernstein, "Who Would Give This Guy Millions . . . ?," *New York Times*.

184 *"Entrepreneur Dryden Brown said"*: Yuliya Chernova, "Tech Utopian Project Praxis Gets $525 Million in Commitments for Planned 'Heroic' City," *Wall Street Journal*, October 15, 2024, https://www.wsj.com/articles/tech-utopian-project-praxis-gets-525-million-in-commitments-for-planned-heroic-city-f4623e98.

185 *"Network States offer a path"*: Gil Durán, "Praxis: Tech Dystopia as the 'Next America,'" *Nerd Reich* (newsletter), October 24, 2024, https://www.thenerdreich.com/praxis-tech-dystopia-as-the-next-america/.

185 *"The next America will be onchain"*: Durán, "Praxis," *Nerd Reich*.

185 *"acceleration zone . . . winning popular narrative"*: Dryden Brown, "National Accelerationism," Praxis, accessed March 25, 2024, at the Wayback Machine, https://web.archive.org/web/20240325054405/https://www.praxisnation.com/writing/national-accelerationism.

186 *Sramek's company had spent $900 million*: Conor Dougherty and Erin Griffith, "The Silicon Valley Elite Who Want to Build a City from Scratch," *New York Times*, August 25, 2023, https://www.nytimes.com/2023/08/25/business/land-purchases-solano-county.html.

186 *branded the project as a "tech utopia"*: Bobby Allyn, "Locals Push Back Against Plans to Build a Tech Utopia in Solano County, Calif.," NPR, September 18, 2023, https://www.npr.org/2023/09/18/1200196497/locals-push-back-against-plans-to-build-a-tech-utopia-in-solano-county-calif.

186 *"the European equivalent of Peter Thiel"*: Hugh Langley and Adam Rogers, "Big Tech's Urban Hero: Here's Why Silicon Valley Is Betting on a Goldman Prodigy to Build a Glorious City of the Future," *Business Insider*, May 5, 2024, https://www.businessinsider.com/california-forever-jan-sramek-goldman-sachs-silicon-valley-city-future-2024-4.

186 *"He seems to combine everything"*: "Has Jan Sramek Quit Goldman for Entrepreneurship?," eFinancialCareers, April 15, 2011, https://www.efinancialcareers.com/news/2011/04/has-jan-sramek-quit-goldman-for-entrepreneurship.

187 *Sramek hired an "A-team"*: Lara Korte and Dustin Gardiner, "Meet California Forever's A-Team," *Politico California Playbook*, December 19, 2023, https://www.politico.com/newsletters/california-playbook/2023/12/19/meet-california-forevers-a-team-00132372.

187 *California Forever also launched*: Adhiti Bandlamudi, "California Forever Hands Out $500K to Solano Nonprofits Ahead of November Election," KQED,

October 15, 2024, https://www.kqed.org/news/11987138/california-forever-hands-out-500k-to-solano-nonprofits-ahead-of-november-election.

187 *Sramek was forced to abandon*: Will McCarthy, "The Scrappy Resistance Looking to Block Big Tech's Urbanist Utopia," *Politico*, June 14, 2024, https://www.politico.com/news/2024/06/14/california-forever-resistance-solano-county-00163018.

187 *accusing the locals of "endless greed"*: Ethan Baron, "'California Forever' Planning Group Wins Big Against Farmers," *Governing*, April 3, 2024, https://www.governing.com/management-and-administration/california-forever-planning-group-wins-big-against-farmers.

187 *Marc Lore searched the land*: "Telosa," City of Telosa, accessed April 13, 2026, https://cityoftelosa.com/.

187 *Isker has described Indians as "cow worshippers"*: Kiera Butler, "Christian 'Theo-Bros' Are Building a Tech Utopia in Appalachia," *Mother Jones*, April 8, 2025, https://www.motherjones.com/politics/2025/04/christian-theobros-are-building-a-tech-utopia-in-appalachia/.

188 *"Nation states are not . . . organize network states"*: Butler, "Christian 'TheoBros,'" *Mother Jones*.

188 *a tech-focused freedom city in the Presidio*: Mark Lutter and Jeffrey Mason, "Build the Presidio Freedom City," *Palladium*, January 17, 2025, https://www.palladiummag.com/2025/01/17/build-the-presidio-freedom-city/.

188 *James Ingallinera proposed the creation of "Frontier Valley"*: Frontier Valley (@_FrontierValley), X profile, accessed April 13, 2026, https://x.com/_FrontierValley. The account describes itself as "a new special regulation district in central SV that will have the most accelerated code in the US for robotics and physical innovation. Pending admin approval."

188 *Devon Zuegel pitched "Esmeralda"*: Gil Durán, "Esmeralda: Network State Comes for Cloverdale," *Nerd Reich* (newsletter), November 12, 2025, https://www.thenerdreich.com/esmeralda-network-state-comes-to-sonoma-county-2/.

189 *"a Chautauqua of the West"*: Amie Windsor, "Edge Esmeralda Visionary Offers First Look at Plan to Create 'Chautauqua of the West' in Cloverdale," *Press Democrat* (Santa Rosa, CA), July 26, 2025, https://www.pressdemocrat.com/2025/07/26/edge-esmeralda-visionary-offers-first-look-at-plan-to-create-chautauqua-of-the-west-in-cloverdale/.

189 *"I went to Greenland"*: Dryden Brown (@drydenwtbrown), "I went to Greenland to try to buy it. Here's what happened:," X, November 14, 2024, https://x.com/drydenwtbrown/status/1856424282823541099.

189 *"the ownership and control of Greenland"*: Rebecca Shabad, "Trump Says Ownership of Greenland 'Is an Absolute Necessity,'" NBC News, December 22, 2024, https://www.nbcnews.com/politics/donald-trump/trump-says-ownership-greenland-absolute-necessity-rcna185197.

189 *Climate change promises*: Sam Meredith, "Greenland's Melting Ice Is Clearing the Way for a Mineral 'Gold Rush,'" CNBC, January 17, 2025, https://www.cnbc.com/2025/01/17/greenlands-melting-ice-is-clearing-the-way-for-a-mineral-gold-rush.html.

189 *"I'm talking about the free world"*: Alys Davies and Mike Wendling, "Trump Ramps Up Threats to Gain Control of Greenland and Panama Canal," *BBC News*, January 8, 2025, https://www.bbc.com/news/articles/c4gzn48jwz2o.

190 *"I think we're going to . . . We're going to get it"*: Christian Ulloriaq Jeppesen, Maya Tekeli, and Jeffrey Gettleman, "Trump Said the U.S. Will 'Get' Greenland. Greenlanders Aren't Impressed," *New York Times*, March 5, 2025, https://www.nytimes.com/2025/03/05/world/europe/trump-greenland-speech.html.

190 *"all of our flags will fly proudly"*: Adrienne Murray and Hafsa Khalil, "US Fires Greenland Military Base Chief for 'Undermining' JD Vance," *BBC News*, April 11, 2025, https://www.bbc.com/news/articles/creq99l218do.

190 *"As the Trump administration intensifies"*: Rachael Levy and Alexandra Ulmer, "Greenland 'Freedom City'? Rich Donors Push Trump for a Tech Hub Up North," Reuters, April 10, 2025, https://www.reuters.com/world/europe/greenland-freedom-city-rich-donors-push-trump-tech-hub-up-north-2025-04-10/.

190 *"He advocates for . . . @elonmusk"*: Dryden Brown (@drydenwtbrown), "We must build a prototype of Terminus on Earth before departing for Mars. I believe Greenland is the place, @elonmusk," X, November 12, 2024, https://x.com/drydenwtbrown/status/1856424526969737669.

191 *"The idea goes like this . . . of Western prowess"*: Zoë Bernard, "Welcome to Praxis: The High-Tech, High-Testosterone Eden That Will Save the World," *Vanity Fair*, June 4, 2025, https://www.vanityfair.com/news/praxis-dryden-brown.

191 *"America cannot compete . . . lose with China"*: Jan Sramek (@jansramek), "America cannot compete with China without building America's Shenzen—a place to build drones, ships, robots, and everything else cutting edge. Where? On @CAForever's 100 square miles in Solano, 60 mile . . . ," X, June 4, 2025, https://x.com/jansramek/status/1930336273295913041.

192 *a "manufacturing park" for "frontier tech"*: "California Forever Unveils the Solano Foundry: A New Home for Frontier Tech, an Hour North of Silicon Valley," California Forever, July 17, 2025, https://californiaforever.com/california-forever-unveils-the-solano-foundry/.

192 *"as many as the market can handle"*: Caroline Haskins and Vittoria Elliott, "'Startup City' Groups Say They're Meeting Trump Officials to Push for Deregulated 'Freedom Cities,'" *Wired*, March 7, 2025, https://www.wired.com/story/startup-cities-donald-trump-legislation/.

192 *"Freedom Cities Coalition has briefed White House"*: Haskins and Elliott, "'Startup City' Groups," *Wired*.

193 *"The United States should . . . a special economic zone"*: Pirate Wires (@PirateWires), "sry cuba, we're building a giant gilded capitalist megafortress on the coast of your failing communist state the one and only @PalmerLuckey with a banger guest take on expanding Guantanamo Bay into Liberty City," X, May 13, 2025, https://x.com/PirateWires/status/1922296163778109522.

193 *"an archipelago" of private cities*: Gil Durán, "The Most Powerful Crypto Bro in Washington Has Very Weird Beliefs," *New Republic*, October 1, 2024, https://newrepublic.com/article/185738/coinbase-brian-armstrong-crypto-lobbying-washington-politicians.

193 *"We need more ... within a small sandbox"*: Brian Armstrong (@brian_armstrong), "We need more special economic zones in the U.S. We should designate ~10 or so like this across different pieces of federal land, each with its own exemption from federal and state law. One for bio, one for drones/aviation, one for crypto, one for robotics, one for mining, etc.," X, May 13, 2025, https://x.com/brian_armstrong/status/1922310910292722116.

193 *"I have concepts ... a freedom zone"*: Aya Batrawy and Franco Ordoñez, "Trump Touts 'Freedom Zone' Plan for Gaza as Ceasefire Talks Stall in Qatar," NPR, May 15, 2025, https://www.npr.org/2025/05/15/nx-s1-5399080/trump-gaza-qatar.

194 *"Beachside luxury resorts ... coastal destination"*: Alexander Ward, Robbie Gramer, and Peter Grant, "U.S. Pitches 'Project Sunrise' Plan to Turn Gaza into High-Tech Metropolis," *Wall Street Journal*, December 19, 2025, https://www.wsj.com/world/middle-east/u-s-pitches-project-sunrise-plan-to-turn-gaza-into-high-tech-metropolis-ebbd96ae.

194 *"Venezuela doesn't need ... allowed to exist"*: Mark Lutter (@MarkLutter), "Venezuela doesn't need to become another Iraq. It needs a Freedom City. The mission is not endless war. It is to end a criminal regime without another trillion-dollar disaster ...," X, January 6, 2026, https://x.com/MarkLutter/status/2008618511111688471.

194 *Lutter, a graduate of George Mason University*: "Mercatus Center Launches Emergent Ventures," George Mason University, July 18, 2018, https://web.archive.org/web/20251223103205/https://content.sitemasonry.gmu.edu/news/2018-07/mercatus-center-launches-emergent-ventures.

194 *A Trump-backed peace plan for Ukraine*: Christian Edwards and Kosta Gak, "US Proposes 'Free Economic Zone' in Parts of Donbas After Ukrainian Pullback, Zelensky Says," CNN, December 11, 2025, https://www.cnn.com/2025/12/11/europe/ukraine-zelensky-free-economic-zone-donbas-intl.

194 *vague plans for a "cryptocity"*: Albert Otkjær, "Alatau, Kazakhstan's Futuristic Crypto City, Faces Ground-Level Realities," *Diplomat*, March 30, 2026, https://thediplomat.com/2026/03/alatau-kazakhstans-futuristic-crypto-city-faces-ground-level-realities/.

195 *Olivier Janssens was buying up land*: Atossa Araxia Abrahamian, "Dubai of the Caribbean, with Crypto? Locals Aren't Buying It," *New York Times*, February 26, 2026, https://www.nytimes.com/2026/02/26/business/st-kitts-nevis-destiny-olivier-janssens-crypto-libertarian.html.

195 *a German crypto entrepreneur was planning CryptoCity*: Tim Stern, "CryptoCity: Shaping the Future of Community Living," Free Cities Foundation, accessed May 3, 2026, https://free-cities.org/cryptocity/.

195 *"global jurisdiction of choice"*: Laurie Clarke and Nelson C. J., "A Peter Thiel–Backed Startup City Wants to Be Africa's Delaware," *Wired*, April 18, 2023, https://www.wired.com/story/itana-binance-charter-cities-institute-africa-tech-startup/.

195 *Pop-up conferences like Edge City*: "Edge City," accessed May 3, 2026, https://www.edgecity.live/.

195 *Srinivasan himself launched a so-called Network School*: Nick Marsh, "Forest City: Inside Malaysia's Chinese-Built 'Ghost City,'" *BBC News*, December 4, 2023, https://www.bbc.com/news/business-67610677.

195 *"a three-month learning retreat"*: Caroline Haskins, "A Mysterious School for the Network State Crowd Is Now in Session," *Wired*, September 23, 2024, https://www.wired.com/story/network-school-balaji-srinivasan/.

196 *the same designer linked to Próspera*: Ryan Scavnicky, "Patrik Schumacher's Liberland Metaverse Is Pure Cringe," *Architect's Newspaper*, April 25, 2022, https://www.archpaper.com/2022/04/patrik-schumacher-liberland-metaverse-cringe/.

196 *"Heya @balajis . . . what we're building"*: Shiv Malik (@shivmalik), "Heya @balajis - the citizens of the network state(s) will need decentralized ID. That's what we're building," Twitter (now X), November 7, 2022, https://x.com/shivmalik/status/1589699240569495552.

196 *Malik replied: "Build cities"*: Shiv Malik (@shivmalik), "Build cities," X, November 28, 2023, https://x.com/shivmalik/status/1729645394022277561.

196 *"At the very moment"*: Nafeez Ahmed, "How Epstein Saved Bitcoin – and Accessed Trump's Tech Inner Circle," *Byline Times*, December 4, 2025, https://bylinetimes.com/2025/12/04/how-epstein-saved-bitcoin-and-accessed-trumps-tech-inner-circle/.

196 *"With his interest first piqued"*: David Morris, "Jeffrey Epstein Saw Promise in Bitcoin—and Its Far-Right Supporters," *Verge*, February 27, 2026, https://www.theverge.com/tech/885252/jeffrey-epstein-bitcoin-cryptocurrency-connections.

CHAPTER 7 ANTICHRIST

199 *He did this in select venues*: Jacob Howland, "Peter Thiel's Visions of Apocalypse," *UnHerd*, May 29, 2025, https://unherd.com/2025/05/peter-thiels-visions-of-apocalypse/.

200 *"The crowd was largely white, male"*: Emily Shugerman and Garrett Leahy, "What the Hell Happened at Peter Thiel's Antichrist Talk? We Asked the Guests," *San Francisco Standard*, September 16, 2025, https://sfstandard.com/2025/09/16/peter-thiel-antichrist-san-francisco/.

200 *"In the most intense kind . . . slightly less extreme kinds of cults"*: Peter Thiel with Blake Masters, *Zero to One: Notes on Startups, or How to Build the Future* (New York: Currency, 2014).

201 *"The Antichrist comes to power"*: Peter Thiel, "Antichrist Lectures," lecture 1 of 4 (Commonwealth Club, San Francisco, September 15, 2025). Transcript obtained by the author.

201 *the Antichrist would be defined by "velocity"*: Thiel, "Antichrist Lectures," 1 of 4.

201 *"It's so strange . . . your other pet passion is the Antichrist"*: Tim Dillon, interview by Joe Rogan, *Joe Rogan Experience*, no. 2375, September 4, 2025, YouTube, https://www.youtube.com/watch?v=hX-oOqnoERY.

202 *"This is my very specific question . . . Antichrist accidentally hastens his or her arrival"*: Peter Thiel, interview by Ross Douthat, "A.I., Mars and Immortality: Are We Dreaming Big Enough?," *Interesting Times with Ross Douthat* (podcast), *New York Times*, June 26, 2025, YouTube, https://www.youtube.com/watch?v=vV7YgnPUxcU.

204 *"Sovereign is he who decides on the exception"*: Carl Schmitt, *Political Theology: Four Chapters on the Concept of Sovereignty* (1922; repr., Chicago: University of Chicago Press, 2005), ebook.

205 *"God created the world"*: Peter Thiel, "The Straussian Moment," in *Politics and Apocalypse*, ed. Robert Hamerton-Kelly (East Lansing: Michigan State University Press, 2007), 202.

205 *"Buddha begins his travels . . . how old Frodo is when he inherits the ring"*: Peter Thiel, "Antichrist Lectures," lecture 3 of 4 (Commonwealth Club, San Francisco, September 29, 2025). Transcript obtained by the author.

206 *"religious but not spiritual"*: Daniel K. Williams, "The Catholic Conversion of J. D. Vance," *Anxious Bench* (blog), *Patheos*, July 22, 2024, https://www.patheos.com/blogs/anxiousbench/2024/07/the-catholic-conversion-of-j-d-vance; Johana Bhuiyan, Dara Kerr, and Nick Robins-Early, "Inside Tech Billionaire Peter Thiel's Off-the-Record Lectures About the Antichrist," *Guardian*, October 10, 2025, https://www.theguardian.com/us-news/2025/oct/10/peter-thiel-lectures-antichrist/.

206 *"My line is always . . . knowledge is more important than belief"*: Thiel, "Antichrist Lectures," 3 of 4.

207 *"wrote about Schmitt's apocalyptic theories . . . National Conservatism movement"*: Laura Bullard, "The Real Stakes, and Real Story, of Peter Thiel's Antichrist Obsession," *Wired*, September 30, 2025, https://www.wired.com/story/the-real-stakes-real-story-peter-thiels-antichrist-obsession/.

207 *"The symbol of the Antichrist . . . prone to demonize their enemies"*: Robert C. Fuller, *Naming the Antichrist: The History of an American Obsession* (New York: Oxford University Press, 1995).

208 *"The whole concept of the Antichrist . . . a duty for the true believer"*: Robert C. Fuller, interview with the author, September 5, 2025.

209 *"Indeed, there is little . . . certain deeply problematic truths"*: Thiel, "The Straussian Moment," 204.

209 *in the eyes of many Christians*: "Peter Thiel," *Forbes*, accessed April 13, 2026, https://www.forbes.com/profile/peter-thiel/.

209 *extremist framework on godless Silicon Valley*: Peter Thiel, "Apocalypse Now? Ancient Prophecies and Modern Tech," interview by Peter Robinson, *Uncommon Knowledge*, Hoover Institution, November 18, 2024, YouTube, https://www.youtube.com/watch?v=qqHueZNEzig.

210 *used to control the world*: Thiel, "Antichrist Lectures," 3 of 4.

210 *"We served caviar bumps"*: Michelle Stephens, interview by Kate Lucky, "'Wouldn't It Be Funny if We Tricked a Bunch of People into Going to Church?,'" *Christianity Today*, August 11, 2025, https://www.christianitytoday.com/2025/08/michelle-stephens-interview-peter-thiel-silicon-valley-revival-evangelism/.

211 *"Everything clicked . . . close to industry demigods"*: Emma Goldberg, "Seeking God, or Peter Thiel, in Silicon Valley," *New York Times*, February 11, 2025, https://www.nytimes.com/2025/02/11/business/silicon-valley-christianity.html.

211 *"Our goal is not necessarily conversion . . . persevering after failure is key to culture"*: Priya Anand, "Christians in Tech Drive Religious Revival in SF," *San*

Francisco Standard, November 9, 2024, https://sfstandard.com/2024/11/09/christians-tech-religion-sf/.

213 *"I guarantee you . . . leveraging Christianity to get closer to Peter Thiel"*: Zoë Bernard, "Christianity Was 'Borderline Illegal' in Silicon Valley. Now It's the New Religion," *Vanity Fair*, March 20, 2025, https://www.vanityfair.com/news/story/christianity-was-borderline-illegal-in-silicon-valley-now-its-the-new-religion.

214 *"LSD and shrooms . . . Guess what might?"*: Garry Tan (@garrytan), "LSD and shrooms won't fill the God shaped hole in your heart. Guess what might?," X, November 9, 2024, https://x.com/garrytan/status/1855317134257328445.

214 *"Tech has an affinity"*: Garry Tan (@garrytan), "Tech has an affinity and needs a connection to Abundance, forgiveness, perseverance and grace," X, November 9, 2024, https://x.com/garrytan/status/1855318028461985934.

214 *"We are creating God . . . God in the form of technology"*: Bryan Johnson, "How Not to Die in 2025," interview by Bari Weiss, *Free Press*, January 7, 2025, video, https://www.thefp.com/p/bari-weiss-bryan-johnson-how-not-to-die-in-2025.

215 *He has subjected his penis*: "Tech Mogul Bryan Johnson Undergoes Shock Therapy on Penis to Get the 'Erections of an 18-Year-Old,'" *New York Post*, November 9, 2023, https://nypost.com/2023/11/09/health/tech-mogul-bryan-johnson-undergoes-shock-therapy-on-penis-to-get-the-erections-of-an-18-year-old/.

216 *"the holy grail of muscle, bone and fat"*: Ashlee Vance, "One Man's Longevity Obsession Now Includes Fountain-of-Youth Injections," *Bloomberg Businessweek*, December 20, 2023, https://www.bloomberg.com/news/features/2023-12-20/biotech-startup-enlists-bryan-johnson-to-show-off-follistatin-gene-therapy.

216 *"No government in the world . . . I want to build it"*: Noah Kirsch, "Bryan Johnson, Blueprint Tech Mogul Trying to Stop Aging, Wants His Own Nation-State," *Daily Beast*, September 19, 2024, https://www.thedailybeast.com/bryan-johnson-blueprint-tech-mogul-trying-to-stop-aging-wants-his-own-nation-state/.

217 *"One is start a company"*: Bryan Johnson, "Building a 'Don't Die' Country," Dear Media Studio, March 19, 2024, YouTube, https://www.youtube.com/watch?v=UDxC3HCejxQ.

217 *"Thiel's quest for longer life . . . co-founder Vinod Khosla "*: Shane Shifflett, Amy Dockser Marcus, and Alex Janin, "The Billionaires Fueling the Quest for Longer Life," *Wall Street Journal*, September 6, 2025, https://www.wsj.com/health/wellness/billionaires-longevity-health-04dd205c.

218 *"This moment would be deeply upsetting . . . even in middle age"*: Max Chafkin, *The Contrarian: Peter Thiel and Silicon Valley's Pursuit of Power* (New York: Penguin Press, 2021), ebook.

219 *"I assume my brain"*: Alex Hern, "Startup Wants to Upload Your Brain to the Cloud, but Has to Kill You to Do It," *Guardian*, March 14, 2018, https://www.theguardian.com/technology/2018/mar/14/nectome-startup-upload-brain-the-cloud-kill-you.

219 *He calls the network state*: Gil Durán, "The Tech Baron Seeking to Purge San Francisco of 'Blues,'" *New Republic*, April 30, 2024, https://newrepublic.com/article/180487/balaji-srinivasan-network-state-plutocrat.

220 *"There is an entire ideology . . . a set of common aims and beliefs"*: Adam Becker, *More Everything Forever: AI Overlords, Space Empires, and Silicon Valley's Crusade to Control the Fate of Humanity* (New York: Basic Books, 2025), ebook.

221 *"The Church is expected to war . . . God will cause this to happen as never before"*: C. Peter Wagner, *Dominion! How Kingdom Action Can Change the World* (Grand Rapids, MI: Chosen Books, 2008), 7.

222 *A 2024 poll by Denison University*: Paul A. Djupe, "Belief in the 7 Mountain Mandate Appears to Be Growing in the Last Year," *Religion in Public* (blog), May 13, 2024, https://religioninpublic.blog/2024/05/13/belief-in-the-7-mountain-mandate-appears-to-be-growing-in-the-last-year/.

223 *It has become part of the culture*: Matthew Boedy, *The Seven Mountains Mandate: Exposing the Dangerous Plan to Christianize America and Destroy Democracy* (Louisville, KY: Westminster John Knox Press, 2025), ebook.

224 *"the man behind . . . machine that remade the legal system"*: Andy Kroll, Andrea Bernstein, and Ilya Marritz, "We Don't Talk About Leonard: The Man Behind the Right's Supreme Court Supermajority," *ProPublica*, October 13, 2023, https://www.propublica.org/article/we-dont-talk-about-leonard-leo-supreme-court-supermajority.

225 *At their core*: George Lakoff, *The All New Don't Think of an Elephant! Know Your Values and Frame the Debate* (White River Junction, VT: Chelsea Green Publishing, 2014), 4–5.

225 *It divides the world*: George Lakoff, "Understanding Trump," *George Lakoff* (blog), July 23, 2016, https://george-lakoff.com/2016/07/23/understanding-trump-2/.

225 *"minority majority"*: William H. Frey, "The US Will Become 'Minority White' in 2045, Census Projects," Brookings Institution, March 14, 2018, https://www.brookings.edu/articles/the-us-will-become-minority-white-in-2045-census-projects/.

226 *"end times fascism . . . hyper-patriarchal Christian supremacists"*: Naomi Klein and Astra Taylor, "The Rise of End Times Fascism," *Guardian*, April 13, 2025, https://www.theguardian.com/us-news/ng-interactive/2025/apr/13/end-times-fascism-far-right-trump-musk.

227 *"The strength of states . . . war between the family and the state"*: Katherine Boyle (@KTmBoyle), "Technology and the Family" (keynote address, American Enterprise Institute, Washington, DC, February 24, 2025), posted on X, February 24, 2025, https://x.com/KTmBoyle/status/1894133112881516994.

227 *"rapidly course-correct"*: Katherine Boyle (@KTmBoyle), "Authoritarian regimes always attack the family first. Christian imagery was removed in the Soviet Union for this reason . . . ," X, February 24, 2025, https://x.com/KTmBoyle/status/1894133116127908295.

227 *"The adage . . . shared hatred of communism"*: Boyle (@KTmBoyle), "Authoritarian regimes . . . ," X.

229 *"She cold-emailed Mr. Thiel . . . national-security-focused portfolio"*: Julia Black, "The Tech Right Gets Its Own Phyllis Schlafly," *New York Times*, October 19, 2025, https://www.nytimes.com/2025/10/19/business/katherine-boyle-andreesen-horowitz-american-dynamism.html.

229 *"AI for warfighting"*: "Vannevar Labs," accessed May 3, 2026, https://www.vannevarlabs.com/.

229 *"Tech must help . . . Meme it and we will be it"*: Katherine Boyle (@KTmBoyle), "The second way technology can support the family is by improving and reducing the cost of education. We are currently experiencing an education revolution . . . ," X, February 24, 2025, https://x.com/KTmBoyle/status/1894133121853128859.

230 *"we are in the midst of a spiritual war"*: Katherine Boyle (@KTmBoyle), "A few months ago, my parish pastor, a former military chaplain, made a security announcement at the end of Mass . . . A lot of Christians are uncomfortable with the idea of fighting back, and we shouldn't be," X, August 28, 2025, https://x.com/KTmBoyle/status/1961073191125754347.

230 *"an era of the martyr"*: Katherine Boyle (@KTmBoyle), "We're entering an era of the martyr. Martyrs for Christ. Martyrs for country. Martyrs for the truth . . . Rest in peace, Charlie Kirk," X, September 10, 2025, https://x.com/KTmBoyle/status/1965955052650061859.

230 *"I'm literally an arms dealer"*: Lauren Goode, "The Silicon Valley Christians Who Want to Build 'Heaven on Earth,'" *Wired*, March 14, 2025, https://www.wired.com/story/christians-silicon-valley-religion-venture-capital/.

230 *"All of modern high tech"*: April Dembosky, "Silicon Valley Rooted in Backing from US Military," *Financial Times*, June 9, 2013, https://www.ft.com/content/8c0152d2-d0f2-11e2-be7b-00144feab7de.

231 *defense tech start-ups raised nearly $3 billion*: Margaux MacColl, "Led by Anduril, Defense Tech Funding Sets a New Record This Year," *TechCrunch*, November 20, 2024, https://techcrunch.com/2024/11/20/led-by-anduril-defense-tech-funding-sets-a-new-record-this-year/.

231 *"Funding to VC-backed startups . . . all-time high for investment in the space"*: Joanna Glasner, "Sector Snapshot: Defense Tech Funding Hits Record High," *Crunchbase News*, December 1, 2025, https://news.crunchbase.com/defense-tech/funding-hits-record-high-2025-snapshot/.

231 *2024 and 2025 investments at $27.2 billion and $49.1 billion*: Rudy Ruitenberg, "Defense Tech Startups Had Their Best Funding Year Ever in 2025," *Defense News*, January 20, 2026, https://www.defensenews.com/industry/2026/01/20/defense-tech-startups-had-their-best-funding-year-ever-in-2025/.

231 *Anduril generated approximately $1 billion in revenue*: Jessica Mathews, "With Massive Funding Round and $31 Billion Valuation, Anduril Is Nearing the Size of Defense Industry Giants It Wants to Displace," *Fortune*, June 5, 2025, https://fortune.com/2025/06/05/anduril-palmer-luckey-funding-30-billion-valuation-founders-fund/.

231 *compared to Lockheed Martin's $71 billion*: Lockheed Martin Corporation, "Lockheed Martin Reports Fourth Quarter and Full Year 2024 Financial Results," press release, January 28, 2025, https://investors.lockheedmartin.com/news-releases/news-release-details/lockheed-martin-reports-fourth-quarter-and-full-year-2024.

231 *"Defense company Anduril . . . the fund's largest check ever, according to the firm"*: Mathews, "With Massive Funding Round," *Fortune*.

232 *Such numbers demonstrate*: Douglas Lindsay, "Trump's 2026 State of the Union: $1 Trillion Defense Budget, 'Warrior Dividend' and What It Means for Troops," Military.com, February 24, 2026, https://www.military.com/feature/2026/02/24/trumps-2026-state-of-union-1-trillion-defense-budget-warrior-dividend-and-what-it-means-troops.html.

232 *"We are seeing Russia . . . we are going to lose the battle of the future"*: Jessica Mathews, "Andreessen Horowitz Defense Tech Investor Katherine Boyle Says 'Ukraine Changed Everything,'" *Fortune*, October 15, 2024, https://fortune.com/2024/10/15/andreessen-horowitz-defense-tech-investor-katherine-boyle-says-ukraine-changed-everything/.

232 *a16z raised $600 million*: Ben Horowitz, "New Funds, New Era," Andreessen Horowitz, April 16, 2024, https://a16z.com/new-funds-new-era/.

232 *"millennial slayer of U.S. defense giants"*: Sam Dean, "Palmer Luckey: Millennial Slayer of U.S. Defense Giants," *Los Angeles Times*, June 30, 2024, https://www.latimes.com/la-influential/story/2024-06-30/palmer-luckey-anduril.

232 *"Manned fighter jets are obsolete"*: Elon Musk (@elonmusk), "Some US weapons systems are good, albeit overpriced, but please, in the name of all that is holy, let us stop the worst military value for money in history that is the F-35 program!," X, November 25, 2024, https://x.com/elonmusk/status/1861088922304160167.

232 *"wiping out nearly $5 billion"*: Daniel Edelson, "Elon Musk Finds New Adversary in Lockheed Martin After F-35 Report," *Ynetnews*, November 25, 2024, https://www.ynetnews.com/article/hytcw1qqyg.

232 *"The system is failing us . . . tools to win the fight of the future"*: David Ulevitch, Katherine Boyle, and Matt Cronin, "Why America Needs Dynamic Defense Reform," Andreessen Horowitz, September 16, 2025, https://a16z.com/why-america-needs-dynamic-defense-reform/.

233 *"state-like power"*: Francesca Bria et al., "The Authoritarian Stack: How Tech Billionaires Are Building a Post-Democratic America—and Why Europe Is Next," xof-research.org, supported by Rosa Luxemburg Stiftung and Friedrich-Ebert-Stiftung, accessed April 13, 2026, https://www.authoritarian-stack.info/.

234 *"No further details . . . propose battle plans"*: Marissa Newman, "Thiel's Palantir, Israel Agree Strategic Partnership for Battle Tech," *Bloomberg*, January 12, 2024, https://www.bloomberg.com/news/articles/2024-01-12/palantir-israel-agree-to-strategic-partnership-for-battle-tech.

234 *"While life in Gaza . . . private and public institutions profit freely"*: Francesca Albanese, *From Economy of Occupation to Economy of Genocide: Report of the Special Rapporteur on the Situation of Human Rights in the Palestinian Territories Occupied since 1967*, A/HRC/59/23 (Geneva: United Nations Human Rights Council, June 30, 2025), https://www.un.org/unispal/document/a-hrc-59-23-from-economy-of-occupation-to-economy-of-genocide-report-special-rapporteur-francesca-albanese-palestine-2025/.

234 *Some Palantir employees quit in protest*: Alex Koller, "Palantir CEO Says His Outspoken Pro-Israel Views Have Caused Employees to Leave Company," CNBC, March 13, 2024, https://www.cnbc.com/2024/03/13/palantir-ceo-says-outspoken-pro-israel-views-led-employees-to-leave-.html.

234 *and Norway's largest asset manager*: Stefania Spezzati and Gwladys Fouche, "Thiel's Palantir Dumped by Norwegian Investor over Work for Israel," Reuters, October 25, 2024, https://www.reuters.com/technology/thiels-palantir-dumped-by-norwegian-investor-over-work-israel-2024-10-25/.

234 *"I think part of the reason . . . more deeply entrenched"*: Michael Steinberger, interview by Calder McHugh, "The Tech CEO 'Making No Apologies for the Work with ICE,'" *Politico Magazine*, November 6, 2025, https://www.politico.com/news/magazine/2025/11/06/alex-karp-book-michael-steinberger-trump-evolution-00638951.

235 *Israel's war on Gaza*: Molly Quell, "Leading Genocide Scholars Organization Says Israel Is Committing Genocide in Gaza," Associated Press, September 1, 2025, https://www.pbs.org/newshour/world/leading-genocide-scholars-organization-says-israel-is-committing-genocide-in-gaza.

235 *72,000 people, including 20,000 children*: Debora Patta, "Gaza War Has Killed an Estimated 20,000 Kids. CBS News Meets Many More Orphaned, and 'Always Scared,'" CBS News, October 8, 2025, https://www.cbsnews.com/news/gaza-israel-hamas-war-children-deaths-orphans-trauma/.

235 *experts call a twenty-first-century genocide*: Emir Nader, "Israel Committing Genocide in Gaza, World's Leading Experts Say," *BBC News*, September 1, 2025, https://www.bbc.com/news/articles/cde3eyzdr63o.

235 *In 2022, a group of Christian ranchers*: Tzvi Joffre, "From Texas to Israel: Red Heifers Needed for Temple Arrive," *Jerusalem Post*, September 15, 2022, https://www.jpost.com/judaism/article-717650.

235 *"bringing red cows"*: Chris Livesay, "What These Red Cows from Texas Have to Do with War and Peace in the Middle East," CBS News, March 5, 2024, https://www.cbsnews.com/news/israel-war-hamas-red-heifers-from-texas-jerusalem-jewish-temple-al-aqsa/.

236 *"In technofeudalism . . . they want eternal life"*: Steve Bannon, "Steve Bannon on 'Broligarchs' vs. Populism," interview by Ross Douthat, *Matter of Opinion* (podcast), *New York Times*, January 31, 2025, https://www.nytimes.com/2025/01/31/opinion/steve-bannon-on-broligarchs-vs-populism.html.

236 *"I argue that the AI industry . . . threats to our kids"*: Tina Nguyen, "MAGA Populists Call for Holy War Against Big Tech," *Verge*, September 6, 2025, https://www.theverge.com/politics/773154/maga-tech-right-ai-natcon.

237 *"All this was also in the hope . . . critical engagement is necessary"*: Barbara Tóth, "Peter Thiel's Secret Visit to the University of Innsbruck," *Falter*, September 24, 2025, https://www.falter.at/maily/20250924/peter-thiels-geheimer-besuch-an-der-uni-innsbruck.

238 *"This text, revered in Silicon Valley . . . intended to control its effects"*: Paolo Benanti, "American Heresy: Should Peter Thiel Be Burned at the Stake?," *Le Grand Continent*, March 14, 2026, https://legrandcontinent.eu/fr/2026/03/14/thiel-heresie-benanti/.

240 *"Fascism is a religious conception . . . a system of thought"*: Benito Mussolini, "The Doctrine of Fascism" (1932), https://bibliotecafascista.blogspot.com/2012/03/doctrine-of-fascism-1932.html.

240 *"[a] form of political behavior"*: Robert O. Paxton, *The Anatomy of Fascism* (New York: Vintage Books, 2004), ebook.

240 *"Since enemies have to be defeated"*: Umberto Eco, "Ur-Fascism," *New York Review of Books*, June 22, 1995, https://www.nybooks.com/articles/1995/06/22/ur-fascism/.

242 *"Maybe if you aren't trying"*: "Hereticon Apocalypse Ball," Founders Fund, https://foundersfund.com/2024/02/hereticon-2024/.

243 *"Nowadays, autocracies are run . . . the evil of America"*: Anne Applebaum, *Autocracy, Inc.: The Dictators Who Want to Run the World* (New York: Doubleday, 2024), ebook.

244 *"complex, networked connections between the entities and individuals"*: Nafeez Ahmed, "The Alt-Right Has Taken the Political Centre. It's Not Too Late to Win It Back," *Correspondent*, February 26, 2020, https://thecorrespondent.com/314/the-alt-right-has-taken-the-political-centre-its-not-too-late-to-win-it-back.

244 *"However ironic or sinister"*: Applebaum, *Autocracy, Inc.*

245 *"The current world is unipolar . . . one point it will be"*: Aleksandr Dugin, *The Fourth Political Theory* (London: Arktos Media, 2012), 16.

245 *"His conviction that the Russian Federation's destiny"*: James Verini, "The Imperialist Philosopher Who Demanded the Ukraine War," *New Yorker*, March 1, 2025, https://www.newyorker.com/news/the-weekend-essay/the-imperialist-philosopher-who-demanded-the-ukraine-war.

246 *"Between 2005 and 2010 . . . together in a single religion"*: Dave Troy, " 'Project Russia,' Unknown in the West, Reveals Putin's Playbook," *Washington Spectator*, December 12, 2024, https://washingtonspectator.org/project-russia-reveals-putins-playbook/.

246 *"All who share negative analysis . . . over the present decadence"*: Dugin, *The Fourth Political Theory*, 203.

246 *"The multipolar world begins"*: Balaji Srinivasan (@balajis), "The multipolar world begins with a multipolar West," Twitter (now X), September 18, 2021, https://x.com/balajis/status/1439348921252282370.

246 *multipolarity "legalizes technology"*: Balaji Srinivasan (@balajis), "How multipolarity legalizes technology, in three steps: 1) The West no longer controls the world 2) So it no longer regulates the world 3) So anyone in the world can innovate. And that is now happening," Twitter (now X), May 31, 2023, https://x.com/balajis/status/1664120463277326336.

246 *"The US will actually do better"*: Naval Ravikant (@naval), "The US will actually do better in a multipolar world, because it'll no longer have to subsidize and police everyone else," X, April 8, 2025, https://x.com/naval/status/1909795284462584087.

247 *". . . America is, at this point"*: Peter Thiel, "Antichrist Lectures," lecture 4 of 4 (Commonwealth Club, San Francisco, October 6, 2025). Transcript obtained by the author.

247 *branded government as "fundamentally evil"*: Peter Thiel, "Peter Thiel at Libertopia 2010," keynote, YouTube, uploaded February 25, 2012, https://www.youtube.com/watch?v=KgH7Lv2gQdk.

249 *"Brexit, just the beginning . . . finding the next bargain"*: Jeffrey Epstein, email to Peter Thiel, June 26, 2016, https://www.justice.gov/epstein/files/DataSet%2011/EFTA02459362.pdf.

CHAPTER 8 THE FUTURE

251 *"exit through the state"*: Olivier Jutel, interview by Gil Durán, *Nerd Reich* (podcast), January 2, 2026, YouTube, https://www.youtube.com/watch?v=u-fThWjJP8A

252 *"for operators, creators and storytellers"*: Erik Torenberg et al., "Introducing the a16z New Media Fellowship," Andreessen Horowitz, November 6, 2025, https://www.a16z.news/p/introducing-the-a16z-new-media-fellowship.

252 *OpenAI joined the fray in April 2026*: Mike Isaac, "OpenAI Buys Streaming Show 'TBPN,' Aiming to Change Narrative on A.I.," *New York Times*, April 2, 2026, https://www.nytimes.com/2026/04/02/technology/openai-buys-tbpn.html.

252 *"And for the price of $2,000"*: Rebecca Bellan, "Can AI Judge Journalism? A Thiel-Backed Startup Says Yes, Even If It Risks Chilling Whistleblowers," *TechCrunch*, April 15, 2026, https://techcrunch.com/2026/04/15/can-ai-judge-journalism-a-thiel-backed-startup-says-yes-even-if-it-risks-chilling-whistleblowers/.

253 *"Peter Thiel and I used . . . industrializes this process"*: Objection, "Top VCs Back Aron D'Souza to Launch Objection: An AI Judge for Investigating Media Claims," press release, April 15, 2026, https://www.businesswire.com/news/home/20260415376479/en/Top-VCs-Back-Aron-DSouza-to-Launch-Objection-An-AI-Judge-for-Investigating-Media-Claims.

253 *"Your case is investigated . . . regardless of whose interests it serves"*: "Objection: The AI Tribunal of Truth," accessed May 4, 2026, https://objection.ai/.

253 *"The second Trump revolution . . . put the administration on the defensive"*: Curtis Yarvin, "You Can't Handle the Truth," *Gray Mirror* (Substack), October 5, 2025, https://graymirror.substack.com/p/you-cant-handle-the-truth.

253 *"making Argentina another Plan B"*: Emma Bubola and Ryan Mac, "Why Peter Thiel Is Decamping to the End of the World," *New York Times*, May 28, 2026, https://www.nytimes.com/2026/05/28/world/americas/peter-thiel-argentina.html.

257 *"The fact that our society . . . power of concentrated wealth"*: Adam Becker, *More Everything Forever: AI Overlords, Space Empires, and Silicon Valley's Crusade to Control the Fate of Humanity* (New York: Basic Books, 2025), ebook.

258 *just under 1,000 billionaires*: "Forbes Billionaires," *Forbes*, accessed April 13, 2026, https://www.forbes.com/billionaires/.

258 *an estimated 3,428 billionaires*: Chase Peterson-Withorn, "World's Billionaires List: Facts and Figures," *Forbes*, March 10, 2026, https://www.forbes.com/sites/chasewithorn/2026/03/10/2026-worlds-billionaires-list-facts-and-figures/.

261 *"This is a tragedy for citizens . . . the public purse will be emptied"*: Marietje Schaake, *The Tech Coup: How to Save Democracy from Silicon Valley* (Princeton, NJ: Princeton University Press, 2024), ebook.

261 *"I'm not just looking . . . take up so much power"*: Marietje Schaake, interview by Gil Durán, "The Tech Coup w/ Marietje Schaake," November 22, 2024, YouTube, https://www.youtube.com/watch?v=GWJ_2j_1J_k.

262 *"We can call bullshit"*: Ruha Benjamin, "Who Owns the Future? The Artificial Intelligentsia and the New Eugenics," Tanner Lecture, delivered April 9, 2025, at the Mahindra Humanities Center at Harvard University, posted May 5, 2025, by Mahindra Humanities Center, YouTube, https://www.youtube.com/watch?v=ZseJigkUhuE.

263 *"universal extreme wealth"*: Sam Altman, interview by Theo Von, "Sam Altman," *This Past Weekend*, episode 599, July 23, 2025, YouTube, https://www.youtube.com/watch?v=aYn8VKW6vXA.

SELECTED BIBLIOGRAPHY

BOOKS

Ahmed, Nafeez. *Alt Reich: The Network War to Destroy the West from Within.* London: Byline Books, 2025.

Applebaum, Anne. *Autocracy, Inc.: The Dictators Who Want to Run the World.* New York: Doubleday, 2024.

Becker, Adam. *More Everything Forever: AI Overlords, Space Empires, and Silicon Valley's Crusade to Control the Fate of Humanity.* New York: Basic Books, 2025.

Ben-Ghiat, Ruth. *Strongmen: Mussolini to the Present.* New York: W. W. Norton & Company, 2020.

Benjamin, Ruha. *Imagination: A Manifesto.* New York: W. W. Norton & Company, 2024.

Boedy, Matthew. *The Seven Mountains Mandate: Exposing the Dangerous Plan to Christianize America and Destroy Democracy.* Louisville, KY: Westminster John Knox Press, 2025.

Borsook, Paulina. *Cyberselfish: A Critical Romp Through the Terribly Libertarian Culture of High Tech.* New York: PublicAffairs, 2000.

Cohn, Norman. *The Pursuit of the Millennium: Revolutionary Millenarians and Mystical Anarchists of the Middle Ages.* London: Secker & Warburg, 1957.

Davidson, James Dale, and Lord William Rees-Mogg. *The Sovereign Individual: Mastering the Transition to the Information Age.* New York: Simon & Schuster, 1997.

Golumbia, David. *Cyberlibertarianism: The Right-Wing Politics of Digital Technology.* Minneapolis: University of Minnesota Press, 2023.

Golumbia, David. *The Politics of Bitcoin: Software as Right-Wing Extremism.* Minneapolis: University of Minnesota Press, 2016.

Hao, Karen. *Empire of AI: Dreams and Nightmares in Sam Altman's OpenAI.* New York: Penguin Press, 2025.

Harris, Malcolm. *Palo Alto: A History of California, Capitalism, and the World.* New York: Little, Brown, 2023.

Popper, Nathaniel. *Digital Gold: Bitcoin and the Inside Story of the Misfits and Millionaires Trying to Reinvent Money.* New York: Harper, 2015.

Roberts, Jeff John. *Kings of Crypto: One Startup's Quest to Take Cryptocurrency Out of Silicon Valley and Onto Wall Street.* Boston: Harvard Business Review Press, 2020.

Sandifer, Elizabeth. *Neoreaction a Basilisk: Essays On and Around the Alt-Right.* Eruditorum Press, 2017.

Schaake, Marietje. *The Tech Coup: How to Save Democracy from Silicon Valley.* Princeton, NJ: Princeton University Press, 2024.

Silverman, Jacob. *Gilded Rage: Elon Musk and the Radicalization of Silicon Valley.* London: Bloomsbury Continuum, 2025.

Slobodian, Quinn. *Crack-Up Capitalism: Market Radicals and the Dream of a World Without Democracy.* New York: Metropolitan Books, 2023.

Slobodian, Quinn. *Hayek's Bastards: Race, Gold, IQ, and the Capitalism of the Far Right.* New York: Zone Books, 2025.

Slobodian, Quinn, and Ben Tarnoff. *Muskism: A Guide for the Perplexed.* New York: Harper, 2026.

Srinivasan, Balaji. *The Network State: How to Start a New Country.* Self-published, 2022.

Turner, Fred. *From Counterculture to Cyberculture: Stewart Brand, the Whole Earth Network, and the Rise of Digital Utopianism.* Chicago: University of Chicago Press, 2006.

ARTICLES AND PAPERS

Eco, Umberto. "Ur-Fascism." *New York Review of Books,* June 22, 1995.

Gebru, Timnit, and Émile P. Torres. "The TESCREAL Bundle: Eugenics and the Promise of Utopia Through Artificial General Intelligence." *First Monday* 29, no. 4 (April 1, 2024), https://doi.org/10.5210/fm.v29i4.13636.

INDEX

ABOUT THE AUTHOR

Gil Durán was born in Tulare, California, the grandson of Mexican immigrant farmworkers. He started his journalism career at the San Jose *Mercury News*. As the newspaper industry hit turbulence, he pivoted to politics and spent fifteen years as an advisor to politicians, including Jerry Brown, Dianne Feinstein, and Kamala Harris. In 2018, he returned to journalism as California opinion editor of *The Sacramento Bee*, and then became editorial page editor of the *San Francisco Examiner*. Now an independent journalist, he publishes two newsletters: *The Nerd Reich*, focused on extremist tech politics, and *FrameLab*, focused on political language.